The Big Book of Jewish Baseball

by
Peter S. Horvitz
&
Joachim Horvitz

S.P.i.
BOOKS

For further information, contact:

S.P.I. Books
99 Spring Street
New York, NY 10012
Tel: 212/431-5011
FAX: 212/431-8646

9 8 7 6 5 4 3 2 1
First Edition

Library of Congress Cataloging-in-Publication Data available.

S.P.I. Books World Wide Web address: spibooks.com

ISBN: 1-56171-973-0

For

Michèle

Preface

"Who is Jewish?" is often the subject of "popular Judaica" books. In this book we include every player that we know of who has at least one Jewish parent or has converted to Judaism. We have made no attempt, in the case of converts, to determine or judge the nature of the conversion. Where only one parent is Jewish, we have indicated which one.

We have generally followed the list published by David Spanner in the 5th edition of Total Baseball. We have been in contact with Mr. Spanner and are deeply impressed with the excellence of his research into the genealogy of major league players. We have varied from his list only in the case of Jake Atz and only after careful consideration of his evidence and that offered by other published sources and the testimony of Mickey Rutner, who knew Atz.

In the case of our minor league lists, we have tried to be as conservative as possible, without being so cautious as to deprive our readers of the most likely Jewish baseball candidates. For instance, we have no certain information that Joseph Katz was Jewish. It does, however, seem far more likely than not. The great majority of the players, however, do not fit into Katz's category and their Jewish backgrounds are certifiable beyond any reasonable doubt.

In the years that we have worked gathering information on Jewish baseball players, we have also incurred many obligations and owe innumerable thanks for the unvarying kindness, interest, and concern that our inquiries have solicited. First, we must thank David Spanner, who has been most generous in sharing the results of his tireless research. Next, we thank Lou Jacobson, who helped us redirect our course, early along our way. Richard Rosen has also shown us great kindness. The help of the staff of Cooperstown's Baseball Hall of Fame Library has been invaluable. In addition, Desiree Horvitz, daughter to author Peter and sister to author Joachim, was always there when we needed her.

We list below everyone else who has helped us, in alphabetical order. In every case, our gratitude and thanks for the assistance we received is significant. (Of course, neither those we have thanked above nor those we thank below are responsible for any faults, flaws, errors or omissions that may appear in this book.)

Cal Abrams	Dennis Bair	Skip Bertman
David Amaro	Ross Baumgarten	Peter C. Bjarkman
Judy Amaro	Jose Bautista	Cy Block
Steve Arffa	Bo Belinsky	Ron Blomberg
Eliot Asinof	Ira Berkow	Erez Borowsky

Danny Buxbaum	Stacy Kleiner	Richie Scheinblum
Bill Carle	Alan Koch	Allan H. ("Bud") Selig
Donald Cey	Steven & Elaine Kolinsky	Larry Shane
Harrry Chozen	Stuart Komer	Harvey Shapiro
Al Clark	Howie Koplitz	George Sherry
Alfred Cohen	Joshua Levey	Larry Sherry
Alta Cohen	Peter Levine	Norm Sherry
Hy Cohen	Jesse Levis	Mr. & Mrs. Harry Shuman
Jim Cohen	Brett Mandell	Al Silvera
Steve Cohen	Ralph Maya	Fred Sington
Bill Corcoran	Ed Mayer	David Solomon
Thomas D. Craig	Marvin Miller	Steve Solomon
Harry Danning	Ron Miller	James Spence III
Nicholas Dawidoff	Sam Nahem	Ethan Stein
Thelma Eisen	Garrett Neubart	Steve Wapnick
Harry Eisenstat	Jeff Newman	David Weber
Al Federoff	David Oliphant	Barry Weinberg
Dave Feuerstein	Charles A. Owens, Jr.	Todd Weinberg
Jason Friedman	Leonard Pill	Jerry Weinstein
Larry Fritsch	Jack N. Porter	Ed Wineapple
Howie Gershberg	Scott Radinsky	Joel Wolfe
Joe Ginsberg	Steve Ratzer	Steve Yeager
Keith Glauber	Allen Richter	Larry Yellen
Lon Goldstein	Al Rosen	Mike Zimmerman
Joe Greenberg	Harry Rosen	Ed Zosky
Stephen Greenberg	Steve Rosenberg	Yvonne Zosky
Steven Greenberg	Wayne Rosenthal	
Walter Haas	Mickey Rutner	
Steve Hertz	Jeffrey Saffer	
Ken Holtzman	Mike Saipe	
Ed Horowitz	Hal Schacker	
Scott Hunter	Jon Schaeffer	

Lastly, we would like to thank the following companies and individuals for their permissions for the reproduction of illustrations and photographs displayed in this book:

Judy Amaro

Yury Arkadin

Eliot Asinof

Best Cards

Brace Photo

Harry Chozen

El Paso Diablos

Fleer Skybox International (National Media Group)

Steve Hertz

Stuart Komer

Joshua Levey

Lansing Lugnuts

Larry Fritsch Cards, Inc.

Marvin Miller

McDag Productions, Inc.

Mother's Cookies

National Baseball Hall of Fame and Museum

Pacific Trading Cards, Inc.

Leonard Pill

Al Richter

Richard Rosen

Mickey Rutner

Score Board, Inc.

Harry Shuman

Sport-Pro

Star Images, Inc.

Sunset Garden Supply, San Francisco, CA

The Topps Company, Inc.

The Upper Deck Company, Inc.

West Michigan Whitecaps

Abbreviations

AB = at-bats
BA = batting average
ERA = earned run average
FP = fielding percentage for stated position
GS = games started
H = hits
HR = homeruns

IP = innings pitched
L = losses
OBP = on base percentage
PCT = percentage of games won
R = runs scored
RBI = runs batted in
SV = saves
W = wins

Lipman Pike, the first Jewish professional baseball player, in the uniform of the 1871 Troy (New York) Haymakers

INTRODUCTION

It was a Jewish poet, F.P. Adams, who immortalized the Chicago Cubs' double play combination of infielders Tinkers, Evers and Chance. Johnny Kling was the catcher for those great 1906-1910 Cubs teams. One of their finest pitchers was "Big" Ed Reulbach, who pitched a shutout double header, the only player in major league history to do so. Despite the claims of earlier authors, neither Kling nor Reulbach, players who richly deserve to join their teammates in the Baseball Hall of Fame, were Jewish. Neither were George Stone, Mike Simon, Sammy Strang, Howie Koplitz, Ralph Winegarner, Eli Gruber, William Kling, Stephen Behel, Billy Nash, "Broadway" Smith, Joseph Strauss, Morrie Aderholt, Robert Katz nor Benny Kauff, the "Ty Cobb of the Federal League."

The reasons for these mistaken notions are complex; they include wishful thinking on the part of identifying fans who fantasize being (baseball) card carrying members of the majority culture. Careful investigation, however, has revealed that these men were not Jewish. Yes, there is a famous Hannukah song on the radio insisting that Rod Carew is now Jewish. While this Twins batting champion sported a Jewish star, his Jewish wife has unequivocally stated that Rod has never converted to Judaism. To be inclusive, we include players with a Jewish parent and those who converted to Judaism, whether before or after their baseball careers. But we do not include someone with a Jewish spouse and never converted, nor someone with proverbial Jewish lineage who joins Jews for Jesus.

No matter how loudly a player may claim to be a Christian, we follow Jewish law in counting every son of a Jewish mother and in not recognizing out conversion. We follow liberal tradition and cues from the women's movement in counting the offspring of Jewish fathers, so some readers will want to mark up the margins of some of our entries. Our responsibility is to be as complete as possible regarding each player's background, even if some of those included wish they were not "outted" in these pages.

Because we want to convey what we can about the lives of these players, not just their baseball careers, there are some great, transcendent moments here in baseball and American Jewish history. Professional highlights include: Hank Greenberg tying the homerun record for a right-hander; Larry Sherry successfully concluding every Dodger victory of the 1959 World Series; Koufax's perfect game; Lou Boudreau leading the Indians both from the bench and from the field to a World Series victory; Bo Belinsky pitching the first no-hitter on the West Coast; Ron Blomberg standing in as the very first Designated Hitter.

There are moments of courage here: Cal Abrams shielding the targeted Jackie Robinson with his body; Moe Berg carefully questioning the German physicist Heisenberg, ready to shoot him dead if Germany were progressing toward the atomic bomb; Sy Rosenthal volunteering to serve in W.W. II after the death of his son; Sam Cantor hitch-hiking across America on artificial legs to seek a job as a batboy.

There are moments of creativity here: Louis Heilbroner and his statistical bureau; Barney Dreyfuss and the creation of the World Series; Arnie Rothstein and the biggest gambling fix in American history. There are moments of tragedy: Herb Gorman dying on the ball field; Cy Malis being medically trapped into drug addiction; Barney Pelty pitching for many years with great skill for a hapless team; Erskine Mayer quitting baseball forever when he learned that his teammates on the 1919 White Sox had taken bribes.

We know the jokes about Jewish athletes. But, no, a book of Jewish baseball heroes is not a short book after all. The book you're now holding is no slight work. Turn to the pages on Sid Gordon, Buddy Myer, and Harry Danning and discover their unsung deeds. Examine the life of Goody Rosen, and you will see a major leaguer who extended his career by playing minor league baseball because he refused to take racial abuse. There are strong and angry men here: Al Rosen walking over to the opposing dugout and offering to fight the guy who called him "Jew Bastard!"; Andy Cohen accepting the title of "Christ Killer" and offering to do the same to a heckling fan; Buddy Myer standing up to the scurrilous Ben Chapman and starting the biggest rhubarb in baseball history.

And there is triumph here: in the swing of the bat and the hurl of the pitch; in the race on the base paths and catching that impossible fly ball. Some of these careers were brief, while many years of effort went into getting called up for that first major league game. For that reason, even those players with brief moments of glory are worth remembering

And, of course, there is much of the humor that follows the conflicts and exaggerated life experience of professional sports. We meet Hank Greenberg's father signing baseballs outside of the Polo Grounds—in Hebrew. We find Saul Rogovin dragged off to a Venezuelan jail by soldiers because he walked a run across. For slapstick shtick, we have the "Clown Princes of Baseball," Al Schacht and Max Patkin.

Of course, the saga of Jewish baseball heroes has not ended. At present, Shawn Green, Jesse Levis, Brad Ausmus, and more are building their own baseball legacies. The Tampa Bay Devil Rays' first manager is Larry Rothschild. Pitchers Scott Radinsky. Doug Johns and Al Levine have been keeping pitches on the corners and their ERA's low. In the minor leagues, a whole new crop of Jewish players is approaching maturity.

Lipman Pike, the first Jewish major leaguer, was also one of the first professional players in the country. His achievements are detailed in our text. From the beginning until now, Jews have played a prominent part in our national pastime, whether as player, umpire, manager, team executive, owner, union leader or commissioner. We have tried to tell the story of Jewish people in baseball as completely as possible. We could have easily gone just beyond the mandatory five innings with, say, The Top One Hundred Jews in Baseball. We hope you will appreciate that we starters held onto the ball through all the extra innings.

Welcome to the game. Batter up!

Table of Contents

Part I
The Jewish Major Leaguers

Part II
Touching Other Bases

Part III
Diamond Tales

2001 Major League Update

Part I
The Jewish Major Leaguers

Cal Abrams

Cal Abrams was born on March 2, 1924, in Philadelphia, Pennsylvania. His father, born in Omsk, Russia, was in the trucking business. His mother was from Atlantic City, New Jersey. When Cal was still a small child, his family moved to Brooklyn. In elementary school, Cal dreamed of pitching for the Brooklyn Dodgers, and it was as a pitcher that he played for his elementary school. When Cal reached James Madison High School, however, he found his natural positions were first base and outfield. Cal graduated from Madison High School in 1941.

In 1942, Cal was signed to a professional baseball contract by the Brooklyn Dodgers, and reported to his first assignment at Olean, New York (Pony League). Two weeks later, however, Cal was drafted into the U.S. Army. He served in Greenland and the Philippines during the war, and was honorably discharged from the Army in 1946.

When Cal returned to baseball—for the 1946 season—he was assigned to Danville, Illinois (3-I League). There he hit .345. In 1947, he was assigned to play in Mobile, Alabama (Southern Association). Mobile became the champion of the Southern Association that year with the help of Cal's .336 batting average. He returned to Mobile in 1948.

Cal began the 1949 season with the Brooklyn Dodgers, debuting on April 20. His first major league hit was off of future Hall of Famer Robin Roberts, at Shibe Park, Philadelphia. Cal finished the season with Fort Worth (Texas League), where he hit .333. Fort Worth captured the league pennant. The next year, 1950, Cal started with St. Paul, Minnesota (American Association), where he batted .333. He finished the season with the Dodgers.

In 1950, Cal played in 38 games for the Dodgers. He had started with the Dodgers with the number 32, but later changed it to number 18. He explained to us, "18 means a lot." Number 32 would later be assigned to Sandy Koufax and is, of course, now retired from the Dodgers. The number 18 stands for the Hebrew word chai, or "life."

In 1950, Cal was involved in a play that is still talked about in Brooklyn whenever his name is mentioned—one that cost the Dodgers a tie with the Phillies for the National League title. It was the final game of the regular 1950 season; the Dodgers were hosting the Philadelphia Phillies at Ebbets Field. The Dodgers were only one game behind the Phillies for the league title. At the bottom of the ninth the score was tied 1–1. Cal made it to second after being walked. There were two outs. Duke Snider was up to bat. He hit a line drive to the shallow part of center field. Centerfielder Richie Ashburn caught the ball on one bounce, as Cal reached third, and the third base coach, Milt Stock, enthusiastically waved Cal home. By the time Cal reached home plate, however, Ashburn had already made a perfect throw to catcher Stan Lopata. Lopata tagged Cal out, to end the ninth. In the tenth inning, Dick Sisler hit a 3-run home run to clinch the pennant for the Phillies.

This event made Cal infamous in Brooklyn and, perhaps, led to his being traded, after 10 games in the 1952 season, to the Cincinnati Reds. Cal's actions are defended by the testimony of Phillies centerfielder Richie Ashburn and pitcher Robin Roberts. Both of them have recently stated that it wasn't Cal's fault that he tried to get home, but instead was the fault of the third base coach, Stock, who had waved Cal on. It was Stock who was fired at the time. Brooklyn's Jewish population also forgave Cal, especially since he batted .280 in 1951. In 1951, Brooklyn's Jewish fans honored Cal with a "Cal Abrams Night."

Cal appeared in 71 games with the Reds in 1952. That year he played in more games, without making an error, than any other outfielder in the National League. (When we interviewed Cal, he was particularly proud of his defensive record. Cal had a lifetime fielding record, as an outfielder, of .977 and 1.000, on first base.) He was traded to the Pittsburgh Pirates in October, 1952. On September 20, 1953, Cal hit his only career grand-slam home run, off Ruben Gomez of the Giants. The Pirates won that game 8 to 4, at the Polo Grounds. Cal was still playing for the Pirates at the beginning of the 1954 season. On May 2, Cal had 4 hits for the Pirates in a single game. He had 2 singles, 1 double, and a triple; he scored 4 runs and had an RBI. The Pirates defeated the Cubs, 18–10. Cal was traded to the Baltimore Orioles, before the June 15 cut-down date, in 1954. He led them in batting that year, with a .293 average. Cal became so popular with the Orioles fans that they organized a second "Cal Abrams Day" for him. Abrams spent one more season at Baltimore, before being traded to the Chicago White Sox in 1956. When the Sox acquired Larry Doby that same year, Cal was sent to Miami (International League). He retired at the end of that season.

Cal was married to May Thaler and they had four children. Towards the end of his life, Cal had financial problems: one of his sons needed to raise money for a kidney and pancreas transplant operation. For the first time in his life, Cal began to charge money for his autograph. Cal Abrams died on February 25, 1997, at the age of seventy-two, in Fort Lauderdale, Florida.

Years	Games	AB	H	R	RBI	HR	BA	OBP	FP
8	567	1611	433	257	138	32	.269	.387	.977

1949-52 Bro-N, 1952 Cin-N, 1953-54 Pit-N, 1954-55 Bal-A, 1955 Chi-A

Lloyd Allen

Lloyd Cecil Allen was born on May 8, 1950, in Merced, California. Of Irish descent, he later converted to Judaism. As a child Lloyd played Little League and Babe Ruth League baseball. Later, he played on the varsity baseball, football, and basketball teams at his high school, Selma High. Lloyd was only the second player in the school's history to play on a varsity team in his freshman year. In his junior year, he pitched a perfect game. When Lloyd was not assigned to pitch, he played outfield. After graduating from high school in 1968, Lloyd attended Fresno City College for one year.

Lloyd was signed by the California Angels as a right-handed pitcher in 1968, as the club's first pick in the free-agent draft. His first minor league assignment was Idaho Falls (Pioneer League). On August 22, 1968, Lloyd pitched a seven-inning, no-hit, shutout game against Magic Valley (Pioneer League). He struck out 13 batters and walked 2. Lloyd was promoted to San Jose (California League) later that year. He married his wife, Sharon (née Raven), on September 7, 1968. In 1969, Lloyd pitched for San Jose and Hawaii (Pacific Coast League), before being promoted to the Angels.

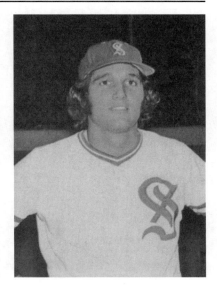

Lloyd made his major league debut on September 1, 1969, at Robert F. Kennedy Stadium, Washington, DC. He pitched a scoreless seventh inning, but the Senators defeated the Angels, 4–0. Lloyd pitched in 3 more games for the Angels in 1969. (His daughter, Shannon Lynette, was born on December 31 that year.) He started the 1970 season with El Paso (Texas League). Even though he led the Texas League in hit batsmen (10), he was elected to the league All-Star team in 1970. Lloyd returned to the Angels in 1970. He pitched in 8 games, with a 2.63 ERA. Lloyd had his first major league victory on September 30, 1970, against the Chicago White Sox. He pitched $7\frac{2}{3}$ innings and gave up 7 hits. The Angels won, 5 to 1, in Anaheim Stadium.

Lloyd had his first full season in the majors in 1971. From June 8 to July 8, he didn't allow an earned run in $23\frac{1}{3}$ innings. He pitched in 54 games with a 2.49 ERA and he had 15 saves. Lloyd returned to the Angels line-up in 1972. When Lloyd arrived at the Angels' training camp with long curly hair, he was ordered by Angels owner, Del Rice, to cut it shorter.

Lloyd became friends with the Angels coach, Jimmie Reese. Jimmie nicknamed Lloyd "Sandy," because he said Lloyd was the "Right-handed Sandy Koufax." Unlike Koufax, however, Lloyd was never shy. He was always flamboyant and colorful, soon becoming a crowd pleaser in Anaheim. Lloyd announced that he would like to become a movie actor, but never did.

Lloyd was traded to the Texas Rangers, after pitching in 5 games in the 1973 season, and pitched in 23 games for the Rangers with a 9.22 ERA. Lloyd played in 14 games with the Rangers in 1974, before being traded to the Chicago White Sox. He spent most of the season in the White Sox's Iowa farm club. Beginning the 1975 season with the White Sox, he appeared in only 3 games, with a 0-2 win-loss and a 12.60 ERA record, before being traded to the St. Louis Cardinals. In 1976, Lloyd pitched for the Cardinals' Tulsa Oilers. He went 9-2, with a 3.40 ERA, in 13 games for the Oilers. Added to the Cardinals' roster at the end of the 1976 season, he never played.

Lloyd Allen retired at the end of the year. He had a lifetime ERA of 4.69, a win-loss record of 8-25, and 22 saves—in 159 games.

Years	Games	IP	W	L	GS	SV	PCT	ERA
7	159	$297\frac{1}{3}$	8	25	19	22	.242	4.69

1969-73 Cal-A, 1973-74 Tex-A, 1974-75 Chi-A

Ruben Amaro, Jr.

Ruben Amaro, Jr., comes from a long line of ballplayers. His grandfather, Santos Amaro, played more than 25 seasons in Mexico. Ruben's father, Ruben Sr., played shortstop in the major leagues for 11 years.

Amaro Jr. was born on February 12, 1965, in Philadelphia, Pennsylvania, the son of a Jewish mother. Ruben did not formally study Judaism, but when he was a boy his family did celebrate the traditional Jewish holidays. In 1980, when his father was a coach on the World Champion Phillies, Ruben became the team's batboy. As batboy, he spent time with Hall of Famers Mike Schmidt and Steve Carlton. After Ruben's graduation from William Penn Charter High School, he attended Stanford University. He graduated from Stanford in 1987, with a BS degree in human biology.

In 1987, Ruben was selected by the California Angels in the 11th round of the free-agent draft. Unlike his father, who was an infielder, Ruben plays outfield. His first minor league assignment, in 1987, was with the Salem Angels. He hit .282, with 27 stolen bases, and was promoted to Palm Springs for the following year. Ruben was promoted to Midland before the end of that year.

Since 1989, Ruben has played in the Venezuelan Winter League. Since 1989, he has played on the Aguilos del Zulia, managed by his father, except for the 1991–92 season. That season he played for La Guaira. His average for his five seasons, as of 1996, is .280, with 151 hits, including 54 extra base hits, in 152 games.

In 1990, Ruben made it to the AAA-level Edmonton Trappers. Ruben was called up to the Angels, from Edmonton, on June 4, 1991, to replace the injured Junior Felix. On June 8, 1991, Ruben made his major league debut with a pinch running appearance in a game against the Detroit Tigers. He made 9 more appearances with the Angels that year.

In December 1991, Ruben was traded to the Phillies, beginning the 1992 season with them. Ruben hit his first major league home run on April 8, 1992. He also had 2 doubles that day, to help the Phillies defeat the Cubs, 11–3. Ruben injured himself in late April and was put on the disabled list. After playing with the Scranton–Wilkes-Barre Red Barons, for rehabilitation, he returned to the Phillies lineup in May. He played in 126 games with the Phillies in 1992, with a .219 batting average.

Ruben played most of the 1993 season with the Scranton–Wilkes-Barre Red Barons. He did play in 25 games with the 1993 National League Champion Phillies. Even though Ruben batted .291 for Scranton and .333 for Philadelphia in 1993, after the season the Phillies traded him to the Cleveland Indians. Ruben again played the majority of the year in the minors, with the Indians' Charlotte Knights (AAA). Ruben also played in 26 games with the Indians. In 1995, Ruben played with the AAA franchise of the Indians again, but the Indians had moved their franchise to Buffalo, New York. Besides playing with the Buffalo Bisons, Ruben played briefly with the Indians, including 2 plate appearances in the World Series. In that year's ALCS, Ruben scored an important run in the conclusive game of the series.

In 1996, Ruben was signed by the Toronto Blue Jays organization, but he was released after playing one month with the Blue Jays' Syracuse farm club. Ruben was re-signed by the Philadelphia Phillies, one day after being released from the Blue Jays. Unlike most players, he was very happy to be signed by the Phillies. He had many happy memories connected with the team and the city was his home. He made an amazing comeback in his second stint with the Phils. In 1996, he had a .316 batting average, in 61 games, and had the third-best average for a pinch-hitter in the National League. Ruben married his wife Virginia (née Machada) on December 6, 1996.

In 1997, Ruben Amaro was used mostly as a pinch-hitter by the Phillies. He batted .234 in 175 at-bats.

Ruben continued during the 1998 season as a valuable contributor to the Phillies organization as a pinch hitter and late inning defensive replacement in the outfield. He also served as the Phillies' third catcher, principally during batting practice.

Years	Games	AB	H	R	RBI	HR	BA	OBP	FP
8	485	927	218	99	100	16	.235	.312	.989

1991 Cal-A, 1992-1993 Phi-N, 1994-95 Cle-A, 1996-98 Phi-N

Morrie Arnovich

Morris "Morrie" Arnovich was born on November 20, 1910, in Superior, Wisconsin. The son of Orthodox Jewish parents, Morrie kept kosher throughout his life. He had two cousins who were rabbis and, as a child, studied Hebrew. Morrie graduated from Superior State Teachers College, where he was a basketball star. He was picked two years in a row for the All-Wisconsin basketball team. Morrie's aptitude at the British style of pocket billiards earned him the nickname "Snooker."

"MOE" ARNOVICH

In 1933, Morrie signed with his hometown team, Superior (Northern League), as an outfielder. He played two seasons there, batting .331 in 1933 and .374 in 1934. In 1934, Morrie hit 3 home runs in one game, against Fargo. In 1935, Morrie was sold to the Philadelphia Phillies, who optioned him to Hazleton (New York–Penn League). He stayed there until 1936, batting .305 in 1935 and .327 in 1936. In 1936, he tied for the league home-run record, with 19.

Morrie was promoted to the Philadelphia Phillies near the end of the 1936 season. He made his major league debut on September 14, 1936, at Philadelphia's Baker Bowl, replacing leftfielder Johnny Moore in the 6th inning. Morrie hit a double off Pirates pitcher Red Lucas and scored 1 run, in 3 at-bats. Pittsburgh defeated the Phillies 6 to 5, in 10 innings. Morrie appeared in 12 more games with the Phillies that year. He had a batting average of .313. Morrie returned to the Phillies lineup in 1937, for his first full season in the majors; he hit a home run to win the season opener, 2 to 1, in Boston. Morrie batted .290 that year, in 117 games. He returned to the Phillies in 1938 to bat .275 in 139 games.

Morrie had his best season in 1939, batting .324 that year, and leading the league in batting for much of the season. The same year, Morrie played for the losing National League

team in the All-Star game. He was even invited to the opening of the National Baseball Hall of Fame, on June 12, 1939. Unfortunately, he played for the cellar-dwelling Phillies, which finished the season over 50 games out of first place. When Morrie got off to a slow start in 1940, he was sold to the Cincinnati Reds for $25,000; he picked up his average with the pennant-winning Reds. Morrie had one appearance in the 1940 World Series: on October 5, he entered the game as a pinch-hitter in the 7th inning. He got 2 at-bats against Detroit Tigers pitcher Archie McKain. He hit two fly balls, and caught the last Detroit pop fly, to end the game, 5 to 2 Cincinnati.

Morrie was traded to the New York Giants in 1941. That year, he batted .280 in 85 games.

Morrie enlisted in the U.S. Army, with his brother, Hyman, in 1942, returning from the service in 1945. He went back to the Giants in 1946, however, when Morrie returned from the Army he was no longer in peak condition to play. After playing in a single game with the Giants, Morrie was optioned to Jersey City. He was later released from the Jersey team.

Morrie returned to his hometown of Superior, Wisconsin, in 1946. He became the basketball coach at a local Catholic high school. He also ran a successful jewelry store and a sporting goods store. Morrie married Bertha Aserson on July 10, 1956. Morrie Arnovitch died on July 20, 1959, in Superior, of a coronary occlusion. He was buried in Hebrew Cemetery, in Superior.

Years	Games	AB	H	R	RBI	HR	BA	OBP	FP
7	590	2013	577	234	261	22	.287	.350	.981

1936-40 Phi-N, 1940 Cin-N, 1941 NY-N, 1946 NY-N

Jake Atz

Jake Atz, a very personable man, a natural leader, and one of the great raconteurs in the history of baseball, had one favorite story he seemed to have told everyone he ever met. It's a funny story, but it has clouded the issue of Jake's origins, so that it is now not certain what name John Jacob Atz was actually born with, on July 1, 1879, in Washington, DC. No one has ever been able to find Jake's birth certificate, so the problem of his family name remains.

Jake's story goes like this: He was born John Jacob Zimmerman. Jake played for a team that paid its players alphabetically. One day, before everyone was due to be paid, the team ran out of money. The team ended up going bankrupt. The players at the end of the list, including of course John Jacob Zimmerman, never got paid. Jake decided he'd never get caught like that again. He changed his last name to Atz, so his name would cover everything from A to Z.

Jake's given names are also a source of mystery. The press of his time and the standard references all give his name as John Jacob Atz. But his wife, in filling in a Hall of Fame questionnaire, listed his name as Jacob Henry Atz. She listed his son's name as Jacob Henry Atz, Jr.

Jake's mother's maiden name is listed on the same document as "Annie Flaherty," so it is pretty clear that he was of Irish origin on the maternal side, presumably Catholic. His father's name is also listed as Jacob Henry Atz, of German origin. Because of all the conflicting evidence, it is not possible to accept Jake's assumed name, but the national origin seems certain. This is the side of his ancestry that was Jewish. That he was Jewish is clear from statements Jake made throughout his life. Some of these statements were made as jokes, as for instance variations on the story about his name. But we have evidence from Mickey Rutner, who worked with him and knew him well, that he also spoke about being a Jew at serious moments and discussed with Mickey questions of anti-Semitism.

Jake began his career in the minor leagues with Raleigh, North Carolina, in 1901. He then was purchased by the New Orleans Pelicans.

ATZ, CHICAGO AMER.

On September 24, 1902, the right-handed utility infielder made his debut with the Washington Senators. In his first game, against Boston, Jake had a hit, scored a run, and made two successful fielding plays on second base. He stayed with the Senators only 3 games, before returning to the minors. Jake's average was only .100 for the Senators, and he did not return to the majors until 1907.

Jake played with Albany, Troy (NY), Memphis, Portland, and, again, New Orleans. It was from the Pelicans that the Chicago White Sox purchased Jake's contract in 1907. Jake came to the team in the same deal that brought Moxie Manuel. Jake, who played mostly at second for Chicago, didn't add much to the power of the previous year's World Series–winning "hitless wonders." His averages with the Sox were .125 in 1907, .194 in 1908, and .236 in 1909.

It was in 1909 that Jake did something very foolish for his team that nearly cost him his life. In a tight game, against Washington, he deliberately moved into the path of a pitch, to get on base. But the pitch, instead of brushing his uniform, hit him squarely on the hip. The pitcher was Walter Johnson and the force of the blow left Jake writhing on the field. Jake never fully recovered from that incident and suffered pains from it for the rest of his life.

The next year, Jake's contract was sold to the Providence Internationals. It was in Providence that Jake was first given managerial responsibilities, taking over the pilot's job from Jimmy Collins in 1911. From there, Jake moved back to New Orleans, where he established his residence. Then it was on to Beaumont, Fort Worth, and Galveston. All this time, Jake was establishing his reputation as one of the finest managers who ever worked in the minor leagues.

Jake first managed the Ft. Worth Panthers (later, the Wildcats or "Cats"), in 1917. Jake set many records in the Texas League as manager. He had seven consecutive first-place finishes for the Cats, 1919–1925. He had the longest service as a manager: 22 years, including 18 with Fort Worth; he had the most first-place teams and the most Dixie Series championships. Jake was one of the winningest managers in the history of organized baseball.

In 1936, on his 58th birthday, Jake was honored by being named manager of the Southern Texas League team, which met the Northern Texas League team, as part of the celebration of the centennial of the Texas Rebellion. Other teams Jake managed include Dallas, Shreveport, Harlingen, and Henderson. Jake's last job as a manager, in 1941, was with Winston-Salem (Piedmont League). It was here that he managed the young Mickey Rutner, who referred to Jake as "a great kibitzer and a very nice man."

Besides managing, Jake did a stint as an umpire in the Texas League. He was also business manager with Galveston. When Jake was manager at Henderson, his son, Jake Jr., served as the team's business manager. Jake Jr. also had experience of his own as a player in the minor leagues.

On January 7, 1907, Jake married Doris Kalman. The couple had a son and a daughter. Jake died on May 22, 1945, in New Orleans, from cancer of the pancreas. At the time of his death, an anonymous reporter described him as follows: "To those who only worked under him he was a driving taskmaster; rough talking and hard handed. That was because he was an earnest competitor and hard loser. To others he was a big-hearted, generous and sympathetic friend. To his opponents he was a snarling, fighting fellow, but to his followers he was a brilliant leader and a happy warrior."

On December 31, 1963, Jake Atz was inducted into the Texas Sports Hall of Fame in Waco.

Years	Games	AB	H	R	RBI	HR	BA	OBP	FP
4	209	605	132	64	49	0	.218	.304	.949

1902 Was-A, 1907-09 Chi-A

Brad Ausmus

Bradley David Ausmus was born April 14, 1969, in New Haven, Connecticut.

He is the son of a Jewish mother and a gentile father. While a student at Cheshire High School, in Connecticut, Brad was a teammate of hockey player Brian Leetch. Brad's high school team won the 1984 Connecticut State Championship.

In 1987, Brad was selected as a catcher by the New York Yankees organization in the 47th round of the free-agent draft. In 1988, Brad played with the Yankees' instructional league affiliate, Sarasota (Gulf Coast League). He was promoted to the Onoenta Yankees (New York–Penn League) at the end of the 1988 season. Brad was promoted to the Prince William Cannons (Carolina League) in 1990 and to the Albany–Colonie Yankees, in 1991.

He was drafted, again, by the Colorado Rockies in the 1992 expansion draft.

He joined the Rockies' AAA club, the Colorado Springs Sky Sox, in 1993. That July, he was traded to the San Diego Padres organization.

Brad made his major league debut, with the Padres, on July 28, 1993. That day, he was walked and got a single in his first two at-bats; he was behind the plate in another 48 games that year. Brad played with the Padres for two more full seasons. In 1994, he led National League catchers in putouts, with 683. That season, he played one game at first base. Brad had his best year in 1995. Besides leading all National League catchers in double plays—with 14—he had his highest batting average, to date: .293. In 1996, still with the Padres, Brad struggled with his hitting. He had a 50-game slump, hitting .181. Brad was traded to the Detroit Tigers during the sea-

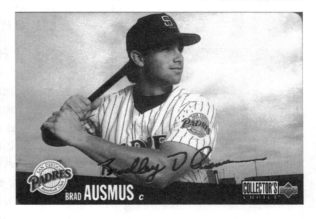

BRAD AUSMUS c

son, finishing the season batting .248 for the team. Brad was again traded in 1997, to the Houston Astros. Since his arrival in Houston, Brad has been improving his swing, and has pulled his average up to the .270 range. His defense and base-running ability are exceptional.

Brad made history on August 12, 1997. He was the first catcher to wear the Fox Sports Catcher-Cam during a major league game. The Catcher-Cam is a small television camera that fits on top of a catcher's mask. The Houston Astros defeated the New York Mets 6 to 0, that day. Brad finished the 1997 season with a .266 batting average in 130 games.

In the off-season, Brad Ausmus lives in Cheshire, Connecticut.

In 1998, Brad took over the position of first string catcher for the Astros.

Years	Games	AB	H	R	RBI	HR	BA	OBP	FP
8	913	3008	791	397	299	48	.263	.338	.991

1993-96 SD-N, 1996 Det-A, 1997-98 Hou-N, 1999-2000 Det-A

Jesse Baker

There were two men who played baseball under the name of Jesse Baker. One was born with that name and pitched for the Chicago White Sox in 1911. The one we are interested in was born Michael Myron Silverman and played shortstop for the Washington Senators in 1919.

Michael Silverman was born in Cleveland, Ohio, on March 4, 1895. His parents had a clothing business, but Michael left it behind, to pursue his dream of becoming a baseball player.

Michael, now calling himself Jesse Baker, obtained a position with the Washington Senators. On September 14, 1919, he made his debut, starting the game against the Detroit Tigers at shortstop. Covering second base, he was spiked by Ty Cobb, who must have seen the 5'4", 140-pound Jesse as a small threat for retaliation. Jesse had to leave the game, never having got an at-bat. That was the end of Jesse's major league career.

Jesse continued playing in the minors for some time. He finally settled down in Los Angeles, where he became a familiar figure at racetracks and prizefights He became friends with the likes of Damon Runyon, Walter Winchell, and the Marx Brothers. Jesse worked in the boxing trade and owned a share of the boxer Sam Cohen.

Jesse Baker was married. He died July 29, 1976, in Los Angeles.

Years	Games	AB	H	R	RBI	HR	BA	OBP	FP
1	1	0	0	0	1	0	NA	NA	1.000

1919 Was-A

Brian Bark

ProCards®

BRIAN BARK
Pitcher
Pulaski Braves

Brian Stuart Bark was born on August 26, 1968, in Baltimore, Maryland. His father is a former minor league pitcher. Brian attended Randallstown High School and North Carolina State University.

Brian was drafted 28th by his hometown team, the Orioles, but he turned them down. He was later picked 11th in the June 1990 draft, by the Braves. That year, he pitched for the Pulaski Braves (A). There, the left-handed Brian pitched 2 wins and 2 losses, and had a 2.66 ERA.

In 1991, Brian was sent to the Durham Bulls (A). Later that year, he was promoted to the Greenville Braves (AA), where he also began the 1992 season. Playing hard in 1992, he accumulated 5 wins had no losses and a 1.15 ERA. Brian was brought up to the Richmond Braves (AAA) during the 1992 season. There he pitched in 22 games with a 1-2 record and a 6.00 ERA. In 1993, he improved, with a 12-9 win-loss record and a 3.67 ERA, but led the International League in walks, with 72.

Brian played with Richmond until June 1, 1995, when he was released. He was quickly signed by the Red Sox on June 2, as a free agent, and brought up to the Pawtucket Red Sox (AAA), where he would stay until his major league debut. Brian was called up by the Boston Red Sox on July 6, 1995. That day, he pitched a third of an inning, in the ninth, against the Minnesota Twins. He gave up no runs, but the Twins won the game, 6–4. That year, Brian pitched $2\frac{1}{n}$ innings. He had a 0.00 ERA, giving up only two hits and no runs.

Brian Bark no longer plays professional ball. He enjoys using the Internet and was considered by his teammates to be a "computer whiz." He resides in Baltimore, Maryland.

Years	Games	IP	W	L	GS	SV	PCT	ERA
1	3	$2\frac{1}{3}$	0	0	0	0	NA	0.00
1995 Bos-A								

Ross Baumgarten

FLEER

PIRATES
34

Ross Baumgarten
PITCHER

Ross Baumgarten was born on May 27, 1955, in Highland Park, Illinois. As a child, Ross was an avid baseball fan; he spent many of his days playing or watching baseball. Ross graduated from New Trier East High School, in Chicago.

In 1977, Ross was the 20th-round selection of the Chicago White Sox in the June Amateur draft. The southpaw pitcher was sent to the White Sox Class A team in Appleton, Wisconsin. He pitched 17 games, with a 3-6 average and a 3.75 ERA. Ross returned to Appleton in 1978. There, he had a 9-1 record and a 1.82 ERA. He was promoted to the Class AAA Iowa team during the season.

After playing in 9 games in Iowa, Ross was promoted to the White Sox. He was called up on August 14, 1978, and made his debut, as a starter, two days later—winning the game, 6 to 2. Ross appeared in 6 more games with the White Sox in 1978, and had a 2-2 record, with a 5.87 ERA. He returned to the White Sox the following year. That year, he suffered throat problems for more than a month, at mid-season, yet finished with a 13-8 record and a 3.53 ERA. He threw a one-hitter on May 25, 1979, against the California Angels. Ross was named "Chicago Rookie of the Year" at the close of the 1979 season.

Ross was a control pitcher. He was never an excellent athlete, but he did know how to use the strike zone and could throw good off-speed pitches.

Ross had his worst season in 1980, although it was not his fault. In his 24 appearances, the White Sox batters scored only 25 runs. In 10 of those games, the White Sox were scoreless while Ross was on the mound. Ross ended the season with a 2-12 record. He threw a second one-hitter against the California Angels on July 2, 1980, and improved his ERA to 3.44. In 1981, Ross pitched with a painful pinched nerve in his left foot. Despite his pain, he managed to pitch in 19 games that year, with a 5-9 record and a 4.06 ERA. At the end of the season, Ross had surgery to remove the nerve. In 1982, he was traded to the Pittsburgh Pirates. He ended his baseball career with the Pirates. Ross retired after pitching in 12 games in the 1982 season. He had a record, that year, of 0-5 and had a 6.55 ERA. He had a lifetime record of 22-36 and a 3.99 ERA.

After retiring from baseball, Ross has never looked back. He became an account executive at the investment firm William Blair and Co. He is married and has three sons and one daughter. Ross Baumgarten lives, with his family, in suburban Chicago.

Years	Games	IP	W	L	GS	SV	PCT	ERA
5	90	$495\frac{1}{3}$	22	36	84	0	.379	4.00

1978-81 Chi-A, 1982 Pit-N

Jose Bautista

Jose Joaquin (Arias) Bautista, who has Russian-Jewish and Dominican antecedents, was born in Bani, Dominican Republic, on July 25, 1964, and is a practicing Jew. He was bar-mitzvah'd and will never play on the High Holidays.

When Jose was young, his family practiced Judaism in private. His family is one of very few Jewish families in the overwhelmingly Catholic Dominican Republic. Most of the Jews in the Dominican Republic are descended from those who fled Nazi tyranny and were accepted by the dictator Leonidas Trujillo, when the democracies of North America had closed their doors to the Jewish people. Most of these immigrants later moved on, but Jose's grandfather stayed put because he had married a local girl, Jose's grandmother. Jose was one of sixteen children. (Four of his brothers have played some form of professional baseball.) Every Friday they baked a challah and lit the shabbat candles.

At age sixteen, Jose was picked by the New York Mets in the 1991 free-agent draft. The right-handed pitcher made his professional debut that year with the Kingsport Mets. He ended the 1991 season with a 4.64 ERA and a 3-6 record. Jose returned to the Kingsporters in

1982 and pitched a 0-4 record with a 8.92 ERA. He began to show promise in 1983. That year, he pitched for the Sarasota Mets and had a 2.31 ERA with a 4-3 record. Jose pitched for the Columbus Mets in 1984 and for the Lynchburg (VA) Mets in 1985. In 1985, Jose pitched a 7-inning no-hitter. That year, he also won 9 consecutive games, from June 21 to August 8. Jose ended the season with a 2.34 ERA and a 15-8 record. He didn't pitch as well the next two years in the Mets system for Jacksonville and Lynchburg, and was released at the end of the 1987 season.

Jose was drafted by the Orioles as their first pick in the December 1987 draft. The Orioles promoted Jose to the majors, the next season. After pitching for 7 years in the minors and a few years in the Dominican Winter League, he finally earned a spot on a major league roster. Jose made his major-league debut on April 9, 1988.

After his debut, he found himself bouncing back and forth between the majors and the minors.

JOSE BAUTISTA
Giants

After pitching in 75 games for the Orioles and 70 for their minor league teams, Jose was released. In 1992, he was granted minor-league free agency and signed with the triple-A Omaha Royals. The next year, 1993, he signed with the Chicago Cubs and reentered the majors. Jose led the Cubs in 1993 with an ERA of 2.81. He remained on the Cubs' roster in 1994, but was released at the end of the season. On April 6, 1995, Jose signed with the San Francisco Giants organization. He spent two years pitching for both San Francisco and their triple-A affiliate, the Phoenix Firebirds. On September 11, 1996, it was announced that Jose would have to miss the rest of the season, because of an aneurysm in his right shoulder and a blood clot in his right index finger. He underwent an angiogram for the aneurysm and was given medication to dissolve the clot.

In 1997, Jose was traded to the Detroit Tigers. He began the season poorly, with a 2-2 record and a 6.69 ERA in 21 appearances, and was released on July 21. It looked as though this would be the end of Jose's 17-year career in professional baseball, but in September, Jose was signed by the St. Louis Cardinals. He pitched in 11 games for the Cardinals and had a 6.57 ERA.

Jose met his wife, the former Lea Robichek, while he was a teenager studying at a Venezuelan engineering school. She is also Jewish, and her family had emigrated to Venezuela from Israel. During the off-season of 1994–1995, Jose's family celebrated the bar mitzvah of their elder son, Leo, and they traveled to Israel to visit Lea's family in Tel Aviv and Haifa, and to see the land of their ancestors. Jose took classes in Hebrew. The Bautistas have two sons, Leo and Jose, whom they are raising to be observant Jews. The family currently lives in Cooper City, Florida.

In a 1994 interview, Jose Bautista stated, "Even though there aren't many Jews in the Dominican Republic, I would like to go back home and build a synagogue in my native land. That way, they will forever have a house of God."

Jose spent the early part of the 1998 season on various minor league teams, including Norwich (AA team in the Yankees organization) and the AAA Calgary Cannons of the White Sox organization.

Years	Games	IP	W	L	GS	SV	PCT	ERA
9	312	$685\frac{2}{3}$	32	42	49	3	.444	4.62

1988-91 Bal-A, 1993-94 Chi-N, 1995-6 SF-N, 1997 Det-A, 1997 StL-N

Bo Belinsky

Robert "Bo" Belinsky was born on December 7, 1936, at Beth Israel Hospital in the Lower East Side of Manhattan. His parents were Edward and Anna Belinsky. Bo's father was a Polish Catholic, his mother a Russian Jew. The Belinskys lived in New York until 1940, when they moved to Trenton, New Jersey, so that Ed Belinsky could take a job at the Roebling plant, which produced steel wire for suspension bridges. Ed had played baseball in the Coast Guard before his marriage and, at 7 or 8, young Robert began to show interest in the game. It was around this time that Robert won his nickname. Robert was a scrapper at school; his friends coined the name Bo from boxer Bobo Olson.

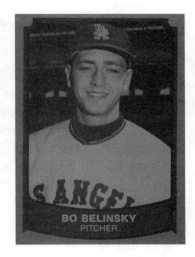

Bo graduated Trenton High School—and also from some of Trenton's seedier pool halls. He had become an excellent pool hustler, but also a star of the local sandlot baseball games. Pirates scout Rex Bowen spotted him in such a game and signed him for one of the Pirates' farm teams, Brunswick, Georgia, a Class D team, in the Georgia–Florida League. Bo was given a ticket to Georgia, but not a penny for the trip. He joined the Brunswick team in 1956, pitching 3 and 3 for 11 games, with a 7.36 ERA. Bo also started the pattern of behavior that would be part of his style and legend throughout his career. He broke the training rules. When he pursued women—women pursued him; he got into fights; he jumped the team; he got drunk; he got other players drunk; he hustled pool. It is hard to understand why Bo was tolerated at all. In addition to all his other faults, he was arrogant. But behind everything else, he had a rich reserve of natural pitching talent and a charisma and charm that got infractions forgiven that for other men would have been unforgivable.

In 1957, Bo, a southpaw, pitched for the Pensacola Dons, an independent team. There he had an ERA of 3.00. The next year was spent with Knoxville (Sally League). In 1959, he was with Aberdeen, Amarillo, Stockton, and Pensacola. Some of these moves were upward ones, rewards for good pitching. Other moves were to get Bo out of harm's way—away from angry fathers and homicidal husbands or, simply, from girls who would not let him alone.

Bo, by this time, was the property of the Baltimore Orioles. During the winter of 1959, they had Bo pitch in Clearwater, Florida, a team in the Instructional League, to help him develop. Then Bo was sent to spring training in 1960 with the Orioles, but he was quickly cut from the roster. He spent that season with Vancouver (Pacific Coast League).

1961 found Bo in Little Rock, during the regular season and in Venezuela for winter league baseball. It was in Venezuela that Bo first showed himself as a mature pitcher. During this same time, his contract was traded by the Orioles to the new American League expansion team in Los Angeles, the Angels. Perhaps no name could have been more inappropriate for Bo.

When the year began, Bo already had drawn publicity to himself by his attempt to hold out for a higher salary. Bo's good looks, his talk of pool hustling, and his cavalier attitude made him an overnight sensation with the California sportswriters. This didn't get him any more money than the $6,000 the Angels had originally offered him, but it won for him the attention of the world. On April 19, 1962, Bo Belinsky made his major league debut. Bo pitched $7\frac{2}{3}$ innings at Chavez Ravine, against Kansas City, and gave up only 2 runs. He had earned his first major league win.

Bo followed this with a victory over the Cleveland Indians and, in his first complete game, a shutout of the Washington Senators. The West Coast, which had idolized its Dodgers and its Giants, and had looked askance at the Angels, had found a new idol. Bo was the man of the hour.

On May 5, Bo made his fourth start and his first against his old team, the Baltimore Orioles. Bo pitched a no-hitter against the Orioles, 2–0. This was the first no-hitter ever pitched at the major league level on the West Coast. Overnight, Bo went from the level of a superstar to a god. If Bo would have taken that no-hitter as a signal from some higher power that he was to dedicate himself to the art and skill of baseball, his reputation, considering his natural abilities, might have eclipsed those of Koufax and Nolan Ryan. But Bo didn't hear such a message. The message he heard was, "You've partied to here, party a hundredfold from here on out." And that is exactly what he did.

Bo finished his first year with the Angels at 10 and 11, a .476 percent. His ERA was 3.56. His career with the Angels continued, moments of greatness interrupting general mediocrity. In 1963 he had only 2 wins and 9 losses. He was sent down to the minors for a period of time, to play for Hawaii. Bo did better, in 1964, with 9 wins and 8 losses. This was the only winning season of his career, with a .529 percentage. A controversy arose over a drunken attack he had made on a much older man, a sportswriter.

Bo was traded to the Phillies for the 1965 season. There he was used primarily as a relief pitcher. He remained with the Phils in 1966, and was honored with a day in his honor. Shortly thereafter, he was sent down to the San Diego Padres (Pacific Coast League).

The next season, Bo was traded to the Houston Astros. Here Bo's genius for publicity helped him start the year, with his demand for a locker for his dog. But his 3 wins and 9 losses got Bo on a plane back to Hawaii, where he spent 1968. During this time, Bo had one last moment of baseball glory. He pitched a second no-hit game for the Hawaii team. At the end of that season, Bo's contract was sold to the Pittsburgh Pirates.

During 1969, Bo was given very little to do by the Pirates. He only appeared in 8 games. Bo's last season in the majors was 1970; his contract had been picked up by the Cincinnati Reds. He appeared in 3 games for the Reds, then was sent to their Indianapolis team for the rest of the season. On September 4, 1970, he was sent home. His career was ended.

A full examination of Bo's "box scores" should include his romances and dates with the likes of Ann-Margret, Tina Louise, Paulette Goddard, and Queen Soroya. He was engaged to Mamie Van Doren, but broke it off. He was married three times. His first wife was a Playboy centerfold, Jo Collins; this first marriage produced a daughter, Stevie. Bo met his second wife, Jane Weyerhauser, while rescuing her from drowning on a Hawaii beach. Jane was quite wealthy, but this marriage also ended in divorce. Bo was married for a third time in 1986.

All these years, Bo has had many problems with addiction to alcohol and prescription drugs. After years of struggle, he finally managed to free himself from these addictions, and has stayed clean for years. Bo Belinsky now resides in Redondo Beach, California.

Years	Games	IP	W	L	GS	SV	PCT	ERA
8	146	$665\frac{1}{3}$	28	51	102	2	.354	4.10

1962-64 LA-A, 1965-66 Phi-N, 1967 Hou-N, 1969 Pit-N, 1970 Cin-N

Joe Bennett

Joseph Rosenblum Bennett was born July 2, 1900, in New York City. He attended elementary school in the Bronx and graduated from Morris High School. He attended NYU and the University of Missouri, but never took a degree.

In 1923, Joe played for the Lancaster Club of the New York–Pennsylvania League. Later in that year, he was called up to play for the Phillies. Joe made his only appearance with the Phillies on July 5, 1923. He was put in the game, against the St. Louis Cardinals, to cover third base. Joe made one assist at his position. He never got an at-bat. The game was held at the Baker Bowl and the Phillies lost, 16–12. Joe claimed he never got paid for his appearance with the Phillies.

Joe once indicated that he had played professional ball from 1922 to 1924. Later, he formed a semi-pro team, the Red Bank Pirates.

Joe tried running a hardware store, in Highlands, New Jersey, and a sporting goods store in Red Bank. In 1926, Joe joined the U.S. Army. He served in the quartermaster's corps through both the Second World War and the Korean War, until 1955. He retired as a lieutenant colonel. Following his retirement, Joe managed Gibbs Hall, the officer's club at Ft. Monmouth, New Jersey.

Joe was married to the former Jean Weisberg in 1929. The couple had two daughters. [Mrs. Jean Bennett died in 1976.] Joe Bennett died in Morro Bay, California, on July 11, 1987.

Years	Games	AB	H	R	RBI	HR	BA	OBP	FP
1	1	0	0	0	0	0	NA	NA	1.000

1923 Phi-N

Moe Berg

Moe Berg was a five-dimensional man in a four-dimensional world. No matter how well one thought one knew him, no matter how close one was to him, there was a portion of his being that was turned away from you, a hidden corner. To almost all who met him, Moe was charming and, apparently, accessible. His charm and immediacy were there for all to experience.

He was, perhaps, the only genius to ever become a major league baseball player. (We don't mean a genius of baseball, like Ted Williams, Satchel Paige, or Ty Cobb, for this he was not—but the real McCoy, à la Einstein, Oppenheimer, or Feyneman.) He was, by every witness's account, a talented linguist, a master spy, a decent second-string catcher, and a myth-maker of the first water. His achievements are a matter of controversy, but enough of his reputation rests on a bed-rock of incontrovertible facts to assure him an immortal reputation unique in the annals of baseball.

Morris Berg was born in Belleville, New Jersey, on March 2, 1902. His parents, Bernard and Rose Berg (née Tashker) had emigrated to this country from the Ukraine. His father, on

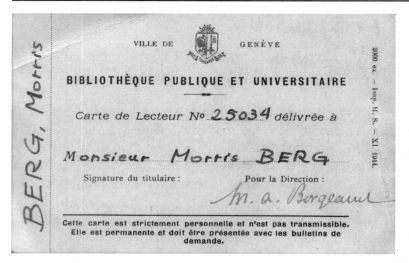

BERG, Morris

VILLE DE   GENÈVE

BIBLIOTHÈQUE PUBLIQUE ET UNIVERSITAIRE

Carte de Lecteur No _25034_ délivrée à

Monsieur Morris BERG

Signature du titulaire :   Pour la Direction :

M. a. Borgeaud

Cette carte est strictement personnelle et n'est pas transmissible.
Elle est permanente et doit être présentée avec les bulletins de demande.

2000 ex. — Imp. H. S. — XI. 1944.

Moe Berg's Geneva, Switzerland Library card, dated to November, 1944. This is the period of Moe's most essential spy mission, the Swiss foray, which included the Werner Heisenberg encounter of December 18, 1944.

his arrival in America, had studied pharmacy. When Morris was four, his parents moved to Newark and his father opened his own drugstore.

As a boy, Morris showed remarkable precocity in intellectual matters and in sports. He was the youngest of three children. His brother, Samuel, would eventually become a doctor and his sister, Ethel, a teacher. Morris spent his youth impressing his friends, both with his baseball prowess and by learning Hebrew. He would buy packs of cigarettes for the baseball cards and throw away the rest of the contents, for he never smoked. When he was old enough, Moe went to Princeton University, where he studied modern languages and graduated with highest honors. He was equally distinguished on the baseball diamond. He was Princeton's star shortstop. He graduated in 1923 and, immediately, found a position with the Brooklyn Dodgers. During a game, Moe was asked to fill in for the catcher. He remained at that position for the rest of his career.

Moe had many good qualities as a catcher. He was wily and knew the batters' weaknesses and his pitcher's strengths. In his latter years, when he was mainly used in the bullpen, he was entertaining to the pitchers warming up. He was always popular with other members of his team. Tales of anti-Semitism always pop up in accounts of the careers of Andy Cohen, Hank Greenberg, Buddy Myer, Al Rosen, and others. But Moe's personality help to minimize ethnic slurs and his apparent aloofness would defuse any question of conflict.

From 1926 to 1930, Moe played with the Chicago White Sox. During the same period he was studying for his law degree at Columbia University and passing the bar exams. Moe did practice law, for a time, in the off-seasons, but baseball was his first love.

Moe's best year was 1929, when he batted .287, had 32 runs, 47 RBIs, and caught 107 games. In those 107 games, he allowed only 5 stolen bases. Chicago's best pitchers at that time, Ted Lyons and Tommy Thomas, always requested Moe as their catcher when they were pitching. Lyons, a Hall of Famer, stated that in all the time Moe caught for him, he never once shook off a sign from Moe.

Injuries led Moe to take a more secondary position as a catcher. In 1931, he was with the Cleveland Indians. He returned briefly to Cleveland, at the end of the 1934 season. From 1932 to 1934, he was with the Washington Senators. It was while with the Senators that Moe set an American League record by catching in 117 consecutive games without committing an error. This record stood for 12 years. While outstanding defensively, Moe was not always dynamite at the plate. In 1933, for instance, he only batted .185. This led one wag to coin the famous line about Moe "He can speak 12 languages, but can't hit in any of them."

Perhaps it was Moe himself who coined the line—he certainly was known for his dry sense of humor and his self-effacing jokes. For instance, Moe liked to tell this story about himself and his friend, Al Schacht: When Moe was catching for Cleveland and Al was with the Senators, Al asked Moe out for a few beers. Moe demurred—his manager, Walter Johnson, being very strict and wanting everyone in bed by 11:30. Al came back, "I'm sure Walter won't mind, Moe, as long as I don't keep any of the ballplayers out." If Moe is the author of the above quote, about his hitting, it would answer one mystery about him: How many languages did he really know? Certainly one he knew was Japanese.

During the winter of 1934, Moe traveled with an all-star lineup for a baseball exhibition tour of Japan. Moe had been to Japan before, in 1932; but this time he was in the company of Babe Ruth and Lou Gehrig. He also traveled with a movie camera with which he made movies of various military installations and defenses. These movies were made at the request of the American government and proved valuable during the Second World War.

Moe was a favorite topic of sportswriters during the 1930s, particularly of John Kieran, columnist for The New York Times. These columns made "The Professor" a familiar figure to the public. On February 21, 1939, the public got a real chance to meet Moe, via the radio show "Information Please," where Moe joined regular panelists John Kieran, F. P. Adams, Oscar Levant, and host Clifton Fadiman. Moe was a great success on the show and the network received thousands of fan letters for him.

From 1935 to 1939, Moe played with the Boston Red Sox. In 1935, he had a surprisingly good year, batting .286 in 38 games. In 1938, he was in only 10 games, but batted .333. From 1940 to 1941, he served as a coach for the team. With the Second World War, the former shortstop, catcher, lawyer, and radio personality found his true calling. He became a full-time spy. Moe began his government work with a tour of duty as a goodwill ambassador to various South American countries. Moe's mission was a great success and he was recruited by the OSS.

Moe served in various capacities, but finally he found his niche as the head of the mission to determine German progress towards the construction of an atomic bomb. This job was particularly difficult because it involved very technical aspects of nuclear physics, excellent linguistic ability, and rare acting abilities.

Moe's most daring exploit was his confrontation with Werner Heisenberg (1901–1976), one of the great physicists of the century and author of the Heisenberg uncertainty principle, one of the cornerstones of quantum mechanics. Heisenberg had received the Nobel Prize in physics in 1932, and was in charge of Germany's program to build a nuclear bomb. Moe had been carefully trained in the fine details that would be necessary to determine the degree of progress the Germans had made. Heisenberg was scheduled to give a lecture in Switzerland, on an abstruse aspect of physics. Moe attended the lecture and asked some very pointed questions of the lecturer.

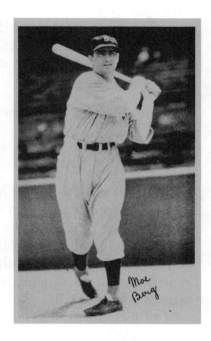

After the talk, Moe walked out with Heisenberg, and continued cross-examining the German scientist. Heisenberg was patient and answered the questions very carefully. This was fortunate for him and for the future of science, for Heisenberg still had many important contributions to make. However, unknown to Heisenberg, Moe had a gun pointed at him all the time, and if any of his answers indicated progress on the part of the Germans towards a bomb, Moe was prepared to kill him. But Heisenberg's replies indicated that they had made no such progress. After the war, Moe's assessment of Heisenberg's statements was proved absolutely correct. Perhaps no other man in the world was competent enough to have carried forth the Heisenberg exploit. It involved complete comprehension of what, at that time, was barely understood by many of those involved in the Manhattan Project. It required linguistic skills and the calmness of a catcher waiting for the most important pitch of the game. Moe was involved in many other exploits during the war. He remained with the OSS for some time after this.

The later years of Moe Berg's life are confusing. He wandered about, seemingly with a purpose, but one known only to himself. He would turn up at ballgames or friends' houses. He would call on the phone and then disappear. He lived off the kindness of his brother and sister or of the many acquaintances who considered it a rare honor to treat him to dinner or put him up for a few days. Moe certainly could have found employment in baseball, but for some reason did not want this. He needed time for his books and newspapers.

Late in May, in 1972, Moe was taken ill and rushed to the hospital. He was suffering from a failing heart. Moe's last words were, "How are the Mets doing today?" He died on May 29, 1972, at the Clara Maass Medical Center in Belleville, New Jersey.

Much has been written about Moe Berg since his death. Our favorite quote is from his old battery mate, Ted Lyons: "He made up for all the bores in the world."

Years	Games	AB	H	R	RBI	HR	BA	OBP	FP
15	663	1813	441	150	206	6	.243	.278	.986

1923 Bro-N, 1926-30 Chi-A, 1931 Cle-A, 1932-34 Was-A, 1934 Cle-A, 1935-39 Bos-A

Nathan Berkenstock

Nathan Berkenstock was born in Pennsylvania in 1831.

Nate played in one major league game. It was on October 30, 1871, the last game of the season. Nate was the rightfielder for the Philadelphia Athletics of the National Association. He didn't get a hit in his four at-bats, but the A's won, 4 to 1, against the Chicago White Stockings. The game was held at Brooklyn's Union Grounds.

Nate Berkenstock died in Philadelphia, on February 23, 1900.

Years	Games	AB	H	R	RBI	HR	BA	OBP	FP
1	1	4	0	0	0	0	.000	.000	1.000

1871 Ath-National Association

Bob Berman

Robert Berman, the son of Morris and Lena Berman, Russian immigrants who fled to this land in the face of the great upsurge of pogroms at the end of the nineteenth century, was born on January 24, 1899, in Manhattan's Lower East Side. While attending P.S. 42, Bob became interested in baseball; there he played with the future Clown Prince of Baseball, Al Schacht. A baseball player throughout his school years, he graduated from Evander Childs High School in 1916, attended two years of college in the City College of New York, then was promptly signed by the Washington Senators as a catcher.

On June 12, 1918, the 19-year-old Bob Berman had his only full inning in the major leagues. He had been used during the 1918 season as a third-string catcher, but on that day he

caught his hero, Walter Johnson, "The Big Train." Walter Johnson won 23 games in the 1918 season and was one of the biggest stars in baseball. On that day, Bob caught the ninth inning as Johnson fanned 2, walked 1, and allowed only 1 hit, in relief of Stanley Reese. This was Reese's only decision, for the Senators beat the St. Louis Browns, 6–4, at Sportsman's Park. Berman later appeared in only one other major league game as a pinch-runner, but never got a chance to have an at-bat. The next year, Bob was sent to Jersey City in the International League, where he played again with his old pal Al Schacht. Bob finished his professional baseball career in Binghamton and Syracuse, New York, three years later.

Returning to college after his baseball career ended, Bob graduated from the Savage School of Physical Education in 1925. He became a health education teacher and baseball coach. During the summers, Bob played for the semi-pro South Philadelphia Hebrews, which was organized by Eddie Gottlieb, the famous owner of basketball's Philadelphia Warriors. Bob eventually became Dean of Boys for the New York City Board of Education. In 1968, he retired after 43 years of work for the New York City School District.

Bob married dance instructor Dorothy Schamps in 1926. After fifty years of marriage, Dorothy died in 1976. They had one daughter, Barbara, who currently lives in Connecticut. Bob remarried after his wife's death; his second wife's name was Lucile, and she too died before Bob, in 1984. Bob Berman died on August 2, 1988, at the age of eighty-nine.

Years	Games	AB	H	R	RBI	HR	BA	OBP	FP
1	2	0	0	0	0	0	NA	NA	1.000

1918 Was-A

Cy Block

Seymour "Cy" Block was born on May 4, 1919, in Brooklyn, New York. As a child, he lived only 5 blocks from Ebbets Field. Cy and his friends would frequently attempt to sneak into the Dodgers games, and he began playing for P.S. 91, as an outfielder, in 1930. When Cy got to high school, he was barred from the baseball team. The coach said that he couldn't catch a cold, much less a fly ball. Since Cy couldn't stay out of baseball, he organized all of the neighborhood into a league. Cy was the captain of his team, "The Falcons."

In 1937, Cy tried out for the Brooklyn Dodgers. He made the final cut and was sent to the minor league club in Elmira for assignment, but when he arrived he was told to go back home. In 1938, Cy went to Florida to attend Joe Stripp's Baseball School. Cy was given special attention by Hall of Famer Joe Tinker. Cy excelled at the school and was given a chance to try out by the Memphis Chicks (American Association).

Cy was signed by the Chicks and sent to their class-D club in Paragould, Arkansas (North East Arkansas League), as an infielder. He hit .322, with 74 RBIs, and that was in the unbearable Arkansas heat. Near the end of the season, he was sent to the Memphis Chicks. Cy played in a few games as a pinch-hitter and one game as a starting player. In 1939, he played with Greenville, South Carolina (Cotton States League), batting .320 with 67 RBIs. Cy played with Macon, Georgia (Sally League), 1940–41. He batted .313 in 1940, and led the league with .357 in 1941. He also led the league in RBIs that year and was voted the league's Most Valuable Player. Cy was promoted to Tulsa (Texas League) in 1942. He batted .276 and was promoted to the Chicago Cubs at the end of the season.

Cy made his major league debut on September 7, 1942, at third base. He got a single and a double and 1 RBI. The Cubs defeated the Cincinnati Reds, 5 to 3, at Crosley Field. At this point, taking into consideration the state of the war, Cy joined the U.S. Coast Guard. While in the service, he was married to Harriet Spektor.

Cy remained in the Coast Guard until 1945. When he left the service, he returned to the Cubs, and had the opportunity to play in 2 games before the end of the regular season. He got 1 hit and 1 RBI, in 7 at-bats. The Cubs won the pennant that year, and went on to the World Series to face the Detroit Tigers. Cy made his only World Series appearance on October 8, 1945. He was used as a pinch-runner for Heinz Becker in the 9th inning of the 6th game. The Cubs won the game, 8 to 7, in the 12th inning, at Wrigley Field. The Tigers, however, went on to win the series, in seven games.

In 1946, Cy played with the Los Angeles Angels (Pacific Coast League). He enjoyed his time with the Angels, but he injured himself, with a leg-muscle pull, some 40 games into the season. His doctor suggested that he should move to a place where it was warmer, so he requested a demotion to the Southern Association. He joined the Cubs' team in Nashville. Cy hit .351 with Nashville and was promoted to Chicago near the end of the year, playing 6 games with the Cubs and batting .231. He started the 1947 season with the Cubs, but had no plate appearances before being returned to Nashville. Cy batted .363 with Nashville and set a new Southern Association record of 50 doubles.

Cy was transferred to the Buffalo Bisons (International League) in 1948. He batted .272 that year, and .255 in 1949. Cy entered the insurance business in 1948.

Following the 1949 season, Cy was offered a place on a team in the Puerto Rican Winter League. He reported to the team of Quadrilla to find that the manager had been fired, and was given the job of manager as well as player. He sent for three players from the States to help him. Two of these were Mickey Rutner and Lou Limmer. Cy and all his players were treated like kings by the locals. Each of them was loaned a chauffeur-driven car and was housed in a beautiful hacienda. Cy's team came in in last place in the league, even though he batted .350, Rutner batted over .300, and Limmer hit 25 home runs.

Cy returned to Buffalo for the 1950 season, and hit .302. He played with the Bisons in spring training in 1951, but received a note to say that he was released—before he had had a reasonable shot at the major leagues. His total lifetime batting average is .325 and his major league lifetime average is .302.

Since his retirement from baseball, Cy has become very successful in the insurance business. He joined the Lee Nashem Group of the Mutual Benefit Life Insurance Company in 1950. Since then, he has qualified every year to be a member of the Million Dollar Round Table, and became a life member in 1954. In 1957, Cy became Mutual Life's leader in both volume and in first-year commissions. He has made himself a multimillionaire.

Cy's charity work has earned him fame throughout the New York area. He and his wife, Harriet, are board members of the charitable organization ITC. Cy is the originator of the New York City Cleanup Contest, where children from Harlem clean up ten blocks of city debris. The Parks Department then rates their work each week, and the overall winning team is given an expense-paid trip to Disney World, courtesy of Cy.

He is very proud of his accomplishments, especially his baseball career. Besides having baseball cards printed up, the license plate of his Rolls-Royce is "LBA 325," which stands for "Lifetime Batting Average .325." In the 1980s, Cy wrote his memoirs with Leonard Lewin of The New York Post; the book was entitled So You Want to Be a Major Leaguer. He has donated all profits from the book to charity.

Cy Block lives with wife Harriet in Lake Success, New York. They have three daughters.

Years	Games	AB	H	R	RBI	HR	BA	OBP	FP
3	17	53	16	9	5	0	.302	.383	.947

1942, 45-46 Chi-N

Ron Blomberg

Ron Blomberg holds a unique place in the history of major league baseball. On April 6, 1973, he became the world's first Designated Hitter, or DH. The DH, who only appears in American League games or inter-league games played by American League rules, is a non-fielding player who bats instead of the pitcher, when the pitcher's turn in the rotation comes up. The idea was to increase the scores of American League games. In this it has been successful, but many have argued that the American League's DH rule has completely changed the strategy of the game. Nevertheless, the rule seems likely to remain in baseball as a permanent feature, at least in the American League. The bat that Ron Blomberg used that April day in Boston—batting for the Yankees—is now preserved among Cooperstown's treasures in the Baseball Hall of Fame.

Ronald Mark Blomberg was born on August 23, 1948, in Atlanta, Georgia. As a kid, he made extra money collecting returnable deposit bottles. At 12, he broke into Little League. Ron attended Atlanta's Druid Hills High School. He won four letters in baseball in his high school career; he also had four letters in both basketball and track.

At his high school graduation, in 1967, Ron was a very hot property. Numerous colleges offered him scholarships. He was also selected as the country's number-one baseball draft pick. Ron turned down all the scholarships, though he did attend part-time at DeKalb Junior College, with a schedule that would not interfere with his baseball. Later, he continued his education at Fairleigh Dickinson University, majoring in psychology.

It was the Yankees who won Ron in the 1967 draft and he joined their organization for the 1967 season. Ron's first assignment was to Johnson City (Appalachian League); he appeared in 66 games with Johnson City, hitting 10 home runs and batting .297. 1968 found him in Kinston (Carolina League), where he batted .251, with 7 homers. Most of the 1969 season, Ron was with Manchester (Eastern League), where he had 19 homers and a .284 batting average. At the end of the season, he was given a brief tryout with the Yankees.

Ron debuted with the Yankees on September 10, 1969. He appeared in only 4 games with them, as an outfielder, in 1969. He made 6 plate appearances and had 3 hits and 1 walk, to give him an on-base percentage that year of .571.

In 1970, Ron played with Syracuse (International League); he hit .273, with 10 homers.

He returned to Syracuse in 1971, with a .326 batting average and 6 homers. But Ron was soon back with the Yankees, in 1971, with a .322 batting average and 7 homers in 64 games. Ron was a regular member of the Yankees' staff from then through the 1974 season. At first, he played outfield or first base. But when the new position of Designated Hitter was created, in 1973, it was a natural for Ron. In 1972, he hit .268; in 1973, .329; and in 1974, .311. In his first at-bat as DH, Ron was walked, forcing in a run.

Starting in 1975, Ron suffered from a series of devastating injuries. These began with a shoulder injury in 1975. This led to an operation in 1976, to redirect tendons in his shoulder. During spring training of 1977, Ron crashed into a fence while pursuing a fly, and shattered his knee. This led to surgery to reconstruct the knee. During the 1975 season, Ron appeared in only 34 games. This number was down to 1 in 1976. He could not play at all in 1977.

Nevertheless, Ron was still considered a hot property, even though his batting average for the period 1975–76 was only .255. Six teams bid for Ron's services in the free-agent draft on November 17, 1977. Bill Veeck was the winning bidder, with an offer of $600,000, over four years, for the Chicago White Sox. But Ron never fully recovered from his injuries and his time with the White Sox was disappointing. There was one last moment of glory, on opening day of 1978, when Ron hit a home run that helped the White Sox beat the Boston Red Sox. Ron had 4 more homers in the next 60 games, and he was hitting just .231. Then, in August, he pulled a groin muscle that put him out of action for the rest of the year. In March 1979, the White Sox released Ron. His historical baseball career was over.

A left-handed batter, Ron was murder on right-handed pitchers, but he had a great deal of trouble with lefties. Very often he was not used in games against southpaw pitchers. He completed his career with a .293 batting average, with 391 hits, including 67 doubles and 52 home runs. Ron also had 140 walks, in a career that embraced 461 games.

Since his time in baseball, Ron has worked in public relations and career consulting. In 1985, he set up his own company in the latter field, USA Career Marketing. Ron Blomberg is married. He and his wife, Beth, have two children: a son, Adam, and a daughter, Chelsey.

Years	Games	AB	H	R	RBI	HR	BA	OBP	FP
8	461	1333	391	184	224	52	.292	.363	.983

1969, 71-76 NY-A, 1978 Chi-A

Jack Bloomfield

Gordon Leigh "Jack" Bloomfield was born on August 7, 1932, in Monti Alto, Texas. He was born to a Jewish father and a gentile mother. Jack never practiced Judaism.

Jack began his professional baseball career as a player with the Savannah club in 1955. After playing there for only 3 days, he was promoted to Harlington. In 1956, Jack was assigned to Jacksonville, Austin, and Topeka—before injuring himself in July. Jack was on the disabled list until September. He finished his minor league playing career with Seattle, Salt Lake City, and Portland. Jack was released in June of 1960.

Jack never played in the major leagues, but his career was not finished in 1960. He went to Japan to play with the Gaijin Stars.

With the Stars, Jack won 2 batting titles, in 1962 and 1963.

In 1969, after returning from Japan, Jack became a scout for the San Diego Padres organization. In 1974, he entered his first major league game, as a second base coach. At the end of the 1974 season, he was traded to the Chicago White Sox organization. He spent 1975 and 1976 as a scout. Jack returned to the field—as a coach—in May 1977. After spending the off-season as a scout, he coached for his final season in 1978. During the off-season, he signed with the New York Yankees. Jack retired from scouting in 1979.

Jack Bloomfield currently lives in McAllen, Texas.

Sam Bohne

Samuel Arthur Bohne was born Samuel Arthur Cohen on October 22, 1896, in San Francisco. He was a member of the Columbia Park Boys organization. It was a youth group that included baseball as one of its activities. Sam joined when he was 9 years old, and he was part of the group for seven years. The Columbia Park Boys organization also included future major league players James "Ike" Caveney and James "Imp" Begley.

Sam Bohne   20

In 1916, Sam began his professional baseball career with Tacoma (Northwestern League). He batted .277 with Tacoma, and was promoted to the St. Louis Cardinals the same year. Sam made his major league debut with the Cardinals on September 9, 1916, against the Cincinnati Reds. Entering the game as a pinch-hitter, he remained in it to play shortstop in the 10th inning, when the Reds scored 3 runs and the Cardinals lost, 3 to 6, at Robinson Field.

Sam played with both St. Paul (American Association) and Milwaukee (American Association) in 1917. He was traded to the Oakland Oaks (Pacific Coast League) in 1919. The next year, Sam was traded to the Seattle Rainiers (Pacific Coast League). With the Rainiers, he hit .333, with 20 home runs.

Sam was promoted to the Cincinnati Reds in 1921. That year, he played in 177 games with the Reds, and hit .285. In 1922, Sam was joined in the infield by some of his old friends from San Francisco: Ralph Pinella, Lou Fonseca, and "Ike" Caveney. Sam had many high moments on the Reds, including hitting 4 home runs in one game and getting a hit with two outs in the ninth inning—to ruin Dodgers pitcher Dazzy Vance's no-hitter.

Sam Bohne
CINCINNATI, N.L.

Sam stayed with the Reds for four more complete seasons, before being traded to the Brooklyn Dodgers, in the 1926 season. Sam finished his major league career with the Dodgers. He played in 668 major league games, and had a .261 lifetime batting average.

Sam played one final year in professional baseball, with

the Minneapolis Millers (American Association) in 1927. During the season, a pitcher on the opposing team, Huck Betts, was angered when he was spiked by a player on the Millers. Betts threw a ball at Sam's teammate after he got hit and was standing on first base. Sam came to the defense of his teammate and knocked out Betts with one punch. When one of Betts's teammates came to his assistance, Sam knocked him cold too. He had learned how to box as a youth in San Francisco, and was also a licensed boxing referee.

After his retirement from baseball, Sam ran a successful business in San Francisco. When his wife, Dorothy, gave birth to their son, Sam named him Roger, after his favorite manager from the Reds: Rogers Hornsby. Roger Bohne became an excellent golfer, but never turned professional.

Sam Bohne died on May 23, 1977, in San Francisco.

Years	Games	AB	H	R	RBI	HR	BA	OBP	FP
7	663	2315	605	309	228	16	.261	.321	.966

1916 StL-N, 1921-26 Cin-N, 1926 Bro-N

Henry Bostick

Henry Landers Bostick was born Henry Lipschitz on January 12, 1895, in Boston, Massachusetts. He played third base in 2 games for the Philadelphia Athletics in 1915. Henry made his major league debut on May 18, 1915. He didn't get a hit in 7 at-bats.

Henry Bostick died on September 16, 1968, in Denver, Colorado.

Years	Games	AB	H	R	RBI	HR	BA	OBP	FP
1	2	7	0	0	2	0	.000	.125	1.000

1915 Phi-A

Lou Boudreau

LOUIS BOUDREAU
CLEVELAND INDIANS. Shortstop.
Born July 17, 1917. Bats right.
Throws right. Ht. 5 ft. 11 in.
Wt. 170 lbs. Batted .295.
No. 132 Double Play

In 1970, Lou Boudreau was inducted into the Baseball Hall of Fame. Lou came into the Hall both as one of the finest shortstops in the history of the game and as one of the game's truly charismatic and original managers. The remarkable thing was that these did not represent two separate aspects of his career, but his almost unique position, in modern baseball, of player-manager.

Lou's career was filled with unique achievements. For eight seasons, he led all American League shortstops in fielding, tying the record. In 1943, he was part of 134 double plays, setting a new major league record. Lou's .982 fielding average, for 1947, also set a new record for shortstops. Lou won the batting title in 1944, with a .327 average. He led the American League in doubles on three occasions, each time with 45. In the best year of his career, 1948, he batted .355; he scored 116 runs; he had 106 RBIs; he had 98 walks; he had a slugging average of .534; he introduced Satchel Paige to the major leagues; he led his team to the American League pennant; and he, then, led them to a victory in the World Series. Lou's lifetime batting average is .295, his lifetime fielding average, at shortstop, is .973.

Louis "Lou" Boudreau was born in Harvey, Illinois, on July 17, 1917. His father was of French-American origin. His mother was Jewish. Lou has emphasized in statements on his background that both of his mother's parents were Jewish and observant. When Lou was just a child, his parents were divorced and Lou was raised by his father, a machinist and semi-pro baseball player. Lou's mother remarried and there seems to have been bad blood between Lou and his stepfather. Lou was raised as a Christian.

Lou was an outstanding basketball player in his high school and he captained his team to the Illinois state championship. Lou won an athletic scholarship to the University of Illinois; he played basketball and baseball for the university, in 1936 and 1937. Lou, a guard in basketball, especially distinguished himself in an Illinois victory over NYU at Madison Square Garden.

In 1938, Lou signed a contract with the Cleveland Indians. When his stepfather informed the university authorities, the Big Ten Conference declared Lou ineligible for further collegiate competition. Lou responded by joining the Cleveland farm team in Cedar Rapids, Iowa. He started playing for the Cleveland Indians on September 9, 1938. He would continue his association with the team until the 1950 season.

Although he had been with the team since 1938, Lou first brought attention to himself in the 1940 season. In that year he hit .295. The club itself, that year, was a scene of dissension. Hal Trosky, Ben Chapman, and Rollie Hemsley led a revolt that soon gathered support from other players on the team—against the management of Ossie Vitt. Vitt stayed at the helm of the club until the end of the season, but the incident had created a sense of malaise in the team. Lou, himself, had stayed clear of the intra-team politics. Roger Peckinpaugh was brought in to lead the Indians in 1941, but he became general manager at the end of the season. Applications were sought for a new manager, and shortstop Lou Boudreau applied. Lou's qualifications were carefully considered, including his rapport with the rest of the team. Lou got the job. Lou, at 24, became the youngest man ever appointed to a regular, full-season manager's job in major league history. Lou began as manager at the start of the 1942 season.

That year, the Indians finished fourth, the same place they had been with Peckinpaugh. The next year they made it to third. But in 1944, the team slipped to fifth. 1945 was not an especially good year, and in 1946 the team's win-loss record was its worst in 18 years. It seemed like something of a victory when, in 1947, Lou was able to pilot his team back to fourth place. Also in 1947, Lou did much to facilitate the integration of the American League, by his diplomatic and compassionate attitude towards Larry Doby. The team's new owner, Bill Veeck, wanted to fire Lou at the end of 1947, but overwhelming support from the fans decided Veeck to give Lou another chance.

All this time he was managing the team, Lou had been playing excellent ball. In 1948, as we have indicated above, everything came together, including the maturation of Larry Doby, the league-leading 164 strikeouts of Bob Feller, the pitching of Bob Lemon and Gene Bearden, and the relief work of Satchel Paige. Nevertheless, the 1948 pennant race was one of the closest in history and actually ended in a dead heat between Cleveland and the Boston Red Sox. A playoff game took place, the first in American League history. Lou made himself look like a genius of a manager by using knuckleballer Gene Bearden to pitch. Bearden kept the Sox down to 5 hits and 3 runs, but it was Lou's own 2 homers and 2 singles that were the measure of victory. Cleveland won the game, 8–3.

Lou's other great innovation as a manager, which he first used on July 14, 1946, was the famous "Boudreau shift." Lou bunched six of his fielders on the right side of second base as a defense against the hitting of Ted Williams. Similar moves had been made before by Peckinpaugh and Jimmy Dykes, but not as effectively as by Lou, who was given credit for the innovation. Lou would continue to utilize this defense through the years, when facing Williams. He claimed that the team was 37 percent more successful against Ted when using the shift.

During the next two years, even though the Indians only finished in third and fourth place, it was a great period for the club, with such stars as Al Rosen, Larry Doby, Bob Lemon, and Bob Feller. But the new owners, who succeeded Veeck, were not satisfied; furthermore, they were looking for a younger man as shortstop. It was General Manager Hank Greenberg who had to tell Lou he had been traded to the Boston Red Sox.

Lou came to Boston in 1951, just as a shortstop, not as a manager. He played at short-stop, as well as at first and third during the year, though not on an everyday basis. In 1952, Lou became manager of the Red Sox. He did insert himself into four games during the year, and these would be his last appearances as a player.

Lou would continue to pilot the Sox through the 1954 season. His first year, the Sox finished in 6th place. He did a little better the next two years, ending in 4th each time. Between 1955 and 1957, he managed the Kansas City Athletics. Lou's first year there was his best, with a sixth-place finish. The other two years, his team ended dead last.

Lou made a return, in 1960, for a final season as a manager. That year, he led the Chicago Cubs to a seventh-place finish.

Lou managed to maintain a good reputation as a manager throughout most of his career, but the record does not justify it. Of the 16 years he coached, only 3 of his teams ended the season in third place or better. His lifetime winning average is just .487. Overall, Lou Boudreau the shortstop and Lou Boudreau the batsman are far more impressive figures than Lou Boudreau the manager. There is, however, the exception to the rule: Lou's 1948 season was genius from beginning to end.

During the hiatus between his assignments with Kansas City and his last year with the Cubs, Lou became the Cubs' radio broadcaster. After the 1960 season, Lou returned to this job and stayed there until 1989.

Lou married and had children. A daughter married pitcher Denny McLain. A son, Jim, had a career in the minor leagues. At eighty, Lou Boudreau currently lives in Oak Lawn, Illinois.

Years	Games	AB	H	R	RBI	HR	BA	OBP	FP
15	1646	6029	1779	861	789	68	.295	.380	.973

1938-50 Clev-A, 1951-52 Bos-A

as Manager

Years	Games	W	L	PCT
16	2404	1162	1224	.487

1942-50 Cle-A, 1952-54 Bos-A, 1955-57 KC-A, 1960 Chi-N

Lou Brower

Louis Lester Brower was born on July 1, 1900, in Cleveland, Ohio.

Lou, or "Old Folks," played shortstop for the Detroit Tigers in 1931. He made his major league debut on June 13, 1931, in a game against the Boston Red Sox in Fenway Park. Lou batted 0 for 4, as the Red Sox defeated the Tigers 7 to 1. Lou got his first major league hit at Yankee Stadium on June 15 the same year. Lou singled and scored 2 runs, as the Tigers beat the Yankees, 8–5. Lou appeared in a total of 21 games for the Tigers. His lifetime batting average was .161 and he had 6 RBIs.

After Lou retired from playing professional baseball, he became a manager in the minor leagues, working with several AAA teams. Lou also worked for Lawton's Baseball School, which taught young ballplayers the fine points of the game.

When Lou retired from managing, he moved with his wife, Rita, to Tyler, Texas.

Lou Brower died there on March 4, 1994.

Years	Games	AB	H	R	RBI	HR	BA	OBP	FP
1	21	62	10	3	6	0	.161	.278	.886

1931 Det-A

Sam Cantor

Sam Cantor (r.) with Connie Mack.

Sam Cantor was a major league batboy. He plied his trade, in 1935, with the Chicago White Sox and, later, with the Philadelphia Athletics.

Sam was from Philadelphia. In 1935, at the height of the Depression, Sam followed two dreams. One of these was simply to get a job, which, for a severely handicapped young man of 17, was extremely difficult when millions of able-bodied adults were seeking work. The other was to be part of the national pastime, the world of major league baseball. Sam read how teams were giving tryouts for various jobs, including batboy positions, in their spring-training facilities. The tryouts were going to take place in Sacramento, California, and Sam was in Philadelphia. Sam didn't have money for a train or a bus. Sam had two artificial legs. Nevertheless, he started to walk. Sometimes a passing car would pick him up and take him part of the way. Sometimes a truck would stop and, at other times, Sam just had to walk along.

He reached the training camp of the Chicago White Sox in Sacramento and was introduced to the manager of the White Sox, Jimmy Dykes. Dykes heard Sam's story and gave him the job he sought. Sam put on the uniform of a Chicago White Sox player.

Years later, from 1951 to 1953, Jimmy Dykes was the manager of the Philadelphia Athletics. He remembered his old batboy from 1935, who lived in the city.

Sam Cantor (r.) with Jimmy Dykes.

Dykes talked with him, and before Sam knew it, he was once again in a baseball uniform. Sam Cantor got to know the owner of the A's, the famous Connie Mack. Now he was more of a team mascot than a batboy.

Some years later, Sam married a Jewish girl and settled in Morrisville, PA. On the weekends, he would make extra money selling things at a local flea market. His neighbor was also a dealer at the flea market, specializing in baseball memorabilia. Having often heard of Sam's baseball exploits, the neighbor had reprints made of a photo of Sam standing with Connie Mack. He arranged for Sam to attend a signing at a sports card show in nearby Levittown. This was a great thrill for Sam, to recall his time in the big leagues.

A few years ago, Sam passed away in Morrisville.

Conrad Cardinal

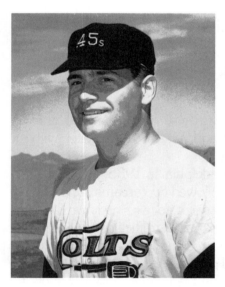

Conrad Seth "Randy" Cardinal was born on March 30, 1942, in Brooklyn.

Randy was signed by the Detroit Tigers in 1962, as a right-handed pitcher. He played the 1962 season in Class D ball and had a win-loss record of 14-7. Randy was sold to the Colt .45s in 1963. He showed up to their spring-training facility in Apache Junction, expecting to return to the minor leagues. Randy pitched wonderfully with the Colt .45s; he had the best ERA on the staff (1.69). A local newspaper said that Randy "looked like the greatest find since uranium."

Randy made his major league debut on April 11, 1963, against the San Francisco Giants. He allowed 1 run and 3 hits, in 3 innings. The Giants defeated the Colt .45s, 7 to 1. Randy pitched in 5 more games for the Colt .45s. His lifetime ERA was 6.08.

Randy Cardinal currently lives in Las Vegas, Nevada.

Years	Games	IP	W	L	GS	SV	PCT	ERA
1	6	$13\frac{1}{3}$	0	1	1	0	.000	6.08

1963 Hou-N

Harry Chozen

Harry Chozen was born in Winnebago, Minnesota, on September 27, 1915. His parents, Abraham and Ida Chozen, had emigrated from the Ukraine, in 1903. Harry was the sixth of 7 children. Harry's father worked in the junk metal and fur businesses. The Chozens were the only Jewish family in a town that was settled by Swedes. In 1923, they moved to Southern California. There, Harry attended Washington Junior High School and Pasadena Junior College, Lower Division. In 1933, after graduating from junior college, Harry began his career as a baseball player.

That year, Harry was signed by the Saint Louis Browns as a catcher, and was sent to San Antonio, Texas. He was released that season. Even so, Harry wasn't discouraged from pursuing a career in baseball. He tried out for almost every team in the country outside of California. He neglected California because he felt there were too many good players there and because it was so warm there that people could practice all year long. Still, try as he might, Harry couldn't make a team.

In 1935, Harry learned that there was a baseball school in Hot Springs, Arkansas run by Ray Doan. It was a six-week course with players like Dizzy Dean, Paul Dean, Burleigh Grimes, and George Sisler as instructors. Since Harry didn't have enough money to pay the $150 tuition, or for room and board in Hot Springs, he wrote a letter to the owner of the school telling him that if he would let him go to school for free, they could use his name in ads, when he became a good ballplayer. Doan accepted, and later did use Harry's name in advertising in The Sporting News.

After the course, Harry was signed by the Lake Charles club. There, he hit .321 in 1935, and was promoted to Fort Worth. After playing in spring training with Fort Worth, in 1936, Harry was sent to El Dorado (Cotton States League). That season, Harry caught every inning of every game and hit .261. In 1937, he batted a league-leading .342 and was voted Most Valuable Player. He was promoted to the Cincinnati Reds at the very end of the season.

With the Reds, Harry made his major league debut on September 21, 1937. He caught for pitchers Joe Cascarella and Bill Hallahan. He had 4 at-bats and got one hit off Phillies pitcher Wayne La Master. But the Reds were defeated by the Phillies, 10–1, at Crosley Field.

During the winter of 1937, the Reds organization optioned Harry to Albany (Eastern League). He was angry because he was supposed to go to spring training with them. He wrote a letter to Judge Kenesaw Mountain Landis, Commissioner of Baseball, explaining that he should be granted free-agency because he signed his contract when he was younger than the contractual age of 21. When spring training began, Harry got a telegram form Warren Giles, president of the Reds. It said that the catcher Ernie Lombardi hadn't signed yet and that they needed him, Chozen, in spring training. Harry left immediately for Florida. When he arrived at the hotel, he was told to go to Giles's room. When Harry got there, he saw Giles holding the letter he'd written to Commissioner Landis. Giles told him to give up his idea of free agency and sign a contract; then, Harry would be given a letter promising him that he would be called up at the end of the year.

HARRY CHOZEN

Harry played with Albany that season; he had a good season and batted .265. He read the newspaper at the end of the year and saw that his name wasn't among the players called up to play on the Reds. Harry called up Warren Giles at 5:00 A.M., asking him what was going on. Giles told him that he was selling his contract to Albany. Harry said that he had a letter that said he had to be called up to the Reds. Giles told him that if he made any trouble he would sell the contract to a team at a lower level. Harry backed down and played in Albany. He played in Albany for another three years and hit between .260 and .270. Giles sent some dozen different catchers during those three years to try to replace Harry, but none of them could hit like Harry. Harry said that he never looked good until they brought in another catcher to try to replace him. While he was with Albany, Harry married Ruth Nelson, on November 1, 1938.

In 1940, Harry went from Albany to Williamsport. The next year, he was traded to the Newport News (Virginia League), where he became player-manager. His brother, Bobby, also played for the News, before being released by Harry. Harry was then transferred to Knoxville, Tennessee.

In 1945, Harry played with Mobile, Alabama (Southern League). That year, he had the highlight of his career: a streak of hitting safely in 49 consecutive games. The manager of the team, Clay Hopper, tried to stop Harry's streak by giving him only one at-bat in some games, but he hit safely in games from May 27 to July 25, 1945. On July 6, Harry's streak looked as if it would come to an end. He was intentionally walked in his first at-bat, then was injured and had to leave the game. The league president ruled that Harry hadn't had a chance to bat and that the streak was not broken. Harry hit in 16 additional games after that date. Harry's streak is the sixth longest in the history of organized baseball.

In 1946, Harry turned his attention to managing. He became a player-manager for the next six years, holding the position with Greenville, Mississippi, and Pine Bluff, Arkansas (Cotton States League), Miami Beach (Florida International League), and Lake Charles (Evangeline League). He retired from baseball at the end of the 1952 season.

After retiring, Harry entered the insurance business. He became district manager for Guaranty Savings Life Insurance Co., in Lake Charles, Louisiana. He was a member of Temple Sinai of Lake Charles, and became president of its board and a member of the choir. He was a member of the synagogue for 25 years.

Harry Chozen died on September 16, 1994, in Houston, Texas. He had two sons, Richard and David.

Years	Games	AB	H	R	RBI	HR	BA	OBP	FP
1	1	4	1	0	0	0	.250	.250	.833

1937 Cin-N

Alta Cohen

Alta Albert "Schoolboy" Cohen was born on December 25, 1908, in New York City, the son of a rabbi. After graduating from South Side High School in 1927, Alta began his minor league baseball career. He won his nickname, "Schoolboy," from his teammates, because of his youthful good looks.

Alta made his major league debut on April 15, 1931, as an outfielder for the Brooklyn Dodgers. He was sent in for defensive purposes in the 6th inning. He went to bat out of order and got a hit. The next inning, Alta batted in his rostered position, to single again and score a run. Brooklyn was defeated by the Boston Braves, 9–3, at Braves Field. This was Alta's only major league appearance in 1931. Alta got 2 out of 3 hits that day, to give him an average of .667 that year.

Alta made his next major league appearance in 1932, with the Dodgers. He appeared in nine games with the Dodgers that year, and had a .156 batting average. Alta was traded to the Philadelphia Phillies for the 1933 season. He played most of the year with the Toledo Mudhens (American Association), but did play in 19 games for the Phillies. He got 6 base hits in 32 at-bats, for a .188 batting average. Alta never returned to the major leagues. He did play 2 more years in Toledo. Even though he played outfield in each of his major league games, Alta became a left-handed pitcher in the minors.

Alta married his wife, Janet, on July 21, 1943. He retired from professional baseball in 1946. After retiring, Alta became an agent for General Electric and a distributor for Altco Products Co.

Alta was inducted into the Brooklyn Dodgers Hall of Fame on April 18, 1997.

Alta Cohen lives in Verona, New Jersey.

Years	Games	AB	H	R	RBI	HR	BA	OBP	FP
3	29	67	13	8	2	0	.194	.289	.925

1931-32 Bro-N, 1933 Phi-N

Andy Cohen

John McGraw, the manager of the New York Giants from 1902 to 1932, had a dream: to have a Jewish star on his team. Part of the roots of this dream were economic: There was a large Jewish population in New York and a large proportion of it would come out to see a Jewish star play. The other source of this dream seems to have been a personal fondness for Jews. For instance, when he met young Moe Berg in Paris, though Berg had never played for him, McGraw greeted him like a long-lost son. Whatever its origins, McGraw followed his dream by trying out such players as Moe Solomon, Harry Rosenberg, and Jake Levy. The closest McGraw ever got to realizing his dream was Andy Cohen, who for a brief moment was the Jewish star he had been seeking.

ANDY COHEN
New York Giants

Andrew Howard Cohen was born October 25, 1904, in Petersburgh, Virginia. His father, Manus, had been born in Lithuania and his mother, Lena, in Kiev. Manus was a cigar-maker by trade, but a great enthusiast of the American game of baseball. Manus even earned for himself a tryout with the Baltimore Orioles. When Andy was seven, Lena, who had respiratory problems, moved with her children to El Paso, Texas, a city that proudly remembers Andy as a native son. Five years later, Andy's parents were divorced.

Andy attended El Paso High School and participated in baseball, football, and basketball. He graduated in 1922 and was almost immediately signed to a contract with Galveston in the Texas League. But Andy was still unsure about his future, so when he was offered a scholarship to the University of Alabama, he accepted. Nevertheless, college could not compete with the lure of the diamond and, in his senior year, Andy quit college and returned to baseball.

In 1925, Andy batted .312 for Waco. This caught the attention of the ever vigilant John McGraw, who had the Giants purchase Andy's contract for $25,000. To show that this was a large amount in 1925, consider that the entire Waco franchise, which had originally been in Galveston, had been purchased shortly before this for exactly the same amount.

Andy made his first appearance with the Giants on June 6, 1926. McGraw put him in to pinch-hit for Frankie Frisch. Andy hit a single off Phillies pitcher Ray Pierce. When he came back to the dugout, McGraw told him, "Young man, congratulations! Today you are leading the National League in hitting." Of course, at that point, Andy was batting 1.000. By the end of the season, however, his average was only .257 and it was felt that he needed more seasoning in the minors.

Andy played for Buffalo (International League) during the season of 1927. He batted .353 and led the team to the league championship. Andy was also called on to represent his team on the International League All-Star Team. In that game, he was asked to play shortstop, but it would be as second basemen that he would return to the Giants, in the 1928 season.

The Giants' very popular second baseman was Rogers Hornsby, but "The Rajah" was sold to the Boston Braves and Andy was called on to take his position. The opening-day game was also Andy's first at second base, with Hornsby on the opposing team. The advanced publicity had built up excitement, and Andy did not fail to deliver. He had 3 hits for the day, 2 runs, and 2 RBIs, in the Giants' 5–2 victory over the Braves and Hornsby.

Of the 30,000 spectators present that day, a large number—as John McGraw had predicted—were Jewish. When the game was over, it was as if Andy had single-handedly won the World Series. Thousands of Jewish fans poured onto the field and lifted him onto their shoulders. They carried him about the stadium, until he was rescued by his teammates and escorted to the team clubhouse. John McGraw called it "the greatest ovation…given any player in all my life." The incident inspired Frank Getty, a newspaper versifier, to write a parody of "Casey at Bat": "Cohen at Bat." The last verse of this spirited ballad runs as follows:

> Then from the stands and bleachers the fans in triumph roared,
> And Andy raced to second and the other runner scored;
> Soon they took him home in triumph, midst the blare of auto-honks,
> There may be no joy in Mudville, but there's plenty in the Bronx.

This was not the only artistic endeavor inspired by Andy Cohen's arrival in the majors. In 1930, there appeared a comic motion picture entitled Hot Curves, directed by Norman Taurog for Tiffany Productions, written by Earle Snell, based on a story by A. P. Younger and Frank Mortimer. The movie starred Jewish comedian Benny Rubin as Benny Goldberg, a rookie player hired by Manager McGraw because "he'll bring plenty of Jewish business through the gate in New York." This line truly indicates the roots of this story in the real life career of Andy Cohen, for the only slightly disguised McGraw, in the movie, would have no interest in the gate in New York, since in the movie Benny is playing for Pittsburgh. The plot of the movie is typical Hollywood fluff, with a mixture of romance, suspense, and misunderstandings. In the final denouement, Benny helps to lead his team to win the World Series.

Andy could not maintain the level of play of his opening day. One problem was his speed, which was not great. Nevertheless, he did finish that year with a .274 batting average and the Giants finished in second place. Andy remained a local hero. The following year, he finished with .294, but the Giants' management was not satisfied and Andy was back in the minors.

In 1930 and 1931, Andy played for the Newark Bears (International League). From 1932 to 1939, he played for Minneapolis (American Association). In 1940, Andy was appointed by the Brooklyn organization to manage their Pine Bluffs team in the Cotton States League. The following year, he managed Elmira (Eastern League) and led the team to the Governor's Cup, the championship for that league.

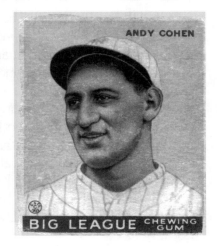

Andy joined the army in 1942 and, as a first sergeant, he took part in the invasion of North Africa. He also served in Italy. After military service in the Second World War, Andy married and became a scout for the Boston Braves. This was followed with various positions as manager in the minor leagues. In 1960, he returned to the majors as a coach with the Phillies. When the manager, Eddie Sawyer, quit and before a new manager, who would be Gene Mauch, could be appointed, for one day Andy Cohen was manager of the Phillies. On April 14, 1960, Don Cardwell pitched the Phillies to victory, 5 to 4, over the Milwaukee Braves, at Connie Mack Stadium. This made Andy one of very few major league managers with a perfect 1.000 average and the only Phillies manager never to loose a game.

Following his year in Philadelphia, Andy returned to his home in El Paso. He took a job with the University of Texas there and for 17 years served as the school's baseball coach. At the same time, Andy also continued to coach for the local El Paso minor league team, the El Paso Sun Kings, an affiliate of the Los Angeles Angels.

Andy Cohen died in El Paso on October 29, 1988. Cohen Stadium, El Paso's luxurious new ballpark, was named in honor of both him and his brother Syd.

Note: John McGraw, after he demoted Andy Cohen, continued to search for his Jewish star. He heard rumors about a boy who played ball in Bronx's Crotona Park. He sent out scouts to look at the boy, but didn't like what he heard from them. When the boy wanted to show off what he could do, McGraw refused to let him try out at the Polo Grounds. John McGraw died, in 1934—without his Jewish star. The boy's name was Hank Greenberg.

Years	Games	AB	H	R	RBI	HR	BA	OBP	FP
3	262	886	249	108	114	14	.281	.317	.964

1926, 1928-29 NY-N

as Manager

Years	Games	W	L	PCT
1	1	1	0	1.000

1960 Phi-N

Hy Cohen

Hyman Cohen at one time considered his baseball career a failure. He pitched only 17 innings in the major leagues with a 7.91 ERA. But recently he has come to understand that he had made it to the top echelon of baseball in a time when the game was at its most competitive: the golden age of Ted Williams, Jackie Robinson, and Mickey Mantle.

Hy Cohen was born January 29, 1931 in Brooklyn New York. His father, Joseph, had come from Warsaw, Poland and his mother, Bessie, was from Brest Litovsk, Russia. Hy began his baseball career in 1948, after being drafted by the New York Yankees. The Yankees drafted him in hopes of finding a young Jewish star. He played for their Class D team in LaGrange, Georgia. After two lackluster seasons, the Yankees neglected to renew Hy's contract. Nevertheless, he was later told that this had been an oversight and that the official who neglected the contract renewal had been reprimanded. His contract was picked up by the Cubs.

Hy began to shine when he pitched for the Cubs' Class A farm team in Grand Rapids, Michigan. His record was 12-9 and he was quickly promoted to the Cubs' team in Des Moines,

Iowa. Hy feels that this was his best year in professional baseball: he ended the season with a 16-10 record, a 2.86 ERA, and 3 play-off victories. Also during this year, he played with such luminaries as Sparky Anderson and Maury Wills. Hy would probably have been promoted to the Cubs the next year, but he was drafted by the U.S. Army, to serve in the Korean War.

Sent to the U.S. Army base in San Antonio, Texas, Hy was assigned to play baseball. He played with such major-leaguers as Bobby Brown, Don Newcombe, Gus Triandos, Bob Turley, Joe Margoneri, Dick Kokos, Owen Friend, and another Jewish player, Marv Rotblatt. He spent two years playing for the Army, before returning to the Cubs system.

Hy returned to professional baseball on the Los Angeles Angels, an AAA team in the Pacific Coast League. He was quickly returned to the Class A Des Moines, Iowa, team, where he had an excellent year, ending up with a 1.88 ERA. This finally prompted the Cubs organization to promote Hy to the parent club.

At Chicago, Hy was allowed to pitch in only 7 games, only one of which he started. He gave up 28 hits in only 17 innings pitched. Stan Musial thanked Hy for helping him out of a batting slump. That kind of gratitude, Hy didn't need. While still pitching for Chicago, Hy was contacted by the Topps trading card company. He was given a substantial amount for permission to have a trading card made of him. Unfortunately, Hy didn't stay in the majors long enough to see a card produced.

He was returned to the Los Angeles Angels in 1955. In 1956, he played again with the Angels and ended up with a 6-0 record. He was then sold to the Tulsa Oilers. From there he went to New Orleans (Southern Association). From New Orleans, Hy was sent to Memphis and Charleston. From Charleston he was sold to Toronto (International League).

Jack Kent Cook, of the Toronto Maple Leafs organization, had been looking for a Jewish star for his Toronto club, to attract the large Jewish population of the city to his team. Cook bought Hy's contract for $50,000. Unfortunately, Hy began to develop arm troubles and this led him to retire from professional baseball.

After retirement, Hy returned to school. He finished college in 1966 with a Master's degree in education and became a teacher in Birmingham High School in the Los Angeles public school system. Hy taught social studies and physical education. He also coached the school's football, tennis, and baseball teams. His baseball team, on two occasions, won the city's championship.

In 1995, Hy was honored at Dodger Stadium in Los Angeles for his outstanding achievements in baseball education. He was joined on the field for this honor by his old teammate, Don Newcombe, and his old rival, Tommy Lasorda, before the start of a Dodger's game.

Hy Cohen is now retired from teaching and lives with his wife Terry. They have two children and three grandchildren. Hy is enjoying his second retirement, and his hobbies include square dancing.

Years	Games	IP	W	L	GS	SV	PCT	ERA
1	7	17	0	0	1	0	NA	7.94

1955 Chi-N

Syd Cohen

Sydney Harry Cohen was born May 7, 1908, in Petersburgh, Virginia. He was the younger brother of Andy Cohen, and like his brother he felt a close attachment to El Paso, Texas, the city where they were raised. While Andy was an infielder, Syd was a pitcher.

In 1928, Syd played for the San Francisco Seals (Pacific Coast League). This famous team would later produce such greats as Dom and Joe DiMaggio. In 1931, Syd was traded to Nogales, Mexico, in the Arizona–Texas League. The team had been having trouble with its fans. Most of these were Mexican and they were upset that the majority of their team were "Anglos." In fact, the team had only one Mexican player, a mediocre pitcher. When the "Anglo" manager of the team tried to get rid of this pitcher, the fans threatened a boycott. Near-riots occurred, and worse was only avoided by soldiers with bayonets patrolling the streets. (One of the owners of the team was governor of the province.) The Mexican pitcher remained on the team, but the fans were still not satisfied. In the midst of this, the manager received the news that he had a new pitcher, Syd Cohen. (You can see why he might not be happy.) But when Syd arrived, the manager's worries turned to smiles. Syd was swarthy and, coming from the border town of El Paso, he spoke perfect Spanish. When Syd was introduced the next day to the fans of Nogales, it was as Pablo García, and it was as Pablo García that he became the left-handed pitching star of Nogales. Twenty years later, Syd returned to Mexico as the manager of the Juárez Indios. Fans were constantly coming up to him and greeting him as "Pablo."

In 1934, Syd made it to the majors, to the Washington Senators, where he joined second baseman Buddy Myer. Syd debuted on September 18. He pitched in only three games that year and in the following year was back in the minors. But in 1936 and 1937, Syd was a regular member of the Senators' staff. He was used mostly as a relief pitcher. Syd did, however, have some historic moments with the Senators. It was he who, on September 29, 1934, pitched Babe Ruth's 708th home run, his last in the American League. It was also Syd who was the last pitcher to strike Ruth out as a Yankee. This was during the same game and, despite Ruth's home run, Syd won the game, 8 to 5.

After Washington, Syd continued his career in the minor leagues, both as a player and as a manager. When he came to Juárez to manage the Indios, he led them to their first league championship. Syd, like Andy, worked for the El Paso minor league teams.

Syd Cohen died in El Paso on April 9, 1988. As stated elsewhere, the El Paso ballpark was named Cohen Stadium in honor of both of the brothers, Andy and Syd.

Years	Games	IP	W	L	GS	SV	PCT	ERA
3	55	109	3	7	3	5	.300	4.54

1934, 1936-37 Was-A

Dick Conger

Richard Conger was born April 3, 1921, in Los Angeles, California. His mother was a Russian Jew. Dick joined professional baseball after attending UCLA for one year.

Dick was signed by the Detroit Tigers as a right-handed pitcher in 1940. He pitched his first professional game with the Tigers. On April 22 that year, Dick was called into the 8th inning of a game against the Chicago White Sox at Comiskey Park. He hurled three innings, winning the game in the eleventh, 6–5. He spent the rest of the year in the minors. Dick was traded to the Pittsburgh Pirates in 1941. He married his wife, Virginia, on May 26 the same year. Dick spent the majority of the 1941 and 1942 seasons in the minor leagues, but he did pitch in 4 games for the Pirates.

In 1943, Dick was traded to the Philadelphia Phillies. There, he pitched in 13 games. One of his victories was a two-hitter against the New York Giants. On August 17, 1943, Dick got his only major league hit, at Shibe Park, against the Cubs. Nonetheless, Dick lost the game, 7–5. He never played in the majors after the 1943 season. He had a win-loss record of 3-7 and an ERA of 5.14, in 70 innings pitched.

Dick served in the Army during World War II. He entered the service in 1944 and was discharged in 1946. When he returned from the war, he also returned to the minor leagues. Remaining in baseball until 1950, he played for Beaumont, Portland, Albany, Toronto, Los Angeles, Nashville, Sacramento, and Tacoma. After his retirement, Dick became a scout for the Dodgers organization. He was also employed as a foreman for the stereotype department of the Los Angeles Times.

Dick Conger died on February 16, 1970, in Los Angeles. He was only forty-eight.

Years	Games	IP	W	L	GS	SV	PCT	ERA
4	19	70	3	7	12	0	.300	5.14

1940 Det-A, 1941-42 Pit-N, 43 Phi-N

Phil Cooney

Phil Cooney was born Philip Clarence Cohen, on September 14, 1882, in New York City. He was the son of Philip and Julia (née Durant) Cohen.

Phil played in one major league game for the New York Highlanders, now the Yankees, under the name of Phil Cooney (he never used the name Cohen as a baseball player). He played third base for the Highlanders on September 27, 1905; he had three at-bats, but did not get a hit. After that game, Phil returned to the minor leagues. In 1917, he was the second baseman for the Omaha Royals (Western League). On July 7, 1917, he was the first Western Leaguer to execute an unassisted triple play, in a game against Denver. Phil had a long minor league career. He married his wife, Loretta (née Keller), on February 1, 1919. After their marriage, Mr. and Mrs. Cohen moved to Paterson, New Jersey.

Phil Cooney died on October 6, 1957, in New York City. He was elected to the Paterson Sports Hall of Fame in 1967.

Years	Games	AB	H	R	RBI	HR	BA	OBP	FP
1	1	3	0	0	0	0	.000	.000	1.000

1905 NY-A

Ed Corey

Edward Norman Corey was born Abraham Simon Cohen on July 13, 1899, in Chicago. Ed changed his name to Corey to stop the ethnic slurs that he faced when playing baseball. He played in only one major league game as a right-handed pitcher for the Chicago White Sox—on July 2, 1918. Ed pitched in two innings and gave up two hits and one run. He has a 4.50 ERA. Ed pitched in other leagues, including the Mid-West League.

Ed Corey died on September 17, 1970, in Kenosha, Wisconsin.

Years	Games	IP	W	L	GS	SV	PCT	ERA
1	1	2	0	0	0	0	NA	4.50

1918 Chi-A

Bill Cristall

William Arthur Cristall was born in Odessa, Russia, on September 12, 1878. He had four sisters and one brother, Samuel. His family moved to Buffalo, New York, when he was young.

Bill began his baseball career as a left-handed pitcher for Woodstock, Ontario (Canadian League), in 1891. There he met his future wife, Marie Gunn. In 1900, he played for Albany. Bill, known as "Lefty," made his major league debut on September 3, 1901, with the Cleveland Indians. He started six games for the Indians that year, winning 1 and losing 5, with a 4.84 ERA. In 1902, Bill returned to the minor leagues to pitch for Oakland (Pacific Coast League). He married Marie that year. Bill played for many minor league teams until his retirement in 1918, including Toledo, St. Paul, Syracuse, Providence, Montgomery, Memphis, and Toronto. He was an exceptional pitcher in the minors and several times pitched, and won, two games on the same day!

The longevity of his career inspired an anonymous poet to write a poem entitled "Just a Line to Old Bill Cristall, Hurler":

Back in the time be-dimmed ages,
Days when I sported short pants,

> Dad used to lamp the sport pages,
> Reading of Candy La Chance,
> Keeler and Kittredge and Kelley,
> Ritchie, McGann and Bill Hall;
> And nightly he read, as they put me to bed,
> "Cristall is pitching good ball."
> Now it seems, centuries later,
> Dad is a grandfather, gray,
> Says the old-timers were greater,
> Yet he still follows the fray.
> Reads about Johnson and Speaker,
> Hap Felsch, O'Neil, and Cutshaw,
> And reads, with a grin, as the "extra" gets in,
> "Cristall is pitching good ball."

After his retirement from playing, Bill managed for the Bay City and Adrian, Michigan, clubs. When his managerial career was over, Bill became an umpire in the International League. Though he did not enjoy the position, he remained an umpire for seven years. While an umpire, he would amuse fans by picking up the peanuts that were thrown at him and putting them in his pocket. He would eat the peanuts as the game progressed.

According to his niece, Mildred Cristall, "He was a wonderful man. Everyone loved him." Bill was an outstanding citizen of Buffalo, New York. Bill Cristall died there on January 28, 1939.

Years	Games	IP	W	L	GS	SV	PCT	ERA
1	6	$48\frac{1}{3}$	1	5	6	0	.167	4.84

1901 Cle-A

Harry Danning

Harry "The Horse" Danning was born on September 6, 1911, in Los Angeles. He was the son of Robert David Danning, originally from Russia, and Jennie Danning (née Goldberg), who had emigrated to this country from Riga, Latvia. He was the fourth of six children, and one of his older siblings was major-leaguer Ike Danning, whose example inspired Harry's interest in baseball.

Harry was always a catcher, even from his sandlot days. His power with the bat and his guile and ability behind the plate made him a natural. In 1928, the same year his brother appeared with the St. Louis Browns, Harry graduated from Los Angeles High School. After selling rugs, and following stints playing semi-pro baseball, Harry was signed by George Washington Grant to play for the Giants' organization. He was sent to Bridgeport (Eastern League) in 1931.

Harry batted .324 his first year in Bridgeport and received excellent instruction in the art of catching from veteran Frank Snyder. Harry started 1932 with the same team, but later in the year he moved up to Winston-Salem (Piedmont League). The next year, he started as the first-string catcher with Buffalo (International League). He did so well there that he got the call to the parent team.

"THE HORSE" DANNING

Harry made his debut with the Giants on July 30, 1933. Gus Mancuso was the first-string catcher for the Giants and Paul Richards was the second-string, so Harry had to patiently perform the duties of a third-string catcher: warm up relievers in the bullpen, catch batting practice, and ride the pine.

In 1937, Harry finally got his chance to serve as first-string catcher. "Harry the Horse," as he had come to be called, after a character in a Damon Runyon tale, did not disappoint. In the bottom of the ninth inning of the second game of a doubleheader on June 9, 1937, a two-run homer by Harry won the game. Overnight, Harry was declared to be the long-sought-after Jewish star of the New York Giants. On July 13, Harry hit home runs in both games of a doubleheader. On August 20 Harry got five hits in a game, four singles and a triple. On August 25, he drove in the final, winning run of an eleven-inning cliffhanger against the Cubs. In 1937, Harry hit .288. His slugging was a major contributing factor to the Giants' capturing the 1937 National League Pennant.

Harry continued to catch excellently and bat with the best of them. In 1938, he batted .306; in 1939, .313; and in 1940, .300. Harry caught the last game at Philadelphia's Baker Bowl, on June 30, 1938, and had 3 hits and 3 RBIs. The last hit in the game and the last in the Baker Bowl was a single by Phil Weintraub, in this 14–1 Giant victory over the Phillies. Harry was one of five Giants to homer in a single inning in a game in 1939. On June 15, 1940, he hit for "the cycle," in a Giants' victory over the Pirates at the Polo Grounds.

Harry was selected for the National League All-Star game, in the years 1938, 1939, 1940, and 1941. He played 10 years with the Giants, from 1933 to 1942. His lifetime batting average is .285. His fielding average for ten years of catching is an outstanding .985.

After the 1942 season, Harry served in the armed forces. During his military service, he developed arthritis in his knees. At his discharge at the end of the war, Harry announced that he would not be returning to baseball. He went into business in Los Angeles.

Harry retired in 1976. Harry Danning is a member of the Maccabee Hall of Fame at the Hebrew University in Jerusalem, of Chicago's Jewish Hall of Fame, and of the Southern California Jewish Sports Hall of Fame.

Years	Games	AB	H	R	RBI	HR	BA	OBP	FP
10	890	2971	847	363	397	57	.285	.330	.985

1933-42 NY-N

Ike Danning

Ike Danning, the elder brother of Harry Danning, was born on January 20, 1905, in Los Angeles, California. His parents were Robert David and Jennie Danning. He was one of six children.

Ike graduated high school from the Los Angeles Polytechnic Institute, where he played baseball, football, and basketball. Like his brother Harry, Ike was a catcher; he batted and

threw right-handed. He was not as tall as Harry, who was 6'1", but was 5'9 ".

Ike started in the minor leagues with Vernon, California (Pacific Coast League). That first year, he batted .179 and had a fielding average of .914. Subsequently, Ike played with Idaho Falls (Utah–Idaho League) in 1926, and with two Eastern League teams, Bridgeport and New Haven, during 1927. In 1927, he batted .309 and had a fielding average of .946. He also had 10 doubles, 1 triple, and 1 home run. Ike played most of the 1928 season with Wichita Falls (Texas League).

On September 21, 1928, Ike got into his first major league game, playing for the St. Louis Browns. Altogether, Ike would appear in only two games with the Browns. He had 6 plate appearances, 3 hits, and 1 RBI. Ike's lifetime batting average is .500.

After his short stay in the majors, Ike continued in the minors. Then, in 1933, he retired from baseball, with no regrets. Undoubtedly, he was pleased that his brother Harry had started with the Giants that same year, and this may have influenced his decision.

After baseball, Ike settled in his native Los Angeles and became Head of Transportation for Twentieth Century–Fox. He continued in this job for 34 years. Ike had married Maryon Powers on May 19, 1926, but she predeceased him. Ike Danning died on March 30, 1983, in Santa Monica, California, of lung cancer.

Years	Games	AB	H	R	RBI	HR	BA	OBP	FP
1	2	6	3	0	1	0	.500	.571	.917

1928 StL-A

Harry Eisenstat

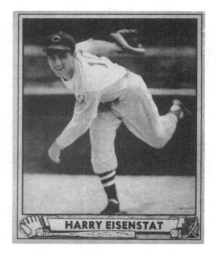

HARRY EISENSTAT

Harry Eisenstat was born on October 10, 1915, in Brooklyn, New York.

Harry made his major league debut with his hometown Dodgers on May 19, 1935, as a southpaw pitcher. He played in 1 more game that year, for the Dodgers, losing both. He returned to the Dodgers in 1936, however, and he had his first major league victory on September 24, 1936, against the Philadelphia Phillies. The game ran only $6\frac{1}{2}$ innings at Ebbets Field, before being called. Harry had a single that day, in 2 at-bats, and the Dodgers won the game, 4 to 2. Harry played one more year on the Dodgers, before being traded to Detroit in 1938.

He had his best year in 1938. On October 2, 1938, Bob Feller set a modern strikeout record with 18. Harry was the opposing pitcher in that game, and won it by a score of 4 to 1. Harry pitched in 32 games in 1938, and had a record of 9-6 and a 3.73 ERA.

While pitching for the Tigers, Harry became a friend of teammate Hank Greenberg. Hank taught Harry how to dress and how to talk to the press. He also introduced Harry to many prominent Jews in the Detroit area.

In 1938, in one doubleheader in which Harry pitched 5 shutout innings in the first game and 4 shutout innings in the second game. In those two games, Hank Greenberg hit 3 home runs. After the Tigers won both of the games, Mickey Cochrane told Hank and Harry, "Fellas, lock yourselves in your rooms tonight because the Jews in Detroit are going crazy."

After pitching 10 games in the 1939 season, Harry was traded to the Cleveland Indians. He remained with the Indians until the end of the 1942 season. He had a lifetime ERA of 3.84, and a record of 25-27, in 165 games.

Harry Eisenstat currently lives in Shaker Heights, Ohio.

Years	Games	IP	W	L	GS	SV	PCT	ERA
8	165	478 $\frac{2}{3}$	25	27	32	14	.481	3.84

1935-37 Bro-N, 1938-39 Det-A, 1939-42 Cle-A

Mike Epstein

Michael Peter "SuperJew" Epstein was born on April 4, 1943, in the Bronx, New York. Mike's father, Jack, had been born in Toronto, while his mother, Evelyn, was a native New Yorker. Jack Epstein was a salesman, Evelyn took care of the children and the home. Mike was the middle child of three. When Mike was still young, the family moved to Los Angeles.

Mike attended Los Angeles' Fairfax High School. There he was a member of both the baseball and football teams. Mike graduated in 1961. He then enrolled at the University of California, Berkeley, where he majored in social psychology. Mike played on the Berkeley baseball team and batted .375 through his junior season. During that junior year, he was offered a contract by scout Tom Lasorda of the Los Angeles Dodgers, but Mike's father insisted he finish his college degree before going into baseball. In his senior year, Mike batted .384 and was named a Collegiate All-American. Mike graduated from Berkeley in 1964. In 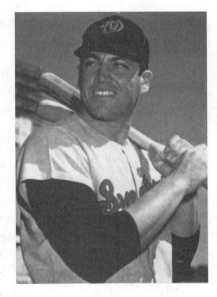 that same year, he represented the United States in the 1964 Olympics, held in Tokyo, as part of this country's Olympic baseball team.

Mike began his professional baseball career in 1965, with Stockton (California League), in the Baltimore Orioles organization. His beginning was most propitious. He led the league in both batting and home runs. He was chosen the league's Most Valuable Player and Rookie of the Year. His average that year was .338 and he hit 30 homers.

In 1966, Mike played for Rochester (International League). Leading his league in homers, with 29, and RBIs, with 102, he was named to the league's All-Star team. His average was .309. Mike was named the league's Most Valuable Player, Rookie of the Year, Sporting News' Minor Leaguer of the Year, and the Topps Minor League Player of the Year. Mike won another title that year, one that he still proudly bears. One of his coaches on the Rochester team, admiring his prowess as a batsman, declared Mike to be "SuperJew"! Mike got a kick out of this title and began marking it on his things—his hat, his shower slippers, and so on. The name caught on and was often used by fans and reporters during Mike's playing days.

Before 1966 was over, Mike was given a chance to debut for the Baltimore Orioles, which he did on September 16. The Orioles went on to win the World Series that year, but Mike hadn't appeared in enough games to qualify to play in the Series.

Mike had just played 9 games for the Orioles, at the beginning of the 1967 season, when he was sent back down to Rochester, for the Orioles preferred playing Boog Powell at first base. Mike refused to report to Rochester, and he soon found himself traded to the Washington Senators. In his early days with the Senators, Mike received batting instruction from Ted Williams. Mike would continue with the Senators until the 1971 season.

It was with Washington, in 1967, that Mike had his first major league homer, off Thad Tillotson of the Yankees, at Yankee Stadium. It was an inside-the-park homer. In 1968, Mike had 13 home runs, plus 5 during an eleven-game appearance with Buffalo (International League). That winter, Mike played for La Guaira Tiburones of the Venezuelan League, and his team won the league pennant.

Mike had his best year in the majors in 1969. He had 30 home runs, including 3 in one game, 85 RBIs, and a .278 batting average. In 1970, Mike had another 20 homers and 56 RBIs, as well as a .256 average. It was during 1970 that the Yankees made strong overtures to the Senators to acquire Mike. This would have been a dream come true for the Bronx-born player. But at the last minute, the deal fell through. During the winter of 1970, Mike played in Venezuela again.

In the 1971 season, after 24 games, Mike was traded to the Oakland A's. This was a break for him, for it gave him an opportunity to play for a team that was a contender and play, in 1971, in the ALCS. The 1971 A's didn't go beyond that series, but the 1972 team, which now included Ken Holtzman and Joe Horlen, went all the way to win the World Series. Mike had a home run in the 1972 ALCS, as well as 4 walks and a stolen base. He had 5 walks in the World Series and scored a run.

Mike was traded to the Texas Rangers for the 1973 season. He played only 27 games with Texas before being moved to the California Angels. Mike continued with the Angels into the 1974 season, before retiring.

Mike had played 9 years in the majors, with a .244 batting average, but a .360 on-base percentage—reflecting his career 448 walks. Mike had 695 career hits, including 93 doubles, 16 triples, and 130 home runs. He was a fine defensive player, with a .991 career percentage on first base, the only position he ever played.

After retirement, Mike headed a precious metals company and had a ranch in Colorado. Currently, he is a hitting instructor with the Sioux City Explorers (independent Northern League). By the first half of the 1997 season, the Explorers were leading their league, with a 28-14 record.

Mike is married to the former Barbara Gluskin. They have three children: Amy, 28; Ashley, 25; and Jake, 19. They have raised their children with a strong sense of tradition, born out of their own convictions as practicing Jews. Mike takes a strong interest in other Jewish baseball players and has maintained contact with many of the great figures of the past. Jake Epstein, Mike Epstein's youngest child, is currently enrolled at the University of Missouri, which he attends on a scholarship. Jake is the catcher on the Missouri baseball team.

Years	Games	AB	H	R	RBI	HR	BA	OBP	FP
9	907	2854	695	362	448	130	.244	.360	.991

1966-67 Bal-A, 1967-71 Was-A, 1971-72 Oak-A, 1973 Tex-A, 1973-74 Cal-A

Reuben Ewing

The man who played baseball under the name of Reuben Ewing was born Reuben Cohen on November 30, 1899, in Odessa, in the Ukraine. His parents were Simon and Bessy Cohen. Reuben's family, after they had emigrated to this country, settled in Hartford, Connecticut. Reuben's father was a dealer in dry goods. Reuben graduated from Hartford High School; in 1920, he entered Lebanon Valley College, Annville, Pennsylvania.

AUTOGRAPH

Reuben Cohen

Reuben Ewing autograph, c. 1960, showing his return to his birth name, after his playing years.

While still attending Lebanon Valley, Reuben appeared, under the name of Reuben Ewing, in 3 major league games, in 1921. On June 21, 1921, Reuben made his debut for the St. Louis Cardinals. Though he appeared in 3 games, Reuben had only one plate appearance. This was on September 27, at St. Louis' Sportsman's Park. Reuben came in to pinch hit for Tink Riviere in the bottom of the 6th inning, in a game between the Cardinals and the Cincinnati Reds. The Reds' pitcher, Eppa Rixey, faced the diminutive Reuben, who was only 5'4 " and weighed 145 pounds. Reuben, who batted and threw right-handed, was struck out. In one of Reuben's other games, he came in as a late-inning replacement at shortstop. In the third, he was put in as a pinch-runner.

Reuben, under his real name of Reuben Cohen, continued his college studies at Lebanon Valley until 1922. He also attended Tufts College. On September 16, 1923, he was married to his wife, Claire.

Reuben Ewing continued to live in Hartford. He died in West Hartford on September 17, 1962.

Years	Games	AB	H	R	RBI	HR	BA	OBP	FP
1	3	1	0	0	0	0	.000	.000	1.000

1921 StL-N

Al Federoff

Alfred Federoff was born on July 11, 1925, in Bairdford, Pennsylvania. He graduated from Etna (PA) High School in 1943. In high school, Al was on both the baseball and football teams. After graduation, Al entered the military and served until the end of the Second World War. Subsequently, he spent two years at Duquesne University.

Al was signed out of Duquesne by scout Ed Katalinas of the Detroit Tigers organization. A right-handed second baseman, Al, broke into organized baseball in 1946 and 1947 with Jamestown, New York (Pony League). He led all second basemen of the league in fielding during both of these years and led the league in assists in 1947. In 1948, Al moved up to Flint (Central League). In that year, he led the Central League in stolen bases and led all the league's second basemen in fielding and assists.

In 1949, Al played with Little Rock (Southern Association), and was named to the league's All-Star team. For 1950 and 1951, Al played for Toledo (American Association). Again, in 1950, Al was an outstanding defensive player, leading the league's second basemen in assists, chances accepted, and double plays. In 133 games, he took part in 134 double plays and 2 triple plays.

At the end of the 1951 season, Al was given his first opportunity to play with the Detroit Tigers. For his entire career, he had been playing within the Tiger farm system. Al made his debut on September 27, but played in only 2 games, with just 4 at-bats—this, due to Al's illness rather than a lack of confidence on the part of the Tiger management.

The start of the 1952 season found Al in Buffalo (International League), where he batted .285. During the season, the Tigers' second baseman, Jerry Priddy, broke his leg. At first they tried to replace him with Don Kollowary, but he didn't work out. Al's outstanding defensive qualifications and his recent improvements in batting got him the job. For the last 74 games of the year, Al was the regular second baseman for the Tigers. He hit .242 for them during the season. Al's highlight of this year, when the Tigers finished dead last, was the no-hitter that Virgil Trucks pitched on August 25, 1952, against the Yankees. The final score was only 1–0, in favor of the Tigers. Al made the final putout of the game, against Hank Bauer.

Al spent 1953 to 1957 in San Diego (Pacific Coast League). In 1954, he led the league in runs scored and bases on balls, as well as leading the league's second basemen in putouts, assists, and double plays. He was also named to the league's All-Star team. 1955 was another excellent year, with Al leading the league's second basemen in putouts and assists. He did the same again in 1956, as well as leading in double plays. That year, he was named San Diego's Most Valuable Player.

During the 1957 season, Al was traded to Seattle, also of the Pacific Coast League. He continued with them the following season. Al then began the 1959 season with Louisville (American Association), but after 5 games he was traded to Atlanta (Southern Association). He finished the season with Atlanta, batting .278 and hitting 4 home runs, the most he ever hit in a season. Nevertheless, Al decided to hang up his spikes after that year. He became a manager.

Al started his managing career in 1960, with Decatur (Midwest League)—Class D. His team finished seventh. The following year, he was with Jamestown (New York–Pennsylvania League)—Class D. During 1962, Al served as a scout for the Detroit Tigers. In 1963, he coached the Class A, Thomasville team (Georgia–Florida). Al led this team to a first-place finish. 1964 found Al in Lakeland (Florida State League)—Class A. The next year, he was back with the same league, but with Daytona Beach.

From 1967 to 1969, Al led Rocky Mount (Carolina League)—Class A. On May 15, 1966, he had the greatest day of his managerial career. Two of his pitchers, Dick Drago and Darrell Clark, both pitched no-hit, no-run games in both ends of a doubleheader, Rocky Mount versus Greensboro. Al's team ended in second place that season in the Eastern Division, but they won the playoff. In 1969, Al's team ended in first place.

While he was still involved in baseball, Al bought a share in a film processing laboratory and helped in the company's operation, particularly during off-seasons. Al Federoff is married. He enjoys hunting and fishing and all sports. He lives in Taylor, Michigan.

Years	Games	AB	H	R	RBI	HR	BA	OBP	FP
2	76	235	56	14	14	0	.238	.290	.973

1951-52 Det-A

Eddie Feinberg

Edward Isadore Feinberg was born on September 29, 1917, in Philadelphia. Eddie's parents were William and Anna Feinberg, who had immigrated from Kiev, Russia. Eddie was the youngest of five children. He dropped out of his Philadelphia high school to sign with his hometown Phillies in 1937, at the age of 17.

In 1937, Eddie was sent to the Phillies' Eastern Shore League team in Centreville, Maryland. He was used as a utility fielder. The next year, he was sent to Montgomery, Alabama (Southeastern League). At the end of the 1938 season, Eddie was promoted to the Phillies, where he joined two other Jewish players, Morrie Arnovich and Phil Weintraub. He debuted September 11, 1938, at the position of shortstop, but didn't get a hit until two days later. That first hit was off Mort Cooper of the St. Louis Cardinals, at Philadelphia's Shibe Park. Eddie also hit a second single that day, but the Phillies lost the game, 3 to 2.

In September 1938, the Phillies were scheduled to play a doubleheader. The problem was that the games were on the same day as Yom Kippur. Arnovich and Weintraub took the day off, but Eddie decided to play. Eddie had only joined the Phillies a couple of weeks earlier and he thought it might hurt his career if he didn't play. Eddie hit 0 for 8 that day. He regretted his decision for the rest of his life.

In 1939, Eddie was assigned to St. Paul, Minnesota (American Association). Later that year, he was again promoted to the Phillies. On May 19, 1939, Eddie tied a major league record, when he had no fielding chances in a twelve-inning game. Eddie did have 2 hits that day, as the Phillies beat the Reds, 4–3. In 1940, when Eddie was told that he would be sold to another team, he opted to retire from professional baseball and to play for the semi-pro Brooklyn Bushwicks.

Later, after retiring from the Bushwicks, Eddie opened and operated a restaurant in Philadelphia. Finally, in 1982, he retired to Florida with his wife, Sally (née Goldstein), at the age of sixty-four. They had three children.

Eddie Feinberg died on April 20, 1986, in Hollywood, Florida.

Years	Games	AB	H	R	RBI	HR	BA	OBP	FP
2	16	38	7	2	2	0	.184	.225	.957

1938-39 Phi-N

Harry Feldman

Harry Feldman was born on November 10, 1919, in the Bronx, New York. In 1937, he was a talented, right-handed pitcher when he pitched two no-hitters for the Bronx's Clark Junior High School. These victories inspired Harry, and when he heard about a tryout camp that the Giants team had organized, he showed up. Harry stayed there three days, but nobody would talk to him. Harry got his courage together and confronted manager Bill Terry, explaining his plight: he was working at a shirt factory, for $14 a week, and he had to take time off to come there. Harry told Terry he wanted to show what he could do, but nobody would look at him—

even though he had been there steadily for three days. Terry told the boy to pitch a few. The camp manager liked what he saw, and signed Harry to a contract for 1938.

Harry played the 1938 season for Blytheville, Arkansas. He had a good year and won 13 games and lost 1, a .929 percentage. For the 1939 season, Harry was promoted to Fort Smith, Arkansas. There Harry met a local girl, Laurette Myatt, and a romance ensued. Harry's average for 1939 was .500, with 7 wins and 7 losses. His next year, still at Fort Smith, showed a .755 average, with 25 wins and 9 losses. This record caught the attention of the Giants brass and Harry was moved up to Jersey City (International League) for the 1940 season.

Harry's record was 5 and 13 for Jersey City in 1940, a .278 average, but his ERA of 3.64 was not bad. Up until August of 1941, Harry went 14 and 16 for Jersey City, a .467 average, with an even better ERA of 3.42. If Harry's good ERAs don't seem to correspond to his poor win-loss records, it should be noted that 18 of Harry's 29 losses at Jersey City were by only one run. This fact won for Harry a new nickname, "Hard Luck Harry." He was also sometimes called "Hank."

But despite his losses, the Giants' management was impressed by what they saw. Harry was called to join the team in August and, on September 10, 1941, he made his major league debut at Forbes Field in a game against Pittsburgh. Harry pitched the first 7 innings of the game, before being relieved. Harry and the Giants both lost, 10–7.

On September 21, Harry had a particularly satisfying start against the Boston Braves. Harry's battery mate in that game was Harry Danning. This was probably the first example of a Jewish battery in major league history. Later Jewish batteries include Larry and Norm Sherry,

Koufax and Norm Sherry, and Bo Belinsky and Norm Miller. The final score of the September game was Giants 4, Braves 0. Both Morrie Arnovich and Sid Gordon had hits for the Giants during this game, Harry Feldman's first major league victory and a shutout.

The year 1941 was an important one for Harry for other reasons. Harry finally married his Arkansas sweetheart, Laurette, and he bought a house in Fort Smith, which became his permanent residence.

Harry finished the 1941 season with the Giants with one win and one loss. His ERA was 4.05. The next year, 1942, was his best with the Giants. He won 7 and lost 1, with an ERA of 3.16. On May 1, 1942, Harry hit his first major league home run, off Cubs pitcher Jake Mooty, in a Cubs 13–9 victory over the Giants at Wrigley Field.

In September 1943, Harry was rejected by the Army because of a lung condition. With one hiatus, Harry played regularly with the Giants all the way through the beginning of the 1946 season. This hiatus took place at the beginning of the 1944 season. Harry, despondent over his mother's recent death and upset because of the illness of his wife, resigned. However, things were soon straightened out and Harry was back with the Giants. His records were 4 and 5 in 1943, with a 4.29 ERA; 11 and 13 in 1944, with a 4.17 ERA; and 12 and 13 in 1945, with a 3.27 ERA.

One interesting game Harry pitched was on April 30, 1944, at the Polo Grounds, against the Dodgers. During the game, the Giants scored 26 runs, a club record since 1900. Harry came into the game as a reliever and pitched $5\frac{2}{3}$ innings, collecting the victory in the 26–8 rout. On September 8, 1945, Harry pitched his last major league victory, against the Cubs, at Wrigley Field, 3–0. This was Harry's 35th victory for the Giants and his 6th shutout.

In 1946, the attention of whole baseball world was focused on Mexico. A Mexican millionaire named Jorge Pasquel was trying to transform his nation's baseball league into a third major league. He was doing this by raiding the U.S. teams, offering fat contracts and fatter signing bonuses to players in the American and National Leagues. Hank Greenberg and Ted Williams were each offered $100,000 to play in Mexico, though both turned the offers down. Pasquel was also raiding the Negro Leagues, producing the first integrated league at the major league level in North America. The Commissioner of Baseball, Happy Chandler, reacted by declaring that any player, with a signed contract, who jumped from the major leagues to play in Mexico would be banned for life from playing in organized baseball.

Harry had started the season with the Giants and had pitched in 3 games, with a record of 0-2. The Giants had been especially hard hit by the Mexican raiders, having already lost 6 players. On May 9, Harry and his good friend and star closer of the Giants, Ace Adams, cleaned out their lockers at the Polo Grounds and caught flights to Mexico. There is some controversy over how much the two men were paid. Newspapers of the day reported that each received $20,000, but Adams later claimed he had received $50,000. It is likely that Harry received something similar.

Harry did not leave any bad blood behind. After his departure, he called Giants manager Mel Ott on the phone and the two men parted amicably. Over 6 seasons with the Giants, Harry had a percentage of exactly .500, 35-35. His major league ERA was 3.80.

Careful records do not seem to have been kept of the 1946 season in the Mexican League, though it should be easy to reconstruct them from the back files of Mexican newspapers. So it is not clear how well Harry pitched during his season "south of the border," pitching for the Veracruz Blues. After the Pasquel raid had fizzled out, the Pasquel family finances a bit shaken, if not seriously harmed, and Jorge hurt by bad publicity, the American players all came home. Eventually, all was forgiven and all refugees from the outlaw league were welcomed back into the fold.

Eventually, Harry's contract was sold by the Giants to San Francisco (Pacific Coast League). He played with the Seals in 1949 and 1950. Both years, Harry had a losing season. He retired from baseball in 1951.

During these years, Harry had maintained his home in Fort Smith. After his retirement, he opened a phonograph record store there. The Feldmans had five children, one son and four daughters. Some time after his marriage, Harry converted to Christianity.

During a fishing trip in March 1962, Harry suffered a seizure. He was rushed to a hospital in Fort Smith. Shortly after, Harry Feldman suffered a heart attack while still in the hospital, and died on March 16.

Years	Games	IP	W	L	GS	SV	PCT	ERA
6	143	666	35	35	78	3	.500	3.80

1941-46 NY-N

Leo Fishel

Leopold H. Fishel was the first Jewish major league pitcher. He was born on December 13, 1877, in Brooklyn.

Leo made his only major league appearance on May 3, 1899. He pitched all nine innings that day for the New York Giants, which were owned by Andrew Freedman. Leo had 6 strikeouts, 6 bases on balls, and gave up 9 hits. The Giants lost the game and Leo got his only decision: one loss. His lifetime ERA is 6.00.

Leo Fishel died of heart disease on May 19, 1960, in Hempstead, New York.

Years	Games	IP	W	L	GS	SV	PCT	ERA
1	1	9	0	1	1	0	.000	6.00

1899 NY-N

Happy Forman

August "Happy" Foreman was born in Memphis, Tennessee, on July 20, 1899. He had three brothers, Mose, Sol, and Frank, as well as two sisters. Happy served in the U.S. Army during World War I. After the war, he took a degree at Chamberlain Hunt College. He then began his career in professional baseball. Happy entered baseball as a left-handed pitcher who batted over .300. His first minor league club was Memphis (Southern League), where he pitched in 1920 and 1921. He played with Clarksdale (Cotton States League) in 1922. In 1923, Happy hurled for both Shreveport and Decatur.

Happy returned to Shreveport at the start of the 1924 season. In 1924, he pitched in three games for the Chicago White Sox. His major league debut came on September 3, 1924. That year, Happy toured with the White Sox in Europe. There he met John McGraw. Happy was very impressed with McGraw, and frequently boasted of their acquaintance. Happy finished the season with Beaumont (Texas League). There he held the 1924 Texas League record for winning percentage, with .640 (16 wins, 9 losses) and with 222 innings pitched.

In 1925, Happy pitched for the Beaumont Explorers. The Explorers were one of the worst teams ever to play. They hadn't won a game in two or three years. One day, Happy pitched a brilliant game against Shreveport and the Explorers won. The next day, Happy got a congratulatory telegram signed "John J. McGraw." He took the telegram and showed it to all of the players, the manager, Dutch Bernson, and several of his friends in Shreveport. Everything was okay—until Happy found out it was a hoax. Four players on the team had really sent the telegram. He tried to sue the Western Union company, but was reminded that the telegram bore a Shreveport date line. For weeks, Happy wouldn't talk with the perpetrators of the hoax.

Happy pitched in three games for the Boston Red Sox in 1926. He played with 2 teams over 2 nonconsecutive years in the majors. He pitched in 6 games, with no decisions. His ERA was 3.18.

Happy returned to the minors in 1926, remaining an active player for several more years. He eventually became the manager of minor league teams in the South and Southwest. One season, he toured with a team of players costumed as Zulus, who played baseball in bare feet!

Happy Foreman died on February 13, 1953, in New York City. He was buried in Beth David Cemetery, Elmont, New York.

Years	Games	IP	W	L	GS	SV	PCT	ERA
2	6	$11\frac{1}{3}$	0	0	0	0	NA	3.18

1924 Chi-A, 1926 Bos-A

Micah Franklin

Micah Ishanti Franklin was born on April 25, 1972, in San Francisco, California. He is the son of a Jewish mother and a black father. Micah was raised Jewish and considers himself a Jew.

After graduating from Lincoln High School, in San Francisco, Micah was drafted by the New York Mets, in the third round of the 1990 draft. Micah has changed positions during the course of his career. He started as an infielder and as a designated hitter, but now plays outfield. In 1990, Micah had his first minor league assignment with the Kingsport Mets. He batted .259 and was promoted, in 1991, to the Pittsfield Mets. Micah was promoted to Erie after playing in 26 games. In 1992, Micah signed with the Cincinnati Reds organization. He was assigned to play with the Billings Mustangs. With Billings, Micah batted .332 with 11 home runs. He began the 1993 season with Winston-Salem Spirits, but was demoted to the Charleston, West Virginia, Wheelers, after 20 games. Micah finished the season with the Wheelers.

In 1994, Micah was promoted back to the Winston-Salem Spirits. That year, he played with both the Spirits and the Chattanooga Lookouts. He batted .300 with the Spirits and .276 with the Lookouts, hitting 31 home runs with the two teams. At the end of the 1994 season, Micah was signed by the Pittsburgh Pirates. In 1995, he played with the Calgary Cannons; Micah batted .293 with the Cannons, with 21 home runs. At the end of the 1995 season, Micah was acquired, on waivers, by the Detroit Tigers organization. He began the 1996 season with the Toledo Mud Hens, but was traded to the St. Louis Cardinals in June, and was sent to play with the Louisville Redbirds. He hit a combined 21 home runs in 1996, making it his fourth consecutive twenty-home-run season. Micah returned to the Redbirds' lineup in 1997.

On May 13, 1997, Micah was promoted to the St. Louis Cardinals. He played his first game that day. Micah got a walk in the 3–0 loss to the Philadelphia Phillies. In his second game, Micah had his first 3 hits, including a home run. A few days later, he homered again, against the Atlanta Braves. Micah played in 17 games for the Cardinals in 1997, with a .324 batting average, .500 slugging average, and 2 home runs. He played the rest of the year with Louisville.

Micah Franklin currently lives in San Francisco.

Micah started the 1998 season with the Iowa Cubs (AAA affiliate of the Chicago Cubs), where his batting average hovered around .350, during the early months.

Years	Games	AB	H	R	RBI	HR	BA	OBP	FP
1	17	34	11	6	2	2	.324	.378	1.000

1997 StL-N

Murrray Franklin

Murray Asher "Moe" Franklin was born in Chicago on April 1, 1914. He was a big and healthy youngster and took to athletics. When he attended Chicago's Carl Schurz High School, he played baseball, basketball, and football. Moe's performances were so impressive that he was offered a scholarship to Northwestern University, but declined it to attend the University of Illinois. There he played second base on the university's baseball team. (The team's third baseman was Lou Boudreau.) While the team was visiting Ann Arbor, to play the University of Michigan, Moe was scouted by Tigers scout Wish Egan. He agreed to sign with the Tigers upon graduation from Illinois. (Egan had ignored Boudreau because Lou had already signed with Cleveland.)

Before the end of the Big Ten season, in 1937, Moe pulled a muscle in his throwing arm, his right. He graduated from Illinois with a degree in physical education, but his injury delayed him from reporting to the Tigers until mid-July. Moe's first assignment was with Beckley (Mountain State League); he made a smash entrance into organized baseball by batting .439 for Beckley. This was the highest batting average of any player, in any league in the country, during 1937. Moe was the recipient of the 1937 Louisville Slugger Award as the Batter of the Year. He hit a league-leading 26 home runs for Beckley in 94 games. Further, he was tied for the league lead for triples, with 13. He also set a league record of ten straight hits.

Moe's next assignment was Beaumont (Texas League), where he played during 1939 and 1940. In Beaumont, in 1939, they tried to shift Moe to the outfield. Then, just three weeks into the season, Moe broke his right leg sliding into home. He was out of the lineup until July 25. When he returned, it was to play third base. Moe batted .288 for the season. In 1940, Moe was back on third and batting .290. During most of the season, he was bothered by some strange disorder. When he finally felt healthy—the last month of the season—he maintained a .600 batting average for that month.

Moe was assigned to the Detroit Tigers for 1941, to play shortstop and third base, and debuted on August 12, 1941. Moe had his first major league hit, two days later, off Thornton Lee, of the Chicago White Sox. Moe was sent in, during the ninth inning, to bat for pitcher Tommy Bridges, and hit a double. Nevertheless, the Sox still beat the Tigers, 3–1, at Comiskey Park. Shortly after this, while the Tigers were visiting the Yankees at Yankee Stadium, Moe, playing in his 13th game, injured his right leg while reaching for a flyball. Up to the time of his injury, he'd been batting .333. He was out for the rest of the year.

Moe played in just 48 games for the Tigers in 1942. He had his first major league home run on May 29, off Cleveland pitcher Al Smith. It came in the 4th inning of a game at Briggs Stadium. It was a 2-run homer and the Tigers won the game, 14–3. Moe would have one more home run that season, for his major league total of 2. His major league average was .262.

Moe joined the Navy during the Second World War and served until 1945. Returning to civilian life, he found himself cut from the Tiger's roster. Moe responded by joining Jorge Pasquel's expanded Mexican League of 1946. He was one of 18 major league players to join the Mexican League that year, including Harry Feldman. Moe continued to play in Mexico and Cuba during the 1947 and 1948 seasons. In 1949, following organized baseball's amnesty for all the men who had played with the outlaw Mexican League, he joined the Hollywood Stars as an infielder. Moe hit .317 that year and his team, which included another Jewish player, Herb Gorman, won the Pacific Coast League Pennant. Moe and Herb Gorman were back with the Stars in 1950, along with another Jewish player, Herb Karpel. Moe played in the Pacific Coast League again in 1951. In 1952, he was with the league's San Diego Padres, along with Herb Gorman and Al Richter. (Jimmie Reese was a coach on the team.)

Moe Franklin died on March 16, 1978, in Harbor City, California.

Years	Games	AB	H	R	RBI	HR	BA	OBP	FP
2	61	164	43	25	16	2	.262	.309	.961

1941-42 Det-A

"Judge" Emil Fuchs

In the twentieth century, there have been two Jewish managers of major league baseball teams who themselves have not been major league players. Lefty Phillips, who did have a minor league career, rose to his position through his proven competence. Judge Emil Fuchs had an easier route to the managership of the 1929 Boston Braves: He owned the team.

Emil Edmund Fuchs was born in Hamburg, Germany, on April 17, 1878. Emil was raised in New York's lower East Side. There he became acquainted with baseball. He was a catcher with the University Settlement House team. He attended NYU Law School and, after graduation, he became a lawyer for the New York Giants organization. At that time the Giant's had a Jewish owner, Andrew Freedman. Emil Fuchs served a term as a New York City magistrate; hence his title, "Judge."

Fuchs formed a syndicate with Christie Mathewson in 1923, in order to purchase the Boston Braves. The price for the club was $450,000. Fuchs put up most of the money, but Mathewson was given most of the authority over the team and the title of president. When Mathewson died in 1925, Fuchs took over full control of the team and in 1927 made himself president.

Fuchs brought many fine players into the Braves organization, including Rogers Hornsby, George Sisler, and Casey Stengel. He was more criticized than praised for bringing Babe Ruth back to Boston in 1935, after "The Bambino" had left the Yankees. Ruth provided a draw for the team, but it soon became clear that he was no longer the player he had been and, eventually, Fuchs fired him.

From 1925 until 1927, Fuchs employed Dave Bancroft to manage the Braves. Every year the team seemed to fare worse. In 1925, they lost 83 games; in 1926, 86; and in 1927, 94. In 1928, he hired Jack Slattery. But of the first 31 games of the season, Slattery lost 20. So then Fuchs hired Rogers Hornsby. Of the remaining 122 games in the season, Hornsby lost 83. Fuchs had had enough. He declared that if his managers were going to lose like that, he might as well do the job himself. So, Fuchs became the manager of the Boston Braves for the 1929 season.

The season started well and Boston won seven of its first nine games. For a few weeks, Boston maintained its position in first place, but soon it began to slide and quickly sank to its familiar position—last place—where it would remain for the rest of the year. It wasn't just that Fuchs was not adequate, it was that he seemed completely out of place in the environment in which he found himself. Tales about Fuchs began to make the rounds:

A player came to Fuchs to tell him that the batter was waiting for instructions with a count of 3 and 1. The "Judge" replied, "Tell him to hit a home run." When Joe Dugan was told to take the shortstop position during a game, Dugan, who did not like Fuchs, asked him where the shortstop was on this field. Fuchs did not care for the jest on his incompetence. He turned to another player and directed him to "Show Mr. Dugan where the clubhouse is and how to take off his uniform."

Fuchs once directed left-handed hitter Ed Brandt to pinch-hit against Phillies pitcher Jumbo Elliott. Brandt told Fuchs that that wouldn't be a good idea, because he was a lefty and so was Elliott. Fuchs hesitated. He looked out at the mound. "So he is," he said.

Fuchs left much of the everyday running of the club to Coach Johnny Evers. Nevertheless, it was often up to him to make the big decisions. Once, a player came to tell Fuchs that the situation in the game called for a squeeze play. Fuchs's reply was, "I'll do nothing of the kind. We'll win this game honorably or not at all." Another observation of Fuchs was: "The time has gone when a manager has to chew tobacco and talk from the side of his mouth."

When Fuchs took over the reigns of the Braves he promised to do better than the managers did in 1928. In 1928, the Braves lost 103 games; Fuchs lost 98. He kept his promise to the Boston fans. However, he did not repeat the experiment. In 1930, the Braves had a new manager.

Fuchs continued as president of the Boston Braves until 1935. Though he was not a great manager and though the Braves' record was poor during his presidency of the team, he, personally, was always very popular with the public and the great majority of his players. With limited resources, he kept the team solvent and provided innovations for the public's benefit, for instance, the first Sunday baseball in Boston.

"Judge" Emil Fuchs died in New York City on December 5, 1961. To keep his memory alive, the sportswriters of Boston annually award a trophy, in his memory, to the outstanding athlete from the city.

Years	Games	W	L	PCT
1	154	56	98	.364
1929 Bos-N				

Milt Galatzer

Milton Galatzer was born on May 4, 1907, in Chicago. When he was young, Milt played ball at the Lawson playground, in the old West Side of Chicago. In 1926 and 1927, he attended Crane Tech. In both years, he was an All-City and All-State outfielder. In 1926, he was a member of the semi-pro Buckeyes team, which won the Chicago city championship.

In 1927, Milt joined his first professional baseball club in Shamokin, Pennsylvania. The next year, he played outfield for Burlington, Iowa. He was released during the season, and did not return to professional baseball until 1930. That year, Milt began the season with Terre Haute (3-I League). He was released to Frederick, Maryland, later that year. A .339 batting average with Frederick won him another chance with Terre Haute in 1931. He hit .371 with Terre Haute and won the 1931 3-I League batting title. In 1932, Milt was promoted to Toledo (American Association).

Milt was then promoted to the Cleveland Indians in 1933, after outfielder Joe Vosmik became ill. He debuted in the first game of a doubleheader on June 25, 1933, in Municipal Stadium in Cleveland. In that game, he was walked 4 times by the Washington Senators' pitcher, Earl Whitehill, to tie the record. The Senators beat the Indians 9 to 0. In the second game, Milt had 2 hits.

During the 1933 season, Milt was involved in a very famous play known as the "Smead Jolley Episode." In a game between the Indians and the Boston Red Sox, Milt hit a ball to right field. He ran to first base. The ball went right between outfielder Smead Jolley's legs. Milt saw this and ran from first to second. The ball bounced off the wall and went through Jolley's legs again. Milt glanced over his shoulder, saw Jolley fumbling the ball, and ran to third. Jolley finally got control of the ball and tried to throw to third, but overshot the third baseman and threw it into the stands. With this, Milt crossed home plate.

Milt played the majority of the 1933 and 1934 seasons with Toledo. He appeared in 57 games for the Indians in 1933 and 49 games in 1934. Milt played his longest major league season in 1935—93 games with the Indians, batting .301. Milt's teammate from the Indians, Hall of Famer Bob Feller, said of him, "There might have been better ballplayers than Milt Galatzer, but there was never a better man."

On August 26, 1936, Milt pitched his only major league game: the final 6 innings of a game against the Washington Senators. Milt allowed 3 runs on 7 hits and ended the game with a 4.50 ERA. He was not credited with a win or loss.

After the 1936 season, Milt was traded to the Cincinnati Reds organization. He played in 3 games with the Reds in 1939. Milt then returned to the minors, after his brief appearance with the Reds. He played in the minor leagues until 1946. Milt had a lifetime major league batting average of .268 in 251 games. He was well known for his fielding, and had a lifetime fielding average of .959 in the outfield and 1.000 at first base.

Milt spent three years in the Army during World War II as a lieutenant. He died on January 29, 1976, in San Francisco.

Years	Games	AB	H	R	RBI	HR	BA	OBP	FP
5	251	717	192	105	57	1	.268	.354	.959

1933-36 Cle-A, 1939 Cin-N

Mark Gilbert

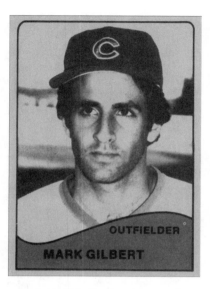

OUTFIELDER

MARK GILBERT

Mark David Gilbert was born on August 22, 1956, in Atlanta, Georgia. Mark is a third-generation Jewish baseball player. His father had been a professional baseball player and his grandfather had played semi-pro ball, pitching to the likes of "Home Run" Baker.

Joseph Gilbert, the grandfather, reached the peak of his pitching career in 1919, in his native Philadelphia, when he was offered a contract by Connie Mack to pitch for the Philadelphia Athletics. Joe's father thought all ballplayers were bums and had threatened to throw him out of the house if he signed. Joe didn't, and limited his playing to weekend semi-pro games. In the war-shortened season of 1919, many of the A's joined local barnstorming teams. It was in a game against such a team that Joe got to pitch against Baker. Baker went 0 for 4 against Gilbert.

Joe didn't discourage his son, Herbert, the way his father had discouraged him. An infielder with the White Sox organization, Herbert went on to reach the triple-A level in the minors.

Both grandpa and father, co-owners of a furniture store in Pompano Beach, Florida, encouraged young Mark. Joe worked with the boy from his birth. Mark played shortstop in Little League and impressed his grandfather, who already dreamed of Mark as the Gilbert who would make it to the majors. Mark played baseball at Fort Lauderdale's Pine Crest High School. He also played at Florida State University in Tallahassee.

Mark graduated from Florida State with a degree in finance, and was signed, in the summer of 1978, by the Cubs. He started with Geneva, NY (New York–Pennsylvania League), that year as a switch-hitting centerfielder. Mark hit .338, in 65 games. During the off-season, he worked in the family furniture store. He drove the truck and made deliveries, as well as sold furniture.

The second year in the minors, 1979, Mark played for Quad City (Midwest League), where he hit .314. Mark built on his reputation as a solid hitter with excellent speed, and he stole 51 bases that year. Of the 43 minor league players Mark played with in 1978 and 1979, Mark was the only one to make it to the majors. One of the great influences on him during this time with the Cubs farm system was Billy Williams, a roving batting coach for the Cubs. Mark felt that Williams helped him a great deal. At the end of the 1979 season, Mark was traded to the Cincinnati Reds organization.

From 1980 to 1982, Mark played with Waterbury, Connecticut. He batted .201, .247, and .301. In 1981, he had 5 home runs, his first in the minors. He repeated that effort in 1982, plus he had 40 stolen bases that year. During the winter of 1982–83, Mark was a baseball instructor. He also got married, and played with the Indianapolis Indians. Mark was moved to Witchita in 1984, where he had an excellent year. He hit .280, with 136 hits, including 6 homers, and 55 stolen bases.

After 1984, because of the length of his service in the minors, Mark became eligible for free agency. He chose to sign with his father's old organization, the Chicago White Sox. Mark was assigned to Buffalo at the start of the 1985 season. He did well there, hitting .265, with 3 home runs and 22 extra base hits. He also had 13 stolen bases.

On July 21, 1985, Mark made his debut with the Chicago White Sox, playing 7 days with them. He had 22 at-bats in 7 games, 6 hits, 3 RBIs, and a .273 average. Two nights before his final game, Mark dove for a line drive and felt his right knee give way. He got up and continued the game. Two nights later, when he made another dive for a line drive, his knee snapped again. This time he couldn't get up. Mark's career was over.

After 4 operations, Mark Gilbert got on with his life. Today he is a financial trader with Goldman, Sachs and Company. He and his wife have two daughters. The Gilberts live in Boca Raton, Florida.

Years	Games	AB	H	R	RBI	HR	BA	OBP	FP
1	7	22	6	3	3	0	.273	.385	1.000

1985 Chi-A

Joe Ginsberg

Myron "Joe" Ginsberg's thirteen-year career in the majors was marked by numerous records and historical moments. He played with the American League team with the most wins and the National League team with the most losses. He holds the American League record for passed balls. He was there when Roger Maris hit his 61st home run. He was the first Mets player to take the field in their first home game.

Ginsberg was born Myron Nathan Ginsberg. His father's name was Joe, and soon friends and relatives were calling the son "Little Joe." The name stuck and he's been known as Joe throughout his life. Although he was born in New York, on October 11, 1926, he was raised in Detroit, and the Tigers were the heroes of his youth. Among those heroes, of course, was Hank Greenberg. When young Joe was signed right out of high school by the hometown team, the Tigers, it was the culmination of his wildest dreams. There he would be, in front of the hometown fans, his friends, and relatives. But first he had to learn his trade, to serve his apprenticeship.

Joe spent five years in the Tiger minor league system. The first year, he played with Class D Jamestown, New York. But then he turned 18 and was drafted. Like many professional ballplayers, Joe discovered that his job in the Army was to continue to play baseball—exhibition games to entertain the troops. He was stationed in the Philippines, where he played with the likes of Early Wynn and Joe Garagiola. Every night, he played before enthusiastic audiences of GIs, sometimes as many as 40,000.

After the war, it was back to the minors, with service in Williamsport and Toledo. Then, in 1948, Joe was brought to Detroit. His real career had begun.

Joe debuted on September 15, 1948. His first at-bat was a walk off Bob Lemon. In that first game, Joe also scored the game-winning run. He was on his way. One of the highlights of his career was the 1950 Detroit club, which missed winning the pennant by only two games. In 1951 and 1952, Joe was Detroit's regular catcher. Then he became part of a platoon, catching and batting against right-handed pitchers, with Bob Swift doing the same against left-handers. Among the most memorable games Joe caught was one in 1952, a no-hitter pitched by Virgil Trucks.

And even as Joe helped Trucks to a no-hitter, he did quite the opposite for Yankee Vic Raschi. Joe hit only 20 home runs in 13 years, but one of his most dramatic was on June 13, 1952. Yankee pitcher Vic Raschi was in the ninth inning of a no-hitter and had one out when Joe hit his home run, spoiling Raschi's no-hitter and shutout with one blow.

In 1953, Joe was traded to Cleveland. There, Joe caught for Bob Lemon and Early Wynn. The 1954 Cleveland team set the American League win record of 111 games, but lost the World Series to the Giants, 4 games to 0.

1955 found Joe back in the minors, with the Seattle Raniers in the Pacific Coast League. He batted .295 that year in Seattle and was named Player of the Year. In 1956, he was back in the majors, in Kansas City, playing for Lou Boudreau. But Boudreau felt that Ginsberg's style of hitting would benefit from a larger ball park. He traded Joe to Baltimore, where he stayed for five years. Again Joe was part of a platoon, catching and batting against right-handers, with Gus Triandos against left-handers. The manager was Paul Richards, who was one of Joe's favorites.

It was while with the Orioles that Joe had the opportunity to catch for Steve Dalkowski. Dalkowski is believed to have been the hardest-throwing pitcher of all time. On a bet, once, Steve threw a baseball through a solid-wood fence. It's believed that Steve's fastball could actually go at about 120 miles an hour. But Steve was incredibly wild. At the point in his career when he seemed to be gaining some control, his arm gave out and he never made it to the majors. Richards wanted to get a true reading of the speed of Steve's fastball, in those days before the radar gun, so he sent Steve and Joe Ginsberg to the U.S. Army Proving Ground at Aberdeen, Maryland, to get a radar reading on Dalkowski's pitch. Alas, Steve was too disconcerted and couldn't get a fastball over the radar box. After twenty minutes of hard throwing, he finally got a little lob over the box at 93 miles an hour. Steve threw a few more pitches, missing the mark, until he pitched right on the box and smashed it.

Joe still remembers a spring-training game against Cincinnati. The Reds' manager, Birdie Tebbetts, after watching Dalkowski warm up, refused to put his regular players in against him. He ordered the rookies that he did send in not to swing the bat—just to make sure they didn't get hit. "This guy is going to kill someone," Tebbetts warned.

It was also with the Orioles that Joe gained his record of three passed balls in a single game. The pitcher was Hoyt Wilhelm, a knuckleballer who was particularly hard to catch. A similar record was set by Gus Triandos, at around the same time, with Wilhelm.

In 1960, Joe was traded to the White Sox and, in 1961, to the Red Sox. It was with the Red Sox, in the dugout, that Joe witnessed Roger Maris' record-setting 61st home run. He finished his career with the 1962 Mets, the "losingest" team in National League history. The opening home game, where Joe was the first player to take the field, was one of only two games Joe played with the Mets.

After leaving baseball, Joe Ginsberg represented the Jack Daniel's Distillery for 16 years. He is now retired in Florida, plays golf, and does an occasional card show. His thirteen years in major league baseball have left him with fond memories.

Years	Games	AB	H	R	RBI	HR	BA	OBP	FP
13	695	1716	414	168	182	20	.241	.334	.983

1948, 1950-53 Det-A, 1953-54 Cle-A, 1956 KC-A, 1956-60 Bal-A, 1960-61 Chi-A, 1961 Bos-A, 1962 NY-N

Jonah Goldman

Jonah John Goldman was born on August 29, 1906, in New York City. He attended Erasmus High School in Brooklyn, where he excelled at baseball and football. He went on to play both sports at Syracuse University, but left without graduating to pursue a career in professional baseball.

Jonah became a player in the Cleveland Indians organization. He played both shortstop and third base. Jonah made his major league debut on September 22, 1928, with the Indians, then he played in 6 more games in 1928, batting .238. Jonah returned to Cleveland in 1930. He got his only major league home run on May 5, 1930. It was a solo home run in the 7th inning of a game against the Boston Red Sox, at Fenway Park. The Indians were defeated 18 to 3. That year, Jonah had his fullest season in the majors: he appeared in 111 games and had a batting average of .242.

Jonah played in 30 games of the 1931 season, before being returned to the minor leagues. He had a lifetime batting average of .224, in 148 games. He finished his playing career in Montreal and Indianapolis, forced to retire in 1935 because of a serious thumb injury.

After retiring from baseball, Jonah turned to business. He became the president of Atlas Men's Shops. Retired from business in 1971, he moved to Palm Springs with his wife, Freda. Jonah Goldman died on August 17, 1980 in Palm Beach, Florida.

Years	Games	AB	H	R	RBI	HR	BA	OBP	FP
3	148	389	87	33	49	1	.224	.293	.941

1928, 1930-31 Cle-A

Izzy Goldstein

Isadore "Izzy" Goldstein was born June 6, 1908, in New York City. His parents were William and Ida Goldstein, who had emigrated from Odessa, in the Ukraine, to the United States. He was the eldest of three children; the family lived in the same part of the Bronx as Hank Greenberg.

By 1928, Izzy had already dropped out of school and joined a semi-pro baseball team. Word of his great pitching skill quickly spread throughout the neighborhood. The James Monroe High School team was one of the best in the neighborhood and was managed by Tom Elliffe, a very enthusiastic and ambitious coach. Though it included such luminaries as Hank Greenberg, the team needed a pitcher badly. Izzy was their man. There was one problem, Izzy had been out of school for a while, and had never been much of a student while he was there. Nevertheless, he was talked into reenrolling in the eleventh grade at James Monroe. Members of the team did Izzy's homework and took his tests—all Izzy had to do was to pitch.

Izzy, Hank Greenberg, and the rest of the team made it to the city finals, held at the Polo Grounds. Izzy pitched a good game, but the team lost 4–1. After the game, Izzy dropped out of high school for a second and final time, becoming pitcher on a semi-pro team at Sea Cliff,

Long Island, and playing with them briefly before being signed by the Detroit Tigers organization, as a pitcher.

Izzy was assigned to the Tigers farm club in Wheeling, West Virginia (Mid-Atlantic League). He ended the season with a strong record of 14-9. In 1929, he was moved to the Evansville, Indiana (Three-I League), where he played for two years. In 1930, Izzy posted a 16-9 record and was transferred, the following year, to Beaumont (Texas League). That year, he also won 16 games and played with such greats as Schoolboy Rowe and Hank Greenberg.

In 1932, Izzy was promoted to the Detroit Tigers, making his debut on April 24, 1932, in the second inning of a game against the Chicago White Sox held at Detroit's Navin Field. He gave up one run in one inning. The Tigers won, 10 to 9, but Izzy wasn't involved in the decision. Izzy got his first win on May 24 in a game against the St. Louis Browns. He allowed 10 hits and 5 runs in $7\frac{1}{3}$ innings, before being relieved by Whit Wyatt. The final score of the game was 6–5. Izzy appeared in 16 games before being demoted to Toronto (International League).

Izzy was known throughout his career as a good batter for a pitcher, ending his stint in the majors with a .294 batting average, with 5 base hits. He finished his 1932 season with Toronto, pitching one more season for the Canadian club before an injured arm forced him to retire at the end of 1933. Izzy attempted to return to baseball. He earned a tryout at the Tigers' 1934 spring-training camp in Florida, but his residual arm difficulties made a comeback impossible.

After Izzy retired from professional baseball, he returned to play semi-pro ball in New York as an outfielder. From 1934 to 1938, he was with the Bushwicks, the Carltons, and the Bay Parkways. After he retired from semi-pro baseball, he entered the retail men's wear business. Izzy also served with the U.S. Army in the South Pacific from 1942 to 1945. After the War he returned to the clothing business. Izzy Goldstein retired to live in Florida with his wife, Caroline. He died on September 24, 1993, in Delray Beach, Florida.

Years	Games	IP	W	L	GS	SV	PCT	ERA
1	16	$56\frac{1}{3}$	3	2	6	0	.600	4.47
1932 Det-A								

Jake Goodman

Jacob Goodman was born on September 14, 1853, in Lancaster, Pennsylvania. He was a first baseman.

Presumably, before he played at the major league level, Jake played in the minors. These teams included Wilmington, the Ironsides of Lancaster, and Trenton. There is a hiatus between Jake's two major league stints, and his minor league experience may have fallen between the two halves of his major league career.

Jake made his major league debut on May 2, 1878, with the Milwaukee Grays. This team, also known as the Cream Cities, existed as part of the National League, which was formed in 1876 to replace the old National Association, only for the season of 1878. It finished that year in sixth and last place.

Jake appeared in 60 games for Milwaukee and batted .246. He had 62 hits, scored 28 runs, and had 27 RBIs. Probably the highlight of Jake's first year was the game of June 25, 1878. Milwaukee was playing the Providence Grays, another now defunct team, and Harry

Wheeler was pitching for Providence. In the third inning, Jake hit a home run. This was the very first home run ever hit by a Milwaukee player. Nevertheless, Providence won the game, 11 to 4. There were 35 errors in the game, 18 of them committed by Providence, including 9 by the pitcher, Wheeler.

Jake returned to the major leagues in 1882 when he played for the Pittsburgh Alleghenys of the American Association. This latter league was formed, in 1882, as a rival to the National League. It lasted until 1891. Its lax rules concerning the consumption of alcohol in the ballparks won for it the nickname of the "beer and whiskey league." Jake played only 10 games with the Alleghenys. His batting average was .317. He had 13 hits, including 2 doubles and 2 triples. Jake scored 5 runs for the team.

During early March, 1890, Jake Goodman suffered a stroke while at his father's home in Reading, Pennsylvania. He lingered for a few days, unconscious, dying on March 9.

Years	Games	AB	H	R	RBI	HR	BA	OBP	FP
2	70	293	75	33	27*	1	.256	.278	.946

1878 Mil-N, 1882 Pit-American Association
* for 1878 only

Greg Goosen

Gregory Bryant Goosen was born on December 14, 1945, in Los Angeles, California. He was the son of a Jewish father, of Russian origin, and a Christian mother. Greg began playing baseball as a catcher when a friend of his broke his finger and couldn't play in a Little League game. Greg was asked to fill in, and remained a catcher for his entire baseball career. He attended Notre Dame High School and played on its baseball and football teams; he was the school's Most Valuable Player in baseball and football, and was elected to the All-League team in his senior year. After his graduation in 1964, Greg was offered athletic scholarships to four universities, but decided to join professional baseball instead.

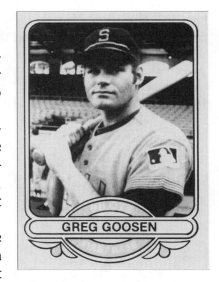

GREG GOOSEN

In 1964, Greg signed with the Los Angeles Dodgers. He had a contract that said that if he didn't make the Dodgers in one year, he would be exposed to waiver claims. His first assignment was Pocatello, Idaho (Pioneer League). He was selected as the League's Topps Player of the Month, in July of 1964. He led the league in putouts, with 316, and in chances accepted, with 332. He was promoted to St. Petersburg (Florida State League) later in the season, but didn't make the Dodgers.

In 1965, Greg was claimed by the New York Mets, on first-year-players waivers. He played with Auburn (New York–Pennsylvania League) in 1965. His batting average of .305, with Auburn, was fifth in the league. Greg played on the league's All-Star team and was voted Most Valuable Player.

Near the end of the 1965 season, Greg was promoted to the New York Mets. He made his Mets debut on September 3, 1965, and played in 11 games. While with the Mets, Greg hit his first major league home run off the Phillies pitcher, Bo Belinsky. It was a 400-foot shot in

Connie Mack Stadium. However, even though Greg batted .290 in his stay with the Mets, he was still assigned to the Jacksonville Suns (International League) the following season. Greg was promoted to the Mets at the end of the season, however, and played in 13 games. He batted .188 with the Mets and was returned to Jacksonville in 1967.

Greg was chosen as the International League Topps Player of the month, for May of 1967. That year, he led the league's catchers in putouts, with 690, and in chances accepted, with 790. He was promoted later the same year and played in 37 games for the Mets. Greg returned to the Mets lineup in 1968. But after batting a .234 average, he was returned to Jacksonville. Greg finished the season in Memphis (Texas League).

In 1969, Greg was traded to the new Seattle Pilots. He began the season with Vancouver (Pacific Coast League), but played in 52 games for the Pilots and batted .309. After 1969, the Pilots moved to Milwaukee and became the Brewers. Greg began the 1970 season with the Portland Beavers (Pacific Coast League), but also played in Milwaukee before being traded to the Washington Senators. Greg retired at the end of the 1970 season. He had a lifetime batting average of .241 in 193 games, played over 6 seasons.

While he was playing, Greg worked as a private detective during the off-seasons. He continued this profession after he retired from baseball, and spent much of his free time in a boxing gymnasium owned by his brother, as well as in pool halls.

Living in Los Angeles also presented another opportunity to Greg: acting in movies. In 1995, Greg had a bit part in the movie Get Shorty. Greg played Duke, "the man at the Ivy." His one line was, "Hey, Harry. That-a-boy, killer." Then he made a gunshot gesture and patted the character Harry on the back. Greg Goosen still lives in Los Angeles.

Years	Games	AB	H	R	RBI	HR	BA	OBP	FP
6	193	460	111	33	44	13	.241	.317	.992

1965-68 NY-N, 1969 Sea-A, 1970 Mil-A, 1970 Was-A

Sid Gordon

Sid Gordon was born in Brooklyn on August 13, 1918. His parents were Morris and Rose (née Meyerson) Gordon. Sid's father, an immigrant from Russia, was a coal dealer. When he was old enough, during the summer holidays Sid would drive his father's coal truck and make deliveries.

Sid played baseball at Samuel Tilden High School. He was so good that his high school coach, Joe Solomon, arranged for a tryout for Sid with Casey Stengel, then of the Dodgers. This was in 1936, just after Sid's graduation. Stengel liked what he saw of the right-handed slugger, but had no place for Sid at that time. Stengel promised to keep Sid in mind, but before he could act on it, he was fired himself. Sid went back to playing second base in sandlot games. It was in such a game that his talents were observed by George Mack, a scout with the Giants.

Mack promised Sid a position on the Giants' farm team in Milford, Delaware (Eastern Shore League), but conditional on his arriving there by a certain date and his being accepted by the manager as good enough for the team. Sid was looking forward to the experience, counting down the days until his departure. Then his father died, and he gave up all ideas of a baseball career. His mother would need him to run the coal business. However, his mother would hear none of it. She would run the business. Rose Gordon made sure that Sid was on the train for Milford, and shoved $32 in his hand as he departed.

Sid was put on third base, an unfamiliar position. He was in every game Milford played that year, and batted .352, with 25 home runs, including two consecutive ones in a single game—the first a grand slam and the second a three-run homer—and seven RBIs with two blows of the bat. Sid led the league in hits, 135; in total bases, 256; and triples, 9. Following the season, Sid was back to his route delivering coal.

The next season, 1939, Sid was sent to Clinton (3-I League). He batted .327 and led the league in triples with 24, an amazing number. Before the end of the season, Sid was moved up to Jersey City (International League), just to get a feel for the team. He appeared in only three games. But in the next two years, Sid proved himself a powerhouse with the Jersey City Giants.

SID GORDON

In 1941, for instance, Sid batted .304. Late in 1940, he married Mary Goldberg. At the end of the 1941 season, Sid was given a chance to debut with the New York Giants. On September 11, he appeared in his first major league game, which took place in the Polo Grounds, in a game against the Boston Braves. This was a very special game in Jewish baseball history. Morrie Arnovich joined Sid in the outfield; Harry Feldman pitched, with Harry Danning as his battery mate. Sid hit a single off Boston pitcher Art Johnson in his first at-bat. Later in the game, he got a triple. Sid's mother was listening to the radio that day and heard the announcement that Sid would start in that day's game. She rushed, with her son's sister, to the Polo Grounds in a taxi—to be there when Sid began his major league career. Sid appeared in just 8 more games before the end of the season. He batted .258 for New York that year.

Sid started 1942 for New York, but his manager, Bill Terry, wanted him to gain more experience in the outfield, so he sent him back to Jersey City for the balance of the season. But this would be the last time Sid would ever play in the minor leagues. He hit .300 for Jersey City.

The next season, 1943, was Sid's first full year in the majors. He was feeling his way, that year, and learning from his new experiences. In the period 1944 to 1945, however, Sid would continue his learning processes in the U.S. Coast Guard.

When Sid returned to the Giants in 1946, he came back as a fully matured player. He was not famous for his colorful personality or glamorous lifestyle. He was an ordinary fellow from Brooklyn: very dependable, flexible, willing to play whatever position was needed, whether in the infield or the outfield. But as he developed, so did Sid's power. He was always a danger to the opposing team, which could expect a hit and often a double or a home run.

An outstanding fielder and hitter, Sid was selected twice for All-Star teams, in 1948 and 1949. He was extremely popular in his native Brooklyn, as well as in the rest of New York. In 1948, when the Giants were visiting Ebbets Field, Sid was honored with a "Sid Gordon Day." This was an unprecedented honor, to have a day honoring an opposing player. (Sid was presented with a Chrysler.) There is a superstition that players usually play badly on days they are honored. Sid proved the exception and hit two homers before his Brooklyn fans that day.

That same year, he was honored by the Men's Club of New York as "the outstanding New York athlete." Sid had had his best home-run year that season, slugging 30.

In 1949, Sid tied a league record by hitting two home runs in one inning. He tied another league record in 1950, with four grand-slam home runs in one season. In three different years, he homered in every park in the league.

In 1950, much to the chagrin of his New York fans, including Giants manager Leo Durocher, Sid was traded to the Boston Braves. Sid responded by having an excellent year with Boston, hitting .304, with 27 home runs. Sid continued with Boston through 1951 and 1952. When, in 1953, the Braves were moved to Milwaukee, Sid went with them. When Sid was traded to the Pittsburgh Pirates in 1954, he had the best batting average of his career, hitting .306. Shortly after Sid had started the 1955 season with the Pirates, his contract was bought back by the Giants. He concluded his major league career that season with the Giants.

Sid's lifetime average is .283. He had 1415 hits, including 220 doubles, 43 triples, and 202 home runs. His fielding average as an outfielder was .985; as a third baseman, .950; and as a first baseman, .991.

In 1956, Sid appeared as a player-coach with the Miami Marlins (International League). After that season, Sid went into business in New York as an insurance underwriter. Sid and his wife, Mary, were married 35 years. They had two sons, Michael and Richard. Michael was a catcher in the minor leagues from 1963 to 1965.

On June 17, 1975, Sid Gordon was playing softball in New York's Central Park when he suddenly collapsed with a heart attack. He was rushed to Lenox Hill Hospital, where he died shortly afterwards.

Years	Games	AB	H	R	RBI	HR	BA	OBP	FP
13	1475	4992	1415	735	805	202	.283	.377	.985

1941-43, 1946-49 NY-N, 1950-52 Bos-N, 1953 Mil-N, 1954-55 Pit-N, 1955 NY-N

Herb Gorman

Herbert Allan Gorman was born on December 18, 1924, in San Francisco. His parents were Harry and Jennie (née Cohn) Gorman. His father was a native of California and his mother of Virginia. Herb began his baseball career after military service during the Second World War.

Herb's first minor league assignment was Three Rivers (Canada–American League) in 1946. He played on first base and in the outfield for the pennant-winning club. Herb was promoted to Spokane (West International League) in 1947. That year, he batted .351 and led the league in RBIs, with 138.

In 1948, he played for Pueblo (Western League), batting .341 and leading the Western League in doubles with 45. Herb was promoted to the Hollywood Stars (Pacific Coast League) in 1949. The Stars won the Pacific Coast League pennant that year. He also played in Hollywood in

1950. In 1952, Herb played on the San Diego Padres (Pacific Coast League); on February 10 that same year, Herb was married to his wife, Rosalie.

Herb made his only major league appearance on April 19, 1952, with the St. Louis Cardinals. He was used as a pinch-hitter for pitcher Willard Schmidt, in the seventh inning. Herb grounded out, as the Cardinals lost to the Chicago Cubs, 8–1, at Wrigley Field.

On April 5, 1953, Herb Gorman collapsed on the field during a game in San Diego, California. He died shortly after of a massive heart attack. He was the shortest-lived of all Jewish major league players, dying at the age of twenty-eight.

Years	Games	AB	H	R	RBI	HR	BA	OBP	FP
1	1	1	0	0	0	0	.000	.000	.000

1952 StL-N

Shawn Green

Shawn David Green was born on November 10, 1972, in Des Plains, Illinois. His family later moved to Santa Ana, California. Shawn entered Tustin High School in 1988, becoming the star of its baseball team. Shawn established school records in stolen bases and in hits. He was named to the 1991 All-American Teams of Collegiate Baseball by USA Today and the American Baseball Coaches Association. Shawn graduated from high school in June 1991, with a 4.0 grade-point average. He ended his high school career with a .430 batting average, 51 stolen bases, 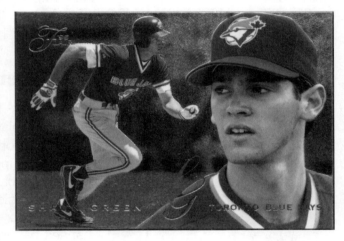 and 147 hits, in 103 games. Shawn's 147 hits, at Tustin, ranked him third on the All-Time State of California Hitters List and tied the California Interscholastic Federation hit record.

Shawn was drafted by the Toronto Blue Jays as their first-round pick in the 1991 free-agent draft. He signed with the Blue Jays with the condition that he could attend Stanford University in the fall and spring, missing instructional league and part of spring training. Shawn was given a fully paid scholarship to Stanford, even though he could not play on the school's baseball team. He was awarded a $700,000 signing bonus by the Blue Jays, the second highest bonus of all time.

Shawn's first minor league assignment was with the Dunedin, Florida, Blue Jays, in 1992. Shawn, who plays any of the three outfield positions, batted .273 in Dunedin. In 1993, he was promoted to the Knoxville Smokies. He played in 99 games with the Smokies and had a .283 batting average, before being promoted to the Blue Jays in September.

Shawn made his major league debut on September 28, 1993. He appeared in two other games with 6 total at-bats, but didn't get any hits. Shawn began the 1994 season with the Syracuse Chiefs; he played in 104 games and had a .344 batting average. That year, he also won the International League's batting championship. Shawn appeared in 14 games with the Blue Jays in 1994. He batted a modest .091 average, but did return to Toronto's lineup in 1995. Shawn

appeared in 121 games in the strike-shortened 1995 season. He began to shine in his first full season with a .288 batting average and 15 home runs, and was the first rookie to lead the Blue Jays in slugging percentage, when, that year, he averaged .509. Shawn returned to Toronto in 1996, batting .280, with 11 home runs. He excelled after the All-Star game, with a .337 batting average. In 1997, Shawn batted a strong .290 batting average for the Blue Jays. He also hit a career-best 16 home runs.

Shawn Green's smooth swing has been compared to that of his former teammate, John Olerud. When asked what he thought of Shawn's potential, veteran teammate Joe Carter said, "The sky's the limit. He's got speed, the best arm in baseball and a natural swing."

Shawn continued into the 1998 season with the Toronto Blue Jays as their regular right fielder.

Years	Games	AB	H	R	RBI	HR	BA	OBP	FP
8	878	3123	882	500	475	143	.282	.349	.985

1993-99 Tor-A, 2000 LA-N

Hank Greenberg

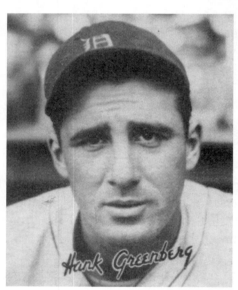

On July 23, 1956, Hank Greenberg became the first Jewish ballplayer to be inducted into Baseball's Hall of Fame in Cooperstown, New York. This was just one of numerous superlatives that marked the career of this extraordinary ballplayer and human being.

Hank holds the record—a record he shares with Jimmie Foxx—of the most home runs hit by a right-handed batter in a season: 58. This record gave Hank the home-run title for the American League in 1938. When comparing Hank's achievement with those of Babe Ruth and Roger Maris, it is important to remember that most ballparks, then and now, favor the left-handed hitter. So Hank's and Jimmie's records should be considered for the true superlatives they are.

Hank also held home-run titles for the American League in 1940 and 1946. In 1932, while playing for Beaumont, Texas, Hank hit 39 home runs, which won him a Texas League title. Probably the most important home run in Hank Greenberg's career was the grand slam he hit in the 9th inning of the last game of the regular 1945 season. This home run won the game and earned for the Detroit Tigers that year's American League pennant. Hank holds the record for the most home runs struck at home in a single season. Hank had 39 homers in Detroit in one year.

Hank led his league in runs batted in for four years between 1935 and 1946. The last of the these years, 1946, is the most remarkable, considering the long hiatus Hank had endured away from baseball because of his voluntary military service during the Second World War. He was fond of pointing out that baseball games were won by runs rather than home runs, and he was proudest of all of his RBI record. In 1935, for example, he had led the American League with 170 RBIs—51 more than Gehrig, who was in second place. Never before in the history of baseball had any player led the RBI column with more than 40 runs over his nearest competitor. In 1937, Hank hit 183 RBIs, an all-time record in the American League for a right-handed batter and just one short of Lou Gehrig's overall American League record.

Perhaps Hank's most impressive RBI record is his record of runs batted in per game, .92. This is the all-time record, one he shares with only two other players, Lou Gehrig and Sam Thompson. (The latter player is a Hall of Famer who played between 1885 and 1906. Sam spent the last year of his career with the Detroit Tigers, Hank's first major league team.)

Hank contributed to the Detroit Tigers' winning four American League pennants while he was with the team. He played in the four subsequent World Series: 1934, 1935, 1940, and 1945. Hank's World Series batting average was .318, even better than his lifetime batting average of .313. Hank contributed significantly to the Detroit World Series victories of 1935 and 1945. He had a total of 5 World Series home runs.

Hank was elected to the American League All-Star Team in 1937 and 1940. He was named honorary captain of the American League All-Star Team in 1983.

Hank was twice elected Most Valuable Player in the American League, in 1935 and 1940. When he was first elected for this honor, he was serving the Tigers as a first baseman. By 1940, he was a leftfielder. Hank was the only player in baseball history to win two MVP awards for two different positions.

Hank Greenberg was not unrecognized for the exceptional talent he showed during his baseball career. He was the first player ever to receive a yearly salary of $100,000.

In 1934, Hank was part of the highest-scoring infield in the history of baseball. The 1934 Tigers infield scored a record 462 runs. Hank, the team's first baseman, scored the lion's share of the runs, with 139; Charlie Gehringer, on second, scored 127 runs; Billy Rogell, shortstop, 100; and Marv Owen, on third base, 96. That 1934 infield, of course, made it all the way to the World Series. The 1934 World Series was the first World Series broadcast on radio. Detroit's own Ford Motor Company put up $100,000 for the rights to broadcast the game, play by play.

The 1945 World Series marked another World Series first for Hank Greenberg. In the sixth game, during the twelfth inning, when a ball struck to the outfield hit a sprinkler head and bounced over Hank's head he was charged by the official scorekeeper with an error. There was a universal protest against this ruling, particularly among the sportswriters present at the game. Some hours later, the official ruling was changed. The batter was credited with a hit and the error charged to Hank was dropped. This was the first time in World Series history that an official decision of a scorekeeper had ever been changed.

Hank is credited with design changes in the mitt of the first baseman that eventually became standard gear. When Hank first introduced his extra long mitt, in 1934, it was the cause of some controversy, especially during the World Series of that year.

Hank was also instrumental in the creation of the pension plan that protects retired players and their families. His interest in the welfare of his fellow players dates from his years as a general manager and team owner. Hank is one of very few players ever to become a general manager or team owner.

Besides Cooperstown's Baseball Hall of Fame, Hank is a member of the State of Michigan Hall of Fame, Texas Hall of Fame, Jewish American Hall of Fame, and Jewish Sports Hall of Fame in Netanya, Israel.

Henry "Hank" Benjamin Greenberg was born shortly after midnight on New Year's day in 1911. His parents were David and Sarah (née Schwartz) Greenberg. Both parents were Jews born in Romania, who had met in New York. His father was in the textile business and quite successful. At the time of his birth, Hank's family lived in Greenwich Village. When he was six or seven, the family moved to the upper Bronx. Hank had an older brother and sister and a younger brother, Joe, who also became a professional baseball player.

"BATTER-UP"
Greenberg
Tigers—1st Base

When he was a boy, Hank was remarkably tall and gangly. He had a bad complexion and, overall, he felt awkward and shy. Near his house in the Bronx was a park where boys played ball. Soon after the family's move there, Henry became a regular in Crotona Park, spending night and day fighting off his sense of isolation by hitting the ball farther and farther, closer and closer to where he wanted it to go. While Hank's siblings would be studying or helping their mother in the house, he was shagging flies. Hour after hour, day after day, year after year, the growing boy honed his strengthened skill.

It was in those days that Hank developed his lifetime habit of constant batting and fielding practice. Before every game, Hank was out there practicing; even after games, he would practice. Many have commented that God made such men as Mantle, DiMaggio, and Ted Williams great players, but Hank Greenberg made himself.

He played baseball, basketball, and football throughout his school and high school years. He played semi-pro ball and attracted the attention of scouts. In 1929, he was offered a $9,000 bonus to sign with the Detroit Tigers while he continued his education and played college ball. But after one semester at NYU, he got tired of college and was anxious to get started in his new career, so he left college and joined the Tigers' minor league system.

Hank began his career in 1930, with Hartford, Connecticut, a single A team, but he was soon demoted to Raleigh, North Carolina, a Class C team. There he did very well, and his progress earned him a single appearance, at the end of the 1930 season, with the parent club, the Detroit Tigers. On his single at-bat, on September 14, 1930, he popped out. Hank started 1931 at Beaumont, in the Texas League, but because Beaumont already had a first baseman, he was quickly transferred to Evansville, in the 3-I League. He did very well, batting .318. In 1932, he did play for Beaumont, batting .290 and leading the league in runs scored, 123, and home runs, 39. Hank was ready for the majors and ready to become "Hammerin' Hank."

The first regular year, 1933, that Hank played for the Tigers he had some difficulty establishing his role on the team. On the recommendation of the manager, Bucky Harris, the Tigers had purchased the contract of first baseman Harry "Stinky" Davis for $75,000. This blocked Hank from his regular position. Hank was tried briefly in the outfield, but mostly he was used as a pinch-hitter. Nevertheless, as the early weeks of the season progressed, Harris's faith in Davis became more and more embarrassing, for Davis was hitting poorly. Hank complained to the team's owner and the owner had a talk with Harris. Finally, on May 6, Harris scratched out Davis's name from that day's schedule and penciled in "Greenberg." In the 8th inning, Hank hit his first major league home run—a scorcher, going over the scoreboard in left center field and landing in the street behind it. From that point on, Hank had the regular job at first base. He ended the season hitting .301.

The next year, 1934, was an outstanding one for Hank. He led his team with runs batted in: 139. One of the most-remembered events of that memorable year took place on September 18. The Tigers were locked in a battle for first place and desperately needed all the help they could get, particularly from their slugging first basemen. But it was Yom Kippur and for that day Hank would not play. This event inspired Edgar A. Guest's famous verses "Speaking of Greenberg":

Two Irishmen are sitting in the stands on that famous occasion. It is clear that Hank has won their respect, but only with difficulty, because of their prejudices. On Yom Kippur, one Irishman turns to the other and says:

> "...We shall lose the game today!
> We shall miss him on the infield and miss him at the bat,
> But he's true to his religion—and I honor him for that."

Hank Greenberg seems to have liked these verses, which were widely quoted. The last two lines were used on the reverse of a medal struck in 1991 by the Magnus Museum's Jewish American Hall of Fame. We feel that this honored Edgar Guest a lot more than it did Hank Greenberg, though the medal, otherwise, was a very beautiful one. The verses are mawkish and condescending. Perhaps they may have sounded liberal and filled with the spirit of mutual understanding in 1934, but reading the complete poem over today, one feels one's teeth grit.

Despite Hank's missing one game, the Tigers won the 1934 American League pennant, although they lost the World Series to the St. Louis Cardinals and, more specifically, to the Dean brothers, who between themselves accounted for all four St. Louis victories. Hank did well in the series, with nine hits, including one home run. In the October 6 game, he tied a World Series record by getting four hits in a single game. By the way, never again in his career was Hank faced with the choice of playing or not playing on Yom Kippur.

1935 was another good year for Hank. He led the American League in RBIs, with 170. His team again took the pennant. In the second game of the World Series, Hank hit a two-run homer, but he also broke his wrist, which finished him for the rest of the series. The Tigers did win, however.

The next year began well, with Hank batting .350, but during the twelfth game of the season, he re-broke his left wrist. He was out for the rest of 1936. In 1937, Hank again led the league in RBIs, with 183, his highest single-year total.

Hank's 1938 season is probably his best remembered. It was during this year that Hank chased Babe Ruth's home-run record of 60 in a single year. Hank made only 58, tying the right-handed home-run record of Jimmie Foxx. Since 1938, it has been a point of controversy whether there existed a conspiracy (or a disorganized movement of individual prejudices) to deny the record to the Jewish Greenberg. Hank, himself, always stated that he did not believe there was any movement to deny him the record. Ruth encouraged Hank in his quest, and Hank was one of very few people that "The Bambino" was willing to talk with near the end of his life. One record that Hank did set in 1938 was the major league record for the most games with two or more home runs in a single season: eleven.

In 1940, Hank was asked to switch his position from first base to left field, to make room on the team for Rudy York. Hank, always a team player, agreed. His success in left field was as marked and as excellent as his defensive play at first had been. Hank was selected as the American League's Most Valuable Player for the second time that year.

After playing only 19 games in the 1941 season, Hank was drafted into the U.S. Army. He had completed his time in the Army and was preparing to return to the Tigers, when the Japanese bombed Pearl Harbor. Although he had no further military obligation, Hank immediately volunteered for the Army Air Corps—the first star of major league baseball to volunteer for military service. While many baseball players passed the war playing exhibition games for the troops, Hank insisted on real combat duty. By the end of the war, he had risen to the rank of captain.

Hank returned to the Tigers during the 1945 season. While he played less than half the year, his .311 batting average was the highest in the league, although he had not played enough games to qualify for the batting title. His grand slam in the 9th inning of the last game of the season clinched the pennant for the Tigers. Hank's seven hits in the 1945 World Series, including three doubles and two home runs, had much to do with the Tigers' victory over the Cubs.

In 1946, Hank returned to first base. Despite an excellent year, in which he led the league in both home runs and RBIs, he was sold to the Pittsburgh Pirates on January 8, 1947. At first, Hank was tempted not to play for the Pirates, a struggling team in a new league. But he was offered a good contract and numerous concessions, including his unconditional release at the end of the 1947 season. Hank proved to be a great attraction in Pittsburgh, where attendance went far beyond anything the team had known. Furthermore, Hank formed a lifelong friendship with Ralph Kiner. Nevertheless, the 1947 season was a kind of twilight to the great playing career of Hank Greenberg.

The 1948 season marked the dawn of a new career for Hank—as baseball executive. On March 27, 1948, Bill Veeck hired Hank to work in an executive position with the Cleveland Indians. Initially, Hank's responsibilities were undefined, but eventually he would run the club's minor league farm system and then serve as the team's general manager. Hank remained with the Indians until 1957. In 1959, he became part-owner and vice-president of the Chicago White Sox. He retired from his position with the White Sox and sold off his share of the team in 1963.

During his playing years, Hank had managed to save a small nest egg. Through wise, or very lucky, investments, he managed to turn this into millions of dollars.

Hank was married twice. His first wife, Caral, whom he married in 1945, was Jewish and a member of the Gimbels Department Stores family. Hank and Caral had two sons and a daughter. Caral was not religious and Hank, despite his Orthodox upbringing, wasn't either, so the Greenbergs did not provide any form of religious education for their children. Their elder son, Glenn, wasn't even aware he was Jewish until it was brought to his attention while he was a student at Yale. Their younger son, Stephen, spent eight years in the minor leagues. He later served as assistant to Baseball Commissioner Fay Vincent.

Hank's first marriage ended in divorce in 1958. Hank retained custody of his children, though Alva, his daughter, later chose to live with her mother. Hank remarried in 1966, and his second wife, Mary Jo, was not Jewish. The couple had no children, but the marriage seems to have been a very happy one. Mary Jo was a former actress who had appeared on the screen under the name of Linda Douglas.

Hank Greenberg spent the years after his retirement enjoying life, the success of his children, the company of his many friends, tennis, charitable work, and the admiration of the world. But the last year of his life was lived in secret and in great suffering. He had contracted kidney cancer and kept his condition a secret from even his closest friends. He died in his sleep on September 4, 1986, in his home in Beverly Hills, California.

Years	Games	AB	H	R	RBI	HR	BA	OBP	FP
13	1394	5193	1628	1051	1276	331	.313	.412	.991

1930, 1933-41, 1945-46 Det-A, 1947 Pit-N

Louis Heilbroner

Louis Wilbur Heilbroner was born in Fort Wayne, Indiana, on July 4, 1861. In 1899, Louis was working in Fort Wayne as an official of a streetcar company owned by Frank de Haas Robison. In that year, Robison closed down his Cleveland baseball team, the Spiders, which had just set a major league record of 134 games lost, and transferred its best players and its manager, Oliver Wendell "Patsy" Tebeau, to his new St. Louis team, the Perfectos. Because Louis had won Robison's trust and respect in his job at Fort Wayne, Louis was asked to become business manager of the Perfectos. This Louis did, even though it meant leaving his home.

Louis Heilbroner's 1915 Season Pass to Ebbets Field

After 92 games had been played in the 1900 season, the team's record was 42 and 50. This win percentage of .457 was a big letdown from the previous year's record of .556. Patsy Tebeau resigned from his position, with 50 games still to be played in the season. Robison turned to Louis, a man he considered as much a friend as a trusted employee, and Louis did not let him down. He agreed to accept the added responsibilities of serving as field manager for the remainder of the season.

Louis stood just 4'6". His voice was weak and high-pitched. He weighed about 100 pounds. The St. Louis team was made up of a bunch of roughnecks. Nevertheless, Louis not only finished the year, but he was able to bring the Perfectos' standing in the league up two places, to a tie for fifth. In the 50 games the Perfectos played under Louis, their winning percentage was .479.

Louis continued to serve as business manager of the St. Louis team through the 1908 season. In the meantime, he had learned a great deal concerning the statistical aspects of the game of baseball. In 1909, he returned to his home in Fort Wayne. There he established the first baseball statistical bureau. His service provided those who were willing to pay for the information, such as scouts and team owners, with full records, statistics, and other relevant information on all baseball players in the country—professional, semi-pro, or collegiate. Also starting in 1909, Louis began publishing the annual volumes of The Baseball Blue Book. This book served as the leading source of information for the National Association of Professional Baseball Leagues, the governing body of the minor leagues.

Louis Heilbroner served as president of the Central League from 1912 to 1914. He died on December 21, 1933.

Years	Games	W	L	PCT
1	50	23	25	.479

1900 StL-N

Eric Helfand

Eric James Helfand was born on March 25, 1969, in Erie, Pennsylvania. Following his family's move to San Diego, California, he attended Patrick Henry High School. Eric also attended two colleges and played on both of their baseball teams: first, at Nebraska State University, then at Arizona State University.

Eric was drafted by the Seattle Mariners in the eighth round of the 1987 free-agent draft. He decided not to sign. Eric was drafted, again, in 1990, by the Oakland A's. He was the 18th overall draft pick. Eric made his professional debut, as a catcher, with the Southern Oregon A's in 1990. His .285 batting average led to his promotion to Madison, at the end of the season. Eric began the 1991 season with the Modesto A's; he spent nearly two months on the disabled list that year, but still had a .250 batting average. Eric returned to Modesto in 1992 to catch in 72 games, before being promoted to the AAA Huntsville, Alabama, Stars.

In November 1992, Eric was drafted a third time—this time by the Florida Marlins, in the expansion draft. But Eric was never to play in their organization, because he was traded back to the A's the same day for shortstop Walt Weiss. Eric played with Huntsville in 1993, before being promoted to the Oakland A's.

Eric made his major league debut on September 4, 1993. He played in another 7 games for the A's that year. Eric then began the 1994 season with Tacoma. He batted .200 before he strained a ligament in his thumb and was put on the disabled list. To his surprise, he was recalled to Oakland when he his thumb healed. Eric played in 7 games with the A's that year. He then played most of the next, 1995, season with the A's. Though he only appeared in 38 games, Eric was used almost the entire season as the backup catcher for Terry Steinbach. At the end of the season, Eric was granted free agency and signed with the Cleveland Indians. He has played 3 major league seasons, with a .171 batting average, in 53 games.

Eric played the 1996 season with the Buffalo Bisons. He was, again, granted free-agency in 1996 and was signed by the San Diego Padres. In 1997, Eric played with the Las Vegas Stars (Pacific Coast League). He hit a career-best .319, with 6 homers and 33 RBIs, despite spending 2 weeks on the disabled list. His fielding percentage was .987.

Eric's hitting has kept him from a steady position in the major leagues. Nevertheless, he is a resourceful catcher and many pitchers are confident with the pitches he signals.

Eric Helfand currently lives in Tempe, Arizona.

Eric began the 1998 season with the Vancouver Canadians (Pacific Coast League) of the Angels organization. By mid-July he had appeared in only 2 games, but he had a .400 batting average.

Years	Games	AB	H	R	RBI	HR	BA	OBP	FP
3	53	105	18	11	9	0	.171	.256	.996

1993-95 Oak-A

Steve Hertz

Stephen Allan Hertz was born on February 26, 1945, in Fairfield Ohio. He was the eldest son of David and Sara Hertz, both of whom were from St. Louis, Missouri. The Hertz family moved to Miami when Steve was young. He played baseball in high school and was selected as an All-City Infielder in both 1962 and 1963. He was also named All-State, in 1963.

In September 1963, Steve signed with the Houston Colt .45s, as a third baseman. He received a $50,000 signing bonus from the new expansion team. Steve had a special clause in his contract: He could attend college in the off-season. (He attended the University of Miami.)

Steve got his first chance to play on the .45s on April 21, 1964, when he replaced Bob Aspromonte. He was fanned by John Tsitouris for his first at-bat. The Colts lost to the Cincinnati Reds, 5–10. After that game, he was sent to the Durham Bulls (Carolina League). Steve returned to the .45s a few times, but he never got a hit in a total of 4 at-bats, though he did score 2 runs.

In 1965, Steve was sent to the Cocoa Astros in the Florida State League. There he made it to the Florida State League All-Star Team, as a third baseman. In 1966, he also made it to the All-Star team in the Western Carolinas League, playing for Salisbury, North Carolina.

In 1967, Steve was drafted by the Dodgers system. That year, he was assigned to Dubuque, Iowa, where he tied a Midwest League record for assists by a third baseman. Steve was sent, in 1968, to High Point, North Carolina. There his team won the Carolina League Pennant. In 1969, Steve was traded to the New York Mets Organization, becoming player-coach with the Pompano Beach Mets (Florida State League). Later that year, he was transferred to the AAA Tidewater Tides (International League). Steve helped the Tides win the International League Championship.

During Steve's stay in the minor leagues there was some confusion over a shipment of bats sent to another player named Steve Hertz. This other Steve Hertz is still mistaken for Steve, and frequently receives copies of his Topps baseball card to sign. This second Steve Hertz, who is not Jewish, is the baseball coach at Gonzaga University in Washington state.

Steve married his wife, Fran, in 1967. He retired from professional baseball two years later, and graduated from the University of Miami with a B.A. in physical education. Steve continued with his education and received an M.A. in administration and supervision in 1978.

In 1970, Steve became a teacher and baseball coach at Coral Park High School, in the Miami area. In 1978, he took his baseball team, at Coral Park High School, all the way to the state championship. He transferred schools, in 1981, to South Ridge High School; in 1984, his team at South Ridge High were runners-up to the state title. In 1986, Steve ended his high school coaching days and became the baseball coach at Miami Dade-Wolfson Community College. The Miami Dade Barracudas were Southern Conference runners-up in 1988, 1991, 1992, 1993, 1994, and 1997 and Southern Conference Champions in 1986, 1987, 1995, and 1996. Steve's high school teams had a 300-95 win-loss record. His junior college teams have a 447-160 win-loss record, an overall winning percentage of 74.6.

Steve Hertz currently lives in Miami and will begin his 14th year of teaching and coaching the baseball team at Miami Dade-Wolfson in 1998. He has two sons: Jeff, 26, and Darren, 21.

Years	Games	AB	H	R	RBI	HR	BA	OBP	FP
1	5	4	0	2	0	0	.000	.000	1.000

1964 Hou-N

Ken Holtzman

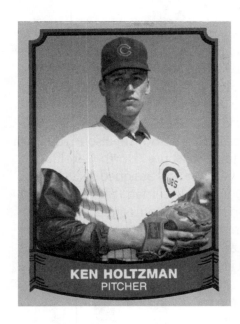

KEN HOLTZMAN
PITCHER

Kenneth Dale Holtzman was born in St. Louis, Missouri, on November 3, 1945, the son of Henry and Jacqueline Holtzman. Ken's father was in the machinery business and both his parents were natives of St. Louis. Ken played baseball at the University City High School, graduating from the school in 1963. Ken then attended the University of Illinois. He graduated with a B.A. in business administration in 1967.

In 1965, he was signed by the Chicago Cubs, receiving a bonus. Ken started his professional career with Caldwell, Idaho (Pioneer League). He had four wins and no losses, and a 1.00 ERA. He was then moved up to Wenatchee, Washington (Northwest League), where his winning percentage was .571 and his ERA was 2.44. Having won four games and lost three, in eight appearances, Ken earned for himself a tryout with the parent team on September 4, 1965. The first batter he faced in the majors, Jim Ray Hart, hit a home run off his first pitch. But, all in all, he pitched in three games for the Cubs in 1965, and had an ERA of 2.25.

Ken started with the Cubs in the 1966 season. That year he won 11 games and lost 16. At least two of those wins were impressive enough to catch the public's attention. His first was memorable because it was against the Dodgers and Don Drysdale. The other impressive win was important because it, too, was against the Dodgers, but also because it was against Ken's boyhood hero, Sandy Koufax. This game took place the day after Yom Kippur in 1966. Koufax had been scheduled to pitch on the High Holiday, but he asked to have his turn switched, which was done. Circumstances therefore brought together the two Jewish southpaws on Wrigley Field that day. Ken preserved a no-hitter for the first seven innings, and only surrendered two hits the whole game. Sandy gave up four hits. The final score was Cubs 2 to Dodgers 1. Ken received a great deal of publicity as a "new Koufax." Sandy, himself, hailed him as "the first Kenny Holtzman." That year, Ken led his team in strikeouts (171) and wins (11).

Ken's 1967 season was abbreviated by his service in the National Guard. He won 9 games that year, with no losses, which earned for him the National League record for the most wins in an undefeated season. His ERA in 1967 was 2.52.

Ken continued to pitch with the Cubs until 1971. During those years, he continued to have excellent numbers. In 1969, he pitched a no-hitter against the Atlanta Braves, and pitched a second no-hitter in 1971 against the Cincinnati Reds. However, despite his good record during these years, Ken was not happy in Chicago. He felt that Manager Leo Durocher did not give him a fair shake or let him live up to his potential. He requested to be traded and, at the end of the 1971 season, his request was granted. He was traded to the Oakland Athletics.

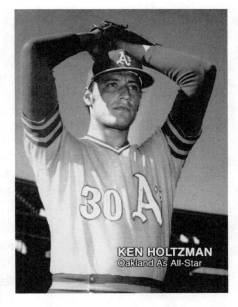

KEN HOLTZMAN
Oakland A's All-Star

In Oakland, Ken truly blossomed. His winning percentage jumped to .633, his ERA dropped to 2.51. He won 19 games, the first time in his career he ever approached the storied twenty-game level. The pitching staff of the 1972 Oakland team was a truly talented one. Besides Ken, the pitchers included "Catfish" Hunter, Vida Blue, and reliever Rollie Fingers. The team also included two other Jewish players, Mike Epstein and Joel Horlen. The team went all the way and captured the World Series victory in seven games against "The Big Red Machine" (Cincinnati Reds). Also during the 1972 season, Ken was picked to represent the American League in the All-Star team.

The following year, 1973, was another excellent one for Ken. For the only time in his career, he broke the twenty-win mark—with twenty-one! Again, the A's went all the way to the World Series and again they took it in seven games, this time against the Mets. Ken was notably impressive in the series, with two of the four victories to his credit. In the first game of the series, even though Ken had not batted all year (because of the designated hitter rule), he doubled and scored the first run of the game. As Ken and the Oakland staff allowed only one Met run, this proved the margin of victory for this 2–1 game. Also in 1973, Ken was picked for the All-Star game and was named by The Sporting News as the American League's best left-handed pitcher.

Again, in 1974, Ken and the Oakland A's went all the way to win the World Series. This time, the National League was represented by the Los Angeles Dodgers, who only managed 1 victory to Oakland's 4. Ken had a World Series ERA of 1.50. He had won 19 games during the regular season.

In 1975, the A's captured the American League Western Division title for the fourth time in four years. However, they failed to win the pennant in the League Championship Series against Boston.

After that season, Ken was traded to the Baltimore Orioles. He remained on Baltimore only part of the year, before being traded to the Yankees. On the Yankees, Ken found himself in conflict with Manager Billy Martin. Martin showed little confidence in him and, as a result, Ken was not able to produce to his potential. In his last year with Oakland, Ken had had 18 wins; in 1976 he had 14, with both Baltimore and New York. In 1977, he produced only 2 wins for the Yankees, and the next year only one. He was then traded, during the course of the season, to the Chicago Cubs. He finished 1978 at Chicago with three losses for the Cubs and no wins. After 1979, and another losing season with the Cubs, Ken retired from baseball.

But Ken left behind a great legacy. In 15 years of major league baseball he had 174 wins and 150 losses, in 451 games, a lifetime average of .537. His lifetime ERA is 3.49. Over the years, he has received 9 votes for entry into Baseball's Hall of Fame.

Ken married Michelle Collons in 1971. The couple has three daughters. Since his retirement, Ken has worked as a stock broker and, subsequently, in the commercial insurance business. The Holtzmans live in Buffalo Grove, Illinois, a suburb of Chicago.

Ken Holtzman is very serious about his Jewish background. He is very open and forthright about his pride in his people and his sincerity in his faith. While traveling with his team, he kept Jewish laws as best he could. He never pitched on a Jewish holiday. The Holtzmans maintain a Kosher home.

Years	Games	IP	W	L	GS	SV	PCT	ERA
15	451	$2867\frac{1}{3}$	174	150	410	3	.537	3.49

1965-71 Chi-N, 1972-75 Oak-A, 1976 Bal-A, 1976-78 NY-A, 1978-79 Chi-N

Joe Horlen

JOEL HORLEN
PITCHER

Joel Edward Horlen was born on August 14, 1937, in San Antonio, Texas, of Christian parents. Later in life, Joe would convert to Judaism.

Joe attended Oklahoma State University and pitched for their team. In 1959, Joe contributed to the Cowboys' victory in the College World Series. In the same year, Joe was signed by the Chicago White Sox, with a $50,000 bonus, and began his professional baseball career with Lincoln (3-I League). He appeared in 18 games, won 1 and lost 9, with an ERA of 5.64. Joe did better in 1960, with Charleston (Sally League), winning 7 and losing 5, with a 2.93 ERA.

But in 1961, in San Diego (Pacific Coast League), Joe really began to click as a pitcher. Much of this improvement, Joe attributes to the tutelage of pitcher Herb Score, who was also with San Diego that year. Joe learned that he mustn't struggle to hit corners, but should relax and simply let his natural ability carry him along. Also, under Score, Joe developed a steady routine of workouts and extra running between starts, to increase his stamina. Joe won 12 for San Diego and lost 9, with an ERA of 2.51. Then the word came from Chicago, and Joe was on his way to the White Sox.

Joe debuted for the Sox on September 4, 1961. He appeared in only 5 games for the team before the end of that season, with 1 win and 3 losses, and with a 6.50 ERA. The team had seen good things, however, and they named him as a starter for the beginning of the 1962 season.

Joe would remain a starting pitcher for the White Sox all the way through the 1971 season. During that time, he came to be considered one of the really premier pitchers of the era. In 1964, Joe had the most strikeouts of his career, 138, and the lowest ERA of his career, 1.88. Yet despite those excellent numbers, Joe's win percentage was only .591, with 13 wins and 9 losses. And Joe did not lead the league in either of the two categories. He came to be called "Hard Luck Horlen" because of such quirks in his career. Another instance was a game, in July of 1963, against the Washington Senators: Joe had a no-hitter going into the 9th inning, with a 1–0 lead. With one down in the inning, Chuck Hinton hit a double and spoiled the no-hitter. Then Don Lock hit a homer and Joe lost the game as well.

Nevertheless, Joe had many outstanding moments that were truly fulfilled. In 1967, he did lead the league in ERA with 2.06. That year, he also led the league in percentage: .731, with 19 wins, including 6 shutouts. He also had a league-leading 6 complete games. But here, too, there would be disappointment. Joe just couldn't manage the 20th win that year. He never again would get close to that magic number. Nor, despite his excellent numbers, did he win the Cy Young Award, which went to Jim Lonborg, who had 22 wins but a lower percentage and a higher ERA. Joe did receive 2 of the possible 20 votes for the award. Also, he did appear in the All-Star Game that year and finally did pitch a no-hitter. Joe's no-hitter came against the Tigers. It was a home game at Comiskey Park, September 10, 1967. The Sox won it, 6–0.

Joe was not much of a batter, in that period before designated hitters, and his lifetime batting average is .134. He gained publicity for himself by his odd habit of chewing tissue paper on the mound. Joe explained that chewing gum made him feel bloated and tobacco made him sick. So, for every game, he would have Kleenex sticking out of his pocket and, before the first pitch, two would go into his mouth.

While Joe never pitched spitballs before in his career, on one occasion he did. He became angered while he was watching a game against the Angels in which the opposing pitcher was quite blatantly using the illegal pitch and the umpire ignored it. The next day, in a game against Kansas City, Joe threw some 20 spitters, without a word of protest. He never repeated the experiment.

Joe had seven 1–0 victories in his career, tying the record of Bob Feller. He started 35 games for the White Sox in 3 consecutive years: 1967, 1968, and 1969. In 1963, 1964, and 1965, the White Sox finished second in the American League, Joe contributing greatly to the team's success.

Nevertheless, the Sox did not renew Joe's contract in 1972 and released him on waivers. Joe was picked up by the Oakland Athletics and given the only chance in his career to pitch in the World Series. Joe's teammates on the A's included Ken Holtzman and Mike Epstein. Joe was used principally as a reliever, though he did start 6 games. His ERA for 1972, going into the World Series, was 3.00. Joe appeared briefly in the 10th inning of the 4th game of the ALCS and was charged with the loss to Detroit. He appeared in the 7th inning of the 6th game of the Series and gave up four runs, in Cincinnati's 8–1 rout of the A's. But the next day, the A's came back to win the seventh game of the hard-fought series and took it all. Joe decided to quit a winner, and retired after the 1972 season, with a 3.11 lifetime ERA and a 116-117 record.

After his retirement, Joe settled down in San Antonio. From 1973 to 1976, he worked as a contractor, building houses. Also, during this period he practiced his golf game. From 1977 to 1978, he served as a peripatetic pitching instructor for the Cleveland Indians. From 1979 to 1986, he continued with his house-building business and started a roofing company. He also helped to start the golf program at the University of Texas at San Antonio. But the lure of baseball was too great for Joe, and in 1987, he returned full-time to the game.

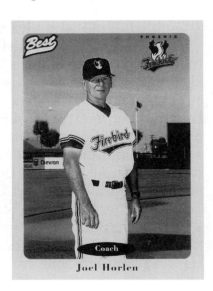

Joel Horlen

Joe started his new baseball career as a pitching coach for

the Mets organization. In 1987, he worked for the Kingsport Mets (Appalachian League), moving in 1988 to Columbia (South Atlantic League). 1989–1990 found him with the St. Lucie Mets (Florida State League). In 1991, Joe coached for the Williamsport Bills (Eastern League).

In 1992, Joe left the Mets and joined the Kansas City Royals organization, coaching for the Omaha Royals. Joe made another move in 1993, changing allegiance to the San Francisco Giants. He started with the Giants' AAA Phoenix Firebirds and has stayed with them through their 1997, and final, season. In 1995, he was asked to take leave from Phoenix, to work with the Shreveport Captains.

Joe is married. His wife, the former Lois Eisenstein, is Jewish. Joe, who has stated, "I had always been interested in the history of the Jews and Judaism," converted to Judaism shortly after their marriage. Lois maintains a special room in their San Antonio house for all of Joe's baseball memorabilia, including pictures, awards, scrapbooks, cards, and his World Series trophy and ring.

Some time after his conversion, Joe Horlen ran into Mike Epstein, his old teammate from the 1972 A's. Joe told Mike about his conversion. Mike told him, "Welcome to the tribe."

Years	Games	IP	W	L	GS	SV	PCT	ERA
12	361	2002	116	117	290	4	.498	3.11

1961-71 Chi-A, 1972 Oak-A

Doug Johns

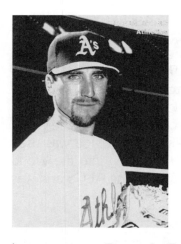

Douglas Alan Johns was born on December 19, 1967, in South Bend, Indiana. His mother is Jewish, but his father is a Roman Catholic. Doug considers himself a Catholic and he attends church regularly. Nevertheless, he maintains a very close relationship with his mother.

Doug, a left-handed pitcher, attended the University of Virginia. He was a sixteenth-round draft pick in the June 1990 draft, and was picked by the Oakland A's organization. In 1990, he played with South Oregon and the Arizona A's. He was 0-2 with the former club (with a 5.73 ERA) and 3-1 with the latter (1.84 ERA). In 1991, he pitched for Madison; there, he was 12-6, with a 3.23 ERA. The following year brought Doug to the Huntsville, Alabama Stars for a brief stay, appearing in 3 games, but with no decisions, before being sent to Reno. In Reno, he went 13-10, with a 3.26 ERA. In 1993, he returned to Huntsville, where he was 7-5, with a 2.97 ERA. The start of the 1994 season found Doug still in Huntsville, where he went 3-0 (1.20 ERA), before being sent to Tacoma (Pacific Coast League). Doug won the 1994 Pacific Coast League ERA title with 2.89. He also led all league pitchers with a .234 opposition batting average. Doug won 9 games for Tacoma and lost 8.

For 1995, Doug went to Edmonton, where he was 5-5, with a 3.28 ERA, and with 55 strikeouts. On July 8, 1995, Doug made his major league debut as starting pitcher in a game against Toronto. He allowed 2 runs on 3 hits, in more than 3 innings. During the game, Toronto pitcher David Cone beaned A's player Mark McGwire. In the 4th inning, Doug threw a pitch behind John Olerud and was ejected from the game. Toronto won the game, 6–3.

Doug pitched in 11 games for Oakland in 1995, with 5 wins, 3 losses, and a 4.61 ERA. He was extremely impressive at the beginning of his career because of the large number of pitches in his repertoire and the various ways that he could throw them. There were many angles to his throws, many speeds, many "looks." Doug showed excellent control, which made up for his lack of extreme velocity.

By September 1995, Doug was inserted as a regular starter in the rotation. At first this was considered a form of surrender to a bad year, a sign that Oakland had given up the struggle to secure a play-off spot. But with Doug replacing Ron Darling in the rotation, the A's took off on a winning spree, Doug contributing mightily. The A's did not make the final cut, but they did act as spoilers, damaging the chances of the Orioles, on two occasions, at the hands of Doug.

In 1996, Doug missed the first week of spring training because of a rib injury. But by the beginning of the season he had become a regular starter for Oakland. Early in the season, Doug was 2-0, but the novelty of his pitching seemed to wear off and batters grew used to his style. By June 27, he was 2-9. Doug's win percentage in 1995 was .625; in 1996, it was just .333, with 6 wins and 12 losses. By the end of the season, his ERA had jumped to 5.98.

Doug was released by the A's on March 10, 1997. He pitched in a total of 51 major league games, with 11 wins and 15 losses. His lifetime ERA is 5.63.

Doug Johns makes his home in Plantation, Florida.

In 1998, Doug became a starting pitcher for the Baltimore Orioles. The early months found him with 2 wins and 2 losses and a 4.88 ERA.

Years	Games	IP	W	L	GS	SV	PCT	ERA
4	114	386	20	22	47	2	.476	5.13

1995-96 Oak-A, 1998-99 Bal-A

Skip Jutze

Alfred Henry "Skip" Jutze was born on May 28, 1946, in Bayside, New York. Skip was born the child of Christian parents, but later converted to Judaism. In 1964, he graduated from Clarke High School in Westbury, New York. He attended Central Connecticut State College, where he practiced his role as a catcher. He graduated from college in 1968.

Skip was signed by the St. Louis Cardinals, just after he finished college. That year, he was assigned to the Sarasota Cardinals (Gulf Coast League). After only 6 games, Skip was promoted to the St. Petersburg Cardinals (Florida State League). He batted .278 with the Cardinals. Returning to the St. Petersburg lineup in 1969, he increased his batting average to .318 and was promoted to Little Rock (Texas League), in 1970. That year, he led all Texas League catchers in games, 116; putouts, 715; assists, 87; and passed balls, 28. He tied for most double plays, with 9. His .243 batting average kept

Skip in Little Rock for another season. Then he was promoted to the Tulsa Oilers (American Association) in 1972. There, he played in 119 games, with a .324 batting average, before being promoted to the Cardinals.

Skip made his major league debut on September 2, 1972. That year, he appeared in 21

games with the Cardinals, and had a .239 batting average. Skip was traded to the Houston Astros organization in 1973. He spent most of the year in Houston, although he did catch 14 games for Class AAA Denver (American Association). Skip's batting average dropped to .204 in Houston. As a result, he spent the majority of the 1974 season in Denver. That year, Skip was elected to the American Association All-Star Team.

In 1975, Skip returned to Houston, to be platooned with catcher Milt May. He played in 51 games, and batted .226. Skip was again platooned with May, in 1976. That year, Skip's batting average dropped to .152. At the end of the season, he was traded to the Seattle Mariners. Playing with the Mariners in their 1977 inaugural season, he was platooned with Bob Stinson and only appeared in 42 games. He hit, that year, all 3 of his 3 lifetime home runs. Skip increased his batting average to .220, but he was still released at the end of the year. He retired at the end of the 1977 season. His good defensive abilities kept Skip employed in major league baseball for five years. He had a lifetime fielding average of .983, but had a lifetime batting average of .215.

Skip Jutze is married and currently lives in Wheat Ridge, Colorado.

Years	Games	AB	H	R	RBI	HR	BA	OBP	FP
6	254	656	141	45	51	3	.215	.255	.983

1972 StL-N, 1973-76 Hou-N, 1977 Sea-A

Harry Kane

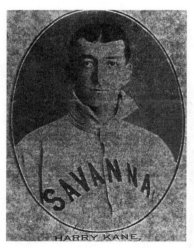

Harry Kane was born Harry Cohen on July 27, 1883, in Hamburg, Arkansas.

Harry was signed by the Philadelphia Phillies system in 1900, as a left-handed pitcher. He made his professional debut with Denver that year. Somewhere along the line, Harry acquired the nickname "Klondike." He was supposed to continue with Denver in 1901, but the salary offer was unsatisfactory, so instead Harry played with the Friar's Point, Mississippi, team. He started the 1902 season with the San Francisco club and was released at his own request to Springfield (Missouri Valley League). There, Harry won 20 out of 21 games, including a remarkable 3 no-hitters. He also won a twenty-inning game against Nevada, 2 to 1.

Harry also made his major league debut that year, on August 8, 1902, with the St. Louis Browns. He didn't shine for the Browns as he did for Springfield. Harry pitched in four games for the Browns, including one complete game. He lost his only decision and finished the season with a .000 average, a 5.48 ERA, and 1 save.

In 1903, Harry returned to Springfield, and again he pitched 3 no-hitters. That year, he also pitched a doubleheader against Leavenworth. He allowed only 3 hits in each game. Both games were shutouts. Harry's fame earned him a short trial, during 1903, with the Detroit Tigers; he pitched in three games for the Tigers, but lost two of them.

In 1904, Harry pitched with Rochester (Eastern League) and Clarksdale (Delta League). While with Clarksdale, Harry did not allow a run to score in 52 innings. The next season, Harry pitched for Savannah. With Savannah, Harry hurled a thirteen-inning no-hitter, but lost the game to Jacksonville, 1 to 0.

In 1905, Harry was given another chance to pitch in the majors. He pitched in two games for the Philadelphia Phillies. Harry won one and lost the other. His win was on September 27, 1905, when Harry yielded only 5 hits as the Phillies shut out the St. Louis Cardinals at Robinson Field, 6 to 0. This was Harry's first major league victory and only major league shutout. He ended his 1905 stint with the Phillies with a 1.59 ERA.

Harry's 1906 season was brief. He pitched in six games for the Phillies, winning one game and losing three, with a 3.86 ERA. Harry pitched during 4 major league seasons in 15 games. He had 2 wins and 7 losses. His ERA was 4.81.

During the 1906 season, Harry gave up playing and became an umpire. He started this career in the Southern leagues. By 1931, Harry had worked his way up to the Pacific Coast League. He quickly became popular in that league.

On September 13, 1932, Harry Kane was umpiring a game in Portland against San Francisco, when he suddenly collapsed on the field. He had had a heart attack. Taken to a doctor, he was told to stay in bed and rest. He died two days later, in his Portland hotel room. The funeral was an occasion of great solemnity, his six pallbearers being fellow umpires. Among the chief mourners were the president of the Coast League, many other league officials, and officials of the various teams.

Years	Games	IP	W	L	GS	SV	PCT	ERA
4	15	86	2	7	9	0	.222	4.81

1902 StL-A, 1903 Det-A, 1905-06 Phi-N

Ryan Karp

Ryan Jason Karp was born on April 5, 1970, in Los Angeles. His father is Harvey Karp, a wealthy Beverly Hills commodities broker. In 1992, Ryan was selected by the New York Yankees, as a pitcher, for their 7th draft selection.

On November 21, 1995, Ryan married his wife, Josette (née Puig). Ryan's father has not spoken to him since his marriage, perhaps upset because of the marriage; Josette is not Jewish and Harvey feels she is an inappropriate match. Also, Ryan apparently converted to Christianity after he married her. He may have done this in retaliation for his rejection by his father over the marriage. Before his first start, Ryan was seen crossing himself in the dugout. Ryan and Josette have had difficulties affording a place to live, since Ryan's father will not assist in supporting them. They have stayed with friends and relatives of Josette's. They even stayed six weeks with the scout who signed Ryan.

After one season with the Yankees Organization, with Oneonta, the southpaw was quickly promoted, in 1993, to the Class A Greensboro Hornets. With the Hornets, Ryan posted a 13-1 record and a 1.81 ERA, in $109\frac{1}{3}$ innings pitched. He was selected as 1993 Yankees organization Player of the Year. At the end of the season he was promoted to the Class AA Albany–Colonie Yankees. In 1994, Ryan was traded to the Phillies organization. He spent the 1994 season with the Class AA Reading Phillies.

In 1995, Ryan pitched in Reading and the Class AAA Scranton–Wilkes-Barre Red Barons, before being called up to the Philadelphia Phillies, on June 19. He made his major league debut on June 23, 1995. Ryan pitched 2 innings in relief of Curt Schilling in St. Louis. He gave up 1 hit and 1 run. On the same day as his debut, Ryan's wife gave birth to their first child.

Ryan returned to the Red Barons for the 1996 and 1997 seasons. He returned to the Phillies lineup on August 18, 1997. On August 25, 1997, he started his first major league game; it was the second game of a doubleheader, and he pitched three innings against the San Diego Padres, in Philadelphia. The Phillies won 6 to 4. Ryan had his first major league win on September 7, 1997, in a game against the Montreal Expos at Olympic Stadium. Ryan ended the season with a 1-1 record and a 5.40 ERA. However, the batting average of opposing batters when he was pitching was only .218.

Ryan Karp now lives with his wife in Miami, Florida.

At the start of the 1998 season, Ryan was pitching for the Durham Bulls, the AAA affiliate of the Tampa Bay Devil Rays. He was used as a middle reliever.

Years	Games	IP	W	L	GS	SV	PCT	ERA
2	16	17	1	1	1	0	.500	5.29

1995, 1997 Phi-N

Herb Karpel

Herbert "Lefty" Karpel was born in Brooklyn, on December 27, 1917. As a boy, Herb became friends with future Hall of Famer Phil Rizzuto. The two boys went to school together. After school, they played baseball together on the same sandlot team. Herb and Phil both attended Richmond Hill High School in Queens, although Phil was two years ahead.

During 1936, Herb played on a New York semi-pro team, Queens Alliance, along with his pal, Rizzuto, while they also worked part-time for a firm in Bush Terminal. Yankee scout Paul Krichell spotted the pair in a Queens Alliance game and signed them both. In 1937, Herb and Phil started their careers in organized baseball with Bassett, Virginia (Bi-St. League). Phil would go on to reach the New York Yankees in 1941, while Herb would not go beyond the minors until 1946.

In 1937, Bassett won the league pennant. Herb had a .572 win percentage and a 3.86 ERA. Later that season, he pitched in a few games for Butler (Bi-St. League). Herb started with Butler in 1938, where he won 6 and lost 5, with a 3.65 ERA. The end of the same season, he played with Thomasville (Georgia–Florida League), where his ERA was 1.54, the best in the league.

Herb was transferred to Amsterdam (Canadian–American League) for the 1939 season. He had a record of 20 and 9, becoming the first pitcher ever to win 20 games in that league. Herb not only led the league in wins, but also led his team to a pennant victory. His ERA in 1939 was 3.86.

In 1940, Herb pitched for Norfolk (Piedmont League), where his record was 11 and 7, with a 2.53 ERA. In 1941, He had a 14 and 13 record with Binghamton (Eastern League) and a 3.27 ERA. Among his victories that year was a no-hitter against Elmira.

1942 was another outstanding year for Herb, as he pitched for the Kansas City team (American Association). Herb won 11 and lost 1, giving him a percentage of .917, the highest in the league. His ERA was 2.47. The last game of the season was a dramatic one, between Kansas City and the Milwaukee Brewers for the league championship. All day it had been storming, and the game, scheduled for 10:00 A.M., was delayed until 4:00 P.M. The field and the 10,000 loyal fans were soaked. Bill Veeck, owner of the Brewers, ordered gasoline poured on the field and the game to begin. Kansas City's starting pitcher was injured early in the game, trying to stop a line drive, and Herb was put into the game with hardly any preparation—a left-handed pitcher against an entire team of right-handed hitters.

The first two men who faced Herb each got a home run off him, and Milwaukee was leading, 2–0. Herb struggled on through the 8th inning, when Kansas City rallied for 9 runs. He held Milwaukee through the 9th. The final score was 9–2 and Kansas City was the champion of the American Association. This was the greatest moment, for Herb, in all his baseball career. It also came at the very end of the first half of that career, for after the 1942 season Herb went into the Army.

There, Herb started with a tank destroyer unit. Later, he was transferred to the infantry, where he became a sergeant in the 410th Infantry of the 103rd Division. He spent seventeen months overseas—in Italy, France, Germany, and Austria—and was awarded the Bronze Star and a unit Presidential citation. Herb was discharged from the Army on November 15, 1945, and returned to his hometown, Elizabeth, New Jersey, where he had lived since 1941, the year he was married. After leaving the Army, Herb took a job as a salesman in the men's furnishings department of a store in Elizabeth. Two months later, he was back in uniform, but this time it was the pinstriped uniform of the New York Yankees.

Herb would rejoin his old friend Phil "Scooter" Rizzuto during 1946 spring training. The Yankees were hard up for pitchers and Herb's outstanding season of 1942, for Kansas City, had not been forgotten. Herb was about to be given his chance. He debuted on opening day of 1946, April 19. The Yankees were hosting the Washington Senators at Yankee Stadium. It was the top of the 8th inning, Yankee pitcher Joe Page had loaded the bases, with 2 out. Herb was brought into the game. He retired Senators rightfielder Buddy Lewis, on a pop-up. The Yankees won the game, 7–6.

Herb would appear in only one other game for the Yankees. In that one, he pitched only $1\frac{1}{3}$ innings and gave up 2 runs. On April 24, just 5 days after his debut, Herb was released to Newark (International League). His major league career lasted 2 games, with a total of $1\frac{2}{3}$ innings pitched. He had a 10.80 ERA.

In Newark, Herb led the league in ERA, with 2.42. He won 14 games that year, and lost 8. In 1947, Herb returned to Newark, with 9 wins and 11 losses. His ERA rose to 4.42.

Herb went west, in 1948, to the Pacific Coast League to join the Seattle Rainiers. Herb was 11 and 14 that first year with Seattle, with a 4.03 ERA. The following year, Herb led the league in winning percentage, with .700, or 14 wins and 6 losses. His ERA was 4.40. In 1950, Herb pitched for the Hollywood Stars (Pacific Coast League). His teammates included Murray Franklin and Herb Gorman.

Herb Karpel lives in North Hollywood, California. In 1994, Herb's old pal, Phil Rizzuto, was inducted into the Baseball Hall of Fame.

Years	Games	IP	W	L	GS	SV	PCT	ERA
1	2	$1\frac{2}{3}$	0	0	0	0	NA	10.80

1946 NY-A

Alan Koch

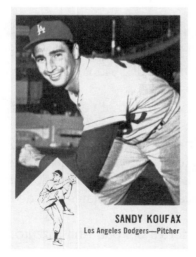

Alan Koch

Alan Goodman Koch was born on March 25, 1938, in Decatur, Alabama. He graduated from Auburn University and began his professional baseball career as a right-handed pitcher with Birmingham in 1960. He pitched two seasons there with a 22-16 win-loss record, 247 strikeouts, and a 3.55 ERA. In 1962, Alan pitched for Denver. The next year, he pitched with Syracuse, where he had a 11-2 win-loss record, 131 strikeouts, and a 3.36 ERA, in 126 innings.

On July 26, 1963, Alan made his major league debut, with the Detroit Tigers. Even though Alan was mostly used in relief, he had one major league win and one loss, in 1963. His first major league victory was on August 8, 1963. Alan entered the game in the tenth inning. The Tigers defeated the Boston Red Sox at Detroit, 6–5. Alan returned to the Tigers in 1964, to pitch in 3 games, before being traded to the Washington Senators. In 1964, Alan pitched in 32 games with the Senators. He won 4 major league games and lost 11. His major league ERA was 5.41.

Alan Koch is currently an attorney in Mobile, Alabama, working for a large hospital and an HMO.

Years	Games	IP	W	L	GS	SV	PCT	ERA
2	42	128	4	11	15	0	.267	5.41

1963-64 Det-A, 1964 Was-A

Sandy Koufax

SANDY KOUFAX
Los Angeles Dodgers—Pitcher

The third Jewish player to be inducted into the Baseball Hall of Fame was Sandy Koufax, the Dodgers' great southpaw pitcher, in 1972. At the time of his induction, Sandy, at age 36, was the youngest man ever so honored. The brilliance of his career made any delay in honoring him practically unthinkable. Not since Walter Johnson, had a pitcher so dominated the opposition as had Sandy. But Sandy's greatness was not a simple tale, a natural genius who arose in the morning to strike out batters. Nor did Sandy gradually learn his trade, getting better from year to year, until he reached perfection. Sandy is actually two different pitchers: the naturally gifted, but often wild, pitcher of 1955 to 1960 and the master of the National League of 1961 to 1966.

Sandy was the first pitcher to ever pitch 4 no-hitters—which he did on June 30, 1962, against the Mets; on May 11, 1963, against the Giants; on June 4, 1964, against the Phillies; and on September 9, 1965, against the Cubs. The last of these was a perfect game. Sandy captured the ERA title five years in a row, from 1962 to 1966, with ERAs of 2.54, 1.88, 1.74, 2.04, and 1.73. Sandy won 25 or more games in 1963, 1965, and 1966. He pitched 11 shutouts in 1963. In addition, he held the strikeout title four times—in 1961, 1963, 1965, and 1966—with 382 K's in 1965, breaking Rube Waddell's season record of 349, which had stood since 1904. On two occasions, Sandy struck out 18 players in a game, tying the major league record first set by Bob Feller. He first did this on August 31, 1959, against the Giants. He did it the second time on April 24, 1962, against the Cubs. At the same time Sandy first tied Feller's record, he set two new records: the most strikeouts in two consecutive games, with 31; and in three consecutive games, with 41.

In 1963, Sandy also set a major league record for most shutouts in a season by a left-hander: 11. The same year, Sandy was chosen as the National League's Most Valuable Player. He received the Cy Young Award in 1963, 1965, and 1966. At the time he received these awards, only one Cy Young was awarded for both leagues.

Sandy pitched in four World Series: 1959, 1963, 1965, and 1966. His combined World Series ERA was 0.95. Nevertheless, of the 7 games he pitched, he won 4 and lost 3. In all 7 games, only 10 runs were scored while he was pitching, but 4 of those runs were unearned.

Sandy pitched in 4 All-Star Games: two in 1961, one in 1965, and one in 1966. In a total of 6 All-Star innings pitched, Sandy surrendered only one run.

SANDY KOUFAX Coach

On December 30, 1935, in the Borough Park section of Brooklyn, New York, a son was born to Jack and Evelyn Braun. They named him Sandford Braun. When Sandford was three, his parents were divorced. When the boy was nine, his mother was remarried, to Irving Koufax. Sandford Braun became Sandford "Sandy" Koufax. Sandy has always shown love and respect for his stepfather and he describes him as "all that a father could be."

Despite the legends created by sportswriters, Sandy was an athletic boy, very interested in sports in general, and basketball in particular. The hero of his youth was Max Zaslovsky (1925–1985), Jewish basketball star of the NBA in the late 1940s and early '50s. Sandy played on Brooklyn's Lafayette High School baseball and basketball teams.

Sandy was offered a basketball scholarship to the University of Cincinnati, but once there, he also joined the university's baseball team. As a kid, Sandy had played first base. His strong throwing arm got him changed to catcher, for he had no difficulty reaching second base, in case of a steal attempt. Finally, Sandy became a pitcher. It was as a left-handed pitcher that Sandy joined the University of Cincinnati baseball team, to get a trip to New Orleans, rather than out of real interest.

But Sandy was extremely impressive. He pitched a 4-hitter against Wayne State and a 3-hitter against Louisville. The scouts began to converge. Before he knew it, he was signed, with a $14,000 bonus, by the Brooklyn Dodgers. Sandy left college behind and became a full-time major league player.

Sandy was signed under a rule that was then in effect that said that bonus players had to stay two years on the parent club. This explains why Sandy never played in the minors and why he had to work out the kinks in his pitching in the full glare of major league publicity.

Sandy debuted on June 24, 1955. He came in, in relief of Carl Erskine, in the fifth inning. The game was in Milwaukee and the Dodgers were down, 7–1. Sandy's first major league pitch was a strike to John Logan, but Sandy ended up giving Logan a hit. Sandy had soon loaded the bases, when Bobby Thompson came up to bat. Sandy bore down and threw his lightning-like fastballs, striking Thompson out. Sandy finished that inning and the next, without giving up a run. He gave up his first run on August 6, 1955, when Roberto Clemente scored off him, during a Pirate 4–1 victory over the Dodgers at Forbes Field.

Sandy's first start came late in the season. The team was leading the league, but most of the starting pitchers were complaining of sore arms. Manager Walt Alston decided to give Sandy a chance. As he was walking by Alston's office, Sandy heard Jake Pitler, the Jewish player for the Pittsburgh Pirates of 1917–18 and the Dodgers' current first base coach, being given the news. Jake let out a loud, "Oh, no!" But Sandy surprised Pitler and everyone else. He struck out 14 batters in a 2-hit shutout! Still, the great days of Sandy Koufax had not yet dawned.

Over the next three seasons, for Brooklyn, and the following three, for Los Angeles, Sandy got into the routine of pitching. Sometimes he was spectacular. On August 31, 1959, he tied the major league record for strikeouts in one nine-inning game: 18. But on other days he would turn wild and would have to be pulled in the early innings. Sandy led the National League in wild pitches in 1958, with 17. For these years, Sandy's winning average hovered around .500. His flaming fastball and elusive curve made him one of the great possibilities of baseball, but not an accomplished fact.

Sandy's transformation began in spring training for the 1961 season. He was scheduled to pitch in a B-squad game against the Minnesota Twins. The game was in Orlando and Sandy was sitting in the bus next to his catcher and roommate, Norm Sherry. Sandy had great respect for Norm as a baseball man, so he listened carefully to what Sherry had to say, which was that Sandy should take it easy, not bear down when he fell behind, but relax and pitch to spots, rather than trying to blow the ball by the batters. He had heard similar things before, but this time it clicked in Sandy's mind and made a miraculous change in his attitude. If Norm Sherry did not have his own excellent career to point to, for these few words of advice to Koufax he would have made his immortal mark in the history of baseball.

Sandy won his game that day. He would go on to win 18 games that year with 269 strikeouts, breaking the league record previously held by Christy Matthewson. From 1961 through the season of 1966, Sandy would win 129 games and lose just 47, a .733 winning percentage.

During the 1965 World Series, Sandy did not play the opening game, as it fell on Yom Kippur. Don Drysdale pitched this game, and the Dodgers lost. That evening in a St. Paul newspaper appeared a virulently anti-Semitic tirade. Sandy could not believe his eyes. The next day, when he pitched, the Dodgers lost again, but the team made a great comeback and Sandy was able to pitch the final victory.

In 1966, Sandy and his friend Don Drysdale made an agreement to hold out against signing their contracts until both men were satisfied about their salaries. The pitchers settled before the season started, but some have seen in this incident a foreshadowing of the coming of the great age of the Players' Association and the influence of Marvin Miller.

During the last few years of his career, Sandy was playing in terrible pain, from a degenerative form of arthritis. At the end of each game he would have to soak his arm in a bucket of ice. At the close of the 1966 season, while he was still at the height of his powers, but when further use of those powers might permanently cripple him, Sandy choose to retire. He completed his career with 165 wins and 87 losses, a .655 percentage; he appeared in 397 games over 12 years; his ERA was 2.76.

Since his retirement, Sandy has continued his association with the Dodgers organization. In 1981, he served as a pitching coach for one of its minor league teams, the Albuquerque Dukes (Pacific Coast League). Sandy has done other coaching through the years.

Sandy Koufax was formerly married to the daughter of actor Richard Widmark.

Years	Games	IP	W	L	GS	SV	PCT	ERA
12	397	$2324\frac{1}{3}$	165	87	314	9	.655	2.76

1955-57 Bro-N, 1958-1966 LA-N

Brian Kowitz

Brian Mark Kowitz was born on August 7, 1969, in Baltimore, Maryland.

Brian was drafted in the eighth round of the 1990 amateur draft, by the Atlanta Braves. The left-handed outfielder was sent that year to the rookie-league Pulaski Braves. Before the end of the season, he was promoted to Class AA Greenville. Brian started the 1991 season with the Class A Durham Bulls, but was sent back to Greenville after two-thirds of the season. He played for both Durham and Greenville again, in 1992. In 1993, Brian was promoted to the Richmond Braves; he batted .267 with Richmond, that year.

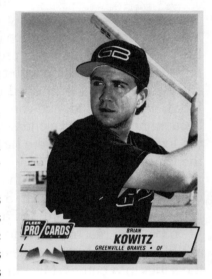

Brian returned to the Richmond lineup in 1994. He was asked to appear, as a left-handed pitcher, in two different games during the season. He had a 1-0 record and a 1.93 ERA. He did give up 8 hits in 4.2 innings pitched, but his only walk was intentional. That year, he batted .300, in 124 games, and was considered a hero in the International League Championships. Brian made two great plays in the final game of the championships, as the Richmond Braves won. He again began the 1995 season with Richmond.

Brian was promoted to the Atlanta Braves on June 3, 1995, when All-Star outfielder David Justice was put on the disabled list. Brian made his debut the very next day. He was used as a pinch hitter in the 5th inning, in a game against the Houston Astros. He doubled down the left-field line for his first at-bat, but the Braves lost 6 to 2. Brian appeared in only 9 more games, until David Justice returned, when Brian was returned to Richmond.

Brian signed with the Detroit Tigers in 1996. He played in spring training with the Tigers. He was then sent to the Toledo Mud Hens. Brian was released in May, and was signed by the Toronto Blue Jays. He finished the year with the Syracuse Chiefs. Brian retired from baseball at the end of the 1996 season.

Brian Kowitz currently lives in Baltimore, Maryland.

Years	Games	AB	H	R	RBI	HR	BA	OBP	FP
1	10	24	4	3	3	0	.167	.259	1.000

1995 Atl-N

Mike Lacoss

Michael James Lacoss was born Michael James Marks on May 30, 1956, in Glendale, California. His father was Jewish, his mother a gentile. Mike changed his last name to that of his step-father, after his parents were divorced. He entered Mt. Whitney High School in Visalia, California, in 1970. There, Mike played on the baseball team as a pitcher. In 1974, he was selected as a first-team All-League in baseball and basketball. That year, he had 5 consecutive shutout games, and allowed 2 earned runs in 50 innings of league play. Mike finished the 1974 season with a 9-2 record and a 1.92 ERA.

In 1974, Mike was drafted by the Reds, as their third selection. He played his first year in professional baseball as a right-handed pitcher with Billings, Montana, (Pioneer League). That year, he had a 6-5 record and a 2.79 ERA in 13 games started. Mike was promoted to Tampa (Florida State League) in 1975. With Tampa, Mike had a 2.86 ERA in 23 games. He was promoted to Three Rivers (Eastern League) the next year. After attending spring training with the Reds in 1977, Mike joined the Indianapolis Indians (American Association). He finished third in the American Association in innings pitched, batters faced, games started, and wins. While on the Indians, Mike was given the nickname "Buffie," because he resembled a character on a popular television series, Family Affair. He returned to the Indians in 1978, where he tied for the lead in shutouts, with 3, before being called up to the Cincinnati Reds.

Mike made his debut, with the Reds, on July, 18, 1978. He had his first major league win on July 21, 1978, in the 10–3 victory over the Montreal Expos. Mike pitched in 16 games in 1978, with a 4-8 record and a 4.50 ERA. He returned to the Reds lineup in 1979, helping "The Big Red Machine" get to the National League Championship with his 14-8 record and a 3.50 ERA. He lost his only game in the championship series, 7 to 1, and the Pirates took the series in 3 games. Mike pitched in the 1979 All-Star Game.

Mike played for the Reds in 1980 and 1981, but was released in 1982. He was then signed by the Houston Astros. Mike had a great year in 1981: He lowered his 1980 ERA of 6.12 to 2.90. Mike returned to Houston in 1983, but missed a month because of a sprained knuckle. He was traded to the Kansas City Royals after the 1984 season. Mike pitched in 21 games for the Royals before being demoted to their Omaha minor league affiliate. He was released at the end of the season.

In 1986, Mike joined the San Francisco Giants in their spring-training camp. Most people thought Mike's career was at his end, but he had studied videocassettes of how he had pitched for the Reds and found it was different from how he was pitching now. Mike changed his delivery back to the way he had pitched when he was a rookie, and ended the season with a much improved 3.57 ERA.

Mike returned to the Giants in 1987 to help them get to the National League Championship Series. That year, he had a 13-10 record and a 3.68 ERA. He pitched in the third game of the series on October 9, 1987. The Giants lost the series and Mike still hadn't reached the World Series. He pitched for the Giants in 1988 and 1989; he had a 7-7 record in 1988 and a 10-10 record in 1989. In 1989, the Giants did get to the World Series, and Mike pitched in 1 inning in the National League Championship Series and in 2 innings of the Series. The

Giants lost the World Series to the Oakland A's in 4 games.

Mike had a shortened season in 1990 because he had to get arthroscopic surgery to repair the cartilage in his left knee. He had a 6-4 record and a 3.94 ERA that year. Mike retired at the end of the season. He has a lifetime record of 97-98 and an ERA of 3.93, over 397 games, during 13 seasons with 4 teams.

Throughout his career Mike was known as a practical joker. He was also famous for his split-finger fastball. Mike Lacoss currently lives in Lemon Cove, California.

Years	Games	IP	W	L	GS	SV	PCT	ERA
14	415	$1739\frac{2}{3}$	98	103	243	12	.488	4.02

1978-81 Cin-N, 1982-84 Hou-N, 1985 KC-A, 1986-91 SF-N

Barry Latman

BARRY LATMAN P.

Arnold Barry Latman was born in Los Angeles, California, on May 21, 1936. He began playing baseball in high school, when he was 16. While he was in high school, he pitched a perfect game. In 1954, Barry was selected to play in the All-Star High School Game, held in New York. His pitching there was so impressive that he was offered a large bonus to sign a contract. However, Barry chose to forego the bonus and accept a baseball scholarship from the University of Southern California.

It was also in 1954 that Barry began a five-year correspondence with Ty Cobb, which eventually led to the two men meeting. Cobb came out, one time, to watch Barry pitch for his high school team. The old man was very impressed with the big (6'3"), right-handed pitcher and encouraged him in his career path. One thing that is not clear is whether Cobb was aware that Barry was Jewish. Cobb was an infamous anti-Semite. We did successfully contact Barry by mail, but he did not answer our question concerning Cobb, so the answer remains a mystery. Barry, himself, is an observant Jew.

It was on the campus of USC that Barry finally signed a major league contract, with the White Sox organization. Barry began his professional career at Waterloo, Iowa, (3-I League) in 1955. He won 18 games that year and lost only 5, with a 4.12 ERA. Barry led the league, that season, in total innings pitched. The next year, 1956, he pitched for Memphis (Southern Association), won 14, lost 14, and had a 3.85 ERA.

In 1957, Barry started with Indianapolis (American Association), where he won 13 games and lost 13 games, but his 3.95 ERA was impressive enough for the pitching-starved Sox to bring him to Chicago for the end of the season. Barry debuted with Chicago on September 10, 1957. He had his first major league victory on September 15, in a game at Griffith Stadium, against the Washington Senators. Barry came into the game in relief of Bob Keegan and hurled two scoreless innings. The White Sox scored 3 runs in the 9th inning, to take the game, 3–1. In his first season, Barry appeared in 7 games, pitching 12 innings, with an ERA of 8.25.

He returned to Indianapolis for the start of the 1958 season. There he pitched in 25 games, with an ERA of 4.62, with 9 wins and 11 losses. When Barry came back to Chicago later in the season, he appeared in 13 games. He won 3 and had no losses, with an ERA of 0.76.

Barry was very impressive with Chicago in 1959, with a .615 winning percentage and an 3.75 ERA. During June, Barry had hurled 18 straight scoreless relief innings. On June 25, he was given a chance to start. He pitched a 5-hit victory over Washington, 4–1. In a July 11 victory over Kansas City, 8–3, Barry had a 4-hit game and got 3 hits himself in his trips to the plate. On August 5, he had a 3-hit shutout against the Orioles. On August 22, he got 8 strikeouts in a victory over Washington. On September 11, he pitched $9\frac{1}{3}$ innings against Baltimore and retired 21 in a row. With Barry's help, the White Sox won the pennant in 1959. Barry was not used in the World Series, which the Dodgers won, 4 games to 2, with the extremely impressive contributions of Larry Sherry.

At the start of the 1960 season, Barry was traded to the Cleveland Indians. With Cleveland that year he had 7 wins and 7 losses and a 4.03 ERA. At the start of the 1961 season, he won 9 consecutive games. He ended the season with a 13 and 5 record, and a 4.02 ERA. Barry was selected to represent the American League in the second All-Star Game of 1961. He did not get a chance to pitch in this game, for it was ended by rain. This was the only All-Star Game to end as a tie, 1–1.

In 1962, Barry had an 8 and 13 record, with a 4.17 ERA. He did pitch another 4-hitter during the season, and continued to combine starts with relief work. His next season, 1963, he had 7 wins and 12 losses, with a 4.94 ERA. Barry was traded for the 1964 season to the Los Angeles Angels, which became the California Angels in 1965. In the first of these years, Barry won 6 and lost 10, with a 3.85 ERA. The following year, he was greatly hampered by physical problems that would plague him for the remainder of his career. He appeared in only 18 games and pitched only $31\frac{2}{3}$ innings. He won 1 game and lost 1, with an ERA of 2.84. Barry was then sent to Seattle (Pacific Coast League), where he had 7 wins and 6 losses, with a 3.09 ERA.

Still suffering from a sore arm, Barry was traded to the Houston Astros for the 1966 season. Despite his problems, he had the best ERA of any right-hander on the Houston staff: 2.71. But even with this excellent ERA, his win percentage was only .222, with 2 wins and 7 losses. The following year, 1967, was Barry's last in baseball. Still with the Astros, he had 3 wins and 6 losses, with a 4.52 ERA.

Barry pitched for 11 years in the major leagues, with 59 career wins and 68 losses. Barry's real value, however, was often as a reliever. He pitched in a total of 344 games, with a lifetime ERA of 3.91. Also, he pitched 28 complete games, including 10 shutouts.

Barry spent some time coaching at the minor league level. Barry Latman is married. The Latmans spent their honeymoon in Israel. Barry lives in Playa del Rey, California.

Years	Games	IP	W	L	GS	SV	PCT	ERA
11	344	1219	59	68	134	16	.465	3.91

1957-59 Chi-A, 1960-63 Cle-A, 1964 LA-A, 1965 Cal-A, 1966-67 Hou-N

Jim Levey

Jim Levey holds the rare distinction of having played two major league sports. Not only did he play baseball, but also was an accomplished football player.

James Julius Levey was born on September 13, 1906, in Pittsburgh, Pennsylvania. He was the son of Mr. and Mrs. Solomon Levey. He had three brothers and sisters. Jim's father worked for a stove company, and when Jim was young he wanted to follow in his father's footsteps. Jim acquired a love of baseball, however, before he started school, although he seldom played because the kids would tell him, "You can't play, you're too small." When Jim entered Thomas Whitman Grammar School, he was told the same thing by the coach. When Jim went to Peabody High School, he was determined to get on the baseball team, but again met with the same remarks about his height.

While Jim was in high school, he became batboy for the Shady Side Triangles, a Pittsburgh semi-pro team. He soon became their mascot. Jim would do anything he could to learn the game.

JAMES J. LEVEY

After two years of high school, Jim dropped out to became an apprentice to a printer. During that summer, he joined the Shady Side Triangles as a rightfielder. While on the Triangles, someone suggested to Jim that he would increase his strength if he got a job that involved more manual labor. Jim followed this advice and got a job as a helper in an iron mill. He got much stronger after handling the heavy iron ingots. At this point Jim's interest in baseball began to wane. He was learning a trade, and decided to continue working in the steel mills of Pittsburgh. Then, in 1923, at the age of 16, Jim decided to join the Marines. In the Marines, his strength continued to increase, and he joined his post's basketball, football, and baseball teams. Jim was soon the regular third baseman on the baseball team. In 1926, Jim was ordered to go to Philadelphia's World's Fair, to play on the All-Marine team at the nation's Sesquicentennial celebration. Jim's team won the Service Championship.

In the spring of 1927, Jim joined the football team in Quantico, Virginia. He played on the Quantico baseball team that summer. Jim reenlisted in the Marines at the end of the season, and played both football and baseball. After two years of service, he met a scout for the New York Giants while on recruiting duty in Boston. The scout told Jim to go to New York and try out for the team. Jim departed in such a hurry that he left his baseball equipment in Boston.

When Jim reported to the Polo Grounds, he met Roger Bresnahan, the assistant of John McGraw. Bresnahan asked Jim if he had brought his equipment.

Jim replied, "No sir. I left Boston in a hurry and I figured I could borrow a pair of old shoes and a glove from one of the players."

Bresnahan told him, "You figured wrong. No equipment, no workout. You better beat it."

Jim was discouraged when he left the Giants tryout. Only a few days later, he signed a contract with a scout for the St. Louis Browns. The scout told him to take a furlough from the Marines and that he would arrange his discharge. Jim was granted a sixty-day furlough and then reported to his first assignment, Tulsa. He played with Tulsa for at least two weeks, but then remembered his furlough would expire on August 23, 1929. As he started packing on August 21 to return to duty, that day he received a letter stating he was discharged. The vice-president of the Browns had enlisted the aid of a U.S. Senator to arrange this.

Jim finished the 1929 season with Wichita Falls, Texas. Wichita Falls won the pennant that year. In 1930, he played with Fort Worth. In 1930, Jim did play in 8 games for the St. Louis Browns. He made his major league debut on September 17, 1930, at Sportsman Park against the New York Yankees. That day, he got two hits, including a two-run double, and scored 2 runs, as the Browns defeated the Yankees, 9 to 8.

Jim wrote to The Sporting News in late 1930, asking them whether he should play professional football on the off-season, because he was having some money problems. The editor suggested that, instead, he should try to get a coaching job, because football was a violent sport and he might get injured. Jim replied that he couldn't get a job coaching because that required a college education. However, he didn't play football that winter, anyway; he played baseball during the 1931 season with the Browns. He hit .209 that year.

Jim was proud of his heritage, and when a sportswriter denied that Jim was Jewish, he angrily replied, "You tell him and everyone that cares to know that I am a Jew...and mighty proud of it."

Jim had his best year in 1932. He had a .280 batting average, with 30 doubles, 8 triples, 4 home runs, and 63 runs batted in. His improved batting was a result of the assistance he got from the Browns' manager, Bill Killefer. Killefer told Jim that he should hit left-handed, instead of right. That year, he was considered to be a star, and was much envied by Giants Manager John McGraw, who was searching for a Jewish star. McGraw said of Jim, "I'd trade my right arm, left leg, and seven ballplayers for that young fellow."

Jim played his final year in baseball in 1933. That year, he had a .195 batting average. His inconsistent hitting and poor fielding, committing 147 errors during his career, led to his dismissal. Jim had a lifetime major league batting average of .230 over 4 years. He later served as a manager in baseball's minor leagues.

Jim returned to organized ball in the winter of 1934—but not baseball. He joined the Pittsburgh Pirates of the National Football League. Jim wasn't used much that year, but in 1935 he became the Pirates' second-highest scorer. Jim retired from the Pirates, and professional football, in 1936.

Jim Levey died on March 14, 1970, in Dallas, Texas.

Years	Games	AB	H	R	RBI	HR	BA	OBP	FP
4	440	1632	375	162	140	11	.230	.272	.936

1930-33 StL-A

Al Levine

Alan Levine P
South Bend White Sox

Alan Brian Levine was born on May 22, 1968, in Parkridge, Illinois. He attended Southern Illinois University at Carbondale.

Al was selected by the Chicago White Sox in the 11th round of the 1991 free-agent draft. The right-handed pitcher was assigned to hurl for the Utica Blue Sox. He ended the season with an impressive 6-4 record and 3.18 ERA. Al was promoted to the South Bend White Sox in 1992. He pitched in 23 games for South Bend, with a 9-5 record and 2.81 ERA. He also pitched in 3 games for the Sarasota, Florida, White Sox, in 1992. In 1993, Al returned to the South Bend White Sox, ending the season with an 11-8 record and a 3.68 ERA. In the winter of 1993, Al pitched in the Venezuelan Winter League for the Caribes de Oriente baseball club. He had a 8-8 record with a 2.31 ERA. Al returned to the Caribes de Oriente in the winters of 1994 and 1995.

In 1994, Al had a very special opportunity. That year, he played on the Birmingham

Barons, with basketball star Michael Jordan. The Barons sold out the ballpark each game and they were constantly being talked about in the media. Al finished the historic season with a 5-6 record with a 3.31 ERA. In 1995, Al pitched for the Nashville Sounds and the Birmingham Barons. His 2.34 ERA with Birmingham earned him a spot on the Chicago White Sox in 1996.

Al made his major league debut on June 22, 1996. He pitched, in relief, in 16 games that year, with 1 loss and a 5.40 ERA. He was then returned to Nashville. In the winter of 1996, he pitched for the Venezuelan League Santurce Crabbers. There he was part of a Jewish battery when his catcher was Jesse Levis. Al began the 1997 season with the White Sox, but when his ERA went over 6.00, he was optioned to Nashville.

Al Levine currently lives in Belleville, Illinois.

On June 7, 1998, Al was recalled from the Oklahoma Red Hawks (Pacific Coast League) to pitch for the Texas Rangers. During the early part of the 1998 season, Al contributed significantly to the success of the Rangers, as a middle relief pitcher.

Years	Games	IP	W	L	GS	SV	PCT	ERA
5	172	284	6	9	6	2	.400	4.25

1996-97 Chi-A, 1998 Tex-A, 1999-2000 Ana-A

Jesse Levis

Jesse Levis was born on April 14, 1968, in Philadelphia, Pennsylvania. He played in both Little League and American Legion baseball. Jesse was raised as a conservative Jew and scheduled baseball practices around his religious studies. He attended Philadelphia's Northeast High School, where he was both a catcher and a first baseman.

Jesse was drafted, in 1986, after his high school graduation, by his hometown Phillies. But instead of entering into the ranks of professional baseball players right away, Jesse chose to attend the University of North Carolina and play on their team. In 1988, Jesse hit .320, with 10 home runs, for North Carolina and was named to the All-ACC's second team. He played in the Cape Cod Summer League that year for the Orleans Cardinals.

In 1989, Jesse was drafted for a second time, this time by the Cleveland Indians, as a catcher, as their fourth-round selection. His first assignment, that same year, was with the Burlington Indians. There, Jesse batted .344, with a .516 slugging average. He was promoted to the Kinston, North Carolina, Indians in the middle of the season, where he batted .299. At the end of the season, Jesse was promoted to the Class AAA Colorado Springs Sky Sox to play in one game. In 1990, he returned to the Kinston Indians, where he batted .296 with 64 RBIs and played in the Carolina League All-Star game. In 1991, he played with the Canton–Akron Indians. That year, Jesse led all Eastern League catchers in chances, with 733; putouts, with 644; and assists, with 77.

In 1992, Jesse played with both the Colorado Springs Sky Sox and the Cleveland Indians. He made his major league debut on April 24, 1992. Jesse played in 28 games with the Indians, with a .279 batting average and a .442 slugging average. With the Sky Sox, he played in 87 games, with a .364 batting average. He spent most of the 1993, 1994, and

1995 seasons in Cleveland's AAA teams in Charlotte, North Carolina, and Buffalo. Jesse played in 31 games in 1993, 1 game in 1994, and 12 games in 1995 for Cleveland. In the strike-shortened 1994 season, Jesse got a hit in his only at-bat for the Indians, making his major league batting average 1.000 that year. When the strike began, Jesse went to work for his parents' restaurant, Levis's (Kosher) Hot Dogs, in Philadelphia. Jesse traveled with the Indians during the 1995 postseason, as their third-string catcher. He warmed up the pitchers in the bullpen in the championship series and World Series, but did not play in any of the games.

On April 4, 1996, Jesse was traded to Bud Selig's Milwaukee Brewers, for pitchers Scott Nate and Jared Camp. Since joining the Brewers, he has been used regularly. In 1996, he appeared in 104 games with a .236 batting average and a .348 on-base percentage. That year, Jesse displayed a good eye, striking out in fewer than 5 percent of his plate appearances. In 1997, Jesse, who bats left-handed, was platooned with right-handed batter Mike Matheny. Jesse batted .285 in 200 at-bats. He was used frequently as a pinch-hitter and he set the club season record for pinch-hit at-bats when he appeared for the 37th time.

Jesse has a bright future with the Brewers. He has both strong offensive and defensive abilities. He is also an important part of the Jewish community. He attends minyan, when possible, and frequently gives talks to Jewish youth groups.

Jesse Levis married Joan Greenspan on October 28, 1995. They currently live in Elkins Park, Pennsylvania, a suburb of Philadelphia.

Jesse began the 1998 season as a backup catcher for the Brewers, playing their first season in the National League. His healthy batting average of .351 had moved him into an advantageous position, as of late May, but then a torn rotator cuff in the right shoulder forced him onto the 60 day disabled list.

Years	Games	AB	H	R	RBI	HR	BA	OBP	FP
8	307	621	159	60	57	3	.256	.337	.995

1992-1995 Cle-A, 1996-98 Mil-A, 1999 Cle-A

Lenny Levy

LENNY LEVY

Leonard Howard Levy was born on June 11, 1913, in Pittsburgh, Pennsylvania. He began his baseball career at the very bottom, as a ticket taker at Pittsburgh Pirates home games in the 1920s. Lenny later became the team's batboy. He graduated from Taylor-Alderdice High School.

Lenny played baseball in the minors. He was signed by the Pirates organization in 1936, and his first assignment was Savannah. In 1937, he was transferred to Portsmouth, then traded to Rock Island later that year. In 1938, Lenny began the season playing with Jackson, Mississippi, but was released that April. After Lenny's playing career was over, he became a scout.

In 1947, Lenny became a coach with the Pirates. He would only coach home games, because he also owned and operated an automobile agency in Pittsburgh's East End. He remained in that position until 1950, returning to scouting in 1951. He scouted and signed Dick Groat, Bill Mazeroski, and Frank Thomas. Lenny returned to coaching, for the Pirates, in 1957. He retired in 1964.

Lenny Levy died on February 2, 1993, in Palm Desert, California.

Lou Limmer

Louis Limmer was born on March 10, 1927, in the Bronx, New York. Lou served in the Army Air Corps during the Second World War.

He began his baseball career as a first baseman for Lexington (NCS League) for 1946 and 1947. He was promoted to Lincoln (Western League) in 1948. In late August of 1948, Lou broke his neck sliding into third base. He was temporarily blinded and could not return to baseball until the 1949 season. In 1949, however, Lou led the league in home runs, with 29, for Lincoln. He was promoted to St. Paul (American Association) in 1950, where he led that league in home runs, with 29; in RBIs, with 111; and in double plays, with 114. He was voted the American Association's Rookie of the Year for 1950.

Lou got his chance to play on the Philadelphia Athletics in 1951. He made his major league debut on April 22, 1951, and appeared in 94 games for the A's that year. Lou's batting average was only .159 and he was sent down to Ottawa (International League) for 1952. He returned to the A's lineup in 1954, for 115 games. Lou had a reputation among Philadelphia fans as the "Babe Ruth of Batting Practice." During practice, Lou would hit one home run after another. Sometimes, during the games, he wasn't quite as good; but on September 25, 1954, Lou hit the last home run for the Philadelphia A's before the team moved to Kansas City. The A's lost the game to the New York Yankees, 10 to 2, in Yankee Stadium. Lou hit 19 major league home runs.

Lou returned to the minor leagues in 1955, playing for Columbus, Toronto, Charleston, Omaha, and Birmingham before retiring from baseball at the end of the 1958 season. Lou Limmer has a lifetime major league batting average of .202 and minor league batting average of .281, in 12 years. Lou is now retired, and still lives in the Bronx.

Years	Games	AB	H	R	RBI	HR	BA	OBP	FP
2	209	530	107	66	137	19	.202	.287	.988

1951, 1954 Phi-A

Andrew Lorraine

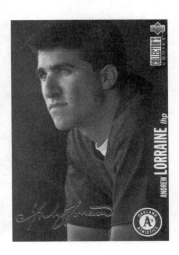

Andrew Lorraine was born on August 11, 1972, in Los Angeles. His family is observant. Andrew's paternal grandparents escaped from Poland, to England, before the German invasion. They changed their name to Lorraine from the original name, Levine. Andrew's father's brother is a rabbi in England. When he was 14, Andrew visited Israel.

Andrew made his professional debut in Venezuela, as a southpaw pitcher. He played in the Venezuelan Winter League with the Tiburones la Guaira baseball club in the winter of 1992–93. He pitched in 9 games, with a 2.51 ERA.

Andrew was drafted by the California Angels in 1993, as their fourth pick. He attended Stanford and pitched on its baseball team during the off-seasons. Andrew played with the short-season Boise Hawks in 1993. His 1.29 ERA earned him a spot on the AAA Vancouver Canadians in 1994, and he had an excellent record with them. His win-loss record was 12-4, with an ERA of 3.42, in 22 games started. That year, Baseball America named him the Pacific Coast League's Number One Pitching Prospect.

On July 17, 1994, Andrew made his major league debut. After only one year in the minors, Andrew pitched for the California Angels. He pitched in 4 games for them that year, losing 2 of them. His ERA with the Angels was 10.62. Andrew graduated from Stanford in 1994, with a B.A. He returned to Venezuela that winter to pitch for the Tiburones la Guaira.

After his disappointing stint with the Angels, he was traded to the Chicago White Sox. Andrew played most of the 1995 season with the AAA Nashville Sounds, although he did appear in 5 games, in relief, for the White Sox. In his second major league outing, he fared better. He gave up only 3 hits, in 8 innings. After the 1995 season, Andrew hurled for the Phoenix Desert Dogs, in the Arizona Fall League. He pitched in 15 games that fall, with a win-loss record of 3-3.

In 1996, Andrew was traded to the Oakland A's organization. He played most of the 1996 and 1997 seasons with the AAA Edmonton Trappers. Andrew was brought into the Oakland A's lineup in August 1997. On August 13, he won his first start in the majors: He pitched 5 innings and allowed only 1 earned run.

Andrew Lorraine, at the end of the 1997 season, was a regular member of the A's pitchers' rotation. Being a southpaw, with 4 different pitches, has marked him as a valuable commodity. He finished the 1997 season with a 3-1 record and a 6.37 ERA in 12 games.

Andrew began the 1998 season as a pitcher for the Tacoma Rainiers (AAA affiliate of the Seattle Mariners). He was used both as a starter and a middle reliever. His contributions to the team helped it to earn its first place position in its division during the early months of the season.

Years	Games	IP	W	L	GS	SV	PCT	ERA
6	54	163	6	10	25	0	.375	6.18

1994 Cal-A, 1996 Chi-A, 1997 Oak-A, 1998 Sea-A, 1999-2000 Chi-N, 2000 Cle-A

Elliot Maddox

Elliot Maddox was born on December 21, 1947 in East Orange, New Jersey. Elliot, who is African-American, was raised in Union, New Jersey, and there made many Jewish friends. He attended the University of Michigan, and while there took a number of courses in Judaic studies. At Michigan, Elliot won the Big Ten batting title with a .467 average. Although he was offered a baseball contract by the Astros, after high school Elliot chose to go on with school and remain at Michigan until graduation.

Elliot was the number-one pick of the Detroit Tigers in the secondary phase of the June 1968 draft. In 1968 and 1969, he had stints with Lakeland, Florida, and Rocky Mount, North Carolina, where he batted .303 for the two years. On April 7, 1970, Elliot debuted for the Tigers. He was a switch-hitting, utility player who could cover in the infield or in the outfield. He got his first major league hit off of Dean Chance, of Cleveland, on April 21. In that game he got two hits and an RBI. The Tigers won the game, 5–3. At the end of the season, Elliot was voted the Tigers' Rookie of the Year, but he was traded to the Washington Senators. In 1972, the Senators moved to Arlington, Texas, and Elliot was now a Texas Ranger. He stayed with the Rangers for 1973. In 1974, he was traded to the New York Yankees.

In that same year, although he did not have any Jewish relatives, Elliot converted to Judaism. He has stated that he believes there are many parallels between blacks' and Jews' experiences in America. He has also emphasized that, despite the press and extreme radicals among both groups, the feelings of the average black person are much warmer towards Jewish people than they are toward any other Caucasian ethnicity.

Elliot had the best years of his career in New York in 1974 and 1975. In the first of these years he hit .303 and in the second .307. Elliot, who had been acquired for his outstanding defensive work, was considered a key to the Yankees' good showing in the 1974 season, when they finished a close second to Baltimore. Though Elliot's 1976 year was abbreviated, he did make it back to the team in time for the World Series. The Yankees, however, were swept by the Cincinnati Reds.

1977 saw Elliot with the Baltimore Orioles. He completed his eleven-year stint in the majors with three years with the Mets, 1978–80. Elliot Maddox's lifetime average was .261, but to see his real value as a player it is also necessary to consider his fielding averages—which include .989 for outfield, .947 for third, and 1.000 for second.

Years	Games	AB	H	R	RBI	HR	BA	OBP	FP
11	1029	2843	742	360	234	18	.261	.361	.989

1970 Det-A, 1971 Was-A, 172-73 Tex-A, 1974-76 NY-A, 1977 Bal-A, 1978-80 NY-A

Cy Malis

Cyrus Sol Malis was born in Philadelphia on February 26, 1907. He learned to pitch on the sandlots there. His older brother, Charles, gave Cy his first chance to pitch by adding him to the roster of the amateur Waco Club.

Cy attended Brown Prep School from 1925 to 1926, and was a star on its baseball, football, and basketball teams. When he was only fifteen years old, he pitched in 19 games for Brown Prep. He won 15 of those games and lost only 4. In one of the games, against Villanova Prep, he struck out 22 batters. During the summers of 1924 and 1925, Cy pitched for the SPHAs (South Philadelphia Hebrew Association). In 1926, he pitched for both the Harrowgate and Germantown clubs.

Cy first pitched professionally in 1927 for Northampton (Eastern Shore League). He won the first six games he pitched. After the first

half of the year was over, Cy was fatigued and felt he needed time off. He asked the club if he could have a short break. They answered by releasing him from the team. He was immediately picked up by the Cambridge team (of the same league). Cy was treated more "humanely" with Cambridge: He was allowed a ten-day break and was used only as a reliever.

At the end of the season, Cy returned to his home in Philadelphia and received a call from the Phillies, offering him a tryout. Signed by them, he reported to their training camp the next spring, in 1928. Cy was used in the Phillies' minor league system for a couple of years before being released. After leaving the Phillies, he returned to the semi-pro ball teams of Philadelphia. Meanwhile, because the Phillies wanted a local player on the team, they re-hired Cy for a trial. He pitched in his only major league outing with the Phillies on August 17, 1934. That day, in relief, he pitched $3\frac{2}{3}$ innings. He gave up four hits and ended his major league career with a 4.91 ERA. Cy was released from the Phillies on September 4, 1934.

Cy joined the U.S. Navy after the Japanese attack on Pearl Harbor. While serving on a naval vessel, a gun mount swung around and hit Cy, breaking his neck and back. The accident produced such horrible pain that Cy could not stop from gnashing his teeth. To ease his pain and quiet him, he was administered morphine. After he became ambulatory, Cy realized he'd become addicted to the drug. He was dependent on it and had to find the courage to attempt to combat his habit. After many months, Cy turned to alcohol to ease himself off his morphine dependency. Nevertheless, he endured years of torturous withdrawal.

After defeating his own drug dependency, Cy began a program that helped others who were addicted to narcotics. The name of the organization was Narcotics Anonymous. It was fashioned after Alcoholics Anonymous. Cy's program had great success. He became, especially, a regular speaker at California prisons. A drug-addicted inmate at San Quentin Prison said of Cy, "He is the best friend we dope fiends have."

Cy soon became an accomplished motion picture and television actor. He first appeared in a movie, appropriately enough, as a ballplayer, in 1943. The film was called Ladies' Day, starred Eddie Albert, and included heavyweight boxing champion Max Baer in the cast. Cy also had parts in The Court Martial of Billy Mitchell (1955), The Alamo (1960), and in the television series "Perry Mason." It was while filming a movie that Cy was kicked by a horse. This forced him to slow down his rigorous pace of activities.

On the advice of his younger brother, Ozzie, Cy began coaching Little League baseball in California. The first year he coached, his team won the league championship. In 1970, the Phillies published a list of all Philadelphians who had played on the team—including Cy—in their yearbook. He was shown a copy and was deeply moved.

Cy Malis died on January 21, 1971, in Hollywood, California.

Years	Games	IP	W	L	GS	SV	PCT	ERA
1	1	$3\frac{2}{3}$	0	0	0	0	NA	4.91

1934 Phi-N

Moxie Manuel

Mark Garfield "Moxie" Manuel was born on October 16, 1881, in Metropolis, Illinois. His father, Isadore Manuel, had been born in Germany. His mother's maiden name was Jane Miller and she was born in Illinois.

Moxie began his remarkable baseball career with the Vicksburg team of the Cotton States League in the 1903 season. He was primarily a pitcher, but throughout his minor league career, he also played in the outfield, in the games he didn't pitch. In that first year, Moxie pitched 26 games for 14 wins and 12 losses. He also had 39 hits and a .204 batting average.

Moxie batted right-handed, but he could pitch with either hand. "Sure, I can slam over with one hand as good as with another," Moxie declared to a reporter in 1907. "When a right-handed batter is at the plate, I serve 'em with my right hand. When a left-handed batter is at the plate, I become a southpaw. That keeps 'em all guessing."

In 1978, when the question of ambidextrous pitching was being investigated by a reporter for The Sporting News, only one major league pitcher was discovered, Tony Mullane. The reporter was contacted by Moxie's son, who provided him with a copy of the 1907 interview we quoted above. The son made it clear that he didn't know whether Moxie had the opportunity to use both right-handed and left-handed pitching in the majors, for he only pitched some 70 innings, and the major league records indicated that Moxie pitched right-handed. Moxie was known, in the Southern Association, to have pitched both halves of doubleheaders—one game with his left hand and one with his right.

Moxie continued with Vicksburg in 1904. He won 21 games and lost 11, in 34 games. Then, in 1905, he started with Baton Rouge of the Cotton States League, but moved on, during the season, to play for New Orleans in the Southern Association. Before the season was over, Moxie had a brief tryout with the Washington Senators. With the two minor league teams he had 22 wins and 18 losses. For Washington, he was only used in relief and had no decisions. He had debuted with Washington on September 25. His ERA with the Senators was 5.40.

Moxie's greatest years seem to have been his 1906 and 1907 seasons with the New Orleans Pelicans. The first of these seasons, he won 17 and lost 15, in 34 games; the second, he won 20 and lost 1, in 32. It was during this period that Moxie achieved some of his most spectacular feats. On one occasion he shut out the Birmingham Barons in both halves of a doubleheader held in New Orleans. Moxie gave up only 2 hits in the first game and 6 in the second. He did not walk a single batter. Both games ended with the score 1–0. Moxie scored the winning run in the first game. It is not clear from the records how Moxie pitched these games. Only one man in the majors ever duplicated his feat of a shutout doubleheader: Ed Reulbach, on September 26, 1908. However, Moxie's achievement was only part of a much greater achievement. This double victory over Birmingham came in the midst of Moxie's string of 58 shutout innings, which set a new Southern Association record.

A journalist of the period described Moxie as "as tough as whalebone, does not lose his head when he is bumped a few times, and when he follows instructions can beat any team in the league." His son, who was born less than a year before his death, tells this story: "Connie Mack once told Rube Waddell to keep an eye on Moxie. 'He's ambidextrous.' Rube replied, 'You're telling me! He would just as soon kill you as look at you.' "

Moxie's son was under the impression that his father's nickname was the origin of the expression "plenty of moxie." Probably the expression and Moxie's nickname have their common origin in the name of the soft drink. According to Moxie's grandson, he loved to hunt and fish. Also, during his days with New Orleans he was considered one of the principal attractions for the "Ladies' Day" games that originated there.

Moxie's excellence with New Orleans brought him to the attention of Charles Comiskey, and his contract was picked up for the 1908 season by the Chicago White Sox. In 18 games with the White Sox, Moxie had 3 wins and 4 losses. However, his ERA was just 3.30. But that year, Chicago had "Big Ed" Walsh, with 1.42; Doc White, with 2.55; and Nick Altrock, with 2.71—among others. And Chicago didn't even win the pennant. Moxie just couldn't compete.

From 1909 to 1911, he returned to the Southern Association, first with Birmingham and then with Mobile. Of the 81 games of this period, he won 30 and lost 36. He finished 1911 with, first, Great Falls and, second, Missoula, both of the Union Association, and finally Kewanee, of the Central Association. In the first two of these teams he won 6 and lost 8, of 15 games. In Kewanee, he played only as an outfielder. Moxie's last season of pitching, 1912, was with Bloomington, of the 3-I League. He won only 3 games and lost 10, out of 13 games. The next year, 1913, his last in baseball, Moxie played as an outfielder with Henderson, Kentucky, in the Kitty League. He batted .237.

After baseball, Moxie Manuel took a job as a clerk. He was married and had children. He died on April 26, 1924, in Memphis, Tennessee, of peritonitis.

Years	Games	IP	W	L	GS	SV	PCT	ERA
2	21	$70\frac{1}{3}$	3	4	4	1	.429	3.58

1905 Was-A, 1908 Chi-A

Duke Markell

Harry Duquesne "Duke" Markell was born Harry Duquesne Makowsky in Paris, France, on August 17, 1923. Duke moved with his family to New York City when he was seven years old. It was the habit of slugger Hank Greenberg to hire boys from the neighborhood to pick up fly balls for him when he was taking extra batting practice. Duke got his first taste of baseball chasing balls for Hank. Duke lived just four blocks from Yankee Stadium. He looked forward, in his youth, to the day when he could pitch in that place, almost in his own backyard.

Duke's plans of being a ballplayer were altered because of the start of the Second World War. He entered the Army in 1942. Duke won a field commission while serving in the Philippines. After three years in the Army, he was given an honorable discharge.

Duke began his minor league career, in 1945, as a right-handed hurler for Hickory, North Carolina. In his second start, he pitched a no-hitter against Thomasville. During 1946, Duke played with Hickory, Manchester, Danville, and Seaford. With Danville, Duke accomplished a very rare feat for a pitcher: He hit 2 home runs in one game. In 1947, he pitched for Seaford; in one game, Duke struck out 11 batters in a row. That year, he set the Eastern Shore League record of strikeouts in a year, with 274. Duke hurled for Schenectady in 1948. In a game against Rome, New York, he struck out 21 batters. (The major league record is 18 K's in a game.) In 1948, Duke set a new

Canadian–American League strikeout record, with 270. Duke played the 1949 season with Utica and Terre Haute. In 1950, he pitched for Portsmouth and Oklahoma City, and began the 1951 season with Oklahoma City (Texas League).

Duke was promoted to the St. Louis Browns at the finish of that season. He made his major league debut on September 6, 1951, pitching three innings in relief of Fred Hutchinson. He allowed 4 hits and 1 run, as the Browns lost to the Chicago White Sox, 4 to 9. Out of his 5 appearances, Duke had 1 win and 1 loss. He pitched his only win on September 27, 1951; that day, he got his only major league hit and scored a run, as the Browns beat the Detroit Tigers, 7 to 4. During his stay on the Browns, Manager Rogers Hornsby never said one word to Duke, which annoyed the hurler. Duke pitched in 5 major league games, including 2 starts, all in 1951. His record was 1-1 and his ERA 6.33.

Despite his great promise, Duke never got another chance to pitch in the majors. He pitched in only 10 innings with the Browns, in spring training, before being returned to the minors in 1952 to pitch for Toronto. During the 1952 season, he was traded from the Browns to the Philadelphia Phillies. Assigned to Syracuse, in the International League, Duke won 11 games and led that league in strikeouts. The next year, he was invited to the Phillies' training camp. He pitched in their spring training, but again did not get picked for the team.

In 1953, Duke wore not only a baseball uniform, but also the uniform of a New York City policeman. During the off-season he had started his new career. Duke would play baseball during the entire season, until his retirement from the sport in 1958, but the rest of the year he was a cop. During the 1953 season, Duke pitched with Syracuse, leading the league in strikeouts. He accomplished the same feat again, with Rochester, in 1955. In 1958, Duke became a full-time policeman.

Duke Markell was married to a one-time model, Charlotte, and they had one daughter, Lynn. Duke died on June 14, 1984, in Ft. Lauderdale, Florida.

Years	Games	IP	W	L	GS	SV	PCT	ERA
1	5	$21\frac{1}{3}$	1	1	2	0	.500	6.33

1951 StL-A

Ed Mayer

Edwin David Mayer was born November 30, 1931, in San Francisco, California. His father had come to this country from Hong Kong; his mother was a native of Pennsylvania. Ed played ball on the team of the University of California, Berkeley, and attracted the attention of scouts from the Boston Red Sox. The scouts were impressed by the big left-hander's variety of pitches and his poise on the mound. When the Red Sox offered him a contract, in 1952, Ed left school and took it. He was later traded to the St. Louis Cardinals, and then to the Chicago Cubs. Ed only made major league appearances with the Cubs.

Ed spent his first five years in baseball playing at the minor league level. He first pitched, in 1952, for Yuma, Arizona. In the next year, 1953, he pitched for San Jose (California League)

Ed Mayer

CHICAGO CUBS

and won 17 games. In 1954, he pitched for Greensboro (Carolina League) and, again, had 17 wins. This was followed with stints in Montgomery, Alabama, and Omaha, Nebraska.

With his bat, Ed helped himself a great deal in the minors. In fact, when Ed was not pitching, he was sometimes called on to play either first base or in the outfield. On a number of occasions, Ed was named to minor league All-Star teams.

While playing winter ball in Cuba, during 1956, Ed badly injured his arm. Following this, at the beginning of the 1957 season, he was assigned to Ft. Worth (Texas League). By this time, Ed had pitched some 165 games in the minors, with a .560 win average and a 3.60 ERA. His success at Ft. Worth and earlier won him a tryout with the Cubs.

Ed debuted on September 15, 1957, at Wrigley Field in a game against the Giants. It was not a propitious beginning. Ed managed to give up 5 runs in 5 innings, including a home run hit by Willie Mays. Nevertheless, the Cubs managed to win the game, 7–6. Ed did not get credit for the win, but he did get a base hit during the game. He appeared in 2 other games in 1957 for the Cubs, ending the year with no decisions and a 5.87 ERA.

The next year, 1958, Ed appeared in 19 games with the Cubs. On April 19, he had his first win. This was a home game against the St. Louis Cardinals. Ed was a relief pitcher in the game, and two home runs in the 8th inning gave him the win. The final score was 6 to 3. Ed would garner one more win for the year and two losses. His ERA for 1958 was 3.80. Ed played 2 years in the majors. His lifetime ERA was 4.31. He had 2 wins and 2 losses, in appearances in 22 games.

During 1958, Ed also played with Portland (Pacific Coast League), appearing in 21 games. In 1959, Ed played for Denver (American Association) and, in 1960, for Monterrey (Mexican League).

After retiring from baseball, Ed Mayer went back to Berkeley and completed his teaching degree. He became an elementary school teacher. Ed was married twice. He was the father of three children. He currently lives in Corte Madera, California.

Years	Games	IP	W	L	GS	SV	PCT	ERA
2	22	$31\frac{1}{3}$	2	2	1	1	.500	4.31

1957-58 Chi-N

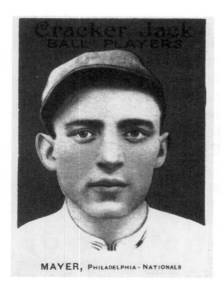

MAYER, PHILADELPHIA - NATIONALS

Erskine Mayer

Erskine John Mayer (originally James Erskine Mayer) was born in Atlanta, Georgia, on January 16, 1889. Erskine's mother was of old English ancestry, including Mayflower pilgrims. She converted to Judaism when she married Erskine's father, Isaac Mayer, who was a German Jew. Erskine's parents originally came from Ohio, but they settled in Atlanta. Erskine's father was a pianist and music teacher. His grandfather, Morris Mayer, had also been a musician and had composed a Hebrew opera. Isaac Mayer was also a baseball enthusiast, who used his spare time playing ball with his three sons, Mark, Erskine, and Sam. Sam would also become a major league player.

Erskine attended Georgia Tech College, but in 1910 left

without graduating, when his reputation as a pitcher, gained on Georgia Tech's team, attracted an offer from the Atlanta Crackers. He was assigned to Fayetteville, in the East Carolina League for the 1910 season. Erskine had 15 wins and 2 losses for 20 starts, and an .882 winning average. In 1911, he played briefly for Atlanta and then for Albany, Georgia. He had 14 wins and 13 losses for 29 starts, for a .519 average. He again started the 1912 season with Atlanta, and appeared in 4 games, with no decisions, before being sent to Portsmouth (Virginia League). He won 26 games for Portsmouth and lost 9, for 37 starts, with an average of .743. His ERA for Portsmouth was 3.02. On August 3, 1912, his contract was purchased by the Philadelphia Phillies.

The right-handed Erskine pitched in only seven games for the Phillies in 1912, with no wins and one loss. He was used that year principally as a reliever. His ERA was 6.33. The next year, 1913, was the first year Erskine began the season with the Phillies. He pitched in 39 games, with 9 wins and 9 losses, for an average of .500. His ERA was 3.11.

It was in 1914 that Erskine established himself as a star of the National League. He produced 21 wins for the mediocre Phillies team, which ended the year in sixth place. He established himself as an outstanding pitcher with a fine curve and excellent speed and control. On July 1, 1914, Erskine pitched his first victory for the Phillies, over the Boston Braves, at Boston's South End Grounds. Erskine gave up just six hits and won, 7–2. During the course of the game, Erskine hit a homer off Boston pitcher George Davis.

One of Erskine's best games of the year was a one-hitter against the St. Louis Cardinals, on July 27, at Philadelphia's Baker Bowl. Dan Griner was the losing pitcher. During the course of the game, Erskine hit a double and scored one of the Phillies' two runs. The final score was 2–0, the only hit against Mayer being a single by St. Louis shortstop Dots Miller.

Erskine was, however, overshadowed on the team by his roommate, Grover Cleveland "Pete" Alexander, who produced 27 wins for the Phils that year, the league record. Alexander's ERA for the year was 2.38, compared with Erskine's 2.58. Erskine lost 19 games and had a win average of .525. Alexander lost 15 and had an average of .643. Mayer once complained, "Every time I pitched well, Alexander topped me."

Erskine Mayer   **P**
1919 CHICAGO WHITE SOX

The friendly competition between the two men continued into the 1915 season, with the salubrious effect that the Phillies, for the first time in their history, won the pennant and went on to the World Series. In 1915, Erskine won 21 games, but this time Pete Alexander won 31. Erskine's ERA was a mere 2.36, but Pete's was 1.22, the lowest in the league for that year and the best ERA he posted in his career—also the eleventh-lowest ERA for a season on the all-time list. Erskine had 15 losses and a winning average of .583; Pete lost 10 and had an average of .756.

There was one area, however, in which Erskine did surpass Pete, and that was in batting. Erskine hit a healthy, for a pitcher, .239, with 21 hits, including a home run. The entire team's batting average was only .247, the lowest average ever for a National League pennant-winning team.

Erskine was married during the 1915 season, on the Fourth of July, and many of his teammates felt that after that, Erskine lost some of his stamina. If this was true, it may explain Erskine's lack of success in the 1915 Fall Classic. The 1915 World Series was the first ever attended by a U.S. president, and President Wilson was present for game two of the Series, which Erskine pitched for the Phillies. The game was a classic pitchers' duel, with Boston scoring only one run in the first inning and the Phils scoring one in the fifth. The deciding run came in the ninth, and Rube Foster won it for Boston, 2–1.

Erskine was not supposed to pitch in the fifth game of the Series, but Alexander injured his arm and Erskine, at the last minute, was called on. The result was not happy and Erskine was taken out after two and a half innings. After Erskine left the game, the Phillies managed to recover the lead, but they lost it again—and the game—in the 9th inning. The loss went to Hall of Fame pitcher Eppa Rixey, and Rube Foster got the win, 5–4. This was the fifth and last game of the Series, which Boston took, 4 games to 1. The Phillies' only victory was in the Series' first game, pitched by Alexander.

The 1916 season was not a good one for Erskine, who had completed the two previous seasons with more than 20 victories each. (By the way, Erskine Mayer was the first Jewish pitcher ever to post 20 victories in a season, or 20 victories in two consecutive seasons. He would be the only Jewish pitcher to win 20 games in a season until 1963, when Sandy Koufax won 25.) Erskine's ERA rose, in 1916, to 3.15 and his average slumped to .500, with 7 wins and 7 losses, in 28 games. The year was a good one for the Phillies, who only missed winning the pennant by a narrow margin. Much of the blame for this loss was directed at Erskine.

In 1917, Erskine snapped back with an ERA of 2.75 and an average of .647, with 11 wins and 6 losses, in 28 games. The next year also began well, with 7 wins and 4 losses in 13 games, an average of .636, with an ERA of 3.12. Despite this successful record for the first part of 1918, Erskine was traded to the Pittsburgh Pirates, at that time owned by Barney Dreyfuss.

Erskine's second part of the 1918 season, with Pittsburgh, was also very successful, with 9 wins and 3 losses in 15 games, to give him a .750 average and an ERA of 2.26. Shortly after he joined Pittsburgh, Erskine participated in one of the most challenging games of his career. He was the starting pitcher against the Boston Braves. The game was deadlocked, 0 to 0, from the start, until Erskine was relieved in the 16th inning, having pitched $15\frac{1}{3}$ innings of scoreless baseball. Erskine was relieved by Wilbur Cooper, who went on to win the game in the 21st inning, 2 to 0.

Erskine's last year in the majors, 1919, began with 5 wins and 3 losses for Pittsburgh in 18 games, an average of .625, with an ERA of 4.48. Erskine was traded to the infamous White Sox team of that year and he pitched 6 games before the season ended, the Sox capturing the pennant. He had only one win and three losses for the Sox, with an ERA of 8.37. The win, Erskine's last, was on August 19 and took place at Comiskey Park. The White Sox defeated the Philadelphia A's, 8–7.

Erskine was the only Jew on the infamous Black Sox team of the 1919 World Series. He was in no way implicated in the plot to throw the Series, though the original instigators of the scheme were Jews, Arnold Rothstein and Abe Attell. Erskine's only contribution to the Series was in the 9th inning of the fifth game. He came in, in relief of Lefty Williams, and allowed one unearned run. This was his last appearance in the major leagues. Erskine pitched for 8 years in the majors with 3 teams. His lifetime ERA was 2.96. He won 91 games and lost 70, giving him a winning percentage of .565.

Erskine played one last minor league game in 1920, for his hometown Atlanta Crackers, where his brother Sam was the captain of the team. He won the game.

When the news of the Black Sox scandal broke, Erskine was heartbroken. He had no idea of what was going on, and felt that the game had completely lost its glory. He swore he would never play ball again—and he never did.

Erskine Mayer afterward became a successful sales manager. He died in Los Angeles, California, on March 10, 1957.

Years	Games	IP	W	L	GS	SV	PCT	ERA
8	245	1427	91	70	165	6	.565	2.96

1912-18 Phi-N, 1918-1919 Pit-N, 1919 Chi-A

Sam Mayer

Samuel Frankel Mayer was born on February 28, 1893, in Atlanta, Georgia, the son of Mr. and Mrs. Isaac Mayer and the younger brother of Erskine Mayer. Sam, like his brother, was infected by the baseball enthusiasm of their musician father, and he spent much of his life in the game. Sam attended both Georgia Military Academy and Georgia Tech.

Sam started his playing career in Blytheville (Northeast Arkansas League) in 1911. Subsequently, he played with Fulton (Kitty League), Savannah (Sally League), Kansas City (American Association), and Topeka (Western League). During 1915, Sam was recalled to Kansas City after a stay in Topeka. He played 17 games with the team and was extremely impressive, so much so that he became the center of a bidding war among several teams. He was first contacted by the Brooklyn team of the Federal League. Sam showed interest, but failed to sign a contract. John McGraw of the Giants showed interest, but the Giants' management refused to get involved because of a potential lawsuit from the Federal League. The Chicago Cubs made Sam an offer, but Sam decided, instead, to accept the offer of Clark Griffith of the Washington Senators.

On September 4, 1915, Sam Mayer debuted at Griffith Stadium in Washington, D.C., as a rightfielder. Sam had no hits in 4 at-bats, but the Senators won over the Yankees, 4–3. Sam's major contributions to the teams that he played for were often defensive.

Two days later, on September 6, the Senators were scheduled for a doubleheader with the Philadelphia A's, at Philadelphia's Shibe Park. In the first game, Sam got his first major league hit, a single, off A's pitcher Tom Sheehan. The Senators won the first game, 5–3. (Later, in 1960, Sheehan became manager of the San Francisco Giants.) In the second game, Sam got his first and only major league home run, off Jack Nabors. The Senators took this game too, 5–0.

On September 17, Sam was called on to make his only appearance as a major league pitcher. This was at American League Park in Washington, in a game against the St. Louis Browns. Mayer was called in to relieve in the 7th inning. He allowed two walks and was then relieved, himself, by George Dumont. The Browns won, 9–0.

After appearing in just 11 games, with a .231 batting average, Sam was sent back to the minors. For the next six years, he was a star of the Atlanta Crackers. Sam's hitting was always good, ranging from .270 to .300, but his defensive work, in center field, was truly spectacular. On many occasions, Sam was known to catch line drives to center, on single hops, and return them so fast to the first baseman as to allow him to tag out the runners. Long before the birth of Willie Mays, Sam patrolled the outfield so effectively that people said of him, when he was in center: "He played all fields." His most spectacular catch was in the park at Memphis. As a slow, fly ball approached, obviously headed for home run history, Sam scurried 8 feet up a flagpole on the edge of the outfield and scooped the ball out of the air. If the team needed an extra pitcher or a first baseman, Sam was always ready to step in.

In 1916, when Sam began playing for the Crackers, the manager of the team was Charlie Frank, with whom Sam would work all of his six years with Atlanta. In 1918, Sam bought a part-interest in the club. He was made the team's captain and also its business manager. In 1919, the team won the Southern Association pennant. The following year, Erskine Mayer, Sam's brother, played his very last professional baseball game with the Crackers.

In 1922, Sam played for Little Rock (Southern Association). Subsequently, he played for Louisville (Southern Association), where his manager was Joe McCarthy, later famous as the manager of the Yankees. (McCarthy won 8 pennants and 7 World Series for the Yankees.) After Louisville, Sam played for San Antonio (Texas League), New Haven (Eastern League), and Pittsfield (Eastern League). Sam retired from playing in 1929.

During his playing years, Sam also worked as a scout for his old major league team, the Washington Senators. He did this for three years, under his old boss, Clark Griffith. Following his retirement, he became a real estate salesman.

In 1958, The Atlanta Journal sponsored a high school All-Star tournament for schools in the area. Sam managed one of the teams. His team lost, but he felt like a winner. "We had 40 boys, many from different environments, and we never had a minute's trouble," he said.

Sam Mayer was married to Marie Stokes. Late in his life, Sam suffered from diabetes. He died of a heart attack on July 1, 1962, in Atlanta. He was buried in Decatur Cemetery in Decatur, Georgia. Earl Mann, the batboy on the Atlanta Crackers during Sam's playing days, said of Sam, when he heard of his death, "I'm sorry to hear it. He was a great fellow, as well as a great outfielder."

Years	Games	AB	H	R	RBI	HR	BA	OBP	FP
1	11	29	7	5	4	1	.241	.333	1.000

1915 Was-A

Bob Melvin

Bob Melvin
Giants

Bob Melvin spent 10 years in the majors, yet he had only a .232 lifetime, major league batting average. His career lasted so long because he was an ideal second-string catcher, worked well with the pitchers, called a good game, and was an excellent defensive player.

Robert Paul Melvin was born on October 28, 1961, in Palo Alto, California. Bob was the son of a Jewish mother and a Catholic father. He attended high school in Menlo Park, California. There, Bob played on the school's baseball, basketball, and golf teams. After his high school graduation, he enrolled in the University of California, Berkeley, and played on the varsity baseball team. After one year, he decided to turn professional and to leave Berkeley. He then enrolled at Canada College, in Redwood City, California.

In 1981, Bob was signed as a catcher by the Detroit Tigers in the January draft. That year, he left California, for the first time in his life, to catch 114 games for Class A Macon. In his first season, he batted .272, with 14 home runs. He also had a league-leading .996 fielding percentage. In 1982, Bob was promoted to the Birmingham Barons. A knee injury shortened his season, but he managed to bat .236 in 98 games. That year, Bob also met his future wife, Kelly Robertson. Bob returned to the Barons' lineup, in 1983. In the middle of the season, he had a .288 batting average and was promoted to the Evansville Triplets, playing in 45 games for them and batting .190. In 1984, Bob started the season with the Triplets, but after 44 games was sent back down to the Birmingham Barons. Bob began the 1985 season with Class AAA Nashville. Before the year was over, he would be called up to play for the Detroit Tigers.

Bob made his major league debut on May 25, 1985. That day, he had his first hit and scored his first run. During the 1985 season, he caught in 41 games. Most of the catching responsibilities were assumed by first-string catcher Lance Parrish. After the 1985 season, Bob was traded to the San Francisco Giants.

For the next 3 years, he shared catching duties with Bob Brenly. Unfortunately for Melvin, Brenly also batted right-handed and was a better hitter. Bob appeared in 89 games for the Giants in 1986, and batted .224. In 1987, however, Bob's batting average dropped to .199. That year, the Giants went to the National League Championship Series. Bob had 7 at-bats during the Series and batted .429. The Giants lost the Series to the St. Louis Cardinals, in 7 games. Bob played one final season with the Giants, in 1988. That year, he got more playing time, but batted only .234.

After the 1988 season, Bob was traded to the Baltimore Orioles for catcher Terry Kennedy. The Giants were intent on acquiring Kennedy because his father worked in their front office. When Bob reached Baltimore, he was platooned with Mickey Tettleton. He stayed with the Orioles for 3 years and batted between .240 and .250 each year. In 1991, Bob broke the Orioles' record for hits in a game, with 5. After the 1991 season, he was traded to the Kansas City Royals. He played in only 32 games in 1992, but had the highest batting average of his career: .314. Bob was also dependable behind the plate for the Royals, not committing one error all year. At the end of the season, he was traded to the Boston Red Sox.

In 1993, Bob batted .222, in 77 games for the Red Sox. In a game against the Baltimore Orioles, in September of 1993, he collided at home plate with the O's shortstop, Cal Ripken. Ripken knocked Bob over and hurt him so badly that he needed three stitches to close a gash above his eye. Before the 1994 season, Bob was traded to the New York Yankees. He played in 9 games there, before being traded to the Chicago White Sox. Bob played in only 11 games for the White Sox. He retired at the end of the season.

Bob Melvin currently lives in Menlo Park, California.

Years	Games	AB	H	R	RBI	HR	BA	OBP	FP
10	692	1955	456	174	212	35	.233	.270	.993

1985 Det-A, 1986-88 SF-N, 1989-91 Bal-A, 1992 KC-A, 1993 Bos-A, 1994 NY-A, 1994 Chi-A

Ed Mensor

Edward "The Midget" Mensor, who stood at 5'6", was born on November 7, 1886, in Woodville, Oregon. Ed was the son of Mr. and Mrs. Henry Mensor and the grandson of Morris and Matilda Mensor of Jacksonville, Oregon. The grandparents ran a store in Jacksonville, Mensor's

MENSOR, PORTLAND. N. W. L.

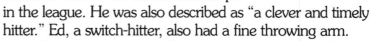

New York Store. They had 17 children, many of whom specialized in playing baseball. The family had its own team and was offered as competition for another family that had advertised, in 1879, to take on all comers. Henry was the pitcher of the family team. He also pitched for the Jacksonville town team.

His son, Ed, played for Portland (Northwest League) in 1910. He was noted as one of the fastest shortstops in the league. He was also described as "a clever and timely hitter." Ed, a switch-hitter, also had a fine throwing arm.

Ed's contract was purchased by the Pittsburgh Pirates and he debuted for the team on July 15, 1912. In his first year, during which he was used in the outfield, he hit .263. He had 26 hits in 39 games.

In 1913, Ed hit only .179 in a year in which he was used in the outfield, on second, and at shortstop. He had 10 hits in 44 games, though in many of these games he was only used as a pinch-hitter. His 1914 numbers are similar, with a .202 batting average in 44 games. But one thing Ed did do this year was hit a home run, the only major league homer of his career. He was used only in the outfield in 1914. Ed had a major league average of .221; he had 54 hits in 244 at-bats, including 6 doubles, 3 triples, and his single homer.

In 1917 and 1918, Ed Mensor played for the Oakland Oaks (Pacific Coast League). Ed died on April 20, 1970, in Salem, Oregon.

Years	Games	AB	H	R	RBI	HR	BA	OBP	FP
3	127	244	54	43	8	1	.221	.367	.964

1912-14 Pit-N

ProCards

MIKE MILCHIN
Pitcher
Louisville Redbirds

Mike Milchin

Michael Wayne Milchin was born on February 28, 1968, in Knoxville, Tennessee, to a Jewish father and a gentile mother. Mike graduated from Tucker High School in Richmond, Virginia, where he played football and baseball. He attended Clemson University and played on its baseball team as a left-handed pitcher, first baseman, and outfielder. In 1988, he was on the gold-medal-winning Olympic baseball team in Seoul, South Korea.

Mike was acquired, as a southpaw pitcher, by the St. Louis Cardinals in the 2nd round of the June 1989 free-agent draft. He split his first professional season between Hamilton (New

York–Pennsylvania League) and Springfield (Mid-Atlantic League).

Mike picked up his first professional win on June 28, 1989, with 7 shutout innings for Hamilton. He finished the season with a combined 4-4 record and 2.16 ERA in 14 games started. In 1990, Mike was promoted to the Arkansas Travelers. He finished the season with a 3-2 record and a 4.31 ERA. He began the 1991 season with the Travelers, but was promoted to the Louisville Redbirds after 6 games. That year, he injured a toe and had some shoulder problems.

Mike had a mediocre season in 1992, which could be blamed on injuries. That year, he broke a toe and required knee surgery, finishing the 1992 season with a 5.92 ERA. In 1993, Mike returned to the Louisville Redbirds to pitch an unimpressive season, and was traded to the Los Angeles Dodgers at the end of it. In 1994, Mike was invited to the Dodgers' spring-training camp, but his shoulder soon became sore with tendonitis. He required surgery to rebuild his left elbow and was forced to miss the entire season. He returned to pitch, however, in 1995, assigned to the Class AAA Albuquerque Dukes (Pacific Coast League). On June 13, he won his third start with the Dukes with a no-hit, 2–0 shutout over the Vancouver Canadians, ending the season with a 8-4 record and a 4.32 ERA. In March 1996, Mike was signed over to the Minnesota Twins as a free agent. He was assigned to pitch for the Salt Lake Buzz (Pacific Coast League).

On May 14, 1996, Mike was called up to the Minnesota Twins. That night, he made his major league debut by getting the final two outs. On August 9, 1996, he was claimed off waivers from the Twins by the Baltimore Orioles, joining the team in Chicago that day. Mike finished the season with the Orioles. In 39 major league appearances Mike Milchin earned 3 wins and 1 loss with a 7.44 ERA. He did not make any appearances during the 1997 season.

Years	Games	IP	W	L	GS	SV	PCT	ERA
1	39	$32\frac{2}{3}$	3	1	0	0	.750	7.44

1996 Min-A, 1996 Bal-A

Norm Miller

Norman Calvin Miller was born on February 5, 1946, in Los Angeles, California. In 1957, when he was 11, Norm was the subject of a TV sports special narrated by Leo Durocher. The heroes of Norm's youth were the Dodgers, and he played hooky from school so he could see the 1962 playoff games between the Dodgers and the Giants. This almost got him expelled. Norm would sit in the left-field pavilion at Dodger Stadium, root for the home team, and scramble for baseballs. The Dodgers were always his team and Tommy Davis was his hero.

Norm, a left-handed batter who threw right-handed, played ball as a boy and also in high school. He graduated from Van Nuys High School in 1964, and was immediately signed by the Los Angeles Angels as a free agent. Norm was assigned to Quad Cities (Midwest League), where he had a .301 batting average. He was used as a second baseman by Quad

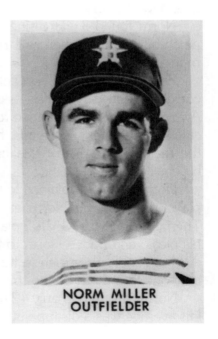

NORM MILLER
OUTFIELDER

Cities. After his first season, Norm was drafted by the Houston Astros. When he got to Houston, Norm was used as an outfielder.

In 1965, Norm was sent to Amarillo (Texas League), where he led the league in bases-on-balls, with 89. He also had 20 homers and drove in 92 runs. Late in the season, Norm was called up to join the Astros. He was told to report to the club at Dodger Stadium. Just one year before, he had been a high school student sitting in the pavilion. Now, at 19, he was in an Astro uniform joining the club in the dugout. Norm didn't expect to get into that game, but during the late innings, on September 11, 1965, he was sent in to pinch-hit. He got a single. Norm got to play in 11 games that season for Houston, with a .200 batting average. He started the 1966 season with Oklahoma City (Pacific Coast League), where he played in 91 games; then he rejoined Houston, before the end of the season, for another 11. This time he batted only .147, but he did pick up his first major league home run.

Norm's career followed similar patterns in 1967 and 1968, starting with Oklahoma City and finishing the year with the Astros. In 1967, he batted .406 with Oklahoma City. While his batting averages were never particularly high with Houston, he began to develop a reputation as an outstanding pinch-hitter. The 1967 Astro team included 4 Jews. Besides Norm, there were Bo Belinsky, Barry Latman, and Larry Sherry. On April 16, 1968, Norm scored the only run in a 24-inning game between the Astros and the Mets, at the Astrodome. This game was the longest night game in major league history.

With the 1969 season, Norm became part of the regular Houston staff, with no further trips to the minors. He was used most consistently in 1969, when he played in 119 games. Norm batted .264 that year, and during the 1969 season he played in two consecutive no-hitters, pitched by Astros Jim Maloney and Don Wilson. Norm had a homer in the season opener in 1970, a repeat of his 1968 opener. In 1971 and 1972, he only batted .239 and .257; but as a pinch-hitter, his average was over .300 each year. Norm lost playing time during 1971 because of a broken wrist. In July 1972, he went 4 for 9 in 2 consecutive games against the Cubs, with 2 home runs and 6 RBIs. During the 1972 season, Norm was reunited with Leo Durocher, who took over the helm of the Astros late in the season. Durocher had interviewed Norm when he was eleven years old.

Norm found it increasingly frustrating to find himself being seen more and more as a pinch-hitter, rather than as a regular field player. Nevertheless, he had carved out a valuable reputation for himself.

But Norm was not content, and he believed he would be a more desirable player if he could broaden his defensive skills. In 1971, following the regular season, he enrolled in the Arizona Instructional League to learn the catcher's position. While Norm had been asked to catch a few times before this, he never got the opportunity to use the newly learned skills in the majors. These new qualifications as a catcher, however, did help him to land his last baseball job.

Norm often complained to the Astro organization that he wanted to be played as a regular player or traded, but Norm was too useful on the bench and Houston hung on to his contract. Then, finally, in 1973, after playing in only 3 games for Houston, the management listened to his pleas, and traded Norm to the Atlanta Braves. In 1973, Norm played in only 12 games, due to injuries; nevertheless, he had 10 pinch-hits and batted .323 as a pinch-hitter. Norm had only one home run during this season, but it was a three-run homer.

Norm was used in only 42 games during the 1974 season, with just 41 plate appearances. His average was a disappointing .171. The highlight for Norm, that year, was being a teammate of Hank Aaron when Hank broke Babe Ruth's lifetime home-run record.

Following the 1974 season, Norm became a free agent. He was approached by both the Yankees and the Dodgers. The Dodgers were particularly interested in Norms's qualifications as a catcher. Norm, as a child, had dreamed of playing for the hometown team. He was signed by the Dodgers, but before the start of the 1975 season a back injury brought Norm's career to an end, at the age of twenty-nine.

Despite his reputation as a pinch-hitter, Norm was a good fielder, with a 1.000 fielding percentage in the outfield during 5 seasons. During his longest season in the outfield, 1969, he had a .984 percentage. Norm's lifetime batting average was only .238, but this overlooks his value as a pinch-hitter. His on-base average was .325.

While he was still playing, Norm was involved in the real estate business in Houston, and worked in it full-time during the winter. Following his retirement, however, he went into the restaurant business and was very successful. Then, starting in the late 1980s, Norm became Director of Advertising Sales and Promotions for the Houston Astros. He also became active in the Greater Houston Sports Association. In 1991, he became a partner in Players Texas Sports, a baseball-card collecting company.

Norm Miller is married. The Millers make their home in Houston, Texas.

Years	Games	AB	H	R	RBI	HR	BA	OBP	FP
10	540	1364	325	166	160	24	.238	.325	.972

1965-73 Hou-N, 1973-74 Atl-N

Buddy Myer

Buddy Myer should be in the Baseball Hall of Fame. This was proved, beyond a doubt, by a careful comparison of his career with that of Hall of Famer Billy Herman. The comparison was performed by statistician and baseball authority Bill James (The Bill James Historical Baseball Abstract, New York: Villard Books, 1986, p. 346). James compared the careers of the two men, number by number, regarding such factors as batting average, runs scored, RBIs, fielding percentage, double plays executed, longevity, assists, and many other factors. James concluded: "How in the world can you put one of those people in the Hall of Fame and leave the other one out?" This question has still not been answered.

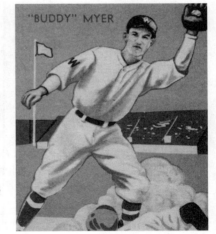

Charles Solomon "Buddy" Myer was born on March 16, 1904, in Ellisville, Mississippi. His father was Jewish, his mother a Christian. Buddy attended Mississippi A&M and starred on its baseball, football, and basketball teams. In 1923, he attracted the attention of the Cleveland Indians and was offered a contract. Buddy accepted, but with the understanding that he would first complete college, which he did in 1925.

When Buddy first reported to Cleveland, that same year, he found that the team was planning to play him in Dallas (Texas League). This was contrary to Buddy's wishes and he soon parted company with the Cleveland organization, making his own deal to play for New Orleans (Southern Association). There he soon showed what he could do. In 99 games he had

125 hits, including 21 doubles, 8 triples, and 3 homers. His batting average was .336. His contract was purchased by the Washington Senators for $25,000 and Buddy was on his way to the majors before the season was out.

Buddy debuted on September 26, 1925, and he played in the last four games of the regular season as shortstop. He batted left-handed, but threw with his right. The Senators won the pennant that year. When the team's regular third baseman, Ossie Bluege, was injured during the World Series, Buddy was called on to play third base for the team. At his very first at-bat during the Series, Buddy got a hit. The Senators lost the Series to Barney Dreyfuss' Pirates in the last game of the seven-game Series.

When Buddy returned, in the 1926 season, he was back to shortstop. That year, he batted .304, with 132 hits, including 18 doubles, 6 triples, and a home run. At the start of the 1927 season, he was hitting just .216. Furthermore, Manager Clark Griffith was not exactly satisfied with Buddy's defensive work at shortstop. Buddy was traded to the Boston Red Sox. This trade has often been pointed out as one of the most stupid in baseball history. The Senators received Topper Rigney, a third baseman hitting only .111 for the Sox and who only lasted 45 games with the Senators, before leaving the major leagues forever. Buddy, on the other hand,

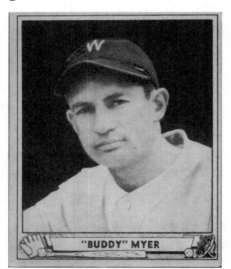

"BUDDY" MYER

hit .288 for Boston. The following year, he hit .313, and led the league in stolen bases, with 30. Griffith couldn't stand it. He had to have Buddy back. Finally, he was able to strike a deal—but the Senators had to give up 5 players to get Buddy.

In 1929, For the first time, Buddy played second base in the Washington infield. He had found his perfect fielding position. That year, his fielding percentage on second was .958. This figure would only improve throughout his career. His lifetime fielding average, on second, is .974. On August 6, 1929, Buddy ended a streak. For 8 consecutive at-bats, he had 8 consecutive hits.

From that time, until the end of his playing career, Buddy's dependable bat, better in the clutch than in normal conditions, and his excellent defensive work on second became a mainstay of the Washington team. Twice, Buddy would represent the American League in All-Star Games.

In 1931, Buddy led American League second basemen in fielding percentage, with .984. That same year, he scored 114 runs. It was the first time he went over 100. He would do this 4 times in his career.

On April 25, 1933, Buddy was guarding second base, when Ben Chapman of the Yankees, trying to prevent a double play, came flying at Buddy, spikes first. Now, undoubtedly, this was not the first confrontation between Buddy and Chapman. Chapman had a reputation as the worst Jew-baiting, anti-Semite in baseball. When Jackie Robinson came to the major leagues and Chapman was manager of the Phillies, Chapman extended his reputation as a hater to include a new title, as the most obnoxious and obscene bigot in both major leagues. Buddy, though not a large man, much smaller than Chapman, came up swinging and Chapman went down. Soon, the entire field had turned into a general melee between the two teams. Then, supporters of the teams began flowing from the stands. Eventually, the umpires restored order, but the incident has gone down as one of the worst rhubarbs in baseball history. Buddy, was of course, thrown out of the game and, later, fined $100. He was also suspended for five games. It must have felt like a bargain. Buddy, himself, never publicly discussed the fight.

In 1933, Buddy had another excellent year with the Senators, hitting .302, and the team won the American League pennant. Much of the credit for this was attributed to him. Clark Griffith, remembering the time he had traded Buddy, once commented that he wouldn't take less than half a million dollars for Buddy's contract. Still, the 1933 World Series was not a good one for Washington. Although Buddy hit .300 for the Series, with 6 hits, the Giants won the Series, 4 games to 1. Game 3 of the Series, Washington's only victory, was a particularly good one for Buddy. Each of his three hits in the game either scored or drove in a run. The final score was 4–0 and was the Series' only shutout—a victory for pitcher Earl Whitehill.

The year 1935 was probably the greatest of Buddy's career. He won the American League batting title with a .349 average. For the fourth, and last, time he scored more than 100 runs—115, to be exact. For the only time in his career he had 100 RBIs—100 exactly. He led his league in number of games played by a second baseman, 151; putouts, 460; and double plays, 138. He came in fourth in the balloting for MVP that year. (The award was won by Hank Greenberg.) After the season, the Yankees made overtures to Washington to purchase Buddy's contract, but they were turned down flat.

In 1936, Ben Chapman joined the Washington Senators. There does not seem to have been any continued ill will between Buddy and Chapman, but Buddy did develop a stomach ailment that put him on the disabled list for a large part of the year. He played in only 51 games that season.

In 1938, Buddy again led the league in fielding percentage, with .982. He also had the second-best batting average of his career, with .336. From 1939 to 1941, Buddy continued to suffer from his stomach problems, as well as the effects of old injuries. Finally, in 1941, he retired.

After his baseball career, Buddy became a banker in New Orleans. He died on October 31, 1974, in Baton Rouge, Louisiana.

When Buddy Myer retired he had a lifetime major league batting average of .303. He had played 17 seasons in the majors, more than any other Jewish player. He had 2131 major league hits, more than any other Jewish player. Indeed, Buddy is the only Jewish player who had more than 2,000 hits. Buddy played in 1923 games, more than any other Jewish player. Buddy had 965 walks, the 83rd most of all time. Buddy had 130 triples (making him 78th on the all-time list), though only 38 homers. Buddy had 353 doubles, 1174 runs, and 850 RBIs.

On the defense side, an interesting comparison can be made to the great Johnny Evers, the second baseman of "Tinkers to Evers to Chance." As a second baseman, Evers executed 688 double plays. Buddy Myer executed, at second base, 963. In all positions, Evers had a total of 692 double plays. Buddy had a total of 1,134. We end where we began: Buddy Myer should be in Cooperstown.

Years	Games	AB	H	R	RBI	HR	BA	OBP	FP
17	1923	7038	2131	1174	850	38	.303	.389	.974

1925-27 Was-A, 1927 Bos-A, 1928-41 Was-A

Samuel Nahem

Samuel Nahem was born on October 19, 1915, in New York City. His family was from Beirut, Syria. He is one of very few Jewish players whose background is Sephardic, rather

than Ashkenazic. The family settled in Manhattan's East Side. They later moved to Ocean Parkway in Brooklyn.

Sam, a side-armed, right-handed pitcher, tried out with the Brooklyn Dodgers while attending college. Casey Stengel told Sam to pitch batting practice to pitcher Van Lingle Mungo. Mungo had a reputation as a savage competitor. Sam threw a couple of pitches, before one hit Mungo right on the butt. Mungo growled with pain, but continued to bat. When Sam was finished, Casey turned to him and said, "We're going to sign you up. If you can hurt that big son of a bitch, you must have something on the ball."

Whereas Sam pitched in the summer, he attended Brooklyn College during the winter. Later he completed law school at St. John's University. Sam made his professional start with Allentown, Pennsylvania, in 1935. He played the next year in Jeanerette, Louisiana. Sam pitched in Clinton, Iowa, in 1937; there, he had a win-loss record of 15-5. Sam, a native New Yorker, was soon given the nickname "Subway" Sam.

Sam started the 1938 season with Elmira, New York. He was promoted to the Dodgers and made his debut on October 2, 1938, at Shibe Park, winning his first major league game. Sam got two hits in the game and one RBI, as the Dodgers beat the Phillies 7 to 3.

In 1939, Sam pitched for both Montreal and Nashville. That year, he won 9 games and lost 9. He was transferred to Houston for the 1940 season; there, he won 8 games and lost 6. Sam played the 1941 season with the St. Louis Cardinals. That year, he had his best major league season. He appeared in 26 games, with a win-loss record of 5-2 and an ERA of 2.98.

The following year, Sam was traded to the Philadelphia Phillies. He pitched in 35 games with the Phillies in 1942. The 1942 Phillies are considered one of the worst teams of the 20th century. They lost 109 games that year, but somehow managed to win 43 and tie one. Sam, principally used as a reliever, registered 1 win and 3 losses. He did have 2 starts.

Sam was sent back down to the minors after the 1942 season. He didn't resurface in the major leagues until 1948. When we asked Sam what minor league teams he had played for, he told us, "There were so many that I used to be known as 'formerly of,' 'Sam Nahem, formerly of,' equal to the trade of several players 'to be named later, several jock straps to be named later.' "

In 1948, Sam returned to the Phillies lineup. He pitched in 28 games that year. At the end of the season, Sam retired from baseball. He looks back on his career with good humor: "I raised mediocrity to new heights, or was it depths?" Sam once met Moe Berg, in the 1930s, at the wedding of a Boston Red Sox player. He told us that he thought Berg was a "very smart, very nice man, very intelligent, considerate, a very nice man."

After retiring from baseball, Sam worked for Standard Oil in California. There he became a very active trade unionist. He even headed his local chapter of the Oil, Chemical, and Atomic Workers Union, before his retirement in 1980. Sam's wife passed away twenty years ago. He currently lives in Berkeley, California. Sam Nahem is the uncle of major leaguer Al Silvera.

Years	Games	IP	W	L	GS	SV	PCT	ERA
4	90	$224\frac{1}{3}$	10	8	3	12	.556	4.69

1938, Bro-N, 1941 StL-N, 1942, 1948 Phi-N

Jeff Newman

Jeffrey Lynn Newman was born on September 11, 1948, in Fort Worth, Texas. He was not born to Jewish parents, but later in life he converted to Judaism.

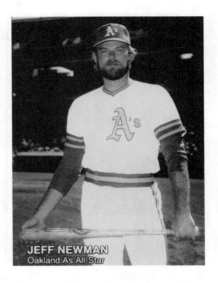

JEFF NEWMAN
Oakland A's All-Star

Jeff attended Paschal High School, in Fort Worth. There, he played on the varsity baseball and basketball teams. After graduation in 1966, Jeff attended Texas Christian University, where he majored in history. He played on TCU's varsity baseball team as a third baseman. In his sophomore year, Jeff batted .350 and was named to the All-Southwest Conference and NCAA All-District first teams. He was also named to the third squad of the NCAA All-American team. In 1969, as a junior, he batted .345 and had 31 RBIs. That year, Jeff was chosen for the for the All-Conference and All-District first teams and he set the TCU record for longest hitting streak, in conference competition, with 14 games. He also set TCU's record for most RBIs, 44; most runs scored in conference play, 32; and he tied the school record for most hits, 57. After graduating from TCU with a B.S. in education, Jeff played semi-pro ball in Fort Worth.

In 1970, Jeff was selected by the Cleveland Indians, in the 26th round of the June free-agent draft. That year, he was assigned to play third base for the Sarasota Indians (Gulf Coast League). With Sarasota, Jeff led the league in RBIs, with 55; tied for the lead in home runs, with 6; and was sixth in the league in batting, with .313. Jeff was selected for the 1970 Gulf Coast League All-Star Game.

In 1971, he was promoted to the Reno Silver Sox (California League). He finished the season with a .269 batting average, in 67 games. Jeff returned to the Silver Sox in 1971, but not as a third baseman. That year, he assumed the position of catcher for the first time in his professional career.

In 1972, Jeff set the California League record for most passed balls in a season, with 51. The next year, he was promoted to San Antonio (Texas League). Jeff improved his catching skills greatly for the 1973 season, when he led all Texas League catchers in assists, with 72; chances accepted, with 720; and double plays, with 10. He also led the league in passed balls, with 30, yet he was still selected for the league's All-Star team.

In 1974, Jeff began the season with Oklahoma City (American Association), before being promoted to Salt Lake City (Pacific Coast League). In 1975, Jeff played for Toledo (International League) and Salt Lake City. In 1976, his contract was purchased by the Oakland A's and he was assigned to play with the Tucson Toros (Pacific Coast League).

In June 1976, Jeff was promoted to the Oakland A's, making his major league debut on June 30. Jeff was used mostly as a catcher, but during his career he played almost every position in the infield, even pitcher. In 1976, Jeff was used primarily in a utility role. He appeared in only 43 games that year, and batted .195. In 1977, he appeared in 94 games for the A's.

On September 14, 1977, Jeff made his only appearance as a pitcher, against the Kansas City Royals. In the 8th inning of the second game of a twinight doubleheader, Jeff was put into the game. He threw one scoreless inning, allowed one hit, and hit one batsman. His lifetime ERA is 0.00. The A's were defeated by the Royals, 6 to 0, in Kansas City.

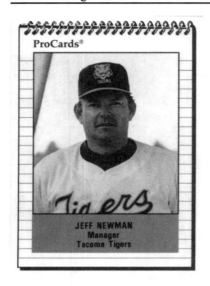

Jeff, during 1978, was used more frequently and in 1979 he appeared in 143 games; that year, he led the club in home runs, with 22. Also in 1979, he was named to the American League squad for the All-Star Game. Jeff's batting averages began to slump between 1980 and 1982. His average slipped in 1980 to .233, then continued to fall below the .200 mark. After the 1982 season, he was traded to the Boston Red Sox. Jeff spent two seasons with the Red Sox before retiring, in 1984. He had a lifetime batting average of .224, in 735 games. His lifetime fielding percentage as a catcher was .981, which is a much better indicator of his real value as a player.

By 1985, Jeff was back in baseball as a roving fielding instructor for the Oakland A's. In 1986, the A's fired their manager, Jackie Moore, before finding a suitable replacement. The A's called up Jeff and asked him if he would like the position. The organization's choice shocked A's fans, who asked "Why Jeff Newman?" The A's organization could offer no real explanation, except that Jeff's appointment was merely temporary. Jeff managed for 10 days. He ended his managing career when Tony LaRussa took over the position on a regular basis. Jeff finished his brief stint as a manager with a 2-8 record.

After managing, Jeff remained with the team, as a coach, for the rest of the season. Following the 1986 season, he was assigned to manage the Modesto A's. He continued his managing career for Huntsville and Tacoma through the 1991 season.

In 1992, Jeff accepted the position as third base coach for the Cleveland Indians. He has held this position through 1997, and his important presence was visible during that year's World Series, which the Indians lost to the Marlins. Jeff Newman lives in Danville, California. He is married and has two children. He enjoys hunting and fishing.

Jeff continued his job as third base coach for the Cleveland Indians into the 1998 season.

Years	Games	AB	H	R	RBI	HR	BA	OBP	FP
9	735	2123	475	189	233	63	.224	.266	.981

1976-82 Oak-A, 1983-84 Bos-A

as Manager

Years	Games	W	L	PCT
1	10	2	8	.200

1986 Oak-A

Max Patkin

Max Patkin was a major league coach and a major league clown. He was the second man to call himself "the clown prince of baseball," a name he adopted after the death of Al Schacht. His gyrations on the base paths, his swinging of 18 bats, his sidewise cap, his rubber legs, his spitting of the same mouthful of water for dozens of eruptions, his filthy, baggy Mets uniform are all the stuff of legend. So are his long rubber face and his gargantuan nose. While Al Schacht always entertained before or between games, Max always performed during the game itself, which made him a target, early in his career, from "purists," who felt he was interrupting the flow of things. Today he is recognized as the spiritual father of all the hundreds of mascots who entertain at major and minor league baseball, and at every other sport, at every level, in this country.

Max Patkin was born in Philadelphia on January 10, 1920, the son of Samuel H. and Rebecca Patkin. Both of Max's parents had come from Russia. Max's father had settled in Philadelphia because he had relatives there. Samuel Patkin ran a delicatessen on Seventh and Dudley Streets, which is the address where Max was born. In 1928, Max's heder class took a trip to Shibe Park. Max fell in love with baseball, a love affair that has lasted him throughout his lifetime.

Max was no great shakes at school, and even managed to flunk a gym class at West Philadelphia High School. But he caught the eye of one of the other gym teachers, the coach of the baseball team, with his high kick when he threw. Max was soon pitcher for the school's second-string team. A wildcat strike by the varsity got Max a chance to pitch in a game against Overbrook High School. Max struck out 15 and won the game. The tall, gangly, and funny-looking pitcher began to attract attention.

Max attended Brown Prep for two years and made a great impression with his victories over college teams. In an exhibition game for the Wentz-Olney amateur club against the House of David, Max won a game, 1–0, against Grover Cleveland Alexander. Max had tryouts with Cincinnati, the Phillies, Brooklyn, and the Red Sox. Finally, he was signed by the Chicago White Sox.

In 1941, Max was assigned to the Wisconsin Rapids (Wisconsin State League). That year he pitched in 27 games, with 10 wins and 8 losses. The next year, he started with the same team, but was fired after he refused to have an operation for bone chips in his shoulder. He was then picked up by Green Bay, in the same league. There he stayed until he was fired for getting into an argument with the pitching coach. That year, 1942, he was in 13 games, for both teams, with 3 wins and 4 losses. During this period, when Max wasn't pitching, he was often used as first base coach. Max would often carry on, in this position, making remarks to the other team's bench, commenting on umpire calls, and so on. These were the first seeds of his great act.

After Max was released by Green Bay, he joined the Navy, and spent most of the Second World War at Pearl Harbor. Often his duties involved pitching baseballs. However, in between duties, he managed to establish a reputation as a kibitzer, a comedian who could "break 'em up on the base paths."

Following the war, Max returned to the minor leagues, to join Wilkes-Barre (Eastern League). After appearing in 5 games—1 win and 1 loss—Max was released. But luck was with him. Right after his release, he was hired to perform his comedy routine during an exhibition game between Harrisburg and its parent team, the Cleveland Indians. Lou Boudreau, the manager of the Indians, liked what he saw and brought Max along to show his stuff to the owner of the Indians, Bill Veeck. Veeck also liked what he saw, and Max was hired as the first base coach for the team. Max served as a coach for the Indians for 1946 and 1947. He would usually coach only during the early innings of games, when his antics would cause less aggravation than later. Nevertheless, his mocking of umpire's calls did get him thrown out of games on several occasions. This led to a nasty editorial in The Sporting News.

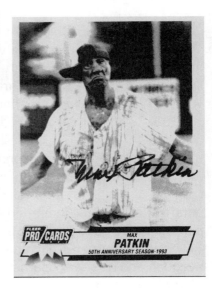

Max went to apologize to Bill Veeck about this. When Veeck heard Max out, he asked him if they had spelled his name right. Max replied yes. Then Veeck asked Max what he could possibly be worried about.

When the Indians became a contender for the pennant, during 1947, Max was released. He began to take his show on the road. He would continue to take his shtick from minor league park to minor league park for practically the next half-century.

When Bill Veeck took over the luckless St. Louis Browns in 1951, Max was back to first base. Max had two further stints in the majors, in 1976 and 1978, with the Chicago White Sox, the team that had originally signed him.

Max was married to Judy Oberndorf, a tall, beautiful blonde. The marriage was not a happy one. Judy was unfaithful and became addicted to prescription drugs and alcohol. She was also violent and abusive to Max and their adopted daughter, Joy. Finally, after 10 years, the Patkins were divorced. Max gave Judy all their property, so he could retain custody of Joy. Judy could not stand the thought of growing old and unattractive. She had several face lifts. On her 50th birthday, she committed suicide. Max's family were very supportive of him during the difficult parts of his life. He was particularly close to his brother, Eddie.

In 1988, Max was featured in the hit motion picture Bull Durham. The picture starred Kevin Costner and Susan Sarandon.

Max officially retired on August 19, 1995, at ceremonies at Reading, Pennsylvania. His uniform and portrait were accepted that day for inclusion in the collection of the Baseball Hall of Fame in Cooperstown. Max is a member of both the Pennsylvania Sports Hall of Fame and the Philadelphia Sports Hall of Fame. Max Patkin lived in King of Prussia, a suburb of Philadelphia, until his death on October 30, 1999 in nearby Paoli.

Barney Pelty

Pelty, St. Louis Americans

While many of the early Jewish ballplayers were content to change their names and hide their Jewish identity, Barney Pelty proudly bore the nickname "The Yiddish Curver."

Barney was born on September 10, 1880, in Farmington, Missouri. He showed natural talent as a right-handed pitcher while still in grammar school. Barney continued his education at Carlton College; the college had offered him free tuition, if he would pitch for their ball team. At Carlton, Barney met his future wife, Eva Warsing. Barney attended and pitched for Carlton College for two years. He then transferred to Blees Military Academy, where he also stayed for two years.

In 1902, Barney received his first bid from a professional ball club. Nashville (Southern League) wanted Barney to pitch for its team. That spring, he injured his arm in practice. Instead of waiting for it to heal, so he could pitch, he decided to try his hand at being a catcher. It didn't take him long to realize that he wasn't cut out for the position, so he returned to his home in Farmington. Following a rest, his injured arm recovered. He returned to pitching with a semi-pro team in Cairo, Illinois.

News of Barney's pitching reached Belden Hill, manager of the Cedar Rapids club (3-I League), and he signed Barney for the 1903 season. Word of Barney's prowess soon spread. There began a bidding war between the Boston Red Sox and the St. Louis Browns over his contract. Unfortunately for Barney, St. Louis won the struggle, because the Red Sox became the first-place club in 1903 and 1904, whereas the Browns ended up in last place for both those years and many more to come.

Barney made his major league debut on August 20, 1903, for the Browns. They were leading the New York Highlanders, 4 to 2, when the Browns' pitcher, Wee Willie Sudhoff, became ill after getting one out in the 9th inning. Barney replaced Sudhoff and retired the two remaining batters, to conclude the game.

Two days later, August 22, Barney made his first start for the Browns. He faced Red Sox pitcher Bill Dinneen. Barney gave up only 8 hits, as the Browns defeated the Red Sox, 2–1. Since Barney won the game without knowing any of the signals, the team considered him good luck. When he didn't pitch, he assisted the team as a coach. On August 31, 1903, he married his fiancée, Eva. Barney finished the year with a 3-3 win-loss record and a 2.40 ERA.

Besides being a ballplayer, Barney was also the proprietor of a notion and bookstore in Farmington. He ran the store in the winter months.

On the Fourth of July, in 1904, Barney pitched a tremendous game against the "Hitless Wonders" Chicago White Sox (the lowest-scoring team to win a World Series). He threw a one-hit, complete-game shutout against the Sox. The Browns won, 3–0. Barney's catcher in that game was Branch Rickey, who would later play a critical role in the integration of baseball, and who would be elected to the Baseball Hall of Fame.

Barney's best year was 1906, when the Browns finished in fifth place. He won 17 games that year, and lost 12, for a percentage of .586. That year, he led the league in opponents' batting average, with .206. Barney pitched an entire three-game series that season, against the White Sox. In 32 innings, Barney gave up just 1 run. But because the Browns scored only 1 run in the series, themselves, they won only 1 of the three games. They lost one of the other games and the third game was a ten-inning, 0–0, tie. Barney's 1906 ERA of 1.59 is still a record for the Browns organization, including their current incarnation as the Baltimore Orioles.

On May 1, 1910, Barney pitched a game for the Browns against the Chicago White Sox. It was the first game held at the new Chicago ballpark, White Sox Park (now known as Comiskey Park). Pelty pitched a shutout, as the Browns defeated the White Sox, 2–0.

Barney served with the Browns until June 1912, when he was claimed on waivers by the Washington Senators. By 1912, Barney was already used up, and the Senators sold him to the minor league Baltimore Orioles after 11 games. He retired from baseball at the end of the season. During the course of his career with the Browns, Barney won 90 games and lost 109. He suffered from a terrible malady that affected all pitchers of the Browns: little run support. If Barney had pitched for a team that gave him the runs he needed, he might today be in the Hall of Fame, like his catcher Branch Rickey.

In 1937, Barney pitched his last game. It was an exhibition game against Hall of Famer Grover Cleveland Alexander. Alexander won the game. After his retirement from playing baseball, Barney did manage a couple of semi-pro teams. Later, he became an inspector for the Missouri State Food and Drug Department and was involved in local politics in his hometown, Farmington. Barney served several terms as alderman of Farmington. He and his wife had one son, who became the city engineer of Farmington.

Barney Pelty died at his home in Farmington, Missouri, on May 24, 1939.

Years	Games	IP	W	L	GS	SV	PCT	ERA
10	266	1908	92	117	217	4	.440	2.63

1903-12 StL-A, 1912 Was-A

Jon Perlman

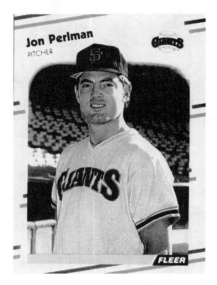

Jonathan Samuel Perlman was born on December 13, 1956, in Dallas, Texas, the son of a Jewish father and a gentile mother. Jon has never considered himself a Jew.

Jon began his professional baseball career in 1979, as a right-handed pitcher for the Midland Cubs. He finished the season with a 4-8 record and a 4.59 ERA. The next season, Jon returned to Midland. That season, he improved his win-loss record to 13-7, with a 4.28 ERA. Jon split the 1981 season between the Iowa Cubs and the Midland Cubs. He pitched his final season for Midland in 1982. That year, he had a 3.66 ERA and a 13-7 win-loss record. Jon pitched for the Iowa Cubs in 1983–85.

Towards the end of the 1985 season, Jon was given a chance to pitch on the Chicago Cubs. He made his major league debut on September 6. He finished the season with a 11.42 ERA in $8\frac{2}{3}$ innings for the Cubs. Despite his high ERA, Jon was not tagged with a loss. After the 1985 season, Jon was traded to the San Francisco Giants organization. He pitched with the Phoenix Giants in 1986 and 1987. In the latter year, Jon pitched in 10 games, in relief, for the San Francisco Giants. He had a 3.97 ERA in $11\frac{1}{3}$ innings. In 1988, Jon was acquired, as a free agent, by the Cleveland Indians organization. He played most of the 1988 season with the Colorado Springs Sky Sox, but Jon did appear in 10 games with the Indians that year. He had a 5.49 ERA in $19\frac{2}{3}$ innings, with 2 losses.

Jon retired from baseball at the end of the season. He had a lifetime ERA of 6.35 and a win-loss record of 1-2, in $39\frac{2}{3}$ innings. Jon Perlman currently lives in Carthage, Texas.

Years	Games	IP	W	L	GS	SV	PCT	ERA
3	26	$39\frac{2}{3}$	1	2	0	0	.333	6.35

1985 Chi-N, 1987 SF-N, 1988 Cle-A

Lefty Phillips

Harold "Lefty" Phillips was born on June 16, 1919, in Los Angeles, California.

Lefty appeared in only five minor league games—as a pitcher with the Bis-bee team in the Arizona–Texas League—before he had to end his playing career because of a sore arm. Lefty continued to work in baseball as a scout for the St. Louis Browns. In 1952, he joined the Brooklyn Dodgers as a scout. With the Dodgers, Lefty discovered and signed many talented players, including Don Drysdale and Ron Fairly.

In 1965, Lefty appeared on the field for the first time as a pitching coach for the World Series–winning Los Angeles Dodgers. He remained a pitching coach with the Dodgers until he took the position of Director of Player Personnel for the California Angels in October, 1968. On May 27, 1969, Lefty was appointed manager of the California Angels. That year the Angels moved from last place to third place in the Western Division. In 1970, they moved up to second place, with a 87-74 record. That year, Lefty was asked to be a coach for the American League All-Star team.

The following year, the Angels fell from second to fourth place, but this was the least of Lefty's problems. That year, one of the players on his team, Alex Johnson, suffered a mental breakdown. Lefty handled Johnson's case poorly by misjudging the player's mental condition. Lefty sided with team owner Gene Autry against Johnson in a way that even further exacerbated Johnson's condition. Johnson was later suspended without pay because of his poor performance; his case went to arbitration, when the Angels refused to put Johnson on the disabled list, where he would have received pay. Later, Johnson, represented by the Baseball Players Association, won the arbitration, on the grounds that mental illness is grounds for disability. Bad feeling arising from this case led to Lefty's being relieved of his job as manager. He did, however, stay on with the Angels organization for one more year as a scout. He was still in this position up to the time of his death.

On June 12, 1972, Lefty Phillips died of asthma at age fifty-three in Fullerton, California. Lefty was married to Roberta and had a son and daughter, Dewayne and Charleen.

Years	Games	W	L	PCT
3	448	222	225	.497

1969-71 Cal-A

Jacob Pike

Jacob Emanuel Pike was born in Brooklyn. He was the younger brother of Boaz and Lipman Pike. Before Jacob began his playing career, he was an umpire for the National Association. He umpired in 1875.

Jacob made his only major league appearance, on August 27, 1877, when he played right field for the Hartford Dark Blues. The Dark Blues played the Cincinnati Red Stockings, the team of Jacob's older brother, Lipman. The game was played in Brooklyn, as were all 1877 home games for the Dark Blues. Amos Booth, pitcher for the Cincinnati Red Stockings, gave up Jacob's only hit, a single, that day. Lip also had one hit that game, and scored the only Cincinnati run. The Dark Blues defeated the Red Stockings, 5 to 1.

The date of Jacob Pike's death is not known.

Years	Games	AB	H	R	RBI	HR	BA	OBP	FP
1	1	4	1	0	0	0	.250	.250	.000

1877 Har-N

Lipman Pike

LIPMAN PIKE

Lipman "Lip" Emanuel Pike was born on May 25, 1845, in New York City. He was the son of Emanuel and Jane Pike. The Pike family were Jews of Dutch origin. Lip had an older brother, Boaz, two younger brothers, Israel and Jacob, and a sister, Julia. His family moved to Brooklyn when he was young.

Boaz was the first of the Pike brothers to play baseball on an organized team. Just one week after his bar mitzvah, Lip appeared in his first recorded baseball game, along with Boaz. This was an amateur game, as were all games before 1866. In 1866, Lip agreed to accept $20 per week to play third base for the Philadelphia Athletics. At the time, many players were being paid by baseball clubs for playing, but the practice was against the rules of the National Association of Base Ball Players. It was made known that Lip was a paid player, and he and two other players were summoned to appear before the judiciary committee of the National Association of Base Ball Players. No one showed up for the hearing, and the case was dropped. Because of this incident, Lip is sometimes referred to as the first professional baseball player.

Lip played in Irvington, New Jersey, in 1867. He left in the middle of the season to play for the Mutuals, known as the Mutes, of New York. This was before the reserve clause; players could simply leave one team to play for another, as they chose. The Mutes were owned by New York political leader "Boss" Tweed. Lip soon left the Mutes because of Tweed's corrupt operation. He then went to Brooklyn to play for the Atlantics.

Lip became famous, on the Atlantics, for excelling in one of the most famous games in history. On June 14, 1870, Lip's team, the Atlantics of Brooklyn, played the Cincinnati Red Stockings, the nation's first fully professional team. The Red Stockings had not been defeated for a season and a half, 130 consecutive games, but on that day their streak was ended by the Atlantics. Lip was crucial in obtaining the final out in the ninth as the Atlantics won, 8 to 7. Lip's fame earned him the nickname "The Iron Batter," and he eventually joined the Red Stockings.

Lip left the Atlantics in 1871 to play for the Troy Haymakers, accepting the position of player-manager. Thus, Lip became not only the first professional Jewish ballplayer but also the first professional Jewish manager. He tied the National Association record for home runs in 1871 with 4, the first year this record was ever kept. This may not sound like many home runs, but Lip played in the era of the dead ball, when it was rare for a player to get a ball out of the infield, much less get a home run. He hit 20 major league home runs during his entire career.

Lip played for Lord Baltimore of Baltimore, in the National Association, for the 1872 and 1873 seasons. He held the National Association undisputed home-run record in 1872 with 6, and in 1873 with 4. Lip became the player-manager of the Hartford, Connecticut, Dark Blues (National Association) in 1874. That year he held records in doubles, with 24, and in slugging average, with .496. Lip was the first batter to win a game by a home run, when he hit a homer in 1874 to win a game, 1 to 0. In 1875, Lip played in the last year of the National Association with the St. Louis Brown Stockings. That year, he had his best batting average, with .343. He again played for the Brown Stockings in 1876, but that year the team joined the National

League in its inaugural season. The National Association collapsed because of gambling and other corruption on the part of both the owners and the players. Lip, however, was always noted for his sobriety, intelligence, and determination.

Lip stayed in the National League in 1877, to play for the famous Cincinnati Red Stockings. He became player-manager for the opening weeks of the season. That year, he held the National League home-run record with 4. Lip played most of the 1878 season with the Red Stockings, but moved to the National League Providence Grays towards the end of it.

In 1879, Lip transferred to play for the Springfield, Massachusetts, National Association team. This new National Association is considered to be a minor league, although at the time it was considered the equivalent of the National League (for a different section of the country). He played for Springfield in order to be closer to his wife and son. Mid-season, Lip became the player-manager of Springfield. The club was forced to close before the end of the year, however, because of financial troubles; Lip finished the year with Holyoke and Albany. He started the next season with the National Association team in Albany, but again money troubles forced the team to fold before season's end. Lip finished the season with the Unions of Brooklyn and the independent New York Metropolitans.

Lip started the 1881 season as co-manager of the new Brooklyn Atlantics and finished the year with the Worchester, Massachusetts, Ruby Legs. Worchester was one of the worst teams in an era when bad teams were being expelled from the National League. The team needed a scapegoat. They decided to blame Lip (who had only played five games with the team) for not fielding a ball up to his potential. Lip was blacklisted from baseball for one year. During that year, he became a haberdasher in Brooklyn. The following year, the Worchester Ruby Legs were thrown out of the National League for their continuing poor record. Lip's haberdashery store became a successful business and a meeting place for local baseball enthusiasts. After the expiration of his year's ban, Lip decided to continue with his business enterprise.

Lip decided to return to baseball only in 1887, at the age of forty-two. He joined the American Association New York Metropolitans, appearing in only one game, because the years had taken a toll on his playing ability. Lip played in 425 major league games in his ten-year career. He had a .326 batting average and 20 home runs. He stayed in baseball as an umpire in the American Association for two more years.

Lip died of heart disease on October 10, 1893, in Brooklyn, at the age of forty-eight. His funeral was a notable event, attended by much of the Jewish and baseball communities of Brooklyn. The services were conducted by Rabbi Geismer of Temple Israel and, according to The Brooklyn Eagle, he "paid fitting tribute to the exemplary life led by the deceased."

In 1914, Francis Richter, editor of Sporting Life of Philadelphia, picked Lip for a fantasy 1870-to-1880 All-Star team, as an outfielder. As a reminder that he was not forgotten, at the very first election for members of the Baseball Hall of Fame, in 1936, Lipman Pike received one vote. He was elected to the Jewish Sports Hall of Fame in Netanya, Israel, in 1985.

Years	Games	AB	H	R	RBI	HR	BA	OBP	FP
10	425	1983	637	433	332	20	.321	.337	.834

1871 Tro-National Association, 1872-73 Bal-National Association, 1874 Har-National Association, 1875 StL-National Association, 1876 StL-N, 1877-78 Cin-N, 1878-Pro-N, 1881 Wor-N, 1887 NY-American Association

as Manager

Years	Games	W	L	PCT
3	71	20	51	.282

1871 Tro-National Association, 1874 Har-National Association, 1877 Cin-N

Jake Pitler

Although Jake Pitler played more than one full year with the Pittsburgh Pirates, he is best remembered as the quirky and good-hearted first base coach of the Brooklyn Dodgers during their "Golden Age." It was Jake who waived on the steals of Jackie Robinson and watched the sacrifices of Podres and Newcombe. It was Jake who watched the first game of Koufax, shaking his head in disbelief. Jake is part and parcel of the legendary past of Brooklyn and its Bums.

Jacob Albert Pitler was born on April 22, 1894, in New York City. He was one of seven children. Jake's family moved to Pittsburgh, Pennsylvania, where he grew up. Jake had two brothers who were active in sports. His brother Harry became a prominent lightweight boxer under the name of Johnny Ray, and later would manage boxer Billy Conn. His brother Dave, in 1918, became a varsity football player at the University of Pittsburgh.

Jake sold peanuts, soda pop, and newspapers at the Pirates' Forbes Field. His deadpan comic wit earned Jake the friendship of many of the players on the team, including Honus Wagner, George Gibson, Lefty Leifeld, and manager Fred Clarke. Jake would frequently work out with the players in their pre-game practice. He became a star in the semi-pro leagues of Pittsburgh.

Jake began his professional career with Connelsville, Pennsylvania, in 1912, but he didn't last long with the team. He reentered baseball in 1913, with Jackson (South Michigan League). The infielder played there again in 1914, and batted .301. At the end of the season, Jake was acquired by the Detroit Tigers; they gave Jake a tryout, but never put him in a game, and promptly returned him to Jackson. Jake played one more season in Jackson, before the club folded in 1915. He managed to join the Chattanooga Lookouts (Southern Association) later that year. Jake batted around .360 with Chattanooga. He remained with the Lookouts until being promoted to the Pittsburgh Pirates in 1917.

Jake had many people helping him get to the majors. Charley Schmidt, of the Southern Association's Memphis club, wrote numerous letters to the Pittsburgh Pirates' owner, Barney Dreyfuss, describing Jake's ability. In one letter he described Jake as "the most peppery kid in the Southern Association and has more ambition than all the rest of the players combined." Jake was touted as the jewel of the Chattanooga Lookouts and one of the greatest infielders to come out of the Southern Leagues. His batting was compared to such former Southern League outfielders as "Shoeless" Joe Jackson and Tris Speaker.

Jake made his major league debut, at second base, in Forbes Field on May 30, 1917. That day, he singled, stole a base, and scored a run, but the Pirates lost, to the Cubs, 6 to 5. On August 22, 1917, Jake set a major-league record for most putouts by a second baseman in one game, with 15. The Pirates lost the game, however, to the Brooklyn Dodgers, in 22 innings.

Jake had trouble hitting in the majors, but one day he hit 2 triples off Hall of Fame pitcher Grover Cleveland Alexander. Jake finished the 1917 season with a .232 batting average, in 109 games. He returned to the Pirates' lineup in 1918. On May 24, Jake stole 2 bases in one inning to tie a major-league record, but the Boston Braves won, 6 to 3, at Forbes Field. Jake had played in just 2 games of the 1918 season before being optioned to Jersey City (International League). On the way to New Jersey, Jake jumped his contract to play "outlaw" baseball in Pennsylvania. For this act, he was banned from the major-league farm system for nine years. He returned to organized baseball in 1928, to play for Binghamton (New York–Pennsylvania League).

In 1929, Jake was not only player, but also was manager of the Elmira, New York, baseball club. He retired from playing in 1933, but continued to manage in Hazelton, Scranton, Springfield, and Portsmouth. In 1938, Jake bought the team that gave him his first baseball job: Jeannette, Pennsylvania. Although he established himself as manager, he was forced to disband the club at the end of the year, due to poor attendance. Later that year, Jake became supervisor of training for an oil company league.

In 1939, Jake got his "big break." He was offered a job as manager for a team that was a farm club for the Brooklyn Dodgers. He became both business and field manager of the Olean club (Pony League), managing for 4 seasons for Olean and winning 2 championships. Jake always considered 1940 his greatest year as a manager. "We were 15 games out of first place, on July 4, and won the pennant by eight games," he would boast. After two seasons at the helm of Newport News (Piedmont League), Jake became a scout for the Dodgers. His greatest achievement was the discovery and signing of Gil Hodges.

In 1947, Jake became first base coach of the Brooklyn Dodgers; he would hold the position until 1957. During the 11 years that Jake coached on the Dodgers, the club won 6 pennants and 1 World Series. During each of those postseason series, Jake would not be present on the High Holidays, either Rosh Hashanah or Yom Kippur. The radio and television announcers would explain why coach Pitler was not present.

Jake became popular with both the new and veteran players of the Dodgers. His straight-faced humor would help create a warm camaraderie with them. He was a specialist in exchanging salty insults. Jake was also known as a great "straight man." He would invite the players to play their practical jokes at his expense and would react with complete surprise.

In 1954, some of Jake's friends suggested a "Jake Pitler Night" at Ebbets Field. At first he refused, but after great urging he consented—only on the condition that all of the money collected would be donated to the children's wing of Beth-El Hospital in Brooklyn. Over $3,000 was collected to establish the Jake Pitler Pediatric Playroom for underprivileged, disabled children. On September 16, 1956, Jake was honored with a second "Jake Pitler Night." This second "Night" was during a twinight doubleheader. Again, all gifts were donated to Beth-El Hospital. The second "Jake Pitler Night" and Jake's Pediatric Playroom were memorialized in a poem by the Pulitzer Prize–winning poet Marianne Moore in 1956. In her poem "Hometown Piece for Messrs. Alston and Reese" there appear the lines: "Jake Pitler and his Playground 'get a Night'—/ Jake, that hearty man, made heartier by a harrier/ who can bat as well as field—Don Demeter."

In 1957, Walter O'Malley launched his "Gold Rush" to the West Coast. The Dodgers opened the 1958 season in Los Angeles, not Brooklyn, but without Jake. Jake would not leave his beloved borough, even to coach for the Dodgers. He did accept a position to scout for the Dodgers in the New York area, but never again returned to the playing field.

Jake Pitler died on February 3, 1968, in Binghamton, New York. He had a wife, Henrietta, and a son, Lawrence. Jake was inducted into the Brooklyn Dodgers Hall of Fame in 1989.

Years	Games	AB	H	R	RBI	HR	BA	OBP	FP
2	111	383	89	40	23	0	.232	.298	.962

1917-18 Pit-N

Scott Radinsky

Scott Radinsky was born on March 3, 1968, in Glendale, California. Scott's mother is Jewish, his father was not. Scott's father died of lung cancer in 1984. Scott has stated that he takes no interest in religion, Jewish or otherwise.

Scott graduated from Simi Valley High School in 1986. That year he was drafted by the Chicago White Sox. Until the time he was drafted, Scott didn't take a strong interest in professional baseball. He was sent to play with the Sarasota White Sox that year, and pitched in 7 games. In 1987, he pitched with both the Sarasota and Peninsula White Sox, with a win-loss record of 4 and 10. Scott didn't see much action in 1988, pitching in only 5 games for Sarasota. In 1989, he had a great year, pitching a 7–5 win-loss record and a 1.75 ERA.

In 1990, Scott was invited to attend spring training camp with the White Sox. He pitched impressively and earned a role on the team as a reliever. Scott was the first pitcher in six years to go from a single-A team to the major league club. The last pitcher to do that was Dwight Gooden.

Scott made his major league debut on opening day in 1990. He earned his first win the next day, against the Milwaukee Brewers, and ended the season with an impressive win-loss record of 6 and 1 and 4 saves. In 1991, Scott was not scored upon in 53 of 67 appearances with the White Sox, and ended with a 2.02 ERA. In 1992, Scott recorded a career-high 15 saves. He led the club in appearances, with 68. The next year, Scott pitched in a career-high 73 games for the White Sox. He finished the season strong, stranding 30 out of his last 34 runners. Scott got a chance to pitch in the 1993 American League Championship Series. He pitched in $1\frac{2}{3}$ innings, in 4 games, and gave up 3 hits and 2 earned runs. His ERA in the championship series was 10.80. The White Sox lost the Series to the Toronto Blue Jays, in 6 games.

Before spring training in 1994, Scott was diagnosed with Hodgkin's disease. He spent the entire season on the 60-day disabled list and underwent chemotherapy and radiation treatment. During the season, Scott coached for his former high school's team in Simi Valley, California. Scott gradually recovered and was well enough to return to the White Sox lineup in 1995. Not fully recovered, 1995 was not one of his strongest seasons, but he did pitch in 46 games.

Scott was granted free agency in 1996 and signed with the Los Angeles Dodgers. He began the 1996 season with 9.2 scoreless innings in 11 outings. Scott was put on the 15-day disabled list on March 30 (retroactive to March 28) with tendonitis in his left middle finger. He ended the season with a 5–1 win-loss record and a 2.41 ERA. In 1997, he had another excellent year; he had a 2.89 ERA in $62\frac{1}{3}$ innings pitched.

Scott is famous for one other thing besides baseball. He is one of the leading punk rock singers in the country. Scott started his music career, with his brother Brian, in the band Scared Straight, which later changed its name to Ten Foot Pole. Scott, who had been lead singer with this group, separated from it because of artistic differences, after recording their 1994 album "Rev." He is now lead singer with the punk rock band Pulley. Pulley has recorded an album titled "Esteem Driven Engine." Scott tours with Pulley in the off-season. He has also played drums with fellow pitcher Jack McDowell's band V.I.E.W.

Scott Radinsky currently lives with his wife, Darlenys (née Cardenas), in Simi Valley, California. In the off-season he enjoys mountain biking.

During the early months of the 1998 season, Scott's position for the Dodgers was shifted from a middle reliever to a closer. He had an excellent ERA, below 2.50, and he wracked up numerous saves.

Years	Games	IP	W	L	GS	SV	PCT	ERA
10	555	$479\frac{2}{3}$	42	25	0	52	.627	3.34

1990-93, 1995, Chi-A, 1996-98 LA-N, 1999-2000 St. L-N

Steve Ratzer

Steve Ratzer was the first Jewish player to play on a major league team in Canada. The team was the Montreal Expos.

Steven Wayne Ratzer was born in Paterson, New Jersey, on September 9, 1953. His parents were Aaron and Florence Ratzer. Steve's father was an executive vice-president of National Shirt Shops. Steve and his two younger siblings were raised in New York City, Steve attending Flushing's John Bowne High School, where he played on the baseball team. A right-handed pitcher, Steve was selected in his senior year for the All-City Baseball Team. Later, he attended St. John's University, graduating in 1975. On graduation, he was signed, as a free agent, by the Montreal Expos.

STEVE RATZER   P

Steve's first assignment, for 1975, was to Lethbridge, Alberta (Pioneer League). At Calgary Airport, while waiting for a connecting flight to Lethbridge, Steve received the news that his father had died of a heart attack. He flew back to New York and sat shiva for his father before flying back to Lethbridge to begin his baseball career. Steve was 3-4 that year with Lethbridge, appearing in 30 games, with an ERA of 2.33. The next year, 1976, he played for West Palm Beach (Florida State League). There, he pitched in 57 games, with an 8-8 record and a 3.42 ERA. For most of the 1977 season, he pitched for Quebec (Eastern League). There, he had a 2-6 record, in 26 games, with a 1.61 ERA. At the end of the season, he was transferred to the Denver Bears (American Association). Steve made two relief appearances in the playoffs, getting a win and allowing no runs.

For the seasons 1978 to 1980, Steve continued to pitch for Denver. In 1980, he had a 15-4 record with a 3.59 ERA. His 15 wins led the league, and he was selected as American Association Pitcher of the Year. Steve had only 29 walks in 163 innings. Before the end of the season, he was given a chance to play for the Expos. Steve debuted on October 5, 1980, starting the game and pitching the first four innings. This would be Steve's only start in the majors. The game was the season finale and the Expos were facing the Phillies at Olympic Stadium. Pete Rose started off the game with a leadoff hit off Steve. Steve went on to give up 9 hits and 5 runs, in his four innings of work. The Expos went on to win the game, 8–7. Steve spent that winter playing for Escogido ("The Chosen") in the Dominican Republic, under the management of Felipe Alou. Steve was 5-1 with Escogido, with an ERA of 1.24. His 14 saves broke the league record, previously held by Kent Tekulve. Steve also won 3 games in the championship series. Also, his team won the pennant and

Steve was selected as Most Valuable Player.

Steve played in 12 games for the Expos during the 1981 season. He pitched his only major league loss on May 14, 1981, a loss to the Dodgers and Fernando Valenzuela. The game was tied up in the 9th, when Pedro Guerrero led off the inning with a home run off Steve. Steve had his only major league victory on May 28, against the Phillies, at Veterans Stadium. He pitched one scoreless inning of relief and got the 6–3 victory. Larry Christenson got the loss.

Steve pitched 13 games for the Expos. He was 1-1. His major league lifetime ERA was 7.17. Steve finished the 1981 season with Denver, where he was 7-3, with a 3.42 ERA. During the winter season, he returned to Escogido, where, once more, his team won the pennant and where he was again selected as MVP. During December 1981, Steve was traded to the Mets. During 1982, he pitched for the Tidewater Tides (International League). Steve was 11-7 for the Tides and was chosen "Rolaids Minor League Fireman of the Year." Steve was then traded to the Chicago White Sox, and this brought him back, for 1983, to Denver.

By this time, Steve had been pitching for 9 seasons, as well as 6 winter seasons in Venezuela and the Dominican Republic. He had played on 9 championship teams. Steve decided to call it quits, so he could spend more time with his family. Steve Ratzer is married to the former Janet Eifert. They have 3 children. Steve left baseball to work in the restaurant business in the Denver area. He currently lives in Palm Harbor, Florida.

Years	Games	IP	W	L	GS	SV	PCT	ERA
2	13	$21\frac{1}{3}$	1	1	1	0	.500	7.17

1980-81 Mon-N

Jimmie Reese

When Jimmie Reese died in 1994, he was still employed as a coach by the California Angels, concluding a seventy-seven year career, the longest in baseball history. Jimmie Reese was born Hymie Solomon on October 1, 1905, in Los Angeles, California.

Jimmie began his career as a batboy in 1917, for the Los Angeles team of the Pacific Coast League. He became a star of that league, as an infielder, in the 1920s, before being purchased by the Yankees in 1929. Jimmie spent the years 1930 and 1931 with the Yankees, primarily as a second baseman. His first-year batting average was an impressive .346, but this slipped to .241 in 1931, and 1932 saw him traded to the St. Louis Cardinals. Following his year in St. Louis, he returned to the Pacific Coast League for a number of productive seasons, being still active in 1936.

After his playing career, Jimmie became active as both coach and scout for various minor league teams. In 1973, he was a coach with the California Angels. In 1992, he served as the honorary captain of the American League All-Star Team.

While a member of the Yankees, Jimmie was roommate and confidant of Babe Ruth. Jimmie commented about Ruth that he could party all night and hit a ball 500 feet the next day. He once quipped that he was the roommate of Babe Ruth's suitcase. But Jimmie said the Babe treated him like a son, and he called Ruth the finest man he ever knew.

Jimmie's longevity in baseball may be attributed to his unique ability as a fungo hitter. This ability—to be able to hit to any corner of a stadium at will, with his fungo bat—made him invaluable for fielding practice. Among the feats attributed to Jimmie and his fungo bat were the abilities to hit a flagpole high above the stadium on the first try and the excellent pitching of batting practice. Jimmie even played rounds of golf with only his fungo bat and a putter. A skilled woodworker, he made a special fungo bat just for himself: flat on one side so he could use it to scoop up balls from the ground.

One of the minor league teams that Jimmie coached was the 1952 San Diego Padres, under the management of the legendary pitcher Lefty O'Doul. This team included three Jewish players, all of whom made it to the majors: Murray Franklin, Herb Gorman, and Allen Richter. Apparently Jimmie did not appear to be Jewish, and the name that he'd taken professionally gave no clue to his origins. Richter, when we contacted him a few years ago, had not been aware that Jimmie was Jewish, though he was well aware that this was true of Gorman and Franklin. A story illustrates this point:

One of the greatest baseball enthusiasts of all time was Jewish songwriter Harry Ruby, whose songs include "Babyface" and "Who's Sorry Now?" Ruby had grown up in the same neighborhood as Al Schacht and the two men were friends from childhood. They often played ball together, and Ruby continued to fancy himself as a pitcher well into his later years. Red Smith called Ruby the "world's greatest baseball fan." Sometime during the mid-1920s, Ruby was pitching in an exhibition game with a mixed team of celebrities and players of the Pacific Coast League. Ruby's catcher was Ike Danning, and the two men decided, instead of using signals, because no one else on the field appeared to be Jewish, to simply indicate their choice of pitches in Yiddish. Jimmie Reese got 4 hits for 4 at-bats. After the game, Ruby, who followed the doings in the Pacific Coast League very closely, complimented Jimmie, but told him he was surprised—as he wasn't aware that Jimmie was such a good hitter. "I guess you also don't know," replied Jimmie, "that my name used to be Hymie Solomon."

Jimmie Reese's uniform number has been retired and other honors have been paid him. Through his playing, his scouting, and his coaching he has left his imprint on four generations of baseball players.

Years	Games	AB	H	R	RBI	HR	BA	OBP	FP
3	232	742	206	123	70	8	.278	.324	.975

1930-31 NY-A, 1932 StL-N

Al Richter

Allen Gordon Richter was born on February 7, 1927, in Norfolk, Virginia. He was the youngest of the three children of Sol and Flora Richter. Al's father had been born in England, but was raised in New York. He was a justice of the peace. Al's mother had been born in Baltimore, Maryland. Al graduated from Norfolk's Maury High School, where he played on the baseball, football, and basketball teams.

In 1945, Al was signed as a shortstop by Louisville, Kentucky (American Association), an affiliate of the Boston Red Sox. He played briefly with Louisville, and then Roanoke, that year, before being drafted by the U.S. Army Air Corps. Al served 18 months with the Air Corps, then returned to Louisville for the start of the 1947 season. He completed 1947 with Lynn, Massachusetts (New England League), and Oneonta, New York (Canadian–American League). Also in 1947, Al began attending college during the off-season, at the University of Miami.

Al played the next two seasons with Scranton, Pennsylvania (Eastern League). He returned to Louisville for 1950. On October 16, however, Al's contract was purchased by the Boston Red Sox. On April 2, 1951, he was optioned back to Louisville, and played most of the season there, batting .321.

On September 20, 1951, Al was recalled to Boston. He made his major league debut, at Fenway Park, three days later. Al was used as a pinch-hitter for Red Sox catcher Les Moss in the 9th inning and hit into a double play. The Yankees won the game by a score of 6 to 1. On September 30, Al got his only major league hit, in Yankee Stadium. It was a single, in 4 at-bats, off Yankee Pitcher Spec Shea. The Yankees won the game by a score of 3 to 0. Al appeared in a total of 5 games for the Red Sox that year. At the end of the 1951 season, in a ceremony at Fenway Park, he was awarded, the "Look Magazine Award," as the minor league All-Star Shortstop of the year.

In 1952, Al played with the San Diego Padres (Pacific Coast League). The Padres were managed by Lefty O'Doul, a close friend of many Hollywood movie stars, who would invite many of the celebrities into the team clubhouse. (It was Lefty who introduced Joe DiMaggio to Marilyn Monroe.) On the Padres, Al played with Herb Gorman and Murray Franklin and was coached by Jimmie Reese. In 1953, Al was returned to Louisville. On September 7 that year, he was returned to the Red Sox. He appeared in one game, as a shortstop, but didn't receive an at-bat. That year, Al graduated from the University of Miami with a degree in business administration.

In 1954, Al was signed by the Saint Louis Cardinals organization. He was assigned to play shortstop for their farm club in Rochester, New York (International League). In 1955, Al was selected Most Popular Player in the International League. After the 1955 season, he played winter ball in the Dominican Republic. 1955 was his last season of professional baseball; he retired with a lifetime major league batting average of .091, in only 11 at-bats.

After retiring from baseball, Al Richter began a career in real estate and in food merchandising. He also hosted a fifteen-minute television show prior to the "Sunday Game of the Week," called "Spotlight on Sports," from 1958 to 1964. Al is married to Ann Fulcher and they have one child. In 1983, Al was inducted into the Norfolk, Virginia, Sports Hall of Fame, which is housed in Harbor Park, home of the Norfolk Tides. Al currently lives in Virginia Beach, Virginia.

Years	Games	AB	H	R	RBI	HR	BA	OBP	FP
2	6	11	1	1	0	0	.091	.286	1.000

1951, 1953 Bos-A

Dave Roberts

David Arthur Roberts was born on September 11, 1944, in
Gallipolis, Ohio. Dave is the son of a Jewish father and a gentile mother.

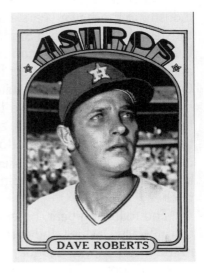

In 1963, Dave was signed by the Philadelphia Phillies organization. He began his professional baseball career with
Spartanburg (West Carolina League). That year, the southpaw
pitcher's 1.79 ERA led the league. In 1964, Dave was promoted to Asheville (Southern League). From Asheville, he moved
to Kinston, North Carolina, (Carolina League), Columbus (International League), and Elmira (Eastern League), until reaching the majors in 1969. He played in the Phillies', Pirates', and
Padres' minor league systems. In 1966, Dave led the Southern
League in shutouts, for Asheville. In 1968, he led the International League in wins, 18, and in complete games.

Dave made his major league debut on September 6, 1969,
with the San Diego Padres. That year, he pitched in a total of 22 games with a 4.78 ERA. In
1971, Dave had the second-lowest ERA in the National League; his 2.10 ERA, in 37 games,
was the lowest in his career.

In 1972, Dave was traded to the Houston Astros. He was again traded, in 1976, to the
Detroit Tigers, and then again, in the middle of the 1977 season, to the Chicago Cubs. In
1979, Dave was traded to the San Francisco Giants. He split the 1979 season between San
Francisco and the Pittsburgh Pirates. In 1980, he pitched for Pittsburgh and the Seattle Mariners. He pitched for the New York Mets in 1981, but retired after the '81 season. Dave
Roberts had a lifetime 3.78 ERA and a 103-125 record, in 445 games, played for 8 different
major league teams.

Years	Games	IP	W	L	GS	SV	PCT	ERA
13	445	2099	103	125	277	15	.452	3.78

1969-71 SD-N, 1972-75 Hou-N, 1976-77 Det-A, 1977-78 Chi-N, 1979 SF-N, 1979-80 Pit-N,
1980 Sea-A, 1981 NY-N

Saul Rogovin

Saul Walter Rogovin was born in Brooklyn, on October 10, 1923,
the son of Jacob and Bessie Rogovin, devoted parents of their only
child. He was also a true son of Brooklyn, attending the borough's
schools and playing in its sandlots. Saul attended Abraham Lincoln
High School and played on its team as an infielder. During the final
game of the 1940 season, he hit a home run that won for his team
the game against James Monroe High School, 11–7, and gave his
school the Public School Athletic League title.

Just out of high school, the Dodgers took a look at Saul at a tryout
in Georgia. They didn't sign the seventeen-year-old. Saul played for a
brief time with Beaver Falls, PA, a Class D team, but the club folded

and he was a free agent once more.

Saul took a job as an assembly worker in the Brewster Aeronautical Plant, an essential industry in those war years. He played with the plant team, and during a game was spotted by the Jewish umpire Dolly Stark. In 1944, on Stark's recommendation, Saul had a tryout at the Giants' wartime training camp at Lakewood, New Jersey. Manager Mel Ott liked what he saw, and signed Saul to a contract for Jersey City. Saul had told Ott that he was a first baseman, but Ott thought he was better suited to the outfield. Saul was used in just 2 games for Jersey City before his contract was sold to Chattanooga (Southern Association), where he was used on third base. Then Red Lucas, a coach for the team, recommended that Saul try pitching. Saul thought about it. On the bottom half of a doubleheader against Birmingham, in the last game of the 1945 season, Saul asked the manager, Bert Niehoff, if he could pitch the game. Niehoff let him, and he shut out Birmingham with just 4 hits. Saul never looked back: He was a pitcher.

The following year, he was traded to Pensacola, but had difficulty finding a place on the team. Wally Dashiell, the general manager, went to bat for Saul and wrote letters to every club in the International League, touting the virtues of his extra pitcher. Buffalo decided to take a look at Rogovin. The manager, Paul Richards, liked what he saw in the big right-hander and liked even more the potential he perceived in Saul. Saul was signed for the 1947 season with Buffalo. Richards brought Saul along slowly. He started him in only six games, and every time he had Saul pitch, Richards himself took over the catching responsibilities, so he could stay close to his young pitcher. That winter, Saul pitched in Venezuela to gain further seasoning.

In 1948, Richards' careful grooming and Saul's extra practice began to pay off. Saul won 13 games for Buffalo. The Detroit Tigers had a deal where they could select two players from Buffalo; they took Saul and Joe Ginsberg. Saul debuted for the Tigers on April 28, 1949. He appeared in only 5 games for the Tigers that year, pitching only $5\frac{2}{3}$ innings, with an ERA of 14.29. The Tigers were not happy and sent Saul back to Buffalo. There, Saul won 19 games, with an ERA of about 3.50.

Saul started 1950 with the Tigers at a night exhibition game in Memphis. The cold night air and overexertion brought on a bout of arm problems that ruined his year and that would haunt Saul for the rest of his career. He managed to pitch in 11 games in 1950 for the Tigers, with 2 wins and 1 loss. His ERA was 4.50. Saul did hit a grand-slam home run during the season. But by August it was clear that he was not improving, and he was sent down to Toledo to try to work it out. Before the end of the season, however, he was sent home.

Saul was back with Detroit for 1951 with a rested arm, but after a few bad games the Tigers placed his name on the waiver wire. His old manager, Paul Richards, now manager of the Chicago White Sox, was quick to pick him up, and Saul was traded on May 15 for pitcher Bob Cain. Richards pitched Saul every 5th day and did not put him in the bullpen. Saul's ERA had been 5.25 with the Tigers; it dropped to 2.48 with Chicago. Even taking the two averages together, Saul led the league in ERA, with 2.78. He ended the season 12-8, a .600 percentage. But even in the games he lost that year, Saul was impressive. Seven of his losses were by only 1 run and the eighth was by 2. The following year, 1952, his record was 14-9, a .609 percentage. In a game against the Boston Red Sox on September 14, Saul struck out 14 batters in 16 innings, before a reliever took over for him. Saul's ERA for the year was 3.85.

Despite his successes, Saul suffered periodic troubles with his sore pitching arm. At first, Richards was sympathetic to him and encouraged Saul not to pitch when his arm was sore. But after a while, when stories started to appear in the press critical of the power pitcher and his temperamental ways, Richards began to grow less patient.

At the start of 1953, Saul was showing good stuff. His first victory was a six-hit shutout of the Tigers. But as the season progressed, Saul's arm became more troublesome. By early August, he was on the disabled list. He returned only in September, and pitched a four-hit shutout of the Cleveland Indians. But Saul finished the year with a 7-12 record and Richards had seen enough. Saul was traded on December 10, 1953, to the Cincinnati Reds.

Saul did not see any major league playing time in 1954. In 1955, he appeared in 14 games with the Baltimore Orioles, before being traded to the Phillies. His ERA was 4.56 with the Orioles, but dropped to 3.08 with Philadelphia. Saul was 1-8 with Baltimore and 5-3 with the Phillies. While being used as a reliever with the Phillies, he retired 32 batters in a row in two games. Saul had a 7-6 record with the Phillies in 1956, with a 4.98 ERA. However, he appeared in only 22 games, still plagued by his sore arm. The next year, 1957, was Saul's last in baseball. After pitching in 4 games—no wins, no losses, and an ERA of 9.00—he decided to call it quits. Saul had played 8 years in the majors. He pitched in 150 games, with 48 wins and 48 losses. His lifetime ERA was 4.06.

After his retirement, Saul went through a period of depression. He found he could not go to ballgames or keep up contacts with his old friends from baseball days, and he became a loner. Even his work for a liquor company gave him no satisfaction.

When he was in his early fifties, Saul decided to go back to school and get a college degree. At first, he attended Manhattan Community College, but then he transferred to City College. Saul graduated with a degree in English education and got a job teaching at Hughes High School in the New York City School System. He taught English primarily, but he was also used for some sections of physical education.

In 1979, after years of silence, Saul returned to the limelight by reintroducing himself to the baseball world through a column in The New York Times, written by Red Smith. After that, Saul began to appear at reunions and at signings. He was no longer a lost man afraid of his past, but a man who had come to terms with it. Saul Rogovin died at St. Vincent's Hospital in New York, of bone cancer, on January 23, 1995. He was survived by his wife, Evelyn.

Years	Games	IP	W	L	GS	SV	PCT	ERA
8	150	883⅔	48	48	121	2	.500	4.06

1949-51 Det-A, 1951-53 Chi-A, 1955 Bal-A, 1955-57 Phi-N

Al Rosen

Albert Leonard "Flip" Rosen was born on leap day (February 29) in 1924, in Spartanburg, South Carolina. As a child he was sickly, suffering from asthma. When he was quite young, his parents, Louis and Rose, were divorced. Al and his brother, Jerry, went to live with their mother, in Miami, Florida. For his health, his mother encouraged Al to participate in sports. The bullies in the neighborhood, often anti-Semitic, encouraged him to learn how to fight. Al's asthma eventually disappeared.

Al became a standout in high school baseball and semi-pro softball. He earned his nickname, "Flip," as a softball pitcher, because of the way he flipped the ball to the batter. Starting in 1941, and at the very lowest

levels, Al began to play minor league ball. Later he would move up through the levels of the minors, while he began to attend college and to participate in college-level sports. As a boxer, Al soon held Florida's intercollegiate title, and he was an enthusiastic participant in college football. He completed his college degree between baseball seasons.

Al served in the U.S. Navy during the Second World War. He left the Navy, in 1946, as a lieutenant.

Beginning in 1946, Al established an outstanding batting record in the minors. That year he played for Pittsfield, Massachusetts, and was chosen as the Most Valuable Rookie for the Canadian–American League. In 1947, he played for Oklahoma City (Texas League) and was chosen as the league's Most Valuable Player. After a brief period with the Cleveland Indians at the start of the 1948 season, Al was assigned to Kansas City (American Association). July 26– 27, 1948, he hit five consecutive home runs—a rare feat. That year, he batted .327 and was chosen the league's Rookie of the Year. At the end of the year, he was recalled to the home club and served as a pinch-hitter in the 1948 World Series. The next year, 1949, was another divided one for Al. He played in 23 games for Cleveland, but spent most of the year with the San Diego Padres (Pacific Coast League).

Al's real arrival in the majors, in 1950, as the regular third baseman for the Cleveland Indians, was remarkable. His rookie year saw him take the American League home-run title, with 37, which set a rookie record. Al also led his league in assists, with 322. That year, he was named Rookie of the Year.

The following year, 1951, he tied a major league record with 4 grand-slam home runs. He also led the league in games played, with 154. He repeated this last feat in 1953. Also in 1953, Al was elected unanimously as the Most Valuable Player—the first person ever to be so elected. Al led his league in RBIs in 1952 and 1953. In 1953, he also again took the home-run title. In the same year, he again led the league in assists, with 338, as well as in double plays, with 38. Al represented the American League in every All-Star team from 1952 to 1955. In the 1954 game, he led his team to victory and tied two All-Star records, with two homers and 5 RBIs. In the 1954 World Series, in which the Giants swept the Indians 4–0, Al batted .250 for 12 plate appearances

Al had a reputation as a player who would not tolerate anti-Semitism and he had the title of a boxing champion to back up his views. On one occasion, a teammate of Saul Rogovin's called Rosen a "Jew bastard." Al walked over to the opposing dugout and asked whether the "son of bitch who called me a Jew bastard" would like to step forward and say it again. Needless to say, no one stepped forward. Once, in 1951, newspaperman Ed Sullivan published a story that Al was really a Catholic. The infuriated Al insisted the paper print a retraction. He added that he'd belonged to a synagogue for most of his life. (As this book clearly demonstrates, many Jewish players changed their names to sound less Jewish. Al is quoted as having said that he wished his name was Rosenthal or Rosenstein, so people could have even less doubt of his Jewishness.)

Starting on May 13, 1954, a series of injuries lessened Al's effectiveness on the field. Soon, the Cleveland fans "got on" Al, booing him when he missed a play at third. A bitter byproduct of his troubles was a conflict with his old friend and strongest supporter, the general manager of the Indians, Hank Greenberg. Though still in demand, Al retired in 1956, not wishing to play at less than his best.

Al played 10 years in the majors, all with the Cleveland Indians. His batting average was .285. He had 1063 hits in 1044 games, including 165 doubles, 20 triples, and 192 homers. He walked 587 times. His fielding percentage on third base was .961 and .981 when covering first.

Following his retirement, Al had a successful career in Wall Street. He followed this with an equally successful third career, in the management side of major league baseball. Al served in executive positions with the Yankees (president and CEO 1978–80), the Astros (president and general manager 1981–85), and the Giants (president and general manager 1986–92). In 1987, Al Rosen was elected Major League Executive of the Year. He lives in Rancho Mirage, California.

Years	Games	AB	H	R	RBI	HR	BA	OBP	FP
10	1044	3725	1063	603	717	192	.285	.386	.961

1947-56 Cle-A

Goody Rosen

Goodwin George "Goody" Rosen is the only Jewish baseball player in the Canadian Baseball Hall of Fame. He was inducted into the Hall in 1984.

Goody was born on August 28, 1912, in Toronto, Canada. His Russian born parents were Samuel and Rebecca Rosen; they had come to Canada from Minsk. Goody was the fifth of eight children. His earliest memories were of playing ball in the streets of Toronto. When old enough, he played in Playground Ball, a Canadian youth league. When he was fourteen, his team won the Canadian Amateur Baseball Championship. A little later, he joined a semi-pro ball team. While with that team, he batted against Satchel Paige. During one at-bat, Satchel struck Goody out before he had gotten the bat off his shoulder.

Goody was determined to make his career in baseball. After many tryouts and disappointments, in 1936 he found a spot on the Louisville Colonels (American Association), a AAA team. During his first year in Louisville, Goody weighed only 135 pounds. (During his entire career, Goody had trouble with managers and owners who didn't think he was big enough for the game. He always proved he was more than big enough.) Goody hit .301 that first year. In 1937, he was selected for the American Association All-Star Team.

Goody debuted with the Brooklyn Dodgers on September 14, 1937. He appeared in only 22 games that year, hitting .312. The next year, 1938, he was a regular starter with the team and played in the outfield. Goody had an excellent year, hitting .281, with 133 hits, 51 RBIs, and 4 home runs. On two occasions, Goody broke up no-hitters, one by Hal Schumacher and one by Bill McGee. One shadow on the year was the occasion when Goody ran into a wall in St. Louis, trying to catch a fly. But this was just symptomatic of Goody's excellent defensive play. He led the league in fielding percentage that year, with .989, and in assists, with 19.

The following year, 1939, marked the managing debut of Leo Durocher and the beginning of Goody's real troubles. He and Durocher could not get along. The conflict started when Durocher insisted that Goody play after he had received an injury to his left ankle. The doctor told Durocher that Goody should not play for a few weeks, but the manager grew furious: Goody was leading the league in hitting, the team needed him! Goody continued to play, but his average dropped to .251. Durocher, whose feud with Goody was getting hotter and hotter, then used this as an excuse to ship Goody off to Montreal.

Goody was scrappy and argumentative by nature, at least with those he felt treated him unfairly. Besides Durocher, he also did not get along with General Manager Larry Macphail. The two feuds, taken together, kept the talented Goody in the minors, though never below the AAA level, until 1944. For the rest of his life, Goody felt that he had wasted some of the best years of his baseball career. He never forgave Durocher or Macphail. His detestation for Leo "The Lip" was something that could not be assuaged even by Leo's death or his own passing years.

After stints with Montreal and Columbus, Goody spent the next four years with Syracuse. In 1944, Goody returned to the Dodgers' lineup. He appeared in 89 games and hit .261.

1945 was the best year of Goody's career. For most of the year, he led the league in batting, and he finished third with a .325 average. He had 197 hits, including 12 home runs, and 75 RBIs. He also scored 126 runs—second in the league, the first being his teammate Eddie Stanky—with 128. No All-Star game was held in 1945, but sportswriters picked a list of players who should have been chosen. Goody was on the list.

At the start of the 1946 season, Goody was asked by Branch Rickey what he wanted for a salary. He told Branch, a man he greatly respected, that he wanted three times his 1945 salary. Rickey agreed, but he warned Goody he would try to trade him if he could. After a few weeks, though Goody had only played three games during the season, Rickey got his chance. It was while riding a subway to the Polo Grounds to play a doubleheader against the Giants that Goody found out he had just been traded to the Giants! It was on that day, April 28, 1946, that Goody got his revenge against the Dodgers and Leo Durocher. In the first game, Goody hit 3 singles and scored 2 runs, the Giants winning 7 to 3. The second game, he had 2 hits, including a home run, 3 RBIs, and he scored 2 runs—the Giants winning 10 to 4.

Shortly after that, Goody ran into another brick wall while chasing a fly, but this time he was seriously injured. He was out of commission for 12 weeks. It would be five years before he could lift his left arm above shoulder level. Goody managed to finish the year with the Giants, and then told them he was retiring.

Goody played 6 years in the majors for 2 teams. He batted .291. He appeared in 551 games, with 557 hits, including 71 doubles, 34 triples, and 22 home runs. He also walked 218 times. His fielding percentage in the outfield was .989.

But meanwhile, Toronto, in the International League, begged Goody to play with them in 1947, just for one year. Goody explained to them about his bad shoulder. They still insisted, for Goody was a national hero in Canada and crowds would come to the stadium just to see him. Goody agreed, though he felt like a thief taking the money. For his first night at Toronto, at least, Goody more than earned his keep: He had 6 hits. For most of the year, though,

Goody could not play at his former level. After 1947, Goody called it quits for good.

In his retirement, Goody went into business in his native Toronto, where he was quite successful. Married to Mildred Rothberg, they had two children. In his later years he became a big fan of the Blue Jays. After 59 years of marriage, Goody's wife died. Goody Rosen never recovered from the shock; he died on April 6, 1994.

Years	Games	AB	H	R	RBI	HR	BA	OBP	FP
6	551	1916	557	310	197	22	.291	.364	.989

1937-39, 1944-46 Bro-N, 1946 NY-N

Harry Rosenberg

Harry Rosenberg was born on June 22, 1909, in San Francisco, California. He was the younger brother of Louis Rosenberg, also a major league player. Harry was a shovel operator for a San Francisco construction firm when, in 1930, he tried out for a position on the Mission team (Pacific Coast League). Harry, a right-handed outfielder, won the position but didn't want to give up his construction job. He would drive a large truck on the construction site in the morning and play ball in the afternoon.

Harry did very well that first year, batting .368, with 60 runs, 53 RBIs, and 11 home runs. Furthermore, he had earned an excellent reputation as a defensive player. One contemporary account said he covered "the center field like a master fly hawk." John McGraw, ever vigilant for a possible Jewish star, scouted Harry and liked what he saw. The Giants bought Harry's contract from Mission for between $35,000 and $50,000. Harry was not pleased, however; with such large amounts of money involved, he felt he was entitled to a percentage, and refused to report to the Giants unless he was paid a $5,000 bonus. The Giants stood firm, and Harry finally had to cave in. He reported as ordered.

When Harry arrived at the Giants, he was met by the usual barrage of publicity that awaited all of John McGraw's Jewish discoveries. He made his major league debut with the team on July 15, 1930, after playing just 70 games in the minor leagues. That first game was at the Polo Grounds, and Harry had a walk. Nevertheless, the Cincinnati Reds won it, 14–8. Harry played in just 9 games for the Giants, but, as he had only 5 at-bats, he was used mostly as a pinch-hitter or pinch-runner or defensive replacement. He never got a major-league hit. The Giants sent his contract to Newark (International League).

In 1931, Harry appeared with Newark, then Bridgeport (Eastern League) and Indianapolis (American Association). He continued with the latter team until the middle of 1933, when he was traded to Fort Worth (Texas League). The next year, he was back with Indianapolis. From 1934 to 1941, he played with various teams of the Pacific Coast League: Sacramento, Mission, Portland, and Hollywood. Then, in 1942, Harry did not play. His final baseball year, 1943, was spent with the San Francisco Seals (Pacific Coast League). After that last season, Harry continued to make his home in San Francisco.

Harry Rosenberg was married. He died in San Mateo, CA on April 13, 1997.

Years	Games	AB	H	R	RBI	HR	BA	OBP	FP
1	9	5	0	1	0	0	.000	.167	1.000

1930 NY-N

Lou Rosenberg

Louis Rosenberg was born on March 5, 1903, in San Francisco. He had ten siblings, including his younger brother Harry, who also became a major league player.

Lou made his big-league debut for the Chicago White Sox on May 22, 1923, as a pinch-hitter in the bottom of the 15th inning of a game between the White Sox and the Yankees. Babe Ruth had just broken the long-standing tie with a two-run home run at the top of the 15th. Lou faced Herb Pennock in that first at-bat. He did not repeat Babe's feat to tie the game; in fact, he didn't get a hit. The Yanks won this game, played at Comiskey Park, 3–1.

In another game at Comiskey, on July 16, 1923, Lou did get a hit, a single, off A's pitcher Slim Harriss. This proved to be Lou's only major league hit. The A's won this game, 4–3. Lou appeared in only 3 games with Chicago, all in 1923. His batting average was .250. He batted right and threw right. He was used mostly as a pinch-hitter, but his ostensible position was second base.

After his playing days, Lou went into the gardening supply business, and he was very successful in this field. His company, Sunset Garden Supply, was in his native San Francisco. Lou Rosenberg died in Daly City, California, on September 8, 1991.

Years	Games	AB	H	R	RBI	HR	BA	OBP	FP
1	3	4	1	0	0	0	.250	.250	1.000

1923 Chi-A

Steve Rosenberg

Steve Rosenberg

Steven Allen Rosenberg was born on October 31, 1964, in Brooklyn, New York. He attended the University of Florida, where he pitched for the Gators. Steve tied a team record, in 1985, by pitching the most complete games in the NCAA post-season, with 10. In 1986, Steve was signed out of the university by the Yankees organization as their number-four pick in the June draft.

He began his professional baseball career with Oneonta in 1986, where the left-handed pitcher had an ERA of 1.00, appearing in relief in 4 games. He was then sent to Fort Lauderdale to finish the season. Here, too, he was primarily used in relief, and had an ERA of 2.12. The following year, 1987, Steve pitched for Albany. Steve saved 15 games that season, appearing in 32, and having an ERA of 2.25. He finished 1987 with Columbus, where his ERA was 4.08 and where he had 2 saves in 21 games. On the basis of these records, Steve was considered one of the Yankees' top pitching prospects. Nevertheless, after the season, the Yankees traded Steve to the Chicago White Sox organization.

Steve began 1988 with Vancouver, where his ERA was 3.33 and where he had 3 saves in 20 games. On June 4, 1988, Steve made his debut, for the Chicago White Sox, at Comiskey Park in a game against Texas. He finished 1988 with a 4.30 ERA for Chicago, with no wins, 1 loss, and 1 save. During the winter of 1988–89, Steve pitched for the Lobos of Arecibo, in the Puerto Rican League. His ERA was 4.10, with 1 win and 4 losses.

The next year, 1989, Steve led the Sox in losses, with 13, against 4 wins; his ERA was 4.94. He spent the winter again with the Lobos of Arecibo. In 1990, Steve returned to Vancouver. There, he had a win-loss record of 6-5 and an ERA of 3.57, with 8 saves. He was called back up to Chicago, but his ERA rose to 5.40. He had 1 win and no losses. During the spring of 1991, Steve was traded to the San Diego Padres organization. In 1991, he began the season pitching for the Las Vegas Stars (Pacific Coast League). During the year, he was called up to appear in 10 games with the Padres. He had a 1-1 record, with a 6.94 ERA. Steve pitched in a total of 87 major league games, with 6 wins and 15 losses, and an ERA of 4.94, plus 1 save. He started 21 games, all in 1989.

Steve Rosenberg lives in Pompano Beach, Florida.

Years	Games	IP	W	L	GS	SV	PCT	ERA
4	87	$209\frac{2}{3}$	6	15	21	1	.286	4.94

1988-90 Chi-A, 1991 SD-N

Max Rosenfeld

Max Rosenfeld was born in New York on December 23, 1902. In his youth, his family moved to Birmingham, where Max attended the University of Alabama, playing both baseball and football there. On the football team, Max lettered as a half-back, from 1920 to 1922. His younger brother, David, followed him to Alabama, where he, too, served as a halfback, from 1924 to 1926. David was considered, in his time, to be one of the leading players at his position in the country, particularly noted for his speed. After he left college, Max changed his residence to Miami, Florida; he formed deep roots in that community which would last him the rest of his life.

MIAMI BEACH   (130)

MAX ROSENFELD
Manager del Miami Beach

In 1924, Max began his professional baseball career with Springfield (Western Association). The following year, the right-hander played shortstop with Jackson (Cotton States League), where his batting average for 118 games was .330. From 1926 to 1928, Max played for Birmingham (Southern Association), with one hiatus, during 1926, when he took a temporary retirement. His batting averages for 1927 and 1928 were .302 and .344. Max played second base and outfield for Birmingham.

The next year, 1929, Max split between Atlanta (Southern Association) and Toledo (American Association). In the first city he batted .328 and in the second he hit .352. In 1930, Max was back with Toledo, again playing second base and outfield and hitting .330. During most of 1931, Max was with Hartford, with a .312 average in 123 games at second and in the outfield. On April 21, 1931, Max was given his first chance to play at the major league level, with the Brooklyn Robins. It was in a game against the Phillies at the Baker Bowl. Max was called in to replace Johnny Frederick, in center field. At his first at-bat, Max flew out, but in the 9th inning he hit a double. Nevertheless, the Phillies won the game, 7–3, behind their pitcher,

Jim Elliott. That first year, Max only appeared in 3 games for Brooklyn, with an average of .222.

In 1932, he appeared in 34 games for Brooklyn. On April 28, 1932, Max had his first major league home run, in another game against the Phillies at the Baker Bowl and again with Jim Elliott pitching. Max's home run came in the 8th inning and was with 2 aboard. Brooklyn won the game, 11–5. Max was playing right field in that game. (During all his time with Brooklyn, he was used as an outfielder.) Max appeared, again, with Brooklyn in 1933, for 5 games. He had just one hit in these games. Max's lifetime major league average is .298, with 17 hits, including 4 doubles and 2 home runs, in 42 games, over 3 years. Max completed 1933 with Jersey City (International League), where he went back to playing both second base and outfield and where he batted .291.

From 1934 to 1939, Max played with Syracuse (International League), Knoxville (Southern Association), Newark (International League), Tulsa (Texas League), Oklahoma City (Texas League), Dallas (Texas League), Jackson (Southeastern League), and Panama City, Florida (Alabama–Florida League). Max's minor league lifetime average is .306, with 1805 hits, including 269 doubles and 42 homers, in 1661 games, over 15 years. He also had 909 runs and 843 RBIs. Starting in 1937, Max not only played part-time on second and in the outfield, but he also managed the Jackson and Panama City teams.

During 1940 and 1941, Max served as president, business manager, and field manager of the Miami Beach Flamingos (Florida East Coast League). He gave up his managing the following season, but continued his association with the Flamingos until 1946. From 1953 to 1955, he served as a scout for Atlanta (International League).

Max was a realtor. He also served as president of the Miami Beach Anglers and Boating Club and as Director of the Miami Beach Fishing Tournament. He was active in a number of organizations, including the Old Timers Professional Baseball Association of Greater Miami. Max was married. He had one daughter, Shirley Berman, and three grandchildren.

Max Rosenfeld died in Miami on March 10, 1969. He was buried in Temple Israel Cemetery.

Years	Games	AB	H	R	RBI	HR	BA	OBP	FP
3	42	57	17	8	7	2	.298	.322	.978

1931-33 Bro-N

Sy Rosenthal

Simon "Sy" Rosenthal, a man whose life was a paradigm of courage and endurance, was born on November 13, 1903, in Boston. Sy learned baseball in the streets of Boston and it was on a Boston playground that he was spotted by a scout and signed for the Red Sox.

Sy, who batted and threw left-handed, started his career in 1922 with Hartford (Eastern League). He then played outfield, his only position, for Albany and Pittsburgh (both of the Eastern League) in 1923. From 1924 to 1925, he played with San Antonio (Texas League). At the end of 1925, he was called up by the Red Sox. His debut was on September 8, 1925, and Sy got a hit off Yankees pitcher Bob Shawkey. He played in 19 games that year, with a batting average of .264.

The next year was Sy's only full year in the majors. He scored 34 runs, had 34 RBIs, 76 hits (including 4 home runs), and a .267 average. He had a reputation as a hard-hitting batter. His career in the majors was cut short by a foot injury he had suffered while in the minors. Sy's lifetime major league batting average, for 2 years, was .266. He played in 123 games, with 95 hits, including 17 doubles, 5 triples, and 4 homers.

Sy's minor league career continued, from 1927 to 1935, with Louisville (American Association), Chattanooga (Southern Association), Dallas (Texas), Atlanta (Southern Association), Galveston (Texas), Mobile and Knoxville (Southern Association), Quincy (Mississippi Valley), Dayton and Beckley (Middle Atlantic), and Peoria (3-I). His lifetime minor league batting average is .333, with 1654 hits (including 80 home runs), 895 runs, and 724 RBIs in 1357 minor league games.

Sy's married life was not happy, but it did produce for him the greatest joy of his life: his son Irwin. When the Second World War began, Irwin, or "Buddy," as he was known, volunteered for the Marines. He was just 17. On Christmas Day, 1943, Buddy Rosenthal was killed in the landings on the beaches of Gloucester Cape, New Britain, in the Solomon Islands.

Although he was already 40 years old, Sy volunteered for the Navy in 1944. At first, he was refused because of an old injury. But Sy paid for corrective surgery and dental work so he would be able to pass the physical. On his second try, Sy was accepted and assigned to the U.S.S. Miantonomah, a minesweeper, cruising off the coast of Normandy near the French port of Le Havre. Sy's ship hit a German mine on September 25, 1944, and he was among the most seriously injured in the explosion. While his life was saved, he was rendered a paraplegic, confined to a wheelchair for the rest of his life.

But Sy was not one to be stopped. He became a warrior in other fields. He was a tireless worker for good causes: for various charities and the ideal of goodwill among peoples of all races and religions. Although he was deeply committed to the Jewish religion, Sy never let that act as an impediment to his charitable work; he worked for charities sponsored by all religious denominations. Not surprisingly, Sy also spent countless hours, often traveling great distances, fighting for the rights of the disabled.

Sy was also very active with veterans' groups, including the Jewish War Veterans. He was also a trustee of the Sports Lodge of B'nai B'rith.

Sy, himself, was not a rich man. In 1947, the Boston Red Sox made it clear that they had not forgotten their old teammate. On September 13, the team sponsored a "Sy Rosenthal Day," and the money raised was used to buy a special house for him, with ramps instead of stairs, so that he could get around in his wheelchair.

One of Sy's most successful charitable campaigns began in 1963, when he was introduced to a black Roman Catholic priest from Bay St. Louis, Mississippi. Sy was convinced of the real need of the priest's seminary, which was trying to raise funds for a gymnasium. Sy put himself heart and soul into the effort to raise the necessary $120,000 for the project. Sy

Sy Rosenthal (r.) and Ted Williams at Bosox charity drive of 1958.

gave $5,000 of his own money towards the cause; from his close friends, he raised $10,000 more. But Sy did not halt his efforts until the gym was completed in 1967. On February 5, 1967, the Divine Word Catholic Seminary of Bay St. Louis dedicated its Sy Rosenthal Gymnasium. The lobby of the gym now houses the numerous plaques, citations, and awards that Sy received during his lifetime. It also has a special plaque dedicated to the memory of his son, who had died in 1943.

Sy Rosenthal died of a heart attack in his native Boston on April 7, 1969. The following Friday morning, on April 11, special services were held at Temple B'nai Moshe, in Brighton, Massachusetts. The synagogue was packed with peoples of all religions and races—to mourn the passing of a great humanitarian and to celebrate a life of good works.

Years	Games	AB	H	R	RBI	HR	BA	OBP	FP
2	123	357	95	40	42	4	.266	.319	.950

1925-26 Bos-A

Wayne Rosenthal

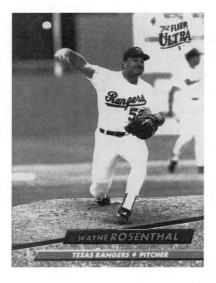

Wayne Scott Rosenthal was born on February 19, 1965, in Brooklyn, New York. Wayne's size, 6'5½" and 220 pounds, made him an impressive figure on the mound. He was acquired by the Texas Rangers in the June 1986 draft. Wayne was used as a reliever and was very impressive at the minor league level. In his first year in professional baseball, 1986, with the Sarasota Gulf Rangers (Gulf Coast League), he pitched in 23 games and ended the year with a 0.73 ERA, the lowest in the league. The next year, 1987, the big right-hander played with Gastonia and was named the Rangers' Minor League Player of the Year, after earning 30 saves.

In 1988 and 1989, Wayne was with Charlotte. During the 1989 season, he was transferred to Tulsa, where he remained for the beginning of the 1990 season. During 1990, he was sent to Oklahoma City, where he played until June 26, 1991, when he made his major league debut.

Wayne's first game pitching for the Texas Rangers was in relief of injured pitcher Rich Gossage. Wayne pitched a scoreless inning. He ended the season with 1 win, 4 losses, 1 save, and a 5.25 ERA in 36 games. In 1992, Wayne Rosenthal pitched in only 6 games for the Rangers. His ERA was 7.71, with no decisions and no saves.

Years	Games	IP	W	L	GS	SV	PCT	ERA
2	42	75	1	4	0	1	.200	5.40

1991-92 Tex-A

Marv Rotblatt

Marvin Rotblatt was born on October 18, 1927, in Chicago, Illinois, the son of Sol and Carolyn Rotblatt. He graduated from Chicago's Von Steuben High School, where he pitched for the school team, and entered the University of Illinois. As soon as he started at Illinois, Marv established himself as a left-handed pitching whiz.

In college, Marv had an outstanding pitching record: 28 wins and 4 losses, for the four years. In one game, he struck out 18 batters, and this was a Big Ten record. So was Marv's junior-year season, when his record was 10 and 0. Marv led his team to the Big Ten championship in both 1947 and 1948. During his summer recesses, Marv pitched for the House of David baseball team. Only 5'6", he was billed as "Little David." During his first season with the House of David, Marv won 14 games in a row. In a game with the Harlem Globetrotters baseball team, Marv struck out 17 players.

The secret to Marv's success was his curve ball. He never had a great fast ball, but his curve ball had remarkable motion. His change of pace was equally impressive and was known to completely confuse batters.

Marv graduated from Illinois in 1948 with a degree in journalism. He had been offered contracts by all but two of the major league teams. He signed with the Chicago White Sox, as they offered the most money, $6,000. Marv debuted in a game against Detroit on the Fourth of July, 1948, at Comiskey Park. He pitched two scoreless innings, giving up only 1 hit, though Detroit won the game, 6–3.

After a few more appearances with the White Sox, Marv was sent down to Waterloo, Iowa (3-I League), for seasoning. He did not meet with any disaster at Waterloo: He had 8 wins in 9 decisions, including 5 shutouts and a no-hitter. Marv was then sent back to Chicago, where he played a few games with the Sox before the close of the season. He ended the year with no wins and 1 loss, in 7 games, and a 7.85 ERA.

In 1949, Marv played with Memphis. His record was 7 and 7. During the year, he was sidelined for about a month with a sore arm. The following year, he started with Sacramento, where he lost two games and was sent back down to Memphis. Marv had an excellent year at Memphis, winning 22 and losing 9. In fact, he led the league in ERA, with 2.67; in strikeouts, with 203; and in innings pitched, with 253. He returned briefly to Chicago to pitch $8\frac{2}{3}$ innings in 2 games. He had no decisions and an ERA of 6.23.

1951 was Marv's most important year in the majors. He began the year as a starter with Chicago, starting the second game of the season. Marv won that game, but he soon found himself being used principally as a reliever. He played only two games that year as a starter; his other 24 games were in relief. Marv ended the year with 4 wins and 2 losses and a 3.40 ERA. This also marked the end of his major league career. Marv pitched for 3 years in the majors, appearing in 35 games. His ERA was 4.82; he won 4 games, lost 3, a winning percentage of .571.

Marv was drafted for military service from 1952 to 1953. He played on a military exhibition team with the likes of Don Newcombe, Bob Turley, and Hy Cohen. During this period Marv injured his arm.

When Marv returned from the service, he continued to play in the minor leagues, playing with Charleston (American Association), Memphis, Atlanta, Monterrey, and Syracuse. With Memphis, in 1954, he had a 13-7 record. In the Southern Association he set a new strikeout record of 202. His record with Syracuse, in 1957, was 9-3, but he suffered another injury in the process—which ended his career.

After leaving baseball, Marv went into the insurance business, where he was very successful. Marv Rotblatt currently lives in Las Vegas, Nevada.

Years	Games	IP	W	L	GS	SV	PCT	ERA
3	35	$74\frac{2}{3}$	4	3	4	2	.571	4.82

1948, 1950-51 Chi-A

Larry Rothschild

Larry Rothschild's place in the history of baseball is secure, which seems like an odd thing to say about a major league pitcher who only pitched $8\frac{1}{3}$ innings. But on his hands, Larry wears 2 World Series rings and he has the unique distinction of being the only Jew to be named inaugural manager of a major league baseball team.

Lawrence Lee Rothschild was born on March 12, 1954, in Chicago, Illinois, to a Jewish father and gentile mother. Larry attended Florida State University and pitched for the baseball squad; in 1975, he led the team to the NCAA tournament.

In 1975, Larry was signed by the Cincinnati Reds. The right-handed pitcher was assigned to the Billings Mustangs (Pioneer League). After pitching in 6 games, Larry was sent to Eugene (Northwest League). He finished the season with Eugene with a 3-0 record and a 2.73 ERA. In 1976, Larry hurled for the Three Rivers Eagles (Eastern League). That year, he had an 11-3 record and 2.05 ERA. Larry was promoted, in 1977, to the Indianapolis Indians. In 1978, Larry played with Nashville (Southern Association), Amarillo (Texas League), and then went back to Indianapolis.

Larry's return to the Indians in mid-season helped stabilize the team's pitching and led them to win the Eastern Division title. Larry pitched in the first game of the 1978 American Association playoffs. That winter, he pitched for Valencia in the Venezuelan League. He played again for the Indians in both 1979 and 1980. In 1981, Larry was signed by the Detroit Tigers organization. He began the season with the Evansville Triplets (American Association), but was promoted to the Tigers at the end of the AAA season.

Larry made his major league debut on September 11, 1981. He earned his only major league save three days later. Larry pitched a total of $5\frac{2}{3}$ innings, in 5 games, with a 1.59 ERA. In 1982, he returned to the Evansville Triplets. That year, he appeared in 2 games with the Detroit Tigers. When he gave up 4 runs in $2\frac{2}{3}$ innings, his major league ERA became 13.50 for the season.

Larry never pitched again in a major league game. He had a lifetime major league ERA of 5.40 and pitched for $8\frac{1}{3}$ innings in 7 games over 2 years. Larry had no major league decision, but he did have 1 save. Larry pitched two more seasons in the minors for the Denver Bears (American Association) and the Iowa Cubs (American Association). Then, in December 1985, Larry returned to the Cincinnati Reds organization as a coach. In 1986 and 1987, he was the pitching instructor of A and AA teams, including the Cedar Rapids Reds (Midwest League). In 1988 and 1989, Larry was the roving pitching instructor between all six Reds farm clubs. On November 16, 1989, Larry was named bullpen coach of the Cincinnati Reds, coaching the 1990 World Champion Reds and the 1991 team. In 1992, he was promoted to the position of pitching coach. In May 1993, he was fired, along with Manager Tony Perez. The next year, Larry became a minor league pitching instructor for the Atlanta Braves.

In October 1994, he was hired by the Florida Marlins as their pitching coach. Larry was very successful in his new role. In only the team's fifth year of existence, his pitching staff led the team to win the 1997 World Series. Larry was credited particularly with helping to develop the Cuban pitcher Livan Hernandez. Hernandez's performances were especially critical in both the NLCS and in the World Series, itself. The rookie right-hander was named the Most Valuable Player for both the League Series and the World Series.

But Larry's part in the victories did not go unnoticed. On November 7, 1997, he was named to the position of manager of the new Florida major league team, the Tampa Bay Devil Rays. He is the initial manager of this expansion team. He was hired by the Devil Ray's general manager, Chuck LaMar. LaMar has been a friend of Larry's since they both worked for the Cincinnati Reds, in 1986. In 1994, LaMar had hired Larry for the Atlanta Braves. Larry Rothschild is now busily planning for the opening of the 1998 season and organizing his new team.

Larry's Tampa Bay Devil Rays fooled the pundits with an outstanding showing at the very start of the 1998 season. However, a few months into the season, the team had sunk to last place in its division, which had been expected, considering the club's weak roster.

Years	Games	IP	W	L	GS	SV	PCT	ERA
2	7	$8\frac{1}{3}$	0	0	0	1	NA	5.40

1981-82 Det-A

as Manager

Years	Games	W	L	PCT
3	485	201	284	.414

1999-2000 Tam-A

Mickey Rutner

Mickey Rutner's baseball career was one filled with triumph and frustration. The triumph was always at the minor league level and the frustration grew out of his inability to find a regular position in the majors. His baseball career inspired his good friend Eliot Asinof to write his first book, a novel, Man on Spikes (1955).

Milton "Mickey" Rutner was born on March 18, 1922, at Hempstead, New York. His parents, Max and Rose Rutner, were immigrants from Lodz, Poland. Mickey was the youngest of five children. He played baseball at St. John's University. After his graduation, Mickey was signed by the Detroit Tigers, with a $2,000 bonus. He was later cheated out of his bonus by the machinations of the Detroit organization. Mickey has commented, "The game of baseball is great, but I disliked the business of baseball."

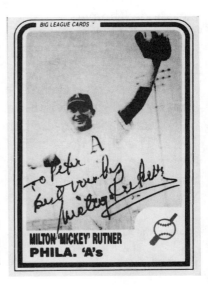

Mickey began his professional baseball career in 1941, with Winston-Salem (Piedmont League). There, Mickey's first manager was Jake Atz—at the very end of his legendary career. Jake confided in Mickey that the Tigers would probably not have signed him if they knew he was Jewish. Jake believed that Mickey's degree from St. John's and his name "Mickey" fooled them. During that

season, Mickey was tried at shortstop and second base; he batted .203. His second year, he played for Wilmington (Inter-State League) and his average jumped to .277. That year, 1942, Mickey was picked for the league All-Star team.

From 1942 to 1945, Mickey served with the 45th Division of the U.S. Army, stationed in Europe. At the conclusion of the Second World War, he returned to Wilmington, where he now played third base. Mickey, who threw and batted right-handed, would hold that position for the rest of his career. In 1946, his first season after military service, Mickey would lead his league in doubles, with 36. He batted .310 and had 126 RBI's. That year, Mickey was selected for a second time as an All-Star for his league. In 1947, Mickey achieved the highest minor league batting average of his career, .327, and got his only opportunity to play in the major leagues.

Mickey played that year for Birmingham (Southern Association), where he appeared in 153 games. On September 11, he got his chance to debut for the Philadelphia Athletics. Mickey had two singles that day, for 4 at-bats, off Joe Haynes, although the A's lost the game, 3–7, to the White Sox. In his first game at Yankee Stadium, Mickey got a hit off of Joe Page that won the game. In all, Mickey appeared in 12 games with the A's. He had 12 hits, including one double and one home run, scored 4 runs, had 4 RBIs, and batted .250.

Mickey was called to spring training with the A's in 1948, but before the season started, he was shipped back to Birmingham. He had another excellent year in Alabama, where he batted .312, with 181 hits, including 46 doubles, 12 triples, and 3 home runs. He also scored 97 runs and had 94 RBIs. Mickey played in the Southern Association All-Star Game that year, and his team won the Dixie Series, beating Fort Worth (Texas League).

Mickey split 1949 between Louisville (American Association) and Tulsa (Texas League). The following year, he split between Tulsa and Toronto (International League). Mickey had a fine year in San Antonio (Texas League) in 1951, where he batted .308, with 159 hits, including 8 homers. That year, he played in the Texas League All-Star Game. 1952 was another divided year, in Memphis (Southern Association) and Tulsa. Mickey's last year in organized baseball was 1953; he was back in the Texas League, with Oklahoma City, where he hit .281.

Mickey spent 10 years in the minor leagues, with a total of 1,160 games and 1,262 hits, including 261 doubles, 58 triples, and 38 homers. His lifetime minor league average is .295.

Mickey had married a dancer with the Radio City Music Hall Rockettes, Leona Schiff, in 1941. They had three sons. One of their boys, Toby, became a psychologist; one, Richard, became an artist; and the third, Paul, became a musician. In 1974, Mickey Rutner became Supervisor of Recreation in his birthplace, Hempstead. He currently lives in Levittown, New York.

Years	Games	AB	H	R	RBI	HR	BA	OBP	FP
1	12	48	12	4	4	1	.250	.294	.885

1947 Phi-A

Roger Samuels

Roger Howard Samuels was born on January 3, 1961, in San Jose, California. He began his professional baseball career as a left-handed pitcher for the Columbus Astros in 1985. Roger played one more season in the Astros organization before being released in 1987. He later signed with the San Francisco Giants, and played on their teams in Fresno and Shreveport that year. Roger was promoted to the AAA Phoenix Firebirds in 1988.

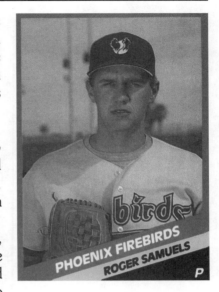

Roger made his major league debut on July 20, 1988, with the San Francisco Giants. That year, he pitched in 15 games with the Giants as a reliever. He had a win-loss record of 1-2, and a 3.47 ERA. Roger returned to Phoenix in 1989, but he was traded to the Pittsburgh Pirates organization on May 10, 1989.

Roger made his debut with the Pirates on May 30, 1989, pitching one scoreless inning against Cincinnati. He made five relief appearances with the Pirates between May 30 and June 8. On June 9, Roger was optioned back to the Buffalo Bisons. He was placed on the disabled list with Buffalo twice, because of shoulder problems. Roger finished the season with Phoenix; he was released at the end of the season, and was signed by the New York Mets. He finished his career, with the Class AAA Tidewater Tides, in 1990.

Roger currently lives in San Jose, California.

Years	Games	IP	W	L	GS	SV	PCT	ERA
2	20	27	1	2	0	0	.333	4.33

1988 SF-N, 1989 Pit-N

Ike Samuls

Samuel Earl "Ike" Samuls was born on February 20, 1876, in Chicago, Illinois. He was a third baseman and shortstop. Ike was signed by the St. Louis Brown Stockings, or Browns, to play for the team during the 1895 season. The Browns were a member of the National League and are an early incarnation of the modern Cardinals. The old American League Browns, today the Baltimore Orioles, had assumed the name of the older St. Louis club after it had discarded it and had taken the designation Cardinals.

On August 3, 1895, Ike, who had not yet played for the Browns, was put into the game to bat for Tommy Dowd, against Chicago Colts pitcher Bill Hutchinson. Hutchinson was, at that time, one of baseball's leading hurlers. Ike had one hit for two plate appearances. The Colts (now the Cubs) defeated the Browns, 6–0.

Ike ended this year, his only one in the majors, with 17 hits in 24 games and a batting average of .230. Ike scored 5 runs and he had 5 RBIs.

Ike Samuls died on New Year's Day, 1942, in Los Angeles, California.

Years	Games	AB	H	R	RBI	HR	BA	OBP	FP
1	24	74	17	5	5	0	.230	.278	.750

1895-StL-N

Moe Savransky

Morris Savransky was born on January 13, 1929, in Cleveland, Ohio. He attended Cleveland Heights High School and pitched for its baseball team. In 1947, he pitched in the Amateur World Series in Brooklyn and the Ohio State High School Championships. Moe graduated from high school in 1948.

In the summer of 1948, Moe was signed by the Cincinnati Reds from a Cleveland sandlot team. He was sent to their Class B team in Sunbury, Pennsylvania. The left-handed pitcher got off to a slow start, but won his last six decisions to end the season with a 6-4 record, allowing only 59 hits in 76 innings, with a 3.67 ERA. During the off-season, Moe attended Ohio State University in Columbus. He remained in the Cincinnati Reds minor league system until his major league debut.

Moe made that debut with the Reds on April 23, 1954. He entered the game in the 9th inning and allowed only 1 hit and no runs. The Reds lost the game to the Chicago Cubs, 10–3, at Cincinnati's Crosley Field. Moe got his only hit in an at-bat on July 11, 1954. He got a single off Milwaukee Braves pitcher Gene Conley in the 3rd inning. Moe scored a run and the Reds defeated the Braves, 6–5, at Crosley Field.

Moe Savransky retired from major league baseball at the end of the 1954 season. He appeared in 16 games, in relief. Moe had a 0-2 record and a 4.88 ERA. He currently lives in Cleveland, Ohio.

Years	Games	IP	W	L	GS	SV	PCT	ERA
1	16	24	0	2	0	0	.000	4.88

1954 Cin-N

Al Schacht

Alexander "Al" Schacht—the first "Clown Prince of Baseball"—was born on November 11, 1892, in New York. Al says of his background in his autobiography, My Own Particular Screwball (Garden City, 1955), "There is talk that I am Jewish—just because my father was Jewish, my mother is Jewish, I speak Yiddish and once studied to be a rabbi and a cantor. Well, that's how rumors get started. The fact is I am Jewish, plenty Jewish."

Al was raised in the mean and very heavily populated streets of turn-of-the-century New York. He was not a good student, but he was a great sandlot pitcher. He seemed to have known everyone. He learned pitching with the assistance of Christy Mathewson. One day, when Al was hanging around the park while the Giants were having practice, Mathewson took Al aside and showed him how to pitch his famous "fadeaway." This pitch is now called the "screwball." Al was a boyhood friend of Harry Ruby and Dolly Stark. He knew Guy Zinn. Harry Cohn, another of his boyhood friends, later became president of Columbia Pictures.

Al pitched for P.S. 42 in the Bronx. He then proceeded to the High School of Commerce in Manhattan, entering the school in 1909 and making the team; but he did not get to pitch. Al then quit school. The next year, however, he returned and found a number of opportunities to show his prowess as a right-handed pitcher. Scouts spotted him in his high school games and got him started on the way to the pros. To assist him in his decision, the New York Public School System expelled Al in 1911—for taking $4.00 to pitch a game in Catskill, New York.

"AL" SCHACHT

Al's first step on the road to the majors was with a semi-pro team in Walton, New York. He played with them in 1910 and 1911. During his tenure there, he won 16 straight games, and also, with his clowning around, planted the first seeds of his later career as a baseball clown. Al's first real minor league team was Erie (Ohio–Pennsylvania League). He started 1912 with them, but never really got a chance to play, before being released because the team had too many pitchers and Al was the smallest one.

Al continued 1912 with the Cleveland team of the transitory U.S. League. He had a great record with this club, including winning 5 games straight, but when the league collapsed, Al was out of work. He finished the 1912 season pitching for the semi-pro New York Metropolitans. From 1913 to 1915, Al hurled for Newark, NJ (International League). During the 1915 season, this team moved to Harrisburg, PA, then, in 1916, returned to Newark. It was during this period that Al roomed with Jim Thorpe, who told him that, with his nose, he looked like "a Jewish Indian." During the 1916 season, Al developed a sore arm and the team laid him off. When he got a chance to complain to John McGraw about this injustice, McGraw, always on the lookout for Jewish players, hired him on the spot. But Al never got a chance to play for the Giants; he just spent the balance of the season on their bench.

Al played the 1917 season with Rochester (International League). Al expected to hear from the army in 1918, so he spent the first half of the season with the Bethlehem Steel Co. team, instead of in the minors. Al was inducted into the Army in 1918, however, and stayed in the service until 1919, all the time playing ball. Al had the best year of his career in 1919, playing for the Jersey City Skeeters (International League). He won 20 games that year, including 10 shutouts, which was a record for the team. As good a record as this was, it was even more remarkable, considering how wretched the Jersey City team was that year. It won only 45 games during the entire season.

Al's magic season did not go unnoticed, and on September 18, 1919, he made his major league debut for the Washington Senators under the management of a man who would come to his aid on many occasions in years to come: the great Clark Griffith. Al pitched in only 2 games in 1919 for the Senators and he won them both, giving him a percentage of 1.000 that year. His ERA was just 2.40. With a record like that, it is not surprising that Al was back in 1920 as a regular part

of the Washington team.

In 1920, Al appeared in 22 games for the Senators. He won 6 games and lost 4. His ERA was 4.44. In 1921, his last year in the majors, Al appeared in 29 games. He had 6 wins and 6 losses. His ERA was 4.90. Al's lifetime major league percentage was .583, 14 wins and 10 losses. His ERA was 4.48. In 3 years, he appeared in 53 games for the Senators.

Al's major league career was brief, despite some remarkable early appearances, because his arm had been overworked during his years in the minors. Furthermore, he had suffered, during his years in the minors, from malaria, ulcers, torn cartilages, and sore arms. Then, during 1920, he suffered a broken shoulder. Al's career was a remarkable mixture of ups and downs.

One of Al's proudest boasts was that Babe Ruth never hit a home run off him during their many encounters in the minor leagues and in the majors. Al pitched the first game Ruth ever started in left field. He once struck out the Babe on three pitches—a rare feat.

From 1922 to 1923, Al played for Reading, PA. Then, unfortunately, the new manager, who took over the team at the start of the 1923 season, didn't approve of Al's brand of humor and he was fired. Al's contract was immediately picked up by Binghamton (New York–Pennsylvania League), where his clowning proved to be a great attraction. Al concluded his playing career in 1924 with New Haven (Eastern League). During these later stints, Al would double as a third base coach—or really triple, for he would also entertain the crowds with his humorous antics.

During his playing days, Al developed a reputation as one of the finest third base coaches in the business. He returned to the majors in 1925, as coach for the Washington Senators, and would hold this job until 1934. In 1935 and 1936, Al was a coach with the Boston Red Sox. It was, however, as a baseball clown, entertaining between innings, and even during play, that Al earned immortality. The act was begun with another ex-pitcher, Nick Altrock, but in 1934 Al went out on his own. The comedy routine, which included humorous stories and broad pantomime—all played out in a battered top hat, tattered frock coat, and huge baseball mitt—took him to 25 World Series, from 1927 to 1952, and 18 All-Star Games and almost countless major and minor league games. He entertained for the USO during the Second World War, including tours in Europe, Africa, and the Pacific. Al boasted that more people, 68 million, had seen him perform than any other player in major league history.

Al's show would begin with his saying a few words to the crowd. Then he would climb into the grandstand and cause all kinds of excitement. He'd kiss girls and escort ladies to their seats, give away bags of peanuts and perform mock weddings at home plate. Then, after he had established an atmosphere of craziness, he would "shadow" the third baseman, copying his every move. Or he would sit on the basepaths, reading a paper, while balls flew about him, until he would snatch a ball from the air. He would then have a batboy deliver it to the first baseman, making sure he signed a receipt. Then Al would go to the mound and do imitations of famous pitchers and batters. He would usually perform his act before the game.

Al Schacht opened a popular New York restaurant and authored three books, including Clowning Through Baseball and his autobiography, My Own Particular Screwball. Al died in Waterbury, Connecticut, on July 14, 1984, at the age of ninety-one. Following his death, Al's title, "The Clown Prince of Baseball," was assumed by Max Patkin.

Years	Games	IP	W	L	GS	SV	PCT	ERA
3	53	197	14	10	18	2	.583	4.48

1919-21 Was-A

Sid Schacht

While Sid Schacht was playing, he was often referred to as "the other pitching Schacht," usually followed by the line, "no relation to the Clown Prince of Baseball, Al Schacht." Sidney Schacht was born on February 3, 1918, in Bogota, New Jersey, and was no relative of Al's.

In 1947, Sid began his professional baseball career as a right-handed hurler with Stamford, Connecticut (Colonial League). He would commute from his Bronx home to the games. (Sid had decided to live at home to take care of his ill mother.) Thanks to his fine control, Sid finished the '47 season with a remarkable 18-7 record. In 1948, he was promoted to the San Diego Padres (Pacific Coast League), but refused to report to the West Coast team that spring because of his mother's continuing ill health. Sid returned to Stamford and finished the season with a 7-8 record, although he did display a league-leading 2.09 ERA. Sid's mother died that fall, and he was sold to the Boston Red Sox organization.

Sid showed, at this point, great confidence in his own abilities. When his new contract was negotiated with the Red Sox, Sid waived his twenty-percent share of the $12,500 purchase price, which his contract brought and which had been specified in his Stamford contract, because he didn't want to be branded as a "bonus-player."

Sid began the 1949 season with Birmingham, but after pitching with the team for a short time, he was demoted to Scranton. Sid began to shine again, with Scranton; he finished the season with a 19-5 record. From 1947 to 1949, Sid displayed uncommon ability to get the ball over the plate, walking only 168 batters in 596 innings. Over the same period, he struck out 383. Despite this feat, Sid was sold to the St. Louis Browns organization, at the end of the season.

Beginning the 1950 season with the Saint Louis Browns, Sid made his major league debut against the Cleveland Indians, on April 23, 1950, at Sportsman's Park. He entered the game in the 7th inning. Sid gave up 1 run, when Ray Boone hit a single to score Al Rosen. After the 7th, the game was called. The Indians defeated the Browns, 7–5.

Sid pitched in a total of 8 games for the Browns that year. He had a 16.03 ERA, for the $10\frac{2}{3}$ innings he pitched. Sid played in 6 games for the Browns in 1951, with a 21.00 ERA, for 6 innings, then was traded to the Boston Braves, to pitch in 5 games during the season. With the Braves, Sid had a 1.93 ERA, but he was responsible for 2 losses.

Sid retired from major league baseball at the end of the season. He had a 14.34 lifetime ERA, pitched $21\frac{1}{3}$ innings, and had a win-loss record of 0-2. Sid Schacht died on March 30, 1991, in Fort Lauderdale, Florida.

Years	Games	IP	W	L	GS	SV	PCT	ERA
2	19	$21\frac{1}{3}$	0	2	1	1	.000	14.34

1950-51 StL-A, 1951 Bos-N

Hal Shacker

Harold "Hal" Schacker was born on April 6, 1925, in Brooklyn.

In 1945, Hal pitched in six games, in relief, for the Boston Braves. Hal was credited with no wins and 1 loss. His ERA was 5.28, for $15\frac{1}{3}$ innings of work.

Hal feels that his baseball career, as a right-handed pitcher, was uneventful. He believes that he never reached the point he wanted to, and he isn't proud of what he accomplished. We respectfully disagreed with Hal Shacker and pointed out that only one minor league player in 20, at the time he played, made it to the majors.

Hal lives in Tampa, Florida.

Years	Games	IP	W	L	GS	SV	PCT	ERA
1	6	$15\frac{1}{3}$	0	1	0	0	.000	5.28

1945 Bos-N

Heinie Scheer

Henry "Heinie" Scheer was born on July 31, 1900, in the Bronx, New York. He was the third of three brothers.

Heinie began his baseball career by playing infield for some of the Bronx amateur teams. In 1914, he played for a team that became the Bronx Borough champions. Heinie went on to play with the Tremont Triangles, the Highbridge Athletics, the Bronx Giants, the Bushwicks, and the Bay Parkways. In 1921, he became a professional player, signing with Hartford.

In 1922, Connie Mack signed Heinie for his Philadelphia Athletics for $5,000. He made his major league debut on April 20, 1922. Heinie struck out in his only at-bat, that day, against Herb Pennock. The A's lost the game, at Shibe Park, to the Boston Red Sox by a score of 15 to 4. On June 25, 1922, Heinie had his first major league hit. He singled in the 9th inning off Senators pitcher Tom Zacher to put the A's ahead, 2–1. Heinie hit his first home run on August 22, 1922, at Shibe Park; it was a two-run homer in the second inning of the second game of a doubleheader. The A's won, by a score of 7 to 2, over the Chicago White Sox. Heinie finished the season with a .170 batting average and 4 home runs, in 51 games.

In 1923, Heinie returned to the A's lineup and batted .238 in 69 games. At the end of the season, he was traded to Shreveport, Louisiana (Texas League), with two other players, for future Hall of Fame outfielder Al Simmons. After this trade, Heinie never returned to a major league lineup. He had a lifetime major league batting average of .212, with 6 home runs, in 120 games.

In 1924, Heinie played for Shreveport. While eating breakfast at his hotel one morning, he met a beautiful waitress, who operated the hotel's switchboard in the afternoons; her name was Ada Caldwell. Heinie played the next two seasons with the Baltimore Orioles (Southern Association) and Peoria, Illinois (3-I League). At the end of the 1926 season, Heinie sent for Ada, to become his bride.

In 1927, Heinie played for Reading (International League) and Baltimore. In 1928, he played for the pennant-winning New Haven Profs. Heinie met many friends while playing on the Profs and made local ties to the community. He played his final season in 1929 for Allentown and Thomas, Ontario (Canadian League).

After retiring from baseball, Heinie moved with his wife from their New York home to New Haven, Connecticut. There, he became a haberdashery salesman with J. Johnson and Son. In 1934, he was a salesman for Eastern Liquor, Inc., and then, later, became a salesman for Eder Brothers, another liquor company. He kept in shape by playing golf. Meanwhile, Heinie helped found Little League Baseball in the New Haven area and later became the local league's commissioner. Heinie retired from Eder Brothers at the age of sixty-five.

In 1973, Heinie suffered a heart attack. He recovered from it, but three years later he suffered a second, fatal heart attack. Heinie Scheer died on March 21, 1976, at New Haven.

Years	Games	AB	H	R	RBI	HR	BA	OBP	FP
2	120	345	73	36	33	6	.212	.259	.973

1922-23 Phi-A

Richie Scheinblum

Richie Scheinblum had a career filled with superlatives. If most of these superlatives were at other than the major league level, his career also had a scope that made him a baseball star of three continents.

Richard Alan Scheinblum was born on November 5, 1942, the second of 5 children, in New York, the son of Fred and Lee Scheinblum. His father was a CPA. Richie's mother, who died when he was seven, had come to this country from the Ukraine. Following his first wife's death, Fred Scheinblum re-married.

Richie was active in Little League as a boy, and one of the great influences on his career was his Little League coach, Janet Murke. It was Janet Murke who advised the naturally right-handed Richie to become a switch-hitter. Later, Richie played for the Babe Ruth League and American Legion ball. At Dwight Morrow High School, in Englewood, New Jersey, Richie played on the baseball, soccer, and basketball teams—helping lead his school to the New Jersey State Basketball

Richie's baseball card from Japan, where local pronunciation rendered his family name as "Shane."

Championship, with a 29-1 record. Richie started on the baseball team as a second baseman, but his wild throws moved him to the outfield. He would stay in the outfield for his entire career.

After graduating from high school in 1960, Richie then attended C.W. Post College, in Greenvale, New York. While there, Richie lettered in baseball, basketball, and track. In 1963, he was named Post's Athlete of the Year. He graduated from Post with a degree in business administration in 1964.

In 1963, Richie played semi-pro baseball for Bloomington (Central Illinois Collegiate League). He batted .287 in 44 games and attracted the attention of scout "Hoot" Evers, who worked for the Cleveland Indians. Richie was offered a contract and a $12,000 bonus for the 1964 season. He signed.

Richie started his professional career with Burlington (Carolina League), hitting .309. He hit only one home run during that initial season, but it was a grand slam that gave Burlington the victory in the bottom of the 13th inning of a tied game against Greensboro. In 1965, Richie played for Salinas (California League), where he hit .318, the best in the league, and was named to the league's All-Star team.

On September 1, 1965, Richie made his major league debut at Municipal Stadium in Kansas City during the 7th inning. He was put in to run for Cleveland's Joe Azcue, and scored on Fred Whitfield's double off Kansas City pitcher John O'Donoghue. Nevertheless, Kansas City defeated the Indians, 4–3. Richie got into 3 more games before the end of Cleveland's season. He ended with a .222 batting average, but a .364 on-base percentage.

In 1966, Richie played for Pawtucket (Eastern League), batting .263. He led the league in doubles and sacrifice flies. During the winter of 1966–67, Richie played in the Nicaraguan League. He led that league in batting: .331. The next regular season, 1967, he played with Portland (Pacific Coast League), and his average was .291. Richie also hit 16 home runs that season. He was tied for honors, in a poll of the managers, as the league's best hitting prospect.

That year, Richie was given another chance to show what he could do on the Cleveland Indians. He hit .318, in 18 games. Starting 1968, again with Portland, he hit .304 and was chosen for the league's All-Star second team. Again he was sent up, during the year, to Cleveland, where he hit .218, in 19 games. But Richie did make a good enough impression, and 1969 would be his first complete year in the majors. He appeared in 102 games and hit .186. He got his first major league home run the same day the U.S. Astronauts first landed on the moon: July 20, 1969.

During the winter season of 1969–70, Richie played the first of two years for the Leones (Lions) of Caracas, Venezuela. During this season and 1970–71, he was very successful in the Venezuelan League. Richie spent 1970 with Wichita (American Association), where he had an outstanding year. He led the league in runs scored, 79; total bases, 265; RBIs, 84; and tied for the lead in hits, 155. Richie was also second in doubles, 32, and home runs, 24. His .337 batting average was third in the league. He was named to his league's All-Star team and also the All-Star team of the Class AAA–East. He was voted the league's Topps Player of the Year and his team's MVP.

By spring training of 1971, Richie had been traded to the Washington Senators. He stayed with them through training and the first month and a half of the regular season. While there, Richie fell under the tutelage of the Senators' manager, Ted Williams. Richie said of this experience, "Ted Williams taught me to think while I'm at bat. That was one of the big things that helped me have such a good year in 1971."

Richie's 27 games with the Senators only gave him a .143 batting average, but the remainder of his year with Denver (American Association) was outstanding. He led the league in batting, .388; total bases, 271; triples, 10; RBIs, 108; and he tied for the lead in doubles, 31. He was second in the league in both runs scored, 83, and home runs, 25. His .388 average was the highest batting average in the league since 1951, when Harry "The Hat" Walker hit .393 for Columbus. Richie's .388 is still the all-time best average for a player on a Denver team. He was named the league's MVP and the league's Topps Player of the Month for August and Topps Player of the Year; he was selected for his league's All-Star team. He was also selected as Colorado's Pro Athlete of the Year. He was equally impressive in that year's American Association playoffs and Junior World Series. In the playoffs, Richie led Denver to victory with 2 two-run homers and a remarkable throw from right field to the plate, which cut off a tying run. In the Series, Richie hit .391, including 2 more homers. Richie finished the post-season with 12 RBIs.

In 1972, Richie was back to the majors, this time with the Kansas City Royals. Richie had an excellent year, batting .300 and hitting 21 doubles and 8 home runs. He was selected for the 1972 All-Star team as the American League's starting rightfielder. In his only at-bat during the game, which was held in Atlanta, Richie grounded out. He started 1973 with the Cincinnati Reds. After 29 games, during which he was batting .222, with his only National League home run, he was traded to the California Angels. Richie appeared in 77 games for the Angels and batted .328.

Richie appeared in only 10 games for the Angels in 1974, before being traded back to the Royals. He played in 36 games for Kansas City and was then traded to the St. Louis Cardinals, where he was in 6 games, with a batting average of .333. This was the conclusion of his major league career.

Richie played in 462 major league games, over 8 years. He had 320 hits, including 52 doubles and 13 home runs. His major league batting average was .263. But this was not the end of Richie's baseball career. Richie played 1975 and 1976 for Japan's Hiroshima team (Central League). In 1975, Richie batted .291 and his team won the pennant. In 1976, Richie hit .308—a very rare achievement in Japan's pitcher-friendly Central League. Richie then tore his Achilles tendon in a mishap, and this finally brought his career to a conclusion.

Richie Scheinblum married the former Mary Almeida. They have a son, Monte. Richie lives in Northridge, California. On August 29, 1992, he was honored at Denver's Mile High Stadium for his All-Time Denver records of .388 batting average and .726 slugging percentage, both accomplished in 1971.

Years	Games	AB	H	R	RBI	HR	BA	OBP	FP
8	462	1218	320	131	127	13	.263	.346	.965

1965, 1967-69 Cle-A, 1971 Was-A, 1972 KC-A, 1973 Cin-N, 1973-74 Cal-A, 1974 KC-A, 1974 StL-N

Mike Schemer

Michael "Lefty" Schemer was born the son of an Orthodox rabbi on November 20, 1917, in Baltimore, Maryland. Sports seem to have been the center of his attention from very early on. By the time Mike was in high school, the family had moved to Miami, Florida, and Mike became a legend, in those days, for his football abilities at Miami High School. His was not a natural talent. His throwing arm was crooked and he ran like a duck—but he was tough. In 1936, in a game against Edison, he scored two touchdowns in the last few minutes of the game, to win it. The following year, in the game against Edison, Mike played most of the game with a broken leg. He thought he just had a charley horse, and he played through his pain, gaining much yardage and scoring a touchdown. Miami won, 28–0. Only after the game was the condition of Mike's leg

Photo by Joe Benetti

MIKE SCHEMER
1947 Solons First Baseman

discovered.

Miami, in those days, was not only the best in the state, but went on to play teams from all over the country. With Mike at their helm, they beat everyone. A sportscaster who saw Mike play said, "He could throw a ball like a rifle." Mike went on to play football at the University of Miami, where he was famous for his passing ability. But he was famous in the Miami community just as much for his abilities in basketball and track. He once tried badminton, as a diversion, and ended up state champion. But above all, he was known for his abilities as a baseball player. In 1940, Mike was scheduled to represent the United States in that year's Olympics, in Tokyo, as part of the baseball team. The start of the Second World War, however, led to the Olympics' cancellation.

Mike served the war years in the U.S. Army. On his return from service, he was picked up by the New York Giants. Mike debuted on August 8, 1945, at the Polo Grounds, in a game against the St. Louis Cardinals. Mike got 2 singles, for 4 at-bats, but St. Louis still beat the Giants, 3–0. During the 1945 season, Mike played first base for the Giants; he batted and threw left-handed. On August 20, 1945, he hit a three-run homer off Cubs pitcher Hank Wyse, at the Polo Ground. The Giants won the game, 9–3. This was Mike's only major league homer. It was symptomatic of Mike's problem in the majors. He was a dependable hitter, as his .333 batting average in 1945 indicates, but he was a short, slap hitter, not the long-ball hitter the Giants were longing for. Mike was given just one more chance, in 1946, to show his stuff. He made one pinch-hit appearance that year, and was out. Mike played in 32 games for the Giants. His lifetime batting average is .330. He had 36 hits, including 3 doubles, 1 triple, and the 1 homer. He scored 10 runs and he had 10 RBIs.

In 1947, Mike played first base with the Sacramento Solons. Then, during the 1950s, he settled down in Miami and turned his attention to softball. During the early part of the decade he played for the North Miami Police team. In softball, his style of hitting proved a great advantage and he became the acknowledged star of Miami's softball leagues. Later, he served as a park supervisor in Miami and as a coach. Mike Schemer died there on April 22, 1983. The fame of Mike's youth had not been forgotten, however, and hundreds turned out for his funeral at Miami's Southern Memorial Park.

Years	Games	AB	H	R	RBI	HR	BA	OBP	FP
2	32	109	36	10	10	1	.330	.365	.993

1945-46 NY-N

Bill Schwarz

William De Witt Schwarz was born on January 30, 1891, in Birmingham, Alabama. He debuted as a catcher on August 20, 1914, with the New York Yankees. He struck out in his only at-bat.

Bill Schwarz died on June 24, 1949, in Jacksonville, Florida.

Years	Games	AB	H	R	RBI	HR	BA	OBP	FP
1	1	1	0	0	0	0	.000	.000	1.000

1914 NY-A

Art Shamsky

Arthur Louis Shamsky was born on October 14, 1941, in St. Louis, Missouri. Art is best remembered as a member of the 1969 "Miracle" Mets, one of the most popular teams of modern times. His .300 batting average for that team was a vital component for its pennant-winning performance.

At his first at-bat in professional baseball, Art hit a home run. His minor league career began in 1960, with Geneva (New York–Pennsylvania League), where the left-handed outfielder hit .271, with 111 hits in 119 games, including 16 doubles, 8 triples, and 18 home runs. He was named to the league's All-Star team that year. He also led the league in assists. Art's roommate at Geneva was young Pete Rose. In 1961, Art played for Topeka (3-I League), where he hit .288, with 116 hits in 116 games, including 20 doubles, 4 triples, and 15 homers. Art batted .284 for Macon (Sally League) in 1962; there, he also had another 16 homers, including 6 in a thirteen-game period. Art spent the next two years in San Diego (Pacific Coast League), where he hit .267 and .272. He had 18 homers in 1963 and 25 in 1964. In the latter year, he also had 12 stolen bases.

The Cincinnati Reds were impressed enough to invite Art to spring training in 1965. He made the team, though as a pinch-hitter rather than a regular player. In this position, Art was most satisfactory. He debuted on April 17. For the year, Art batted .260, .289 when pinch-hitting, proving himself one of the team's best left-handed pinch-hitters. In 1965, he hit only 2 home runs. This number jumped to 21 the following year, when Art was platooned against right-handed pitchers—and this was in only 96 games. This total was second only to Deron Johnson on the Reds. August 12–14, 1966, Art tied a major league record by batting 4 home runs in 4 straight at-bats. (This record was tied again, in 1971, by Mike Epstein.)

In 1967, Art batted .197, with just 3 homers. Before the start of the 1968 season, he was traded to the New York Mets. He hit .238 that year, hitting 12 home runs. Then, Art was sent to Tidewater (International League) at the start of the 1969 season. His .289 average and his 4 homers, in just 11 games, brought him back to the parent club in a hurry. Art's 91 hits—including 9 doubles, 3 triples, and 14 homers—did a great deal to get the Mets to compete in the first-ever National League Championship Series. Once the team was in the Series, against Atlanta, Art's .538 batting average was critical in the Mets' 3–0 victory. His 7 hits led all batters in the Series. Art was not as impressive in the World Series itself, but the Mets still took the Series, 4–1, over the Baltimore Orioles. Art, by this time, had become a hero to the Jews of New York. The triumph of the "Miracle" Mets solidified his position as one of the most popular people in all the city's 5 boroughs.

Art had another good year in 1970, with a .293 batting average and 118 hits, including 19 doubles, 2 triples, and 11 homers. His next year, 1971, was a bit of a letdown, with just a .185 average in just 68 games. At the end of the season, Art was traded to the St. Louis Cardinals. Before the 1972 season started, however, he was traded again, to the Chicago Cubs. Art was suffering from back problems during this period. He appeared in 15 games for the Cubs, batting .125; he got 2 singles for the Cubs, the last hits he would ever get. After these 15 games, he was traded to the Oakland A's. Art appeared in 8 games for the A's, but with just 7 at-bats. He got no hits and ended his stay with Oakland with a .000 average. Art's back problems had become too serious to ignore. Before the end of the 1972 season, he called it quits.

Art batted .253 in 8 years of major league ball. He played in 665 games, with 4 teams. He had 68 career home runs. His on-base percentage was .333 and his slugging average was .427.

Since his baseball career, Art has been successful in real estate, sports broadcasting, and the restaurant business. Art Shamsky still makes his home in the city that took him to its heart: New York.

Years	Games	AB	H	R	RBI	HR	BA	OBP	FP
8	665	1686	426	194	233	68	.253	.333	.987

1965-67 Cin-N, 1968-71 NY-N, 1972 Chi-N, 1972 Oak-A

Dick Sharon

Richard Louis Sharon was born on April 15, 1950, in San Mateo, California. Dick was the child of a Jewish father and a gentile mother. In high school, he was All-League in baseball, basketball, and football.

Dick was chosen as Pittsburgh's number-one draft pick in the June 1968 free-agent draft. He would spend five years in the Pirates' farm system. Dick began his career with Bradenton (Gulf Coast League), where he hit .166. He spent 1969 with Gastonia (West Carolina League), where he hit .216 and began to develop a reputation for excellent defensive work in the outfield, even as his batting averages slowly mounted. In 1970, he hit .254 with Salem (Carolina League), with 22 home runs. In the following year, his average rose to .255, with Waterbury (Eastern League). Dick played with Charleston (International League) in 1972, where he hit .268, with 14 home runs.

He was traded to the Detroit Tigers on November 27, 1972, for Jim Foor and Norm McRae, and was sent, at the start of the 1973 season, to Toledo (International League), where he hit .208 in the first 16 games of the season. On May 13, 1973, Dick made his major league debut with the Detroit Tigers, put in late in the game as a defensive replacement. On the following day, Dick made his first plate appearance in a game against the Yankees, at Yankee Stadium. On his first at-bat he got an RBI. In the 8th inning, he got his first major league hit, a run-scoring double off Mike Kekich. On May 31, Dick got his first major league home run, off White Sox pitcher Eddie Fisher. The Sox beat the Tigers 10–2, at White Sox Park. In a game against the Rangers on July 10, Dick had a perfect 4-for-4, with 2 home runs and a double. On September 9, he stole twice on 2 attempts.

At the end of his first season, Dick was awarded the Tiger Rookie of the Year for 1973. Previous winners of this award included Elliott Maddox, who won the award in 1970. Dick's excellent work in right field, which gave him a .970 fielding percentage in 1973, continued to improve in '74, when his percentage was .989. His offense, however, slipped and his batting average dropped from .242 to .217. In November, 1974, Dick was traded to the San Diego Padres, along with Bob Strampe and Ed Brinkman, for Nate Colbert. Dick batted only .194

for the Padres in 1975, and his fielding percentage dropped to .948. On October 20, 1975, Dick was traded to the St. Louis Cardinals for Willie Davis; he was assigned to the Cardinals' AAA farm club in Tulsa.

Dick would never return to the majors. He had a major league batting average of .218 in three years. He played in 242 games, had 102 hits, including 20 doubles and 13 home runs.

Dick Sharon is married. He lives in Dillon, Montana.

Years	Games	AB	H	R	RBI	HR	BA	OBP	FP
3	242	467	102	46	46	13	.218	.294	.969

1973-74 Det-A, 1975 SD-N

Larry Sherry

Lawrence "Larry" Sherry, the MVP of the 1959 World Series, was born with two club feet on July 25, 1935, in Los Angeles, California. His mother had fallen just before she gave birth to Larry and the family believes this may have had something to do with Larry's malformed feet.

LARRY SHERRY

The first 12 years of his life were a struggle for Larry. For six weeks, he struggled through a series of operations. Then he had to wear braces on his feet. When Larry was 10, he entered a foot race. His father, Harry, a studio worker in one of the Hollywood movie lots, was there to cheer him on. Larry struggled with grim determination against his opponents and his handicap, to come in third. By twelve, he could stand on his own two feet, without braces, although he still needed special shoes. There was nothing that Larry wanted to do more than follow in the footsteps of his three older brothers, Stan, Norm, and George, all of whom played baseball for their high school team.

Larry played for John Burroughs Junior High. In the summer, he played for the Hollywood Post 43 American Legion team. All this time, brother Norm coached Larry. This was a constant feature of Larry's youth and his career. In 1949, Larry entered Fairfax High School, where his three brothers had all been athletic stars. But still, Larry was not a good runner and he still needed special orthopedic shoes if he was to play sports. The baseball coach at Fairfax came to the rescue. He arranged for special shoes for Larry and pulled Larry out of the infield, putting him on the pitcher's mound. There, Larry would share duties with his classmate Barry Latman.

In his first year, Larry was already a star of the baseball team, earning his first letter. By his senior year, he was a star of the basketball team too, setting a new record for the school in scoring—22 points in a game—and captaining the team. He was also named All-City.

In 1953, when he was working as a clerk in a grocery store, Larry was approached by Lefty Phillips, then working as a scout for the Los Angeles Dodgers. Larry was given a modest bonus, the day before his eighteenth birthday, and assigned to Santa Barbara (California League). In 1953, his first year in the minors, he won 1 game and lost 2, giving him a percentage of .333. This set a pattern for his early career—which was basically a losing one. The Dodgers hierarchy, however, continued to see great promise and progress in the young right-hander, and they continued to advance him up the levels of the minor leagues until he would reach the majors.

In 1954, Larry was with Great Falls (Pioneer League) and Bakersfield (California League). He won 6 games that year, and lost 8. His ERAs for the two teams were 7.82 and 5.15. The next season found him in Newport News (Piedmont League), where he won 5 and lost 10, with an ERA of 4.90. During the 1955 season, Larry seriously considered quitting baseball, but brother Norm talked him out of it. In 1956, Larry was sent to Pueblo (Western League). For the first time, he did not have a losing average; he won 13 and lost 13, with and ERA of 4.39. While in Pueblo, Larry happened to walk into a sporting goods shop, and struck up a conversation with a girl working there, Sally Swearingen. They began dating, and two days before Christmas 1956 Larry and Sally were married.

In 1957, Larry was sent to Los Angeles—not to the Dodgers, who were still in Brooklyn—but to the Pacific Coast League team. He continued the season with Fort Worth (Texas League). Again, it was a losing one: 10 wins against 11 losses. However, his ERA with Fort Worth was down to 3.07. Larry started 1958 with the parent club, the Los Angeles Dodgers. On April 17, 1958, he debuted. He was only used as a reliever, however, during 5 games, pitching less than 5 innings. His ERA was a whopping 12.46, however, and he was sent to Spokane (Pacific Coast League), where he won 6 and lost 14. For the only time in their minor league careers, the two Sherry brothers played together on this team.

Larry's great year of 1959 began for him in St. Paul (American Association). There, he pitched 6 wins and 7 losses, with a 3.60 ERA. For the first time in his career, however, he had found an effective third pitch. He had first developed this pitch during the winter of 1958–59, playing in Venezuela, his brother Norm catching for him. Up to this time, Larry had depended on his fastball and his curve. But now he introduced a very effective slider. By mid-season, Larry was leading the American Association in strikeouts. In addition, he had pitched, among his six wins, some very impressive shutouts. When Johnny Podres' back forced him out of the pitching rotation, the Dodgers sent out the call for Larry.

Larry, who had staggered along in the minors, came to the major leagues and looked wonderful. While his first start for the Dodgers was a loss, 2–1, he gave up no earned runs. He would be excellent throughout the regular 1959 season, ending with the first winning record of his career, 7 wins and 2 losses, with a 2.20 ERA. But this was just a prologue to the 1959 World Series.

Of the 4 Dodger victories in the series over the Chicago White Sox, Larry, used only in relief, had two wins and two saves. He completed all 4 victories. His Series ERA was 0.71. He pitched $12\frac{2}{3}$ innings of the Series, more than any Dodger starter and any Dodger pitcher. To add frosting to the cake, Larry's batting average for the series was .500. Rookie reliever Larry was chosen as the Series' MVP.

He became the toast of the West Coast and the nation, and was awarded a car and prizes of all kinds. He was the guest of honor at 25 banquets over the next few months, also appearing on 78 radio and TV shows. When the next season began, he was out of practice and not up to his best. In the first half of the year, he had only 6 wins against 7 losses. But in the second half of 1960, Larry was 8-3, with a 2.58 ERA. He had become the king of the Dodger relievers. Larry started only 3 games in 1960, but he relieved in 54, leading the National League in relief victories that year.

On May 7, 1960, Larry was teamed for the first time, on the Dodgers, with his brother Norm, as a battery. The Sherry brothers were the only Jewish brother battery in major league history, only the 10th brother battery in the majors at all! During that first game, Larry got the win and Norm hit a home run. Since the Sherrys, there has never again been a brother battery in the big leagues. They last appeared together in 1962. Larry continued in his position, as reliever, for Los Angeles through the 1963 season. His ERA in 1961 was 3.90; in 1962, this figured dipped to 3.20; his ERA for 1963 was 3.73.

Larry was traded to the Detroit Tigers in 1964. He was the team's top reliever, until injuries slowed him down. He finished the year with 7 wins, 5 losses, and a 3.66 ERA. The following year, his ERA dropped to 3.10. In 1966, he had 8 wins and 5 losses, as well as 20 saves. During 1967, Larry's ERA with the Tigers rose to 6.43 and he was traded to Houston during the season, finishing the year with Houston with a 4.87 ERA and leading the team in saves. On the 1967 Astros, Larry was reunited with his old high school mound mate, Barry Latman. There were two other Jews on this team, Bo Belinsky and Norm Miller. All this time, Larry was increasingly bothered with injuries and arm problems. He was traded to the California Angels for the 1968 season, but after just 3 games decided to call it quits.

Larry finished his career with 53 wins, 44 losses, 82 saves, and a lifetime ERA of 3.67. He appeared in 416 games and pitched $799\frac{1}{n}$ innings in 11 major league seasons. Larry's greatest moments of glory came early in his major league career, but he had a long career as a dependable and steady reliever. The World Series of 1959 will always be remembered in terms of his contributions.

Larry worked for the Seattle Rainiers (Pacific Coast League) as a pitching coach for the balance of the 1968 season. He continued coaching, finally returning to the majors as a pitching coach in 1977, with the Pittsburgh Pirates. He stayed with the Pirates for 1978. From 1979 to 1980, he coached with the California Angels.

Larry Sherry and his wife, Sally, have a son, Scott, and a daughter, Suzanne. He enjoys golf. He lives in Mission Viejo, California.

Years	Games	IP	W	L	GS	SV	PCT	ERA
11	416	$799\frac{1}{3}$	53	44	16	82	.546	3.67

1958-63 LA-N, 1964-67 Det-A, 1967 Hou-N, 1968 Cal-A

Norm Sherry

Norm Sherry would be a major figure in baseball history for three things, even if he did not have a fine record as a catcher to point to, a winning record as a manager, and a long run as a coach: Norm was part of the last brother battery in baseball, he was a major influence on the pitching career of his brother Larry, and he gave the advice that started Sandy Koufax on his climb to greatness.

Norman Burt Sherry was born on July 16, 1931. He had three brothers, all of whom played baseball at Fairfax High School. Brother George would play in the minors. Norm and Larry would both play major roles in the major leagues. While at Fairfax, Norm played basketball as well as baseball. He began at Fairfax as a pitcher, but Coach Frank Shaffer needed a catcher, so Norm was recruited. In 1949, Norm was All-City catcher and his team won the city championship.

After high school, he attended a tryout at Gilmore Field, where he was signed by the Hollywood Stars, at that time a part of the Dodgers organization, with a $6,000 bonus. He was assigned to Santa Barbara (California League) for the 1950 season. Right-handed Norm hit .241 that year, with 4 home runs. The 1951 season was divided between Fort Worth (Texas League) and Newport News (Piedmont League). During 1952 and 1953, Norm was in the Army. Afterward, the 1954 season was a repeat of 1951, divided between Fort Worth and Newport News.

Norm was very successful at his catching duties, but his batting averages kept him in the minors. In 1955, Norm began to turn this around with his work with Fort Worth. But then he had trouble with his elbow, which eventually led to an operation. After this, Norm broke his thumb. Following the season, he had an operation for a ruptured disc, so that by the time Norm reported for 1956 spring training he could barely walk. He caught in 66 games during that season, however, which was divided between Fort Worth and Buffalo (International League).

Norm did well in spring training during 1957, and until two days before the season started his name appeared on the Dodgers' roster. But then he was sent to St. Paul (American Association). On May 20, Norm's right wrist was shattered by a foul tip. Two days later, as had been planned, Norm, his hand in a cast, was wed to Mardie Brockway. Larry Sherry served as best man during the ceremony.

Things looked up for Norm in 1958. He played for Spokane (Pacific Coast League), where he caught 131 games, hit 27 doubles, and had 41 RBIs, for a .278 batting average. On June 14 of that year, Norm's wife had their first child, Cynthia. On the same day, brother Larry also had a daughter, Suzanne. The girls were delivered by the same doctor.

Norm got a brief appearance with the Dodgers at the start of the 1959 season. He made his debut on April 12, but then was sent back to Spokane, after appearing in only 2 games. His batting average during his brief time with Los Angeles in 1959 was .333. His average with Spokane was .253, but there he had 47 RBIs to his credit. During that winter season, Norm played for Escogido, Venezuela. When health problems sent player-manager Pete Reiser back to the United States, Norm took over as skipper of the club, as well as catcher, and led them to the league pennant. This certainly brought him to the attention of the Dodgers management. The following season, when the Dodgers decided to carry three catchers instead of two, Norm was on board for good.

The 1960 season saw Norm catch in 47 games for the Dodgers and hit .283. His season was cut short when he was hit by Giants pitcher Stu Miller and his wrist was shattered. Norm also played in 47 games in 1961, but he hit .256. In 1961, Norm suffered a kidney injury when he was knocked over by pitcher Curt Simmons of the St. Louis Cardinals while protecting the plate. It was during spring training of 1961 that Norm had his famous conversation with Sandy Koufax, which began the latter's climb to greatness. Norm's final year with the Dodgers was 1962. He caught in only 35 games and hit .182. During that year, he became one of very few catchers to accomplish an unassisted double play. That winter, Norm was traded to the Mets; he caught 63 games for the Mets in 1963 and hit .136, his career low.

Norm played 5 years in the majors with a .215 batting average. He had 107 hits in that time, including 18 home runs. But his real value as a player was his defensive work. His lifetime fielding average as a catcher is .989. To put this in perspective, we can compare this to his fellow Dodgers Roy Campanella and John Roseboro, universally recognized as two of the greatest catchers of all time. Campanella's percentage was .988 and Roseboro's was exactly the same as Norm's, .989.

Norm left major league baseball with a reputation as a pretty smart fellow. He had done well during his stint as a manager in Venezuela. He had done much to guide the careers of his brother Larry and Sandy Koufax. In 1970, Norm was hired as a coach for the California Angels, which job he continued through 1971. In 1976, he returned to the Angels as a coach, but before the season was over became the team's manager, when Dick Williams proved unsatisfactory with a .406 winning percentage. Norm raised the team's percentage to .561. In 1977, his percentage fell to .481 and he was replaced after 81 games. It is interesting to note that Jimmie Reese was part of the Angels staff throughout Norm's regime as skipper.

Norm Sherry has continued his career as a major league coach with a number of different organizations. From 1978 to 1981, he worked for the Montreal Expos. From 1982 to 1984, he was with the San Diego Padres. His latest stint has been with the San Francisco Giants, from 1986 to 1991. He currently lives in San Diego, California.

Years	Games	AB	H	R	RBI	HR	BA	OBP	FP
5	194	497	107	45	69	18	.215	.280	.989

1959-62 LA-N, 1963 NY-N

as Manager

Years	Games	W	L	PCT
2	147	76	71	.517

1976-77 Cal-A

Harry Shuman

Harry "Handsome Harry" Shuman was born in North Philadelphia on March 5, 1916. He graduated from Philadelphia's Central High School.

In 1936, Harry was majoring in pre-law at Temple University, when he was invited by a friend to pitch batting practice for the Philadelphia Athletics. Harry was pitching on Temple's team, but he had only dreamt about a career in baseball. Connie Mack was watching practice that day, and liked what he saw. He offered Harry a minor league contract. Harry forgot about college and the law, and signed. He started his career in the A's farm system, and had considerable success playing with the Toronto Maple Leafs (International League).

Harry was a right-handed pitcher with a good fastball and a good curve. After playing on a variety of farm clubs, his contract was purchased by the Pittsburgh Pirates. Harry debuted for the Pirates on September 14, 1942. Harry appeared only in relief in the majors, and has no wins or losses to his credit. In fact, in 1942 he played in only that one game with the Pirates. That day, he pitched for 2 innings and gave up no runs, so his ERA for the year was 0.00.

Harry appeared in 11 games for the Pirates in 1943, pitching 22 innings. His ERA for 1943 was 5.32. Harry was traded to the Phillies for the 1944 season. He pitched in 18 games, pitching 26⅔ innings, with an ERA for the year of 4.05. At the end of the season, Harry's contract was traded to the Los Angeles Angels (Pacific Coast League). But he had had enough of traveling and didn't want to be that far from his family. His years of baseball had been a source of great pleasure to him, but he was married and he had children.

Harry had been making about $5,000 a year pitching. But now he wished for something more secure, so Harry decided not to report to the Angels. He took a job working for a steamship line. Later, he worked as a supervisor for the Pennsylvania State Department of Revenue. He then spent some 12 years working for the Veterans Advisory Council of the Philadelphia City Council. Later, until his death, Harry worked for the Philadelphia Democratic Executive Committee. Harry and his wife, Phyllis, were married during Harry's minor league days. Both he and Phyllis were very proud of their Jewish background. The Shumans had three daughters and seven grandchildren.

Harry Shuman died on October 25, 1996, of heart failure while working at his desk in the Center City office of the Democratic Executive Committee.

Years	Games	IP	W	L	GS	SV	PCT	ERA
3	30	$50\frac{2}{3}$	0	0	0	0	NA	4.44

1942-43 Pit-N, 1944 Phi-N

Al Silvera

Aaron Albert "Al" Silvera was born on August 26, 1935, in San Diego, California. He is the nephew of major league player Sam Nahem. Al attended the University of Southern California, played on its baseball team, and batted .405, with 14 home runs, including 5 grand slams.

When Al left college, he had offers from many different teams, but chose to sign with the Cincinnati Reds, as a bonus player. On June 12, 1955, Al made his major league debut with the Reds. That season, he played in 13 games for the Reds and batted .143. Al briefly returned to play for Cincinnati in 1956. That year, the Reds changed their name to the Redlegs. This was done because of the contemporary atmosphere of Commie-phobia, inspired by the witch hunts of the House Committee on Un-American Activities and Senator "Tailgunner" Joe McCarthy.

The Redlegs organization got over their wimpiness the very next year and went back to being the Reds—as they had been for 75 years before this. Al did not get an at-bat in 1956, but he did appear in 1 game. He had a lifetime batting average of .143.

Al Silvera currently lives in Beverly Hills, California.

Years	Games	AB	H	R	RBI	HR	BA	OBP	FP
2	14	7	1	3	2	0	.143	.143	NA

1955-56 Cin-N

Fred Sington

Frederic William Sington was born on February 24, 1910, in Birmingham, Alabama. He attended Phillips High School. From 1927 to 1930, Fred attended the University of Alabama. From 1928 to 1930, he played on the university's football team. He was the team's star tackle and was selected, in 1929, for the All-America Third Team; in 1930, he was named to the All-America First Team by Grantland Rice.

Fred was a leading figure in Alabama's 1930 team, which was undefeated for the season and triumphed in the Rose Bowl. Fred also played on the university's baseball team. He began his college career as a pitcher, but was converted to an outfielder by coach Hank Crips. While attending college, Fred was a member of the Jewish fraternity, Zeta Beta Tau. He graduated Phi Beta Kappa in 1930.

After graduating from college, the 6'2", 219-pound, football tackle spurned offers to become a professional football player or professional wrestler and set out to become a baseball player. He signed with the Washington Senators. In 1932, Fred batted .368 with Beckley, West Virginia (Mid-Atlantic League). In the off-seasons between 1931 and 1934, Fred was an assistant football coach at Duke. In 1933, he played with the Atlanta Crackers.

In 1934, Fred was promoted to Albany, New York (International League); he batted .345 for Albany before being further promoted to the Washington Senators. Fred made his major league debut on September 23, 1934. That day, he hit a single that scored Buddy Myer. The Senators defeated the A's, 2–1, at Shibe Park. In 1934, Fred appeared in a total of 9 games with the Senators. He had a .286 batting average in 35 at-bats. In 1935, Fred played most of the season with Chattanooga (Southern Association), where he won the batting crown with his .384 batting average. He did get to play in 20 games with the Senators in 1935, with a .182 batting average; in 1936, he played in 25 games with them. On September 9, 1936, Fred hit his first major league home run, off Jake Wadew of the Detroit Tigers. It was a solo homer in the 9th inning. The Senators won the game, 11–4, at Navin Field. Fred ended the 1936 season with a .319 batting average.

In 1937, he had his only full major league season. He appeared in 78 games and batted .237, with 3 home runs. At the end of the season, Fred was traded to the Brooklyn Dodgers, where, in 1938, he appeared in 17 games and batted .358, with 2 home runs, and where, in 1939, he appeared in 32 games with a .274 batting average. Fred retired at the end of the season. He had a lifetime batting average of .271 and 7 home runs, and appeared in 181 games.

During World War II, Fred coached the All-Service football champions at Norman, Oklahoma. Fred then returned to his hometown of Birmingham, and was active in the community. He also was chief umpire and president of the Southeastern Conference Officials Association for many years. In 1955, Fred was inducted into the College Football Hall of Fame, the only Jewish baseball player ever so honored. In 1957, his son, Fred Sington, Jr., was drafted in the 12th round of the NFL draft by the San Francisco 49ers. Both Fred, Jr. and his brother David were prominent tackles on Alabama football teams during the 1950s. Dave was a co-captain of the Crimson Tide

In 1987, an award was named after Fred; the Sington Trophy is an award given to outstanding professional, collegiate, and disabled athletes from Alabama. The awards are presented annually at a ceremonial dinner. Fred was also a life member of the Birmingham Board of the Salvation Army. It has been reported that Fred converted to Christianity at some point in his life. Fred Sington died in Birmingham, Alabama on August 20, 1998.

Years	Games	AB	H	R	RBI	HR	BA	OBP	FP
6	181	516	140	66	85	7	.271	.382	.961

1934-37 Was-A, 1938-39 Bro-N

Mose Solomon

This 1977 Topps cartoon is Mose's only appearance on a baseball card.

Mose Solomon was born on December 8, 1900, on the famous Hester Street when it was the center of Jewish activity on the Lower East Side of Manhattan. He was the son of Benjamin and Anna Solomon. Mose's father had been born in Russia, his mother in Austria. Benjamin Solomon was a peddler by trade and the family was poor. When Mose was young, they moved to Columbus, Ohio. Mose's given name has been a matter of some controversy. When he first came to public attention, in 1923, it was given in the press as Moses or Moe. His birth certificate, through a mistake of the attending midwife, gives the name as Morris. Mose, however, is what he called himself, what his family called him, and the only proper form.

His parents were observant. Their children took special interest in sports. Mose's brother was a boxer, and fought under the name of Henry Sully, becoming a champion in Ohio. Mose became a professional in both baseball and football.

Among the events of his football career, he went barnstorming one year, as a ringer with the Carlisle Indian School team. Among his teammates was Jim Thorpe. With the Indians, Mose became a talented dropkicker, but he had to quit the team when he was spotted by a Columbus sportswriter and was offered free tuition by Ohio State University to play on its football team. This may be one of the earliest instances of an athletic scholarship on record. Unfortunately, Mose's financial situation wouldn't allow him to accept the offer.

Mose began his baseball career in 1921 with Vancouver (Pacific Coast International League.) A left-hander, he played first base and outfield while in the minors. He was a steady batter, and his first year's batting average, .313, matches his lifetime minor league average. Mose had 13 home runs his first year; he played in the same league in 1922, first with Vancouver, then with Tacoma.

It was while he was still in the minors that Mose earned the reputation as a Jew who would not brook ethnic slur or insult. On more than one occasion, he enforced respect for himself and his religion with his fists. The word soon went round, "Better lay off the big Jew." In 1923, Mose played with Hutchinson, Kansas (Southwestern League). It was with Hutchinson that Mose gained notoriety. During the season, he hit 49 home runs, to break the old minor league record of 45, set in 1895. No one except Babe Ruth had ever hit more home runs in a season. Furthermore, Mose hit .421, leading the league. He also led his league in runs, hits, and doubles, besides home runs, and was dubbed by the press the "Jewish Babe Ruth" and the "Rabbi of Swat." John McGraw, who was ever questing to find a great Jewish star for his ball club, convinced the Giants' owners to buy his contract. The press reported various figures for this transaction from $4,500 to $100,000.

Mose debuted for the Giants on September 30, 1923, at the Polo Grounds. The game was tied, at the bottom of the 10th inning, 3–3, and Frankie Frisch was on second. Mose doubled off Joe Oeschger of the Boston Braves, and drove in the winning run. Mose, who played right field for the Giants, appeared in only one other game for them. He was never called back after that year, even though his batting average had been .375.

At the time, it was speculated that Mose's fielding skills were weak. This has been denied in an interview given by his son in 1987. According to Joseph Solomon, John McGraw demanded that Mose stay with the team through the World Series, even though he wasn't eligible to play, nor would he be paid. Meanwhile, Mose had an offer to play football for Portsmouth. He told this to McGraw, who replied that he would have to decide whether he was going to be a baseball player or a football player. He couldn't be both, at least not while on the Giants. Mose took the football offer and the Giants sold his contract to Toledo (American Association).

However, Mose was not a great fielder. His fielding average on the Giants was only .833; and with Hutchinson, he had made 31 errors in one season.

Mose continued to play minor league ball until 1929. After Toledo, he played with Pittsfield, Bridgeport, Waterbury, Hartford, and Albany, all of the Eastern League. Throughout his career, however, he was bothered by injuries, and many of his seasons were abbreviated ones. His son noted that he had brittle bones in his ankles and he often broke them. Mose was in the hospital 23 times. In 1927, with Albany, Mose led the league in doubles, with 43. He concluded his baseball career in 1929, with Canton (Central League).

After his playing career, Mose Solomon became a building contractor in Miami, Florida, and was quite successful. He was married and had a son, Joseph, who was a minor league player. Mose died of heart failure on June 25, 1966, in Miami; he was buried in the city's Mt. Nebo Cemetery.

Years	Games	AB	H	R	RBI	HR	BA	OBP	FP
1	2	8	3	0	1	0	.375	.375	.833

1923 NY-N

Bill Starr

William "Chick" Starr was born on February 16, 1911, in Brooklyn. He was the son of Isaac and Esther Starr, immigrants from Russia who met and married in New York. Bill's father and uncle had rabbinical training, but his father didn't make his living as a rabbi. Bill attended Joseph Medill High School in Chicago after the family moved.

In 1931, Bill made his professional baseball debut with Lincoln (Nebraska State League) as a catcher. The next year, he played with the Norfolk club (Nebraska State League), which won the league pennant. In 1933, he caught for St. Joseph, Missouri (Western League), which also won the pennant. The next two years, he was with Albany, New York (International League), and Harrisburg (New York–Pennsylvania League).

Bill made his major league debut with the Washington Senators on July 23, 1935. He replaced catcher Sammy Holbrook in the 10th inning at Chicago's Comiskey Park. The Senators defeated the White Sox, 4–3. In 1935, he played in 11 more games for the Senators. He had 5 hits in 24 at-bats, for a batting average of .208. He also had 1 RBI and scored one run. In 1936, Bill joined the San Diego Padres (Pacific Coast League). He was called up to the Senators to play in one game in 1936, but had no plate appearances.

Bill returned to the San Diego Padres for the 1937 season, and was platooned as catcher with George Detore. The team included Jimmy Reese and Ted Williams. In one game, Bill was called upon to replace Williams with a one-strike count. Bill was chosen because the manager wanted a player that could bunt. He bunted foul for the second strike, then flied out. The Padres won the Pacific Coast League Pennant in 1937. Ted Williams was sold for the next year to the Boston Red Sox.

Bill played one more full season in the minor leagues, before a broken leg ended his career during the 1939 season. In 1944, however, he returned to baseball—not as a player or as a coach, but as an owner. Bill was head of the group that purchased his former team, the Padres.

During his tenure as owner of the Padres, Bill became a very public figure. In 1948, he hired the first African-American player in the Pacific Coast League, John Richey. Bill negotiated, unsuccessfully, with the National and American Leagues to make the Pacific Coast League the third major league. On one occasion, Bill paid $500 dollars for a player named Tom Alston, and then sold him to the St. Louis Cardinals for $150,000 and four players. What's more, Bill created an innovative scouting system years before such a system was used by major league teams.

Bill's Padres won the Pacific Coast League Pennant in 1955. He sold them, a year later, for $300,000 to C. Arnholt Smith. Since then, the Padres have gone on to become a National League expansion team.

After leaving the Padres, Bill turned to the development of condominiums, apartment buildings, and shopping centers. He also wrote a book in 1989 entitled Clearing the Bases. In his book Bill criticized the new methods of player training. He also voiced his distaste for the one-handed catching techniques that are employed by modern catchers.

Bill Starr died on August 12, 1991, in La Jolla, California. He was married three times and had four children.

Years	Games	AB	H	R	RBI	HR	BA	OBP	FP
2	13	24	5	1	1	0	.208	.208	.971

1935-36 Was-A

Steve Stone

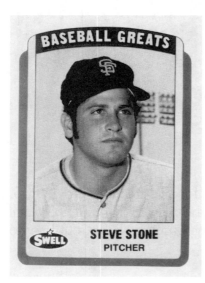

BASEBALL GREATS

STEVE STONE
PITCHER

Steven Michael Stone was born on July 14, 1947, in Euclid, Ohio, a suburb of Cleveland. At his high school, Steve was a Ping-Pong champion. In his youth, he also played golf and tennis, as well as sandlot baseball.

In 1963, Steve pitched victories in both halves of a double-header in Class D City Playoffs. Steve pitched in the Cape Cod League in 1968, and had a 2.00 ERA. At Kent State University, he played on the bowling and volleyball teams. He also played pool. But Steve's outstanding interest in college was baseball. As a pitcher, Steve was selected for the All Mid-American Conference Team. As a junior, Steve was named captain of the Kent State baseball team. His catcher at Kent State was future big-leaguer Thurman Munson. Steve graduated with a teaching degree in social studies in 1970.

By the time he graduated, Steve already had in hand a contract from the San Francisco Giants. He began pitching for the Giants organization during the summer of 1969 with a stint at the farm club at Fresno (California League). Steve was most impressive. On May 23, his lightning fastballs helped him strike out 17 Lodi batters in a complete game. From July 17 to August 22, he won 7 consecutive games, including 3 shutouts. Steve finished the season with a 12–13 record and a 3.61 ERA.

STEVE STONE
ORIOLES   PITCHER

The following year, the right-handed pitcher started the season with Amarillo (Texas League). He pitched in 19 games for them, with a 9-5 record, before moving up to Phoenix (Pacific Coast League). There his record was 5-3, with a 1.71 ERA. With this record, it's not surprising that Steve started 1971 with the San Francisco Giants. He made his major league debut on April 8, and would appear in 24 games for the Giants, with 5 wins and 9 losses and a 4.15 ERA. Before the end of the season, he returned to Phoenix. There his record was 6-3, with a 3.98 ERA.

Steve returned to the majors in 1972, this time permanently. His record was 6-8 and his ERA was 2.98. At the end of the season, Steve, suffering from a sore arm, was traded to the Chicago White Sox. He was 6-11 for the Sox in 1973, with a 4.24 ERA. Steve was used as both a starter and a reliever by the Sox. He pitched the last game of the season for the White Sox on September 30 in a three-hit shutout against the pennant-winning Oakland A's, striking out his career high, to that point: 12 batters. On December 11, 1973, Steve was traded across town and across leagues to the Chicago Cubs. The Cubs seemed to suit Steve; in 1974, for the first time in his major league career, he turned in a winning season, winning 8 and losing 6, with a 4.14 ERA. He had an even better year in 1975, going 12 and 8, with a 3.95 ERA for 33 games, 139 strikeouts, and 6 complete games, including a shutout.

Despite the fact that Steve had one of the best records on the pitching staff of the lackluster Cubs, instead of offering him encouragement for the start of the 1976 season, they suggested he take a voluntary pay cut. Steve refused, though he agreed to play out the final year of his contract; but he made it clear that he would go the route of free agency in 1977. All this became academic during the season, however, when Steve suffered a torn rotator cuff in his right shoulder. The Cub management wanted him to undergo an operation. Steve refused. They then suggested that he allow himself to be injected with cortisone so that he could continue to pitch with his injury. Again Steve refused.

Steve believes that he was the first player ever to refuse a course of treatment suggested by a team doctor. Instead, he found his own doctor, a kinesiologist from the University of Illinois. The doctor put his arm into a series of treatments in which the shoulder was frozen and then exercised. The theory was that this would increase the blood circulation to a part of the body where the blood flow is usually reduced. The exercises were also designed to strengthen the arm. The treatment was a resounding success, Steve showing excellent stuff by the end of the year. Even though a question mark hung over the rest of Steve's career, five teams bid for his services for 1977. Steve went back to his former team, the White Sox, now being run by Bill Veeck. Veeck bet $60,000 that Steve wouldn't fall apart during the year. He was more than repaid when Steve turned in a 15-12 record. The 15 wins were the highest in his career, to this point.

The following year, Steve was given $125,000 by the White Sox. He finished 1978 with a 12-12 record and the determination to become the first player in history to enter the re-entry draft for free agents for a second time. Again Steve received 5 offers, including one from the kind of team he wanted to work for, a team with a chance at a pennant: the Baltimore Orioles.

Steve was given a four-year contract by the Orioles, for $760,000—then an excellent sum. But disappointment met him at the beginning of the 1979 season. It was made clear to Steve, by manager Earl Weaver, that he was fifth pitcher in a four-man rotation—an insurance pitcher, not a regular starter. By the All-Star break, Steve's record was not good, just 6-7, and a 4.40 ERA. So Steve took himself in hand and began a search for self-improvement. He sought advice from the other pitchers on the staff, including Jim Palmer and Mike Flanagan, and he began to follow fixed routines. He would listen over and over to the same music. He would eat the same meals. He put a toy elephant inside his locker. He meditated, he tried positive thinking, and he talked to a psychic. Also Steve tried to reestablish his connection with his boyhood idol, Sandy Koufax, reading Koufax's autobiography five times. He changed his uniform number from 21 to 32, Sandy's number. All this could have meant little or nothing. Instead, Steve did not loose another game for the rest of the year. His ERA dropped to 3.77, and he won 5 more games before the year was out, ending on a lucky 11-7 record.

Steve was not given a chance to pitch in that year's American League Championship Series against the Angels. He pitched only 2 innings in the World Series, in one of Baltimore's 3 victories in a losing series against the Pirates. But the stage was set for one of the most remarkable seasons ever experienced by a Jewish pitcher: In 1980, Steve Stone became the first Jewish pitcher since Koufax to win the Cy Young Award, making him only the second Jewish player to gain this award. To date, this feat has not been repeated.

From 1971 to 1979, Steve had won 78 games and lost 79—a win percentage of .497. One would be hard pressed to find a better example of mediocrity. But Steve did not wish to go down as just another fair pitcher, just another hurler trying to fill in the innings. He longed for greatness and knew he had the possibilities of greatness within himself. Steve was a curve ball pitcher. To throw a great curve ball takes a great deal out of the pitcher. During 1980, more than half the pitches he threw were curve balls. Like a tenor who knows if he hits the high notes too truly and too strongly he will destroy his own instrument, the pitcher must take something off his curve if he will continue to pitch. Steve made his decision: "I knew it would ruin my arm. But one year of 25-7 is worth five of 15-15."

Steve got his magic year. He won 25 games and the Cy Young Award. He led the league in wins and in winning percentage. He pitched in the 1980 All-Star Game and pitched 3 perfect innings. He led his team to the brink of winning the pennant, missing by only 3 games. Through May, June, and July, Steve was practically unbeatable, and encompassed a winning streak of 14 games. He ended 1980 with a 3.23 ERA.

But the injury that Steve was betting against was there to claim him in 1981. Steve did pitch in 15 games, with 4 wins and 7 losses, and his ERA was 4.60. Nevertheless, before the end of the year, Steve read the handwriting on the wall and, suffering from tendonitis, retired.

He ended up with 107 career wins and 93 losses, a percentage of .535. His lifetime ERA is 3.97. Steve did not go very far from the ballfield on his retirement, just up a bit, to the broadcast booth. He became a sportscaster in Chicago, doing the play-by-play for the Cubs, beginning in 1983. Steve Stone also keeps himself busy running his own restaurants, in Chicago and Scottsdale, Arizona, writing poetry, playing chess, and continuing to indulge his lifelong enthusiasm for ping-pong. Steve makes his home in Chicago.

Years	Games	IP	W	L	GS	SV	PCT	ERA
11	320	$1788\frac{1}{3}$	107	93	269	1	.535	3.97

1971-72 SF-N, 1973 Chi-A, 1974-76 Chi-N, 1977-78 Chi-A, 1979-81 Bal-A

Bud Swartz

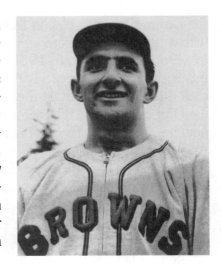

Sherwin Merle "Bud" Swartz was born on June 13, 1929, in Tulsa, Oklahoma. He was raised in Los Angeles. Bud's father, Art, was a minor league catcher. Bud attended University High School and was the star southpaw hurler of the baseball team; he pitched the team to the Greater Los Angeles scholastic title with seven victories and no defeats.

When he graduated from high school, in 1947, Bud became a hot commodity with many of the major league clubs. He received definite offers from the St. Louis Cardinals, New York Yankees, Brooklyn Dodgers, Boston Braves, and Cincinnati Reds. Bud and his mother decided, however, to sign with the St. Louis Browns after meeting General Manager Bobby DeWitt. Bud's contract stipulated that he would pitch his first season with the Browns.

On July 12, 1947, Bud made his professional and major league debut with the team. He pitched a scoreless 9th inning as the Browns lost to the Yankees, 12–2, in St. Louis' Sportsman's Park. On July 24, 1947, Bud raised his batting average to a perfect 1.000. He hit a single off Yankees reliever Vic Raschi in his only at-bat. Later in the season, Bud was sent to pitch for the Browns farm team in Springfield, Illinois (3-I League); he never appeared in another major league game after the 1947 season. Bud had a lifetime ERA of 6.75 in $5\frac{1}{3}$ innings.

Bud Swarz died on June 21, 1991, in Los Angeles of complications from pneumonia.

Years	Games	IP	W	L	GS	SV	PCT	ERA
1	5	$5\frac{1}{3}$	0	0	0	0	NA	6.75

1947 StL-A

Don Taussig

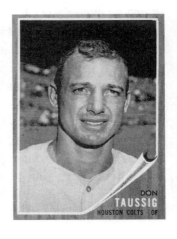

Donald Franklin Taussig was born in New York City on February 19, 1932. His family later moved to Long Beach, NY, and Don graduated from Long Beach High School. Don attended Rutgers University, Columbia University, and Hofstra College; he is a graduate of the last.

Don was signed to his first contract by the Yankees organization. His first assignment was in 1950 to La Grange (Georgia–Alabama League), where he appeared in only 2 games. In 3 at-bats, Don scored a run, but had no hits. The right-handed outfielder was quickly sent to Independence (K-O-M League) to spend the balance of the 1950 season. There he batted .195, with 42 hits in 54 games, including 8 doubles, 4 triples, and 3 home runs.

In 1951, Don played with Sunbury (Interstate League), where he batted .245, with 112 hits in 136 games, including 25 doubles, 3 triples, and 12 home runs. The following year, 1952, was a good one for Don. He hit .263 for Jacksonville (South Atlantic League) and led the league outfielders in assists, with 26. He spent the start of the next year with Sioux City (Western League), where he was hitting .182 in 9 games; then he was called to serve in the Army. Don spent 21 months in the service, from 1953 to 1955.

Don returned to play in Dallas (Texas League) in 1955. He played 46 games with Dallas, with a .210 batting average, before being moved back to Sioux City. There, his average rose to .296, in 93 games. In 1956, Don returned to Dallas. With Dallas, in 1956 he hit .251, but this rose, in 1957, to .281. Also, in 1957, Don led the Texas League outfielders in putouts, with 445. He was named the league's All-Star centerfielder.

Don began the 1958 season with the San Francisco Giants, who had just arrived in their new home—across the continent from Manhattan. He made his debut on April 23. Then, on April 29, he got his first major league hit off of Curt Simmons. This was at San Francisco's Seals Stadium, the first West Coast home of the Giants. The Phillies won the game, 7–4. On June 6, Don got his first major league home run, off Harvey Haddix of the Cincinnati Reds. Cincinnati won this game, 6–5. After appearing in 39 games, Don was sent back to the minors, to finish the year with Phoenix (Pacific Coast League). It is believed that he was sent down because the Giants' manager, Bill Rigney, had too many outfielders. Don had been hitting .200 at the time; his defensive work, on the other hand, had been outstanding, with a 1.000 fielding percentage.

Don hit .212 for Phoenix in 1958, where he played in 70 games. The next year, 1959, was spent with Fort Worth–Charleston (American Association), where he hit .246. Don had a great year with Portland (Pacific Coast League) in 1960. He started slowly, hitting just a little above .250 at mid-season. But then he went on a tear. He finished the year with a .286 average, hitting 23 homers, 8 triples, and 23 doubles and knocking in 101 runs. For the second half of the season, his average was well over .300. Don also led all league outfielders in fielding percentage. With the expansion of the leagues and Don's fine year, he became a hot property.

In 1961, Don was back to the majors, with the St. Louis Cardinals. Don was used that year mostly as a substitute or a pinch-hitter. He appeared in 98 games and batted a very presentable .287. This record, along with his .992 fielding percentage, led to Don's being selected by the new Houston Colt .45s for their inaugural season, 1962. However, he was on the disabled list for the first 3 months of the season due to torn ligaments in his left knee and subsequent surgery. After his return to active duty, Don's batting average of .200, in 16 games, did not strongly impress the management and he was sent down to the minors.

Don played 3 years in the majors on 3 different teams. His lifetime batting average was .262. He appeared in 153 games, had 69 hits, including 14 doubles, 5 triples, and 4 home runs. He scored 38 runs and had 30 RBIs. His lifetime major league fielding percentage was .994. Don finished the 1962 season with Oklahoma City (American Association), where his batting average was .250, appearing in just 24 games for this team. Don played on 4 different teams in 1963: Toronto (International League), Denver (Pacific Coast League), Albuquerque (Texas League), and Binghamton (Eastern League). He played in only 38 games with the first 3 of these teams, but played 74 games with Binghamton and had a .245 average for them. Don had 17 home runs in 1963.

Don Taussig now lives in Long Beach, New York.

Years	Games	AB	H	R	RBI	HR	BA	OBP	FP
3	153	263	69	38	30	4	.262	.317	.994

1958 SF-N, 1961 StL-N, 1962 Hou-N

Eddie Turchin

Edward Lawrence "Smiley" Turchin was born on February 10, 1917, in New York City.

In 1937, Eddie began his professional baseball career, as an infielder, in the Dominican Republic. Later that year, he was offered a contract with the Cleveland Indians. Eddie played one more season in the Dominican Republic before reporting to Batavia in 1939. In 1940, Eddie played with Syracuse. In 1941, Eddie was promoted to Wilkes-Barre. He spent two seasons there, before being promoted, in 1943, to the Cleveland Indians.

Eddie made his major league debut on May 9, 1943, at Sportsman's Park. He replaced shortstop Rusty Peters in the 9th inning of a tied game against the St. Louis Browns. Eddie had 2 singles off of Fritz Ostermueller, including a thirteenth-inning hit that scored pitcher Mike Naymick for the winning run. The Indians defeated the Browns, 6–5. Eddie appeared in another 10 games for the Indians; he had a .231 batting average in 13 at-bats.

Although he appeared in only 11 games for the Indians, Eddie made quite a reputation for himself. When he first arrived at Cleveland's spring-training camp, he was asked by a group of reporters to go to a room to answer questions. Eddie nodded, but never appeared. The reporters theorized that Eddie couldn't understand English since he was constantly talking to teammate Paul Calvert in French or Spanish. The truth was that Eddie spoke not only English, but five other languages as well.

In July of 1943, Eddie was told to report to the Buffalo Bisons by Manager Lou Boudreau. Instead of reporting to the Bisons, Eddie enlisted in the service. Eddie returned to baseball in 1946, playing the 1946 season with the Bisons. In 1947, he played his final season of baseball for the York White Roses in York, Pennsylvania.

Eddie Turchin died on February 8, 1982, in Brookhaven, New York.

Years	Games	AB	H	R	RBI	HR	BA	OBP	FP
1	11	13	3	4	1	0	.231	.375	1.000

1943 Cle-A

Steve Wapnick

Steven Lee Wapnick was born on September 25, 1965, in Panorama City, California. Steve, a right-handed pitcher, attended Fresno State University in Fresno, California. In June 1985, he was drafted by the Yankees but did not sign with them. Steve was drafted again, two years later, by the Blue Jays as their thirtieth-round pick in the June 1987 draft. This time, Steve signed.

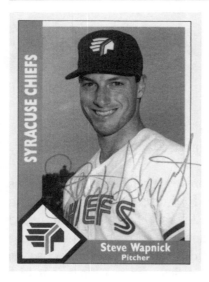

Steve Wapnick
Pitcher

He had his first assignment in St. Catherines (New York–Pennsylvania League) in 1987. Steve started 6 games and relieved in 14. He had a very impressive 3.02 ERA and his record was 3-4, plus 6 saves. In 1988, he played with Myrtle Beach (South Atlantic League), where he saved 12 games and had a 4-3 record, a 2.24 ERA, and 69 strikeouts, in 54 games.

Steve played in three Blue Jays farm teams in 1989: Dunedin, Knoxville, and Syracuse. His combined record for the three teams was 6-0, with a 1.80 ERA. Steve began the 1990 season with the Detroit Tigers as a Rule 5 draft player; he debuted for the Tigers on April 19, 1990. Steve appeared in only 4 games for the Tigers, however, pitching only 7 relief innings. He had no wins or losses, but a 6.43 ERA. On May 1, Steve was returned to the Jays. He was then assigned back to the Syracuse Chiefs (International League), and on September 5, Steve was traded to the Chicago White Sox.

In 1991, Steve pitched 5 relief innings in 6 games for the Sox. He had no wins and 1 loss, with a 1.80 ERA. Steve's major league career total is 10 games, in 2 years, with a 0-1 record and a 4.50 ERA. In the winter season of 1992–93, Steve played in the Venezuelan League, for Oriente. He appeared in 10 games, starting 9. His record was 1-6, his only victory coming, on November 26, 1992, against the Sharks (Los Tiburones) of La Guaira. His ERA was 7.68.

Steve pitched with Calgary (Pacific Coast League) in 1993. He was 1-5, with a 4.96 ERA. In September 1993, he went on the disabled list. During the winter season of 1993–94, Steve again played in Venezuela, with Oriente. During spring training of 1995, he was a replacement player with the San Francisco Giants during the players' strike.

Steve Wapnick is married. He lives in Sepulveda, California.

Years	Games	IP	W	L	GS	SV	PCT	ERA
2	10	12	0	1	0	0	.000	4.50

1990 Det-A, 1991 Chi-A

Phil Weintraub

Philip Weintraub was born on October 12, 1907, in Chicago. His parents were from Kiev, Russia. Phil was the third of six children.

Phil (whose nickname was "Mickey") began his baseball career as a left-handed pitcher. After graduating from Loyola University, he joined the Rock Island, Illinois, club (Mississippi Valley League) in 1926. In the next two years, he pitched for Waco (Texas League) and Tyler (Lone Star League). Phil didn't excel in pitching, but his batting was excellent. He threw hard, but was not destined to be a pitcher.

After playing three seasons in the minor leagues, Phil had to take a temporary hiatus from baseball. Following the death of his father, Phil was obliged to take on the family's auctioning business. He returned to baseball two years later.

When Phil returned, in 1930, he came as an infielder, playing for Dubuque, Iowa (Mississippi Valley League). That year, he almost won the league batting title, missing it by one percentage point. In 1931, Phil played for Terre Haute, Indiana, which won the 3-I League Pennant. The next two seasons, he was with Dayton, Ohio (Mid-Atlantic League), and Birmingham (Southern Association).

In 1933, Phil became part of the New York Giants lineup as an utility outfielder. He debuted with the Giants on September 5, 1933. Two days later, Phil got his first major league hit from Pittsburgh Pirate's pitcher Heine Meine, at Forbes Field. It was a solo home run, in the sixth inning. Phil appeared in only 8 games with the Giants in 1933.

Phil played with the Giants during spring training of 1934. Then, when it was reported that he would not start the season with them, the Giants office was inundated with calls, telegrams, and letters from Jewish fans protesting the move. For a time, Manager Bill Terry was about to call Phil back from his minor league assignment with Nashville; but he stood his ground and, as the Giants' season opened, you could hear the "Oi gewalts" across Manhattan.

Phil had a great year with Nashville (Southern Association) in 1934. He batted a league leading .401, and his average was the first .400 recorded in the league for over 30 years. Phil was a hero in Nashville that year. He also got to play briefly with the Giants, towards the end of the season. Phil appeared in 31 games and batted .351.

He spent most of the 1935–36 seasons in the minors, with a few appearances with the Giants as a utility player. In 1936, he played with the Rochester Redwings (International League). There, he nearly won the batting title, just missing because of a dislocated shoulder. Then, Phil was sold to the Cincinnati Reds in 1937. After playing in 49 games with them, however, he was returned to the Giants. Phil played in 6 games with the New York team, before returning to the minors for the remainder of the season.

In 1938, Phil was traded to the Philadelphia Phillies. He played in 100 games with the Phillies and had a .311 batting average. He got the last hit at the Baker Bowl, before the Phillies moved to Shibe Park. During both the 1935 and 1938 seasons, Phil followed the lead set by Hank Greenberg and did not play ball on Yom Kippur. At the end of the 1938 season, the Phillies sold Phil to Minneapolis (American Association). He played with Minneapolis for the 1939 and 1940 seasons, and was selected to be in the American Association All-Star Game in 1940.

Phil retired briefly, but returned to play for the Los Angeles Angels (Pacific Coast League) in 1941. He remained in the minors until 1944. However, he played the 1944 season with the Giants, and had his fullest major league season that year, with 104 games. On April 30, 1944, Phil batted in 11 runs, in the first game of a doubleheader against the Brooklyn Dodgers. He had a home run, a triple, two doubles, and a bases-loaded walk. This was one RBI less than the record, which is 12 in one game, set by Jim Bottomly of the 1924 Cardinals. The Giants beat the Dodgers that game, 26–8. Babe Ruth, who had retired nine years earlier, was sitting in the front row at the game. When it was finished, Ruth told Phil, "Kid, that was some performance. You knocked in enough runs for a month. Some guys don't get that many in a season." This was one of Phil's finest memories.

Phil scored 5 runs in a single game twice during the season. The major league record is 6 runs, set by the Giants' Mel Ott. That year, 1944, Phil had a .316 batting average in 361 plate appearances. He played his final season with the Giants in 1945, when he was in 82 games.

Phil retired from baseball, after 20 seasons, at the age of 38. He explained that he had no problem with hitting, but had trouble running.

Phil completed his major league career with a .295 batting average in 7 seasons, on 3 teams. He appeared in 444 games and produce 407 hits, including 32 homers. He scored 215 runs and had 207 RBIs.

After his retirement from baseball, Phil worked in the wholesale food business, in New York. He later sold real estate in Palm Springs, Florida. Phil was elected to the Chicago Jewish Sports Hall of Fame in 1982.

Phil Weintraub died on June 21, 1987, in Palm Springs, Florida. He and his wife, Jeanne, had two children, Phil Jr. and Jill.

Years	Games	AB	H	R	RBI	HR	BA	OBP	FP
7	444	1382	407	215	207	32	.295	.398	.990

1933-35 NY-N, 1937 Cin-N, 1937 NY-N, 1938 Phi-N, 1944-45 NY-N

Ed Wineapple

Ed "Lefty" Wineapple was born August 10, 1906, in Boston, Massachusetts. His father owned a leather company.

Ed attended one year at Syracuse University and became captain of the Freshman baseball, football, and basketball teams. Ed then attended Providence College, a Catholic school, where he played on both the school's basketball and baseball teams. In 1929, he was the nation's second-highest basketball scorer, with 278 points in 20 games. Ed was selected that year as an All-American in basketball in the first nationwide poll. He was also selected for the All-American baseball team, while at Providence College.

After Ed finished college, he thought about playing on a professional sports team. He couldn't play professional football because of a leg injury that he sustained in high school and reinjured in college. He decided to become a professional baseball player, signing with the Washington Senators as a pitcher, for $5,000, in 1929.

Ed debuted with the Senators that year on September 15, at Griffith Stadium, against the Detroit Tigers. He was used as a reliever, and gave up 7 hits and 2 earned runs, in 4 innings. Fortunately for Ed, he was not credited with the loss, because the Senators were already losing, 14–2, when he entered the game. The final score was 16–2. Ed was sent back to the Senators' farm club in Chattanooga (Southern League). He then pitched for Toronto (International League) and Wilmington, North Carolina (Piedmont League). Altogether, Ed spent three years in professional baseball. He finally had to leave because of his old leg injury, which never properly healed.

Ed also played professional basketball with Syracuse, in the ABL, during the winter months. He was a forward from 1929 to 1930.

After Ed finished his career in sports, he began working for a sportswear company, and eventually became its vice-president. Ed was later inaugurated into the Sports Hall of Fame at his alma mater, Providence College. He was the first person ever to be elected to the Providence College

Sports Hall of Fame.

Ed Wineapple died on August 23, 1996.

Years	Games	IP	W	L	GS	SV	PCT	ERA
1	1	4	0	0	0	0	NA	4.50

1929 Was-A

Steve Yeager

Steve Yeager will probably be continued to be remembered, in years to come, for three reasons. He invented a throat protector that hangs from the catcher's mask; he shared the MVP honors with two other players for the 1981 World Series; and he was involved in a marketing scam with a company called Collectibles International. Hopefully, the complexities of the last of these three activities will be cleared up and Steve will be exonerated. For Steve had a fine 14-year career that deserves to be remembered for its excellence, rather than any connection with a shady sports-card brokerage firm.

Stephen Wayne Yeager was born November 24, 1948, in Huntington, West Virginia. Neither of his parents was Jewish, but Steve converted to Judaism later in his life. In high school, he was a star in three different sports. Once, in a single baseball game, Steve hit 2 grand-slam homers.

Steve signed with the Los Angeles Dodgers as their 4th selection in the June 1967 free-agent draft. Steve was first assigned, in 1967, to Ogden, but was switched before he even had an at-bat, to Dubuque. It was soon clear that Steve was an outstanding defensive catcher, with a cannon of a right arm, always ready to throw out players trying to steal second. At this point, however, Steve was not a great hitter. His average in Dubuque was just .171, with just 6 hits.

The following year, 1968, Steve played with Daytona Beach. Here his average dropped to .153. He managed to raise his average to .154 in 1969, at Bakersfield. While his average was a hairline better, he had 1 homer fewer than in 1968, when he did have 1. Steve played from 1970 to the start of the 1972 season with Albuquerque. Here his hitting improved, with averages between .274 and .280. He got 12 homers over the 3 seasons. Meanwhile, the Dodgers needed a new catcher and decided to give Steve a try.

Steve made his debut with Los Angeles on August 2, 1972. He would catch 35 games for the Dodgers in the 1972 season. His .274 batting average of 1972 would actually be the highest average of his entire major league career. For the seasons 1972 to 1973 and the start of 1975, Steve served the Dodgers as their second-string catcher, his reputation growing all the time for the excellence of his defensive abilities. When Joe Ferguson, the Dodgers' number-one catcher for 1973 and the start of 1975, broke his arm in a brawl with the San Diego Padres, on July 1, 1975, Steve was graduated to the lead position. Steve would remain behind the plate for the Dodgers until 1985. Aside from injuries, Steve's possession of the number-one catcher's position was undisputed until his last two seasons with the Dodgers, when he worked as backup to Mike Scioscia.

For his entire career, Steve's fielding percentage was .987. This can be compared to fellow Dodger Roy Campanella, at .988; Moe Berg, at .986; and Johnny Bench, at .990. There is no question that Steve was one of the finest catchers of all time. Further, during the years that Steve was with the Dodgers, the team went to the league playoffs 6 times. They won the pennant in 1974, 1977, 1978, and 1981, a year they also won the World Series.

Steve tied the major league record for most putouts by a catcher in an extra-inning game with 22, in a 19-inning game, on August 8, 1972. In the same game, he also set a new National League record for chances accepted, with 24. During the 1974 season, he had one of the longest winning streaks for a catcher in major league history, catching in 24 straight victories. Steve led the league in putouts in 1975, with 806. He stole home on April 30, 1976. His best overall season was 1977, when he hit 16 homers and drove in 55 runs. One of Steve's 1977 homers was a grand slam. He had also hit grand slams in 1974 and 1975. Steve hit two game-winning homers in the 1980 season. In the 1981 World Series, he hit .286, with 2 home runs and 4 RBIs. Steve shared the honors of MVP for the Series with Pedro Guerrero and Ron Cey. In his 4 World Series, Steve hit .298.

Steve's career was not free of injuries. On September 6, 1976, he suffered one of the most unusual injuries in baseball history. Bill Russell was batting and Steve was standing in the on-deck circle, waiting for his turn. The next pitch shattered Russell's bat and the jagged end struck Steve in the neck, piercing his esophagus. He was rushed to the hospital and underwent 98 minutes of surgery. Nine fragments of wood were removed from his throat. Steve was back in 2 weeks. In 1982, Steve suffered a knee injury; after arthroscopic surgery, he was back in 19 days, and hit .245 that season—his best in years. On July 31, 1983, Steve broke his wrist when he was hit by a pitch.

Steve remained with the Dodgers for 14 seasons, then was finally traded to the Seattle Mariners on December 11, 1985. He played in 50 games for the Mariners in 1986, with a .208 batting average and a 1.000 fielding percentage. Steve got 2 home runs during the year. He retired after that season.

In 15 years of major league baseball, 14 of those years with the Dodgers, Steve played in 1269 games, had 816 hits, including 118 doubles, 16 triples, and 102 home runs. He walked 342 times. His batting average was .228, but his on-base percentage was .300. He scored 357 runs and had 410 RBIs.

Steve was married on the steps of City Hall in Los Angeles. The mayor was his best man. In 1989, Steve appeared in the movie Major League, where he played the part of Duke Temple. Steve reprised the role of Temple, now Coach Temple, in a 1994 sequel, Major League II.

In 1996, Steve came back into the news when a baseball card franchise company, Collectibles International, was accused of fraud. He had served as the celebrity spokesman for the company in newspaper ads and television commercials. The case is still under investigation, and it is not at all clear to what extent, if any, Steve was involved in the firm's deceptive practices.

Steve Yeager lives in Granada Hills, California.

Years	Games	AB	H	R	RBI	HR	BA	OBP	FP
15	1269	3584	816	357	410	102	.228	.300	.987

1972-85 LA-N, 1986 Sea-A

Larry Yellen

Lawrence Alan Yellen was born on January 4, 1943, in Brooklyn. After graduating from Brooklyn's Lafayette High School, he attended Hunter College, and pitched on Hunter's baseball team—twice named Most Valuable Player. In 1962, Larry pitched in the Hearst All-Star Game.

In 1963, Larry was signed with the Houston Colt .45s, as a right-handed pitcher. That year, he played with San Antonio (Texas League). Larry had pitched in 18 games before his 2.82 ERA got him promoted to Houston. He would pitch in only one game for the Colt .45s, during 1963. On September 26, 1963, Larry made his debut, starting a game against the Pirates. He pitched 5 innings before being relieved, giving up 7 hits and 2 earned runs. The Colt .45s won the game, 5 to 4, in 11 innings.

By the time Larry returned to the Houston lineup, in 1964, the name of the team had been changed to the Houston Astros. Larry pitched in 14 games for the Astros in 1964, including 1 start. That year, he also pitched for Oklahoma City (Pacific Coast League). Larry Yellen's lifetime major league ERA is 6.23. He currently makes his home in Atlanta, Georgia.

Years	Games	IP	W	L	GS	SV	PCT	ERA
2	14	26	0	0	2	0	NA	6.23

1963-64 Hou-N

Guy Zinn

Guy Zinn was born on February 13, 1887, in Hallbrook, West Virginia, one of five children. He had three brothers, Edmin R. "Romeo," P.E. "Pete," and Archie "Roster." His sister became Mrs. Hugh McLane.

Guy began his career with Grafton (Pennsylvania–West Virginia League) in 1909 as an outfielder. He played well there and had a .294 batting average. In 1910, Guy played in Memphis, Macon, and Toledo, batting approximately .230 at each club.

Guy began the 1911 season with Altoona (Tri-State League). On September 11, 1911, he was promoted to the New York Highlanders, later known as the Yankees. He replaced player Harry Wolter, who was injured. Guy finished the year with the Highlanders, but played in only nine games in 1911. He had his most complete season in the majors, 106 games, in 1912, when he batted .262 and hit six home runs for the Highlanders. His batting earned him the nickname "The Gunner."

Late in the 1912 season, Guy was sold to Rochester, but he didn't like the idea of returning to the minors, so he refused to report. As a result, the Highlanders had to send a different player to Rochester and Guy was suspended. Finally, he caved in and reported to Rochester for the 1913 season. With Rochester, Guy got the opportunity to get a hit off Al Schacht.

After playing 110 games for Rochester, he returned to the major leagues: He was sold to the Boston Braves, late in the 1913 season. Guy played in 36 games for the Braves, with a .297 batting average. However, the Braves were disappointed with Guy's playing and they sent him back to Rochester, which sold his contract to Louisville. Instead of reporting to Louisville, for the 1914 season, Guy tried out for the Baltimore Terrapins, in the newly founded Federal League. He was selected for the team and played there in 1914 and 1915, but the league collapsed after the 1915 season. Guy was the only Jew to play in the Federal League.

Guy was signed by Scranton–Wilkes-Barre in 1915, and played 75 games there before returning to Louisville. Near the end of the season, he played in New Orleans. During the 1917 season, he played in Bridgeport (Eastern League), and in the 1918 season with Newark (International League).

In 1919, Guy was traded to Hamilton (Michigan–Ontario League). He played there for three years, batting .324, .307, and .267. He hit a combined 17 home runs for Hamilton, in 258 games. Guy finished his career in Brantford (International League), playing in 20 games for Brantford in 1922.

Guy Zinn died on October 6, 1949, in Clarksburg, West Virginia.

Years	Games	AB	H	R	RBI	HR	BA	OBP	FP
5	314	1103	297	136	137	15	.269	.338	.927

1911-12 NY-A, 1913 Bos-N, 1914-1915 Bal-Federal League

Eddie Zosky

Edward James Zosky was born on February 10, 1968, in Whittier, California. He is the son of a gentile father and a Jewish mother, Yvonne Zosky (née Katzman). Eddie attended St. Paul High School, in Santa Fe Springs, California. In 1986, graduating from high school and enrolling in Fresno State University, Eddie became the right-handed shortstop of the varsity baseball squad at FSU. He batted .370 in his junior year and was named to the All-American teams of both The Sporting News and Baseball America.

In 1989, Eddie was the first-round draft pick of the Toronto Blue Jays. He skipped the lower leagues and was sent directly to the Double-A affiliate of the Jays, the Knoxville Blue Jays (Southern League). There, he batted .221, in 56 games. Eddie returned to Knoxville in 1990 to bat .271, in 115 games. On February 2, 1991, he was married to Shelly Snylander. When the 1991 season began, Eddie was promoted to the Syracuse Chiefs (International League); there, he led International League shortstops with 221 putouts, 371 assists, and 88 double plays. That year, he was also chosen for the International League All-Star Team. Eddie was called up to Toronto on September 1.

On September 2, Eddie made his debut with the Toronto Blue Jays, at the Skydome. He played shortstop in the 12-inning, 5–4 win over the Baltimore Orioles, getting a single in his first at-bat off Orioles pitcher Dave Johnson. In 1991, Eddie batted .148 in 18 games for the

Blue Jays. In 1992, Eddie returned to the Syracuse Chiefs' lineup. There, he hit .350 in June, after hitting .160 in April and .170 in May. He finished the season with a .231 average, returning to Toronto after the minor league season ended in September. Eddie batted .286 in 8 games for the Jays.

In 1993, he underwent surgery to remove a bone spur from his right elbow. That year, he played in only 33 games for the Hagerstown, Maryland, Suns (South Atlantic League) and the Syracuse Chiefs. In 1994, Eddie was invited to spring training with the Toronto Blue Jays, but he was cut from the team before the season began and spent the entire season with the Chiefs. He played 41 games at second base, 34 at shortstop, and 1 at third base. This was the first time Eddie played second base in professional baseball. He batted .264 in 85 games and hit 7 home runs.

On November 18, 1994, Eddie was traded to the Florida Marlins, and in 1995 appeared in 6 games with them, before being sent to the Charlotte Knights (International League). With the Knights, he played in 92 games and batted .247. In 1996, Eddie was signed, as a free agent, by the Baltimore Orioles and played the 1996 season with the Rochester Red Wings (International League). Eddie batted .256 in 95 games for the Red Wings. On November 9, 1996, Eddie's son, Levi, was born.

In 1997, Eddie was signed as a free agent by the San Francisco Giants. That season, he played with the Phoenix Firebirds (Pacific Coast League). Eddie played most of the season on third base; he batted .278, with a career-best 9 home runs.

Eddie has a lifetime major league batting average of .179 in 39 at-bats. He played in 32 games, over 3 years, with 2 teams. He is regarded as one of the finest defensive shortstops in the minor leagues. In the majors, he has been mostly used as a defensive replacement.

Eddie currently lives with his wife, Shelly, and son in Fresno, California. In 1996, Eddie Zosky was inducted into the Fresno State University Sports Hall of Fame.

Eddie started the 1998 season with the Louisville Redbirds (AAA affiliate of the Milwaukee Brewers).

Years	Games	AB	H	R	RBI	HR	BA	OBP	FP
5	44	50	8	4	3	0	.160	.173	.967

1991-92 Tor-A, 1995 Fla-N, 1999 Mil-N, 2000 Hou-N

Part II
Touching Other Bases

Chapter 1
Minor League Players I

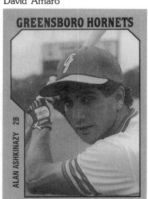

David Amaro

Eliot Asinof

David Mario Amaro Born: September 3, 1962, in Philadelphia, Pennsylvania. Position: First base.

David is the older brother of major-leaguer Ruben Amaro, Jr. He was selected in the 20th round of the 1984 free-agent draft, by the Chicago Cubs. David played one season with the Geneva Cubs, but injured his wrist and was forced to retire. That same winter, he tried to make a comeback, playing a season in the Mexican League, but his injury prevented him from continuing.

David is currently National Sales Manager for Lysias, a computer company with its headquarters in Willow Grove, Pennsylvania.

1984 Geneva Cubs (Cubs).

Alan Ashkinazy Born: December 7, 1961. Position: Infield.

1984 Winter Haven; 1985–86 Greensboro Hornets.

Eliot Asinof Born: July 13, 1919, in New York City. Position: First base and outfield.

Eliot Asinof was brought to the Phillies' camp by their scout, George Earnshaw, after he saw Eliot play at Swarthmore College. Earnshaw told him, "You know, because you're a Jew, you're gonna take a lot of shit." Eliot replied, "I can take shit." And Eliot did face anti-Semitism, but he kept on playing—"for the love of the game."

When playing on the semi-pro Plattsburg team, he was a teammate of Mickey Rutner, and, even though Eliot was batting .400, Mickey was the better player. The club had been losing. Near the end of the season, Manager Bill Barrett, whom Eliot describes as a "real bastard," told him, "There's too many Heebs on this club, you're fired." To this day, Mickey Rutner—who stayed on the team—remains one of Eliot's closest friends. They talk with each other at least once a week.

In 1941, Eliot was a leading star of the Wausau Timberjacks.

During one at-bat, the pitcher threw a pitch just past Eliot's nose. The umpire, named Reagan, yelled, "Strike!" Everyone in the stands knew that the pitch wasn't a strike. The crowd started yelling, "Reagan, you Jew bastard, you kike," though certainly he wasn't Jewish. Eliot, the real Jew, laughed so hard he fell out of the batter's box. Reagan turned to Eliot and asked him what he could do. Eliot said, "You're through!" After that, every time Reagan returned to officiate at Wausau he was met with the same insults.

Eliot's lifetime batting average in the minor leagues was .296. He served in the Aleutian Islands during the Second World War, as part of the Eleventh Air Force.

After Eliot's baseball career was over, his life's work still involved baseball. He wrote many prominent articles and books, including Eight Men Out (the story of the Black Sox Scandal). It

Rob Blumberg, Jr.   Kane Co. Cougars

has been a best-seller over the decades since it was first published in 1963, and is considered the standard work on its subject. It was turned into a major motion picture, in which Eliot briefly appeared, in 1988. His other works include Bleeding Between the Lines (1979) and Nineteen Nineteen (1990). Eliot still loves the game of baseball and continues to write about it.

1939 Plattsburg (semi-pro); 1940 Moultrie (Georgia–Florida League); 1941 Wausau (Northern League).

Jake Atz, Jr. (son of Jake Atz) Born: November 29, 1910. Died: September 18, 1976, in New Orleans, LA.
1941–42 Texarkana.

Bark (father of major leaguer Brian Bark. No first name available.) Position: Pitcher

Steve Blomberg
1976 Shreveport Captains (Pirates; AA).

Rob Blumberg, Jr. Born: December 10, 1967. Position: Pitcher
1989 Knoxville Blue Jays; 1989 St. Catherines Blue Jays; 1990 Myrtle Beach Blue Jays; 1991 Kane County Cougars.

Erez "Ez" Borowsky Born: August 1, 1960, in Reus, Spain. Position: Catcher

Erez was born to Itzhak and Miriam (née Zaidman) Borowsky. His parents were both born in Israel and Erez still has a large family there. Erez moved with his family to New York City in 1965. He played his first baseball game in New York. The Borowskys later moved to Los Angeles, where Erez played baseball on his high school team.

In June 1982, Erez was drafted by the Minnesota Twins. He spent his $2,000 signing bonus on a pilgrimage to Israel at the end of the 1982 season. In 1983, Erez played on the Visalia Oaks with Kirby Puckett.

Erez considers his most outstanding achievement in baseball to be two league records which he set while with Visalia.

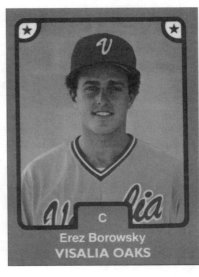

Erez Borowsky
VISALIA OAKS

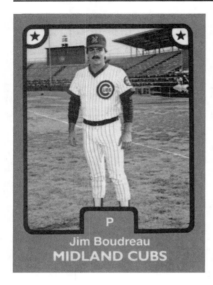
Jim Boudreau
MIDLAND CUBS

He set a new California League record for the most games caught in a season and a new record for fielding percentage. Erez said, "If I had to do it again, I would play baseball again, because it is through baseball that I had the ability to see and meet many people from all over this wonderful country. It has enriched my life."

Since 1986 and his retirement from professional baseball, Erez has become president of Health Sports Technology Group. He married Donna Farmer in 1988. They have one daughter, Sophia, and live in El Segundo, California.

1982 Wisconsin Rapids Twins (A; Twins), 1983–84 Visalia Oaks (A; Twins), 1985–86 Orlando Twins (A; Twins).

Jim Boudreau (son of Lou Boudreau) Born: 1960. Position Left-handed Pitcher.

1984 Midland Cubs; 1985-86 Charlotte O's.

Robert "Bobby" Chozen (Harry Chozen's brother)

Bobby played briefly for the Newport News before being released by his brother Harry, who was the player-manager.

1942 Newport News.

Myer Kenneth Chozen (Harry Chozen's brother)

1932 Portland; 1933 Oakland Oaks (Pacific Coast League); 1934–35 Tulsa; 1937 Jackson, Mississippi; 1945 Hollywood.

H. J. Cohen

1908 Girard, Pennsylvania; 1909 Lexington, Kentucky; 1910–11 Nashville, Tennessee; 1912 Keokuk, Iowa and Jackson, Mississippi.

H. J. Cohen

John Cohen Born: September 21, 1966. Position: Outfielder

1990–91 Visalia Oaks.

Randy Phillip Cohen

1967 Aberdeen; 1968 Miami & Stockton; 1969 Rochester; 1970 Dallas–Fort Worth; 1970 Rochester; 1971 Dallas–Fort Worth; 1972 Amarillo & El Paso; 1973 Waterbury.

John Cohen   Visalia Oaks

Tonny Cohen Born: October 14, 1965. Position: Pitcher.

1987 Macon Pirates; 1988 Augusta Pirates.

Leon Feingold Position: Pitcher.

1994 Butte Copper Kings.

Randy Phillip Cohen

Jerry Feldman Born: 1946. Position: First base and outfield.

1968 Idaho Falls & San Jose (A's); 1969 Davenport (A's); 1970 El Paso (Angels); 1971–72 Salt Lake City (Angels); 1972 Shreveport (Pirates); 1973 Salinas (Pirates).

Jason Friedman Born: August 8, 1969. Position: Infield.

Jason is the son of a Jewish father and a gentile mother. In 1990, while with Elmira, Jason led the league's first baseman in assists, with 56. In 1994, He led the Sarasota Red Sox in extra-base hits, with 56. He was a replacement player with the Boston Red Sox during 1995.

Jason had to end his playing career in 1996, because he never fully recovered from a pitch that struck him.

1989 Gulf Coast (Red Sox; A) & Winter Haven (Red Sox; A); 1990 Elmira Pioneers (Red Sox; A) & Winter Haven (Red Sox; A); 1991 Elmira Pioneers (Red Sox; A); 1992 Lynchburg Red Sox (Red Sox; A); 1993 New Britain (Red Sox; AA); 1994 Sarasota Red Sox (Red Sox; A); 1995 Pawtucket, Bowie Baysox, & Rochester; 1996 Port City Roosters (Mariners).

Bruce Clark Gardner Born: 1938. Died: 1971. Position: Left-handed pitcher.

One of the saddest stories in the history of Jews in baseball is the story of Bruce Gardner, a promising pitcher with the Dodgers organization. When he failed to make it to the majors and his minor league career was over, he found himself deeply depressed. He took his own life in 1971.

From 1958 to 1960, Bruce won 40 games for the University of Southern California Trojans, to become their winningest pitcher. This record was unbroken until 1997, when Randy Flores won his 41st game.

1960 Montreal; 1961 Reno; 1962 Spokane; 1963 Salem & Great Falls; 1964 Salem.

Eric Genden Position: First Base, Outfield.

1995 Kane County (Marlins; A).

Howard Stuart Gershberg Born: June 9, 1936, in Bayport, New York. Position: Right-handed pitcher.

Howie pitched for the Los Angeles Dodgers and San Francisco Giants organizations. He coached baseball for 12 years for Johns Hopkins University. Howie entered the Anaheim Angels organization in 1985, as a pitching coach. He is now the pitching coach of the Vancouver Canadians, Class AAA. In the off-season, Howie coaches in the Hawaiian Winter League for the Hilo Stars.

1955 Shawnee, Kokomo, & Thomasville; 1956 Sandersville & Mushoyee.

Herbert Gilbert (father of Mark Gilbert) Position: Infield.

TONNY COHEN   RHP

Jason Friedman

Bruce Clark Gardner

Howie Gershberg
PITCHING COACH • LAKE ELSINORE STORM

VISALIA

IKE GOLDSTEIN   C

STEVE GREENBERG
infielder - Spokane
40

ProCards®

ED HOROWITZ
Catcher
Frederick Keys

ProCards®

BRAD KANTOR
Infield
Watertown Indians

Barry Goldman Born: August 24, 1969. Position: Right-handed pitcher.

Barry was ranked second among all Northern League relief pitchers in 1993. He was third on the team in strikeouts, with 59 in 66.2 innings. Barry also set the team record for the least hits given, with 58. In 1995, Barry was a replacement player for the Colorado Rockies.

1993–95 Sioux City Explorers (independent).

Ike Goldstein Born: March 25, 1964, Position: Catcher.

1986 Kenosha; 1987 Visalia Oaks.

Michael David Gordon (son of Sid Gordon) Position: Catcher.

1963 Dubuque; 1964 Aberdeen & Stockton; 1964 Lexington & Twin Falls.

Joe Greenberg (brother of Hank Greenberg) Born: 1916. Position: Infield.

1936 Charleston & Johnstown; 1937 Toledo & Fort Worth; 1938–39 Baltimore; 1940 Shreveport; 1941 Fort Worth; 1942–55 military service; 1956 Montgomery.

Stephen Greenberg (son of Hank Greenberg) Born: September 1948. Position: First base.

Steve served as deputy to baseball commissioner Fay Vincent. He currently works for the Classic Sports Network.

1967–69 Falmouth (Cape Cod League); 1970 Geneva (New York–Pennsylvania League); 1971 Burlington (Carolina League); 1972 Denver (American Association); 1973–74 Spokane (Pacific Coast League).

Monroe Greenfield

1977 Phoenix Giants (Giants; AAA).

Stu Greenstein

1977 Lynchburg Mets (New York Mets; A).

Edward Neil Horowitz Born: November 1, 1967, in Brooklyn, New York. Position: Catcher.

Ed became a professional baseball player after receiving a BS in accounting from Rider College. In 1990, he played on the Frederick Keys, the Carolina League Championship team. In 1991, Ed played on the Carolina League All-Star Team. Ed is currently a comptroller with Morcom, Inc. He lives in Lawrenceville, New Jersey.

1989 Erie Orioles; 1990–92 Frederick Keys (Orioles).

Bradley Jason Kantor Born: August 8, 1971 in Hollywood, Florida. Position: Infield.

1991–92 Watertown Indians.

Mike Kaplan

1928 New Haven Profs (Eastern League).

Joseph Katz Position: Outfield and (in 1898 only) first base.

1889 Greenville; 1890 Burlington & Seattle; 1891 Grand Rapids & Kansas City; 1892 Minneapolis; 1893 Chattanooga; 1894 Rock Island & Moline; 1895 Jacksonville; 1896 Portsmouth & Birmingham; 1897–98 Mansfield & Youngstown.

Steve Kolinsky Born: November 30, 1943. Position: Outfield.

Steve was a scout for the Cubs organization and the manager of the Huntington Cubs from 1993 to 1994.

1964–65 Miami, Little Rock, & Chatanooga; 1966 Macon; 1967 San Diego; Reading Phillies & Portsmouth; 1968–69 Reading Phillies; 1970 Pawtucket; 1971 Winston-Salem & Pawtucket; 1972 Toledo.

Stuart Komer Born: March 23, 1926, in Detroit, Michigan. Position: Catcher.

Stu Komer was born and raised in Detroit. As a boy, he often attended Tigers games and got to see his idol, Hank Greenberg, in action. In high school, Stu, a right-hander, joined the baseball team. It was then, that he first met, and played against, another catcher from Detroit, Joe Ginsberg. In the minors, the two men would again play against each other. During his high school years Stu also met Al Richter and Al Rosen.

Stu attended Ohio State University, where he played on the baseball, basketball, football, and track teams. When he graduated, he signed a bonus contract with the St. Louis Browns organization. The bonus was $5,000. Stu remained within the Browns' farm system his entire baseball career. His most memorable game was an exhibition one, in 1946, when he had the opportunity to catch for Satchel Paige. In 1948, Stu played on the Elmira Pioneers, alongside Pete Gray.

After he left baseball, Stu spent a year as athletic director and coach, and was teacher, in Horseheads High School in New York State. He then spent a year working for his father's soft drink company in Detroit. Afterward, Stu worked for a time with a Chicago mail-order firm. In 1966, he returned to Elmira, New York, and became president and chairman of the board of Artistic Greetings. Stu still lives in Elmira and serves as chairman. On September 2, 1997, he was honored at an Elmira Pioneers game by being asked to throw out the ceremonial first pitch.

1945 Newark (Ohio State League); 1946 Springfield, Illinois (3I League); 1947 Gloversville, NY (Canadian–American League); 1948 San Antonio (Texas League); 1948–1949 Elmira, NY (Eastern League).

Rube Levy. Played 1887–89, in the California League. Position: Center Fielder.

Levy (first name unknown).
1910 Lynchburg (Southern Association)

Stu Komer (l.) with Pete Gray,

Rube Levy

Levy (of Southern Association)

Julius Leo Mack, Jr

Jacob Levy

In 1932, Jake was called up by John McGraw, in his last year as manager, to play on the New York Giants. He sat on the bench, but the right opportunity never arose for him to enter a game. His name is always included in the list of players from whom, John McGraw hoped, would appear a great Jewish star.

1929 Allentown; 1932 Knoxville.

Marc Lipson Born: November 27, 1966. Position: Right-handed pitcher.

1989 Elizabethton Twins; 1989 Gulf Twins; 1990 Visalia Oaks; 1990 Kenosha; 1991 Visalia Oaks; 1992 Orlando Sun Rays.

Lou List (born **Paul Michael List**) Born: 11-17-65, North Hollywood, California, Died: 1998, Position: Outfield.

Lou List was born Paul List; he changed his name to that of his grandfather on the occasion of his grandfather's death, July 22, 1992.

In 1994, Lou was traded to the New Haven Ravens and with them Lou became a fan-favorite. Whenever the outfielder/designated hitter came to the plate, he was serenaded by a chorus of "Lou, Lou, Lou." He became so popular that the Lou List Fan Club was founded by a local high school student.

In 1997, Lou was diagnosed with Hodgkin's disease. He was not able to play that year. He died from the disease in January 1998. In his honor, the New Haven Ravens retired his uniform number, 7, on August 7, 1998, during a special "Lou List Night." This is only the second number ever retired by the Ravens; the only other one retired was Jackie Robinson's number 42.

1987 Salem; 1990 Arizona Mariners (Mariners; A); 1991 Carolina, Salem, & Augusta Pirates (Pirates; A); 1992 Carolina Mudcats, Tulsa Drillers, & Gastonia Rangers; 1993 Tulsa Drillers; 1994 New Haven Ravens (Rockies; AA); 1995 Replacement player with Colorado Rockies, New Haven Ravens; 1996 Minot Mallards (Independent).

Julius Leo Mack, Jr.

Julius had a batting average of .235 in 1916.

1916 Jacksonville Tarpons (South Atlantic League).

Brett Mandel Born: May 10, 1969. Position: Infield.

Brett Mandel is the Henry Thoreau of minor league baseball. Brett put aside a career with Philadelphia city government in order to pursue a season of baseball with the Pioneer League, Southern Division. He was lucky enough to find a team, the Ogden (Utah) Raptors, willing to take him on and allow him to ride the bench, collect a salary, appear on two baseball cards, and shmooze with the rest of the team—in order to write a book about life at the very bottom rung of professional baseball. Brett's Minor Players, Major Dreams (Lincoln: University of Nebraska Press, 1997), like Thoreau's Walden, is a book ground in the reality of things, the texture of life, and the passage of time. If we get no great philosophical revelations, we do get to meet Brett and discover a fascinating observer. We also get to learn a great deal about how organized baseball really works, though the view Brett gives us is from the lowest depths—like looking at the Statue of Liberty, standing on top of its big toe and staring up toward the crown. Brett found some difficulty finding a publisher for his book. It was turned down by some thirty publishers before finding a home, but has attracted excellent reviews since its publication.

Brett believes that in 1994 he was the lowest-ranked professional baseball player. He got only five official at-bats during the entire season. In his first at-bat he got a successful sacrifice and earned his only RBI. Brett's only minor league hit came during an exhibition game against the all-girl Silver Bullets team.

Brett is a graduate of Northeast High School in Philadelphia, which also produced major-leaguer Jesse Levis and minor-leaguer Scott Hunter. Since his retirement from professional baseball, Brett has returned to work in the Philadelphia city government and currently is an assistant city comptroller.

Brett selected as his Raptors uniform number the number 5, that of his favorite player, George Brett. It was in 1980, during the only successful run for a World Series title by the Phillies, his hometown team, that Brett actually met George Brett. George signed an autograph for Brett: "To the other Brett—best wishes—George Brett."

1994 Ogden Raptors.

David Oliphant Born: July 23, 1935 in the Bronx, New York, Position: Right-handed pitcher.

In 1953, Dave signed a contract with the New York Yankees organization to pay for his tuition to college. He was paid a $3,000 signing bonus. Because he was a professional baseball player, Dave had to attend a small, private college, Curry.

In 1955, Dave was sent to a club managed by a rabid anti-Semite. He asked for his release from the New York Yankees. The Yankees refused to grant him free agency, but they did transfer him to a team owned by the Cleveland Indians for the remainder of the season. At the end of it, his father had to buy Dave's contract for $2,000. Later that year, Dave signed with the Brooklyn Dodgers.

When playing with Monroe, Louisiana, in 1958, Dave got to room with both of Mickey Mantle's twin brothers, Roy and Ray. He attended two Brooklyn Dodgers spring-training camps, where he played with Sandy Koufax, Carl Erskine, Carl Furillo, Tommy Davis, Roy Campanella, and Jackie Robinson. During one of the two spring trainings, Dave wore Robinson's number, 42.

One of the most important friendships Dave made while playing was with an African-American player, Curt Flood. He met Flood in 1955, when Flood was an opposing player in a game. Flood was playing for Savannah, Georgia, and Dave was pitching for Macon, Georgia. They bonded because there were few players who would talk to Flood because of racial prejudice. After retiring from baseball, Dave became a consultant for Simon and Schuster Publishers. When the Curt Flood Case challenged the player reserve clause, Dave offered him help in getting a book

David Oliphant

SAM PERLMAN
Tigers

Leonard Pill

Richie Richman

published in order to get out his side of the case. Dave also assisted Flood in writing his book, The Way It Is.

In 1958, when Dave graduated from Curry College, with a B.A. in education, he quit his position as a right-handed pitcher in the Dodgers organization. Dave has always believed he was blessed because he was able to receive an education while playing baseball.

1953 Olean Yankees (Pony League); 1954 Bristol, Virginia (Appalachian League); 1955 Monroe, Louisiana (Cotton States League) & Pine Bluff (Cotton States League); 1956 Hornell, New York (Pony League) & Macon (South Atlantic League); 1957 Macon (South Atlantic League); 1958 Atlanta Crackers.

Sam Perlman
In the 1920s he played for a Canadian team.

Leonard Pill Born: August 21, 1920. Position: outfield.
Leonard signed with the Dodgers in 1941, with a $1,500 bonus. During his playing career, Leonard could never understand why, during spring training, he was always a great hitter, yet would fall into horrible batting slumps during the season. He played until 1942, when he entered the Army. Leonard returned to play for his friend Mel Steiner's team in Bisbee in 1948. He was replaced by a younger player and then tried out for Phoenix. Leonard played briefly in Phoenix, before settling in Albuquerque for the 1948 season.

That year was the best season of Leonard's career. But he was already 28 at its end, had just gotten married, and wanted to go back to school. So Leonard decided to retire at the end of the 1948 season. He states, "I had a lot a fun as a ball player, and I met a lot of interesting people."

1939 Troy, AL; 1941 Santa Barbara, 1942 Dayton Ducks and Durham Bulls; 1942–46 military service; 1948 Bisbee, Phoenix, & Albuquerque.

Jeff Pinkus
1977 Salem Pirates (Pirates; A).

Richie Richman
Richie played baseball, basketball, and football for Villanova University.
1963 Bakersfield (Phillies).

Alexander "Petey" Rosenberg Born 1918 in Philadelphia, PA. Died 1997 in Philadelphia.
"Petey" played basketball with the SPHAs from 1939–1946 and the Philadelphia Warriors from 1946–1948. His 1946–1947 team won the Basketball Association of America championship.
c.1935 Tarboro, N.C. (Costal Plain League).

Todd "T.J." Rosenthal Born: May 10, 1971. Position: Infield.
1992 Salt Lake Trappers & Thunder Bay Whiskey Jacks; 1993 Thunder Bay Whiskey Jacks.

Max B. Rosner Played: 1903–? Position: Player-manager & manager.

Harry Ruby (born Harry Rubinstein) Born: January 27, 1895, in New York. Died: February 23, 1974.

Harry was world famous as a composer, songwriter, and screenwriter, but he always had a passionate interest in baseball. In 1931, Harry batted against Walter Johnson in an exhibition game between the Washington Senators and the Baltimore Orioles. Harry played in a number of other major league exhibition games.

Four times in the 1950s, Harry actually played, already over fifty, during the last innings of official Pacific Coast League games. He appeared with either the Hollywood Stars or the Los Angeles Angels.

Harry is the composer of such standards as "Who's Sorry Now?", "I Wanna Be Loved by You," "Watching the Clouds Roll By," "Baby Face," and "Three Little Words." He also wrote screenplays, including two for the Marx Brothers: Horsefeathers and Animal Crackers. The latter contained Harry's theme song for Groucho Marx, "Hooray for Captain Spaulding." Harry's life story was made into a movie, Three Little Words, released in 1950. He made an appearance in the 1951 baseball movie classic, Angels in the Outfield.

George S. Sherry (brother of Larry and Norm Sherry) Position: Pitcher.

1951 Modesto, Bartlesville, & Eugene; 1952 Waco & Mayfield; 1953 Mayfield; 1954 Salinas.

Aaron Silverman (also played under the name of Ernest Sills) Born: October 29, 1922. Position: Right-handed pitcher.

When Aaron began his baseball career, he played under the name of Ernie Sills. He had gotten the nickname in college. He later played under the name Aaron Silverman. In 1949, an article was printed about Aaron in the Yiddish newspaper The Forward. In 1952, he played for Jack Kent Cook's Toronto Maple Leafs.

1947 Williamsport; 1949–51 Buffalo Bisons; 1952 Toronto Maple Leafs.

Allan Edward Silverstein Born: January 21, 1964. Position: Right-handed pitcher.

1987 St. Catherines; 1988 Myrtle Beach Blue Jays; 1989–90 Dunedin Blue Jays.

Sandy Silverstein Born: Brooklyn, New York.

1951 Buffalo Bisons.

Joseph Solomon (son of Mose Solomon) Position: Pitcher.

Harry Ruby

Aaron Ernie Silverman

Barry Weinberg

c. late 1940s or early 1950s South Miami (Dade County League).

David Steinberg Born: November 18, 1960, in the Bronx, New York. Position: Right-handed pitcher.
1983 Wisconsin Rapids Twins.

Paul "Twister" Steinberg Born: July 4, 1880. Position: Catcher.
1902–1904 Houston (Texas League).

Art Swartz (father of Bud Swartz) Position: Catcher.

Barry Weinberg
Barry is currently a trainer with the St. Louis Cardinals, formerly of the Oakland A's. While serving in a similar position in Shreveport, during August of 1977, the team found itself short of players. Barry was signed to a player's contract as an emergency measure, and actually got to play. He had 8 at-bats and produced 1 hit.
1977 Shreveport.

Randy Weisner Position: Catcher.
1995 Sarasota White Sox (White Sox; Short-season A).

Al Zigelman Position: Catcher.
1941 San Bernardino.

Addenda

Mark Brownstein Position: Right-handed Pitcher. Jewish American player in Japan.
1962 Hanshin Tigers minor league team.

Al Goldis Position: Outfielder.
1960's Cincinnati Reds farm system

William Phillip Granok Position: Pitcher.
Bill had one of the speediest fast balls in the Dodger's farm system, but with, alas, little control.
1961-4 Reno, Orlando, Ozark (later Andalusia,) St. Petersburg, Kingsport, Kinston, Gastonia, Batavia.

Kermit Kitman Born: Brooklyn. Position: Center Fielder.
1943 Harrisburg, Toronto, Durham; 1944 Montreal, Trenton; 1945-6 Montreal.

Marvin Lieb Position: First baseman. Died: February 5, 2000, in Florida.
1948 Dodger's farm system

Chapter 2
Minor League Players II: Active

Steven Eliot Arffa Born: January 26, 1973, in Pasadena, California. Position: Left-handed pitcher.

In 1991, Steve was drafted by the Dodgers, but decided to finish college before entering professional baseball. He did play in the Alaska Summer League. He was drafted again in 1994, this time by the New York Mets. In 1994, Steve played in the New York–Pennsylvania League All-Star Game. On August 30, 1995, he pitched a three-hit shutout against Vero Beach (Florida State League).

1994 Pittsfield Mets (Mets; A); 1995 St. Lucie Mets & Binghamton (Mets; A); 1996 St. Lucie (Mets; A).

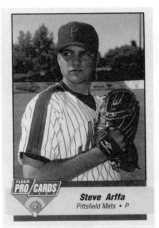

Steve Arffa
Pittsfield Mets • P

Dennis Bair Born: November 17, 1974, in Pittsburgh, Pennsylvania. Position: Right-handed pitcher.

Dennis was selected by the Cubs in the 1995 draft. He pitched a 1.60 ERA with Williamsport that year and a 1.51 ERA with Rockford. In 1996, Dennis led the Daytona Cubs in innings pitched, with 174, and in games started, with 26. He came in second with strikeouts with 127. Dennis underwent knee surgery in 1996 and missed the entire season.

1995 Williamsport (Cubs; Short-season) & Rockford (Cubs; A); 1996 Daytona Cubs (Cubs; A).

Dennis Bair

Danny Buxbaum Born: January 17, 1973, in Tallahassee, Florida. Position: First base.

Danny may be the best current Jewish prospect for the major leagues. He was the MVP of the Northwest League in 1995, and led the Texas League in batting, doubles, hits and extra-base hits throughout the early part of 1997. He is considered one of the best prospects in the Angels system. In 1997, Danny played in the AA All-Star Game.

1995 Boise Hawks (Angels, Short-season); 1996 Lake Elsinore (Angels, A); 1997 Midland (Angels, AA).

DANNY BUXBAUM
BOISE HAWKS

Dan Cey Born: 1975, in Los Angeles, California. Position: Short-

29 IAN EPSTEIN
PITCHER

stop.

Dan is the son of Ron Cey, star third baseman for the LA Dodgers and the Chicago Cubs. His mother is Jewish. In 1996, Dan injured his shoulder and missed much of the year. He began the 1997 season with a bang: an eleven-game hitting streak. He led the league in doubles, with 34, for Fort Myers.

1996 Fort Wayne (Twins, A); 1997 Fort Myers Miracle (Twins, A).

Ian Epstein Born: March 29, 1971, in Piedmont, California. Position: Left-handed pitcher.

Ian signed with the A's in 1994, after graduating from the University of Southern California.

1994 South Oregon A's (A's; Short-season); 1995 West Michigan Whitecaps (A's; A).

David Feuerstein

Dave Feurstein Born: July 19, 1973, in Scarsdale, New York. Position: Outfield.

Dave was drafted by the Rockies in 1995. He contributed to Yale University's three consecutive Ivy League Championships.

1995 Portland Rockies (Rockies; Short-season); 1996 Asheville Tourists (Rockies; A); 1997 Salem (Rockies, A) & New Haven Ravens (Rockies; AA).

Joel Garber

Joel Garber Born: October 14, 1973, in Manhattan Beach, California. Position: Left-handed pitcher.

In his first professional season, Joel led the Appalachian League with a 1.20 ERA. That year, he also was the team leader in winning percentage with .833, and in strikeouts with 66.

1995 Bristol (Rookie); 1996 South Bend Silver Hawks (Short season).

Ronald P. Gerstein Born: January 1, 1969, in Santa Cruz, California. Position: Left-handed pitcher.

In 1997, Ron played for the Kao-ping Fala in the Taiwan Major League. He ended the season with a 7-5 record and a 3.01 ERA.

1990 Salt Lake (A); 1991 Sumter Flyers (Expos; A); 1992 Rockford Expos (Expos; A); 1993 Stockton Ports (Twins; A); 1994–95 El Paso Diablos (Twins; AA); 1996 El Paso Diablos (Twins; AA) & Lubbock Crickets; 1997 Kao-ping Fala (Taiwan Major League).

*Keith Glauber Born: January 18, 1972, in Brooklyn, New York. Position: Right-handed pitcher.

Keith was drafted by the Cardinals in

Ron Gerstein P
Rockford Expos

Keith Glauber
PITCHER • NEW JERSEY CARDINALS

1994. In 1997 he played with the Mesa Saguaros in the Arizona Fall League.

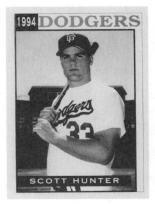

1994 New Jersey Cardinals (Cardinals; A); 1995 Savannah (Cardinals; A); 1996 Peoria Chiefs (Cardinals; A); 1997 Arkansas Travelers (Cardinals; AA) & Louisville Redbirds (Cardinals; AAA).

Jason Halper
1997 Oneonta Yankees (Short-season A; Yankees).

Scott Hunter Born: December 17, 1975, in Philadelphia, Pennsylvania. Position: Outfield.

Scott's mother is Jewish; his father is a gentile. Scott played with the Grand Canyon Rafters in the Arizona Fall League in 1997.

1994 Great Falls Dodgers (Dodgers; A); 1995 San Bernadino Spirit (Dodgers; A) & Capital City (Mets; A); 1997 Binghamton Mets (Mets; A).

Gabe Kapler

*Gabe Kapler Born: August 31, 1975, in Hollywood, California. Position: Outfield.

In 1995, Gabe was named "Best Raw Power in the Detroit Organization." He was named to the Florida State All-Star Team. He played in the Hawaii Winter League's Honolulu Sharks in 1997.

1995 Jamestown Jammers (Tigers; Short-season); 1997 Lakeland (Tigers; A) & New Britain (Twins; AA).

John Myrow

Stacy Kleiner Born: January 12, 1975, in Tarzana, California. Position: Second base.

1997 Prince William (Cardinals; A).

Stacy Kleiner

Joshua Levey Born: 1975, in St. Louis, Missouri. Position: Right-handed pitcher.

Josh was a four-year letterman in baseball at Northwestern University. In June 1997, he graduated with a Bachelor's degree in communications and a 3.0 grade point average.

1997 New Jersey Cardinals (Short season; Cardinals).

John Myrow Born: February 11, 1972, in Los Angeles, California. Position: Outfield.

John's mother is Jewish, his father African-American.

Garrett Neubart

Joshua Levey

Howard Prager
Louisville Redbirds • IF

Jeffery Saffer

Jon Saffer
Vermont Expos • OF

Mike Saipe

1993 Bend; 1994 Central Valley Rockies; 1995–96 New Haven Ravens.

Garrett Neubart Born: November 7, 1973, in Livingston, New Jersey. Position: Outfield.

Garrett graduated from Columbia University, where he was made Ivy League Player of the Year in 1995 and GTE Academic All-American.

Garrett has a younger brother named Adam who is an outfielder at Rutgers. In 1998, he will be a junior.

1995 Portland Rockies (Rockies; A); 1996 Asheville Tourists (Rockies; A); 1997 Salem Avalanche (Rockies; A).

Gus Ornstein Position: First base

In 1997, Gus signed with the New York Yankees. He also plays football for Notre Dame.

Howard Prager Born: April 6, 1967, in Austin, Texas. Positon: Infield.

1989 Auburn Astros (Astros; Short-season); 1990 Osceola; 1991 Jackson & Osceola; 1992 Jackson; 1993 Louisville Redbirds & Arkansas; 1994–95 Louisville Redbirds.

Jeff Saffer Born: June 30, 1975, in Scottsdale, Arizona. Position: Outfield.

Jeff is the younger brother of Jon Saffer. The two brothers work out together in the off-season.

1995 Tampa Yankees (Yankees; A); 1996–97 Greensboro Bats (Yankees; A).

Jon Saffer Born: July 6, 1973, in Inglewood, California. Position: Outfield.

Jon was the International League Player of the Week for May 19–25, 1997. During that week he had a batting average of .600 (15 hits out of 25 at-bats), with 2 doubles, 1 homerun, 3 RBIs and 5 runs scored.

1992 Gulf Expos; 1993 West Palm Beach & Jamestown (Expos; A); 1994 Vermont Expos (Expos; A); 1996 Harrisburg (Expos; AA); 1997 Ottawa Lynx (Expos; AAA).

*Mike Saipe Born: September 10, 1973, in San Diego, California. Position: Right-handed pitcher

Mike was the Eastern League Pitcher of the Week for June 2–8, 1997. That week, he won both of his starts, allowing 3 hits in 14 shutout innings, including a complete game (seven-inning) one-hitter. He also hit a home run. That year, Mike played in the Eastern League All-Star Game. In 1997, he played with the Scottsdale Scorpions in the Arizona Fall League.

On June 25, 1998, Mike Saipe was called up to the majors to

make his debut as a starter for the Colorado Rockies. In his first outing he pitched 6 innings against the Houston Astros and gave up 3 runs on 9 hits. On July 1, 1998, Mike started his second game, against the Seattle Mariners, and completed 4 innings, giving up 9 runs, including a home run to Ken Griffey Jr. After his second outing, Mike was sent back to the AAA level to further develop his skills. Mike finished his 2 game stint with 1 loss, 2 hit batsmen, 5 home runs rendered, and a 10.80 ERA, all in 10 innings.

1994 Bend; 1995 Salem Avalanche; 1996–97 New Haven Ravens (Rockies; AA).

Jon Schaeffer Born: January 20, 1976, in Tarzana, California. Position: Catcher.

Jon was drafted out of Stanford University in 1997 by the Minnesota Twins. Because of his .330 batting average with Elizabethton, he was quickly promoted to AA.

While growing up in the Los Angeles area, Jon played with Dan Cey and frequently played against Gabe Kapler.

1997 Elizabethton Twins (Twins; Short season) & New Britain Rock Cats (Twins; AA).

Justin Siegel Born: September 3, 1975, in Hollywood, California. Position: Left-handed pitcher.

1996 Hudson Valley Renegades (Texas Rangers; A).

Justin Siegel

David Solomon Born: September 30, 1971, in Torrance, California. Position: Left-handed pitcher.

1994 Billings Mustangs (Reds; Rookie).

David Solomon
Billings Mustangs • P

Steve Solomon Born: April 9, 1970, in Los Angeles, California. Position: Outfield.

1992 Batavia Clippers (Phillies; Short-season); 1993 Spartanburg Phillies (Phillies; A); 1994 Clearwater Phillies (Phillies; A); 1995 Reading Phillies (Phillies; AA); 1996 St. Paul Saints.

Al Sontag Position: Right-handed pitcher

1997 Saskatoon Stallions (independent Prairie League).

Steve Solomon
OUTFIELDER • CLEARWATER PHILLIES

Ethan Stein Born: November 11, 1974, in Raleigh, North Carolina. Position: Right-handed pitcher.

In 1993, Ethan graduated from Apex High in North Carolina. He was drafted by the Kan-

David Waco
INFIELDER • SPARTANBURG PHILLIES

#21 Ethan Stein
PITCHER
1997 MEIJER
LANSING Lugnuts

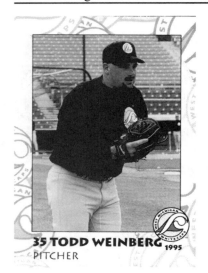

35 TODD WEINBERG 1995
PITCHER

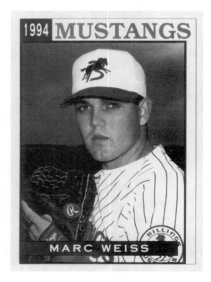

1994 MUSTANGS

MARC WEISS

INF

Joel Wolfe

sas City Royals in the 12th round of the June 1996 free-agent draft. Ethan currently attends the University of North Carolina and lives in Cary.

1996 Spokane (Royals; Short-season; A); 1997 Lansing Lugnuts (Royals; A).

Dave Waco Born: December 8, 1969, in Panorama City, California. Position: Infield.

1993 Sioux Falls Canaries; 1994 Clearwater Phillies (A) & Spartanburg Phillies; 1995 Clearwater Phillies (A).

Todd Weinberg Born: June 13, 1972, in Fall River, Massachussets. Position: Left-handed pitcher.

In 1997, Todd became the closer of the Huntsville Stars. He played for the Phoenix Desert Dogs in the Arizona Fall League that year.

1994 South Oregon A's; 1995–96 West Michigan Whitecaps (A's; A); 1997 Visalia (A's; A) & Huntsville Stars (A's; AA).

Marc Weiss Born: August 3, 1973, in Los Angeles, California. Position: Right-handed pitcher.

1994–95 Billings Mustangs (Reds; Rookie).

Joel Wolfe Born: June 18, 1970, in Northridge, California. Position: Infield-Outfield.

1991 Southern Oregon A's; 1992 Reno; 1993 Huntsville Stars & Modesto; 1994 Huntsville Stars; 1995 Huntsville Stars & Edmonton Trappers; 1996 Arkansas Travelers.

Mike Zimmerman Born: February 6, 1969, in Brooklyn, New York. Position: Right-handed pitcher.

1990 Welland Pirates & Salem; 1991 Salem; 1992 Carolina; 1993 Buffalo & Carolina; 1994 Carolina, Buffalo, & Edmonton; 1995–96 Charlotte Knights (AAA; Marlins); 1997 Omaha Royals (AAA; Royals) & Wichita Wranglers (AA; Royals).

*Now major leaguers, see pages 274-280.

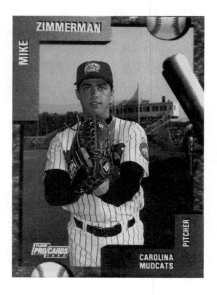

ZIMMERMAN

MIKE

CAROLINA MUDCATS

PITCHER

Chapter 3
Jewish Umpires

Jews have been umpiring in major league games almost as long as they have been playing in them. Even though the first Jewish ballplayer was Lipman Pike, it was his brother, Jacob Pike who had the honor of being the first Jewish umpire, when he officiated in the National Association in 1875. Lip, however, did umpire—in 1887 in the National Association, and again, in 1890, in the National League. There was one other early Jewish umpire, a man named Cohen. Not much is known about him, not even his first name. He umpired in the National League in 1893.

Albert "Dolly" Stark

The first Jewish umpire of modern times was Albert "Dolly" Stark. Dolly was born on November 4, 1897, in New York City. He came from a poor family on Manhattan's Lower East Side and was a boyhood friend of Al Schacht. In 1916, Dolly started his baseball career as a minor league player for Jersey City in the Washington Senators' minor league system. His small stature earned him the nickname "Dolly."

In 1918, Dolly played with Schacht in a league started by the Bethlehem Steel Company called the Steel League. They both played for the team in Bethlehem, Pennsylvania. Dolly went on to play in Newark, before getting a chance to try out with the Washington Senators in 1921. Dolly fared poorly at his try out. He was especially weak at hitting. As he was preparing to return to the minor leagues, a friend asked him to umpire a college game in Vermont. He accepted the invitation and did a magnificent job of umpiring. Dolly was so adept at it that he was induced to try umpiring as a career. He umpired in college games until 1927, when he began working in the Eastern League. People were so impressed with his skill in the blue suit that, the next year, he was promoted to the National League. He was helped to this position by a written recommendation sent by the Giants' manager, John McGraw, to National League President John Heydler.

When Dolly began umpiring in the National League, he became the protégé of Hall of Fame umpire Bill Klem. Klem called Dolly "a natural" and taught him the finer points of the job.

Dolly went on to be a highly respected umpire. He changed the role of the base-line umpires by introducing mobility to the position. In 1934, he was voted as the "League's Best

"DOLLY" STARK

Umpire" by the National League players and he umpired during the All-Star Game. On August 24, 1935, Dolly was commemorated with his own "Day" at the Polo Grounds and was presented with an automobile.

In 1936, Dolly held out for a better salary. He was the first umpire ever to do this. The league refused to meet his demands, however, so that year he was employed as a baseball radio announcer in Philadelphia. Dolly returned to umpiring in 1937. He retired in 1939. But Dolly returned to umpire one more year, in 1942.

In the off-seasons, Dolly would coach basketball at Dartmouth College. He coached the freshman team from 1925 to 1928. In 1929, he was appointed head coach at Dartmouth, remaining in that position until 1936. Dolly returned to coaching at Dartmouth in 1945. He retired once more after the end of the 1946 season. His coaching record was 102 wins and 59 losses.

Al Forman

Dolly died on August 24, 1968, in New York City.

Between 1942 and 1954, there was no Jewish umpire at the major league level.

Stanley Landes was born in the Bronx. After serving four years with the Marines in World War II, Stanley began his baseball career as a minor league pitcher. From 1946 to 1947, he pitched in the North Atlantic League and in the Border League. When he retired from minor league ball, in January 1948, Stanley was advised by umpires Bill Grieve and Red Jones to take up umpiring.

Stanley began as an umpire in the North Atlantic League, in 1948. By July of that year, he had already moved up to Class C ball, in the Mid-Atlantic League. In 1950, he was promoted to umpire in the Class A Sally League, but returned to the Marines in 1951 to serve in the Korean War. In 1952, he returned to umpiring in the Sally League. Stanley was also married that year. He was purchased by the American Association in 1952. Stanley joined the National League at the close of the 1954 season. He continued umpiring until his retirement in 1972. Stanley died in 1994.

While Stanley Landes was umpiring in the National League, he was joined by another Jewish umpire, Al Forman, who was born on July 7, 1928, in Morristown, New Jersey. His parents were Seymour and Mollie Forman. After graduating from high school, Al worked in various jobs for five years, before enrolling in the U.S. Army in 1950. After a military discharge in 1954, he attended Fairleigh Dickinson University. Upon graduation, with an associate degree in business management, Al enrolled in the Al Sommers School of Umpires in Daytona, Florida. In 1956, he started his new career in the Florida State League. In 1957, Al umpired in the Northwest League. The next year he worked not only in the Northwest League, but during the winter also umpired in the Nicaragua Winter League. In 1959, he was promoted to the Texas League. After a two-year stint there, in 1961 Al was promoted to the National League.

Al umpired many great games, including Koufax's third no-hitter on June 4, 1964, at Philadelphia's Connie Mack Stadium. After the 1965 season, Al's National League contract was not renewed. He retired from major league umpiring until the 1978–1979 umpires' strike; Al became a replacement umpire in the American League during the strike. After

1965, he umpired at the college level, becoming a prominent umpire in the Eastern Collegiate Conference and in the NCAA. He made eight appearances in the College World Series. Al currently lives in Kitty Hawk, North Carolina.

The next Jewish umpire also worked in the National League. Alfred Cohen was born in 1927 in Pittsburgh. Between 1946–1947, he spent a year in the U.S. Army as a Military Police officer. Alfred was married in 1950. He began umpiring in Little League games in 1959, then worked his way up to umpiring high school games. Next, he worked at semi-pro games. After these experiences, he became the National League backup umpire in Pittsburgh. Alfred retired in 1976. After retiring from baseball, he became Director of Safety and Security in the suburban school district of North Hill, Pennsylvania. He is now retired from that position and lives with his wife in Pittsburgh.

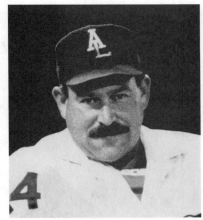

Al Clark

Currently, there is only one Jewish umpire at the major league level. Al Clark was born in Trenton, New Jersey, on January 9, 1948. He started his career in sports as a sportswriter in Trenton. Al studied education at Eastern Kentucky University, then began his career as an umpire in the Midwest League. Al was promoted to the Texas League; then, he umpired in the Venezuelan Winter League. Al's last minor league assignment was in the American Association, before he joined the American League umpiring staff, in 1976. Since 1976, Al has worked in Championship Series, World Series games, and All-Star games. On September 6, 1995, Al was one of the four umpires at Camden Yards during the famous game when Cal Ripken broke Lou Gehrig's record for consecutive games played.

In the off-season, Al does public relations work. He also volunteers at a local anti-drug program. He is known, in addition, to be a talented amateur magician. Al lives, with his wife, in Newtown, Pennsylvania.

Chapter 4
Jewish League Officials
& Club Executives

Commissioner of Major League Baseball:

1992–98 Alan H. "Bud" Selig (Interim Acting Commissioner)

1998– Commissioner

The idea for a baseball commissioner was first proposed by a Jew, Albert Davis Lasker (1880–1952). Lasker was a minority stockholder in the Chicago Cubs, when the Black Sox scandal rocked the baseball world. Lasker's original proposition called for a three-man board, but this was changed into a single commissioner.

Bud Selig, born in 1934, is the first Jew to hold the commissioner's position. He is the first person in his office who is also an owner of a team, although the commissioner of baseball has always been paid by the team owners. Bud owns the Milwaukee Brewers. On July 9, 1998, his position was formalized after he had acted in the position on a "temporary" basis for almost six years. Bud was unanimously elected by the team owners and he became baseball's ninth commissioner. At that time, Bud placed his shares of the Milwaukee Brewer's baseball team into a trust.

Bud resurrected an idea first proposed by Hank Greenberg—interleague play, which started in 1997. Since accepting the position of commissioner, Bud has also introduced the ideas of revenue sharing among owners; wild cards; and a new round of playoffs. For the future, Bud has introduced the idea of team realignment, which would use a regional division system instead of leagues. Part of Bud's legacy will always be the players' strike, which cost baseball the 1994 World Series. Peter Ueberroth, a former commissioner, has said of him, "He has done an incredibly good job navigating baseball through tough times."

Bud was selected, in 1978, as the Major League Executive of the Year.

National League

VICE PRESIDENT

1929–32 Barney Dreyfuss

Barney Dreyfuss (1865–1932) was born in Germany, but came to America when he was seventeen to avoid serving in the German Army. He first got involved in baseball as a means of recovering from his poor health. His playing interest was soon converted to an interest in investment and management. When his first team, the Louisville Colonels (American Association), folded he purchased an interest in the Pittsburgh Pirates. Barney brought his stars from the Colonels to the Pirates—including Honus Wagner and Rube Waddell.

BARNEY DREYFUSS

Barney is credited with originating the World Series. During his term of president with Pittsburgh, his team won 6 pennants and ended in the first division 26 times. In 1909, Barney built Forbes Field as a new home for the Pirates.

Barney was uniquely honored in 1929 by being named the National League's first vice president. He is also a member of the Jewish Sports Hall of Fame in Israel. Further, he is listed on a special honor roll of baseball executives at the Baseball Hall of Fame in Cooperstown.

CLUB PRESIDENTS

BOSTON BRAVES

1927–35 Emil E. Fuchs [See Major Leaguers section]

CINCINNATI REDS

1880 Nathan Menderson

Like Barney Dreyfuss, Emil Fuchs, and Albert Lasker, Nathan Menderson (1820–1904) was born in Germany.

Emil Fuchs

1890 Aaron Samuel Stern

Aaron Stern (1853–1920) already owned the Reds in 1882, when they became the first team to win an American Association pennant. Aaron introduced such innovations as "Ladies Day," the sale of seat cushions, and candy concessions. He was noted for his generosity to his players, often rewarding critical hits with $10 gold coins.

1930–33 Sidney Weil

Sidney brought to the Reds the great talents of Ernie Lombardi and Paul Derringer, favorites of the Reds' fans.

HOUSTON ASTROS

1981–85 Albert L. Rosen (also General Manager) [See Major Leaguers section]

LOUISVILLE COLONELS

1899 Barney Dreyfuss

MONTREAL EXPOS

1969–90 Charles R. Bronfman (also Chairman of the Board)

NEW YORK GIANTS

1895–1902 Andrew Freedman

In 1895, Andrew Freedman (1860–1915), a realtor-politician, with close connections to Tammany Hall, purchased the practically bankrupt New York Giants for $50,000. This price represented one tenth of Freedman's estimated fortune of that time: $500,000. Andrew was brusque and ruthless in methods of handling his team and in trying to rebuild it. He quickly offended players, sportswriters, fans, and fellow owners.

Yet many of his ideas were farsighted. He wanted his fellow owners to admit that baseball was in business to make a profit and that it should be run like a business. His suggestions were practical and, if they had been followed, would have been very profitable. But all they led to was having Andrew being denounced in the public press as a "God-damned Sheeney" (Sporting Life, November 25, 1899).

Andrew became furious at such blatant anti-Semitism. His supporters saw Andrew as a prophet, who wished to bring reason and modern business methods to the National Game. His detractors depicted him as a violent, ill-mannered brute who would explode at mere nothings, like being called a "Sheeney" by a player on an opposing team. In 1898, "Ducky" Holmes of the Baltimore Orioles used this slur during a game, and Andrew wanted Holmes thrown out of the game. The umpires refused, and he appealed the case to the arbitration committee, which laid Holmes off. The case aroused a great deal of passion, the great majority of it aimed against Andrew.

Andrew sold out his interests in the Giants in 1902, for $125,000. One of the last acts of his tenure was the appointment of a new manager, the last in a long line, for Andrew had not gotten along with his managers. This manager was John McGraw, perhaps the most influential one in the history of the game. Andrew now turned all of his attention to his major life's work, the building of the New York City subway system.

PITTSBURGH PIRATES

1900–32 Barney Dreyfuss

1932–46 William Edward Benswanger (also Treasurer)

When Barney Dreyfuss' son, Samuel, died in 1931, his father never recovered from his grief. Bill Benswanger (1892–1972), Barney's son-in-law, took over the reigns of the Pirates on Barney's death. During his 15 years at the helm, the team finished in the first division 11 times. Bill was also responsible for bringing Ralph Kiner to the major leagues.

SAN FRANCISCO GIANTS

1976–79 Robert A. Lurie (also Co-Chairman)

1980–85 Robert A. Lurie

1986–92 Albert L. Rosen (also General Manager)

American Association

LEAGUE PRESIDENT

1891 Louis C. Kramer

Louis Kramer (1848–1922) was part-owner of the league's Cincinnati Reds. Louis, who helped to found the American Association, held the presidency of the league for some 6 months.

CINCINNATI REDS

1883–84 Aaron S. Stern

1887–89 Aaron S. Stern

American League

EXECUTIVE VICE-PRESIDENT

1983–88 Robert Fishel

CLUB PRESIDENTS

BALTIMORE ORIOLES

1901 Sidney W. Frank

Andrew Freedman issued this silver pass to a Jewish patron in 1898

Sidney and his brother, Moses, were responsible for bringing an American League franchise to Baltimore in 1901. Unfortunately, it didn't last there long, but was moved to New York, where it became the New York Highlanders and, later, the Yankees. Baltimore did not get a major league team back until 1954.

1966–79 Jerold C. Hoffberger (also Chairman of the Board; see below)

   Jerold Hoffberger gained his position with the Orioles—a different team from that which had been led by Sidney Frank—by his presidency of the National Brewery Co., which owned the team. Jerold was also distinguished for his activities within the Jewish community, both nationally and in Baltimore.

1980–82 Jerold C. Hoffberger

CHICAGO WHITE SOX

1940 Harry Grabiner (also Vice President)

Harry Grabiner worked for the Chicago White Sox for 40 years. In 1940, on the death of Louis Comiskey, he was named acting president, while retaining his title of vice president.

JERRY REINSDORF

1981–90 Eddie Einhorn

1981– Jerry M. Reinsdorf (also Chairman)

The current chairman of the White Sox is considered one of the most influential owners in baseball today. Jerry, who also owns the Chicago Bulls basketball team, is usually considered the head of the conservative wing among team owners.

CLEVELAND INDIANS

1963–71 Gabriel Howard Paul (also Treasurer/General Manager)

Gabe Paul (1910–1998) spent most of his life as part of the baseball world. He began his career as a shoeshine boy in the ballpark in Rochester, New York. He slowly rose up the ranks of responsibility until he became general manager of the Cincinnati Reds in 1936. In 1956, Gabe was named "Major League Executive of the Year" by The Sporting News.

1978–85 Gabriel H. Paul (also CEO)

KANSAS CITY ROYALS

1969–93 Ewing Kauffman (also Chairman of the Board)

MILWAUKEE BREWERS (NOW NATIONAL LEAGUE)

1970–98 Allan H. "Bud" Selig (also CEO)

1998– Wendy Selig-Prieb (also CEO)—Daughter of Bud Selig

NEW YORK YANKEES

1973–77 Gabriel H. Paul

1978–80 Albert L. Rosen (also CEO)

Gabe Paul

OAKLAND ATHLETICS

1990–95 Walter J. Haas (also Chairman/CEO)

SEATTLE MARINERS

1977–79 Danny Kaye (also Managing General Partner)

Born David Daniel Kominski, the great movie star and comedian Danny Kaye (1913–1987) was a lifelong baseball enthusiast. During his later years he was known for his TV appearances and his work for UNICEF.

Danny Kaye

Chapter 5
Marvin Miller and the
Players Association

For more than a hundred years, there had been a conflict between the players and the team owners over the distribution of profits. The players tried to get a fare share of the revenues many times, in many ways, but they consistently failed; that is, they failed until Marvin Miller became head of the Baseball Players Association. Hank Aaron has called Marvin Miller "as important to the history of baseball as Jackie Robinson." Marvin was well versed in labor laws and precedents, and his many years of experience in the Steelworkers' Union had tempered him. He took on the owners and won: he enriched the players to an extent never conceivable before and made the public change their perception of these men.

Marvin was born on April 14, 1917, in Brooklyn, New York, the son of Alexander Miller, a ladies' coat salesman, and his wife Gertrude, a teacher in the New York public school system. Marvin's father was a kind and generous man; he always made special efforts to help the less fortunate. As a child, Marvin was athletic, even though he had a limited range of motion in his right shoulder because of an injury at the time of his birth.

As a boy, Marvin was a great fan of the Brooklyn Dodgers. He could recite all of the Dodgers' statistics, by heart, and those of most of their competition as well. Whenever Marvin is asked why he accepted the position of Chief Executive of the Baseball Players Association—when he had such a prestigious position with the United Steel Workers Union—he replies, "I grew up in Brooklyn, not far from Ebbets Field." He has never needed to say anything else.

After graduating from P.S. 153, in Brooklyn, Marvin attended James Monroe High School. He then enrolled in New York University. It was while at NYU that Marvin met his future wife, Theresa Morgenstern. After graduating, with a degree in economics, he attended graduate school courses at the New School for Social Research. Marvin worked for the War Labor Board during WWII. After the war, in 1950, he began as a staff economist for the United Steel Workers Union, and rose up the ranks to be chief research director of the union and assistant to the union's president.

Marvin became Executive Director of the Baseball Players Association in 1966, after a dramatic series of events which began when he was interviewed by Robin Roberts. Marvin led the Players Association through two strikes, in 1972 and 1981, and a lockout in 1990. He used reason to make his decisions. That is why he was more successful than the owners he opposed. They were far less interested in the health of their sport than in maintaining their control over the players and maintaining an outdated system. They were like the Bourbons: They never forgot anything and they never learned anything.

In 1976, Marvin and the Players Association were involved in their most important decision. They defeated the reserve clause with the Messersmith-McNally Case and brought about free agency. The reserve clause is the clause in the standard baseball contract that says once a player signs with a team he is not allowed to leave it to go to another, unless he is traded. Free-agency rules allow that after seven years' experience and the termination of his contract, a player can take offers from all interested teams and sign with whomever he wants. Free agency has benefited the players by increasing their salaries; benefited the fans by better distributing the most talented players; and benefited the owners by creating more interest in baseball and, therefore, increasing their profits.

Marvin headed the Players Association for only 24 years. This was but a brief moment, considering the vastness of his accomplishments. He resigned from his position in 1984. Nevertheless, he played a major role in the negotiations of the 1990 contract. Marvin continued to work for the Association as a consultant for the next few years.

Marvin is now retired. He lives with his wife, Terry, in New York. They have one son and one daughter and a grandson. In 1991, Marvin published his best-selling memoirs, A Whole Different Ballgame.

The current executive director of the Players Association is Donald Fehr, who is also Jewish. He has held this position since 1984.

Chapter 6
Jewish Participation in Baseball in the Olympic Games

The earliest of the modern Olympic Games did not include baseball as part of their roster of sports. Baseball was only included as a demonstration sport on a few occasions during some of the Olympics held in the first half of this century. In most of these instances, there was Jewish participation. Since 1984, baseball has become a regular part of the Summer Olympics.

Abel Richard Kiviat was born on June 23, 1892, in New York. He was one of the great middle-distance runners of all time. On June 8, 1912, during the United States Eastern Olympic Trials, Abel set a new world record for the 1,500 meter race, with a time of 3:55.8—which record would stand until 1917 and would remain the U.S. record until 1928. Abel was not quite as effective in the Stockholm Olympics themselves, where he won the silver medal with a time of 3:56.9. Even though he competed primarily in track and field events, he was also part of the 1912 U.S. Olympic baseball team. This was the first year in which baseball was played at the Olympics and was included in the venue as a demonstration sport. Abel served in the Army during the First World War. He continued his running career after the war, until 1925. For more than a quarter of a century Abel served as press steward for track meets in the New York area. Abel died, at the age of ninety-nine, in 1991.

After 1912, the next occasion when America's national sport was demonstrated at an Olympic game was 1936. The 1936 Olympics were held in Nazi Germany. After the final Olympic events were completed, after the triumphs of Jesse Owens had demonstrated to the world the absurdity of Adolph Hitler's racial theories, America staged an exhibition of baseball.

The U.S.A. Baseball Congress had selected the two teams to compete. Planning had not been started early enough and the nation was forced to pick the two teams just a few weeks before they were scheduled to depart. The Baseball Congress asked managers of college and amateur leagues to nominate players, and when the two teams were selected, they had only a few days to practice. The American teams were called the "U.S.A. Olympics" and the "World

Herman Goldberg

Herman Goldberg's Jersey

**1996 LSU TIGERS
NATIONAL CHAMPIONS**

Skip Bertman – Head Coach

Amateurs." Both teams wore the same red-white-and-blue uniforms, with a big "US" across the chest. The U.S.A. Olympics and World Amateurs did play a series of ten practice games in Hakenfeld Stadium, Berlin. The official exhibition game was played on August 12, 1936, at the same stadium. The German audience broke the record for the largest crowd ever seen anywhere in the world at a baseball game, with 125,000 people in attendance.

There was one Jewish player in this game. His name was Herman Goldberg. He played on the World Amateurs team. Herman was born in Brooklyn and attended Brooklyn College. The World Amateurs defeated the U.S.A. Olympics, 6 to 5. After playing in the Olympics, the two teams toured Europe and America, playing various amateur and military teams.

As baseball was only a demonstration sport in the 1936 Olympics, the participants were not eligible for prize medals, but were awarded participation medals. Herman's participation medal and jersey from the World Amateurs is now on display in the Baseball Hall of Fame.

In 1940, the Olympic games were planned to be staged in Tokyo, Japan. Due to the war, however, the games were canceled. It had been planned that the 1940 Olympics would have teams competing from all over the world. Nine teams had signed up to compete in baseball in Tokyo, including those of both the U.S. and Japan. The U.S. Team was picked from amateur and college players throughout the country. Mike Schemer was picked as part of that team.

The next Olympics to include baseball were held in 1964. These games were played in Tokyo. Another Jewish player was chosen to compete on the U.S. Team: Mike Epstein.

Jewish players and coaches have been involved in U.S. Olympic baseball teams in recent years. Mike Milchin played on the gold-medal-winning 1988 team. Ivan Zweig was picked to be part of the 1992 team, though he never had the opportunity to play. Skip Bertman and Jerry Weinstein coached the 1996 team, which went on to win the bronze medal. Skip's connection with the Olympics goes back to the gold-winning team of 1988, which he served as pitching coach. Skip, who was born in 1939, earned his B.A. in health and physical education from the University of Miami (Florida) in 1961; he took his M.A. from Miami in 1964. Skip served as assistant coach at Miami from 1976 to 1983.

In 1984, Skip was named as head coach of the Louisiana State Tigers baseball team, and the years since then have proven Skip to be one of the greatest collegiate coaches in the history of the game. He has piloted LSU to winning season after winning season since he first took over the helm—for fourteen consecutive seasons—and he is still going strong. Nine times Skip led the Fighting Tigers to College World Series appearances. Six times his team took the Southeastern Conference championship. And, in 1991, 1993, 1996, and 1997, Skip led LSU to the NCAA Championship, the national college title.

Skip Bertman – Head Coach

But Skip is not merely a great coach, he has proven himself time after time to be a teacher and guide to the young men who form his team. Of the players who have played four years with Skip, nearly all have graduated from LSU. Of the ballplayers whom he has coached, over 200 have gone on to play professional baseball. During the 1995-96 period, when Skip was guiding the U.S. Olympic team, he led his men to a 71-11 record and a bronze medal in the Olympics itself.

Skip is a member of the University of Miami Sports Hall of Fame. He was named National Coach of the Year in 1986, 1991, and 1993. He and his wife, Sandy, have four daughters.

Skip's assistant coach for team USA, in 1995-96, was Jerry Weinstein of Sacramento City College. Jerry was born on November 9, 1943, in Los Angeles. He is the baseball coach of Sacramento and has led his team to conference championships or co-championships 15 times in 19 years. He led Sacramento to the state title in 1988.

In 1992, Jerry first served as assistant coach for team USA, under Head Coach Ron Fraser. Jerry served as the manager of the Geneva Cubs in 1993, and the Williamsport Cubs in 1994. Like Skip Bertman, many of the young men whom, Jerry has coached have gone on to professional baseball careers—including some 15 major-leaguers.

Chapter 7
A Whole Other Ballgame

Who is the greatest Jewish pitcher of all time? Is it Sandy Koufax, with his four no-hitters (including one perfect game), his three Cy Young awards, and his election as the youngest member ever to the Baseball Hall of Fame? Perhaps it is Barney Pelty, with his lifetime ERA of 2.63 (compared to Koufax's 2.76)? Or then, perhaps, it is a pitcher who first came to public attention during the Chicago World's Fair of 1933: Harry "Coon" Rosen.

Harry who? You've never heard of him?!

Well, during his career, Harry Rosen pitched some 300 no-hit games, including 195 perfect ones. Harry won more than 3,000 games in a pitching career that spanned more than 50 years, but his chosen game was not major league baseball, although he was offered a contract by the St. Louis Cardinals in the early 1930s. His game was softball. Harry was born in Lincoln, Nebraska, on June 25, 1908. He and his family soon left the state, and Harry was raised in Chicago. It was on the politically incorrect streets of Chicago of the 1920s that Harry's luxuriant, curly black hair and swarthy complexion earned him the nickname of "Coon," a cognomen he proudly bore.

Harry "Coon" Rosen

At age twelve, Harry led the Von Humboldt Grammar School to the Chicago YMCA championship. Later, he attended the University of Illinois, whose baseball team he led to the Big Ten championship in 1931. Harry appeared on the team as both a pitcher and a first baseman. His father discouraged him, however, from accepting the Cardinal contract because he thought being a ballplayer was "the equivalent of being a bum."

But Harry did not let his love of the game fade with his hopes of a professional career, and he joined the J. L. Friedman Boosters softball team, an amateur club. And then came the World's Fair of 1933. What innovations the world saw in that fair! There was Sally Rand and her fan dance. There was the first All-Star Baseball Game. There was a special

224

day set aside to honor Jews; a special token was issued to mark the day. And there was the first World Series of Softball, an event that has been repeated every year since, to this day.

The World Series of Softball was the idea of Leo H. Fischer, a Jew and a sportswriter for the Chicago American, a newspaper owned by William Randolph Hearst. Fischer's enthusiasm for softball lead him to found, in 1933, the Amateur Softball Association, the recognized governing body of organized softball in the United States. Fischer was elected first president of the organization and he held that position for eight years. Born in Chicago on September 20, 1897, he was also the author of a classic book on softball, How to Play Winning Softball (New York: 1940).

Fischer used the power of the Hearst chain to advertise the new World Series across the entire country. There were many innovations in that Series, including a new rule book—which became standard for softball, which up until that time was played with an unbelievable diversity of rules and equipment. Even the softball itself had no standard size. It was during the 1933 World's Fair that the game was divided into "fast pitch" and "slow pitch." It was also during the fair that women took their rightful place as softball players. Leo Fischer was tireless in his promotion of the first World Series of Softball. Though he was given only ten days to organize the event, he managed to gather 24 regional championship teams from around the country to compete. Sixteen of these teams were men; eight, women. The Series was the surprise hit of the Fair, with some 350,000 spectators.

In that first softball World Series, Harry Rosen pitched eight games in three days and led his team, the J.L. Friedman Boosters, to the championship over Detroit's Briggs Beautyware, 5 games to one. The importance of this event cannot be overemphasized, for it marks the beginning of the modern history of the game of softball, a game that has become one of the most popular participatory sports known to both men and women.

Harry's sport was fast-pitch softball and he was famous for the figure-eight arm motion of his pitch, which sailed in over the plate at about 100 mph, with a two- to three-foot rise and a sudden drop. Even the greatest hitters of the game found it impossible to hit "Coon" Rosen. Harry participated in the softball World Series for the next twelve years. In eight of those years, he was named a first-team All-American. For five years in a row, Harry was chosen Most Valuable Player.

In 1950, Harry stopped playing softball on a regular basis. Though he was living in San Diego, California, he took a job in Tijuana, Mexico, as general manager of both the Caliente Race Track and Tijuana's jai alai fronton. In 1973, he came to Las Vegas to direct the newly opened MGM Grand Fronton.

In 1976, Harry was chosen to pitch for a celebrity team, led by Dale Robertson, playing against the Houston Astros in an exhibition fast-pitch softball game at the Astrodome. Harry's pitch was timed at over 100 mph and, in 5 innings of work, he fanned between 10 and 12 major league players. He was 68 at the time! Even into his eighties, Harry continued to practice his pitching two or three times a week. According to a witness, even at that age Harry's pitch could make the catcher's mitt "pop like a firecracker."

Harry was often honored for his prowess. In 1935, he was featured by Robert L. Ripley in his cartoon "Believe It or Not." Harry was a member of the Amateur Softball Association's National Hall of Fame, in Oklahoma City; the Chicago Sports Hall of Fame; the Arizona Sports Hall of Fame; the Softball Hall of Fame, in Chicago; the Arizona Softball Hall of Fame; and the San Diego Hall of Champions. In 1993, he was elected as a member of the International Jewish Sports Hall of Fame in Netanya, Israel.

25 Fanny "Bobbie"
Rosenfeld, Toronto

Harry Rosen died on January 4, 1997, in Sun City, California. He was survived by two daughters, seven grandchildren, and four great-grandchildren. At the time of his death, he was engaged to be married to Anne La Sala of Sun City.

"Coon" was not the first or only Jewish star of softball—a game that traces its origins to Thanksgiving Day 1887, in Chicago, when it began as an indoor version of baseball. The game quickly moved outdoors and became as popular among women as men.

Probably the first Jewish softball star was a remarkable woman named Fanny Rosenfeld (1903–1969). Fanny, who was often known as "Bobbie" because of her bobbed hair, was born in Katrinaslav, Russia, but was raised in Canada. She was a remarkable athlete who excelled in basketball, tennis, bowling, hockey, and track and field. She won two medals in the 1928 Olympic Games: a gold in the 400 meter relay race and a silver in the 100-yard dash.

Even as a girl in the streets of Barrie, Ontario, before the family moved to Toronto, Fanny learned to play softball from the other kids. In 1922, she joined the factory softball team for the Patterson's Chocolate Company of Toronto, and was a member of a number of other championship teams, besides softball. After her Olympic victories, however, she returned to her participation in softball.

In 1929, Fanny suffered a serious attack of arthritis; it left her disabled for the next eighteen months. While, after her recovery, she was no longer able to compete in track events, she did continue her participation in softball until 1933, when a second attack of arthritis permanently ended her sports career. She coached softball for some time after that.

In 1937, Fanny began writing on sports for a Toronto newspaper and soon became a leading sports journalist. In 1950, she was selected by the sportswriters of Canada as Canada's Female Athlete of the Half-Century. She is honored in the Canadian AAU Sports Hall of Fame. In 1981, she was selected for Israel's Jewish Sports Hall of Fame.

The name of Rube Goldberg (1883–1970) has become part of the English language in the phrase "Rube Goldberg Invention." The artistic achievements of this great American original cartoonist and sculptor, are too vast and diverse to discuss here, except to mention that a number of his early cartoons have baseball themes. It is Rube Goldberg the softball pitcher that we wish to focus on here.

In the late thirties and early forties, President Franklin Roosevelt managed his own softball team, consisting of his sons, members of his cabinet, Secret Service men, and members of the White House press corps. Roosevelt's favorite opposition was a team fielded by Lowell Thomas and consisting of various celebrities and newsmen. Babe Ruth was on the team, as well as Edward R. Murrow, Heywood Broun, and Franklin P. Adams. The name of the team was the "Nine Old

Men"—a joke on Roosevelt's view of the Supreme Court. The team's pitcher was often Rube Goldberg, who pitched the entire game with a lit cigar clenched between his teeth. These games, fast-pitch softball, would stop with America's entry into the Second World War.

The debility of major league baseball during the war led to the All-American Girls Professional Baseball League. This league was the creation of Philip K. Wrigley, owner of the Chicago Cubs, with some help from Branch Rickey and others. The league started in 1943, with six teams, and lasted until 1953. The league was the inspiration for the hit movie A League of Their Own (1992). The brand of ball played by the AAGPBL was a cross between softball and baseball, with both overhand and underhand pitches allowed. The ball used was halfway in size between a baseball and a softball. There were four Jewish players in the AAGPBL: Thelma Eisen, Anita Foss, Blanche Schachter, and Margaret Wigiser.

Thelma "Tiby" Eisen, a native of Los Angeles, born on May 11, 1922, had the longest career of any of these Jewish women in the AAGPBL. Tiby played from 1944 to 1952, for four different cities: Milwaukee, Grand Rapids, Peoria, and Fort Wayne. Tiby had been working at the shipyard in Los Angeles in 1944, when she was recruited by the Milwaukee Chicks, as an outfielder. The Chicks, who were managed by major league star Max Carey, took the championship that year, but still had poor attendance, so the franchise was moved to Grand Rapids.

In 1946, Tiby, playing for the Peoria Redwings, had the best year of her career, with nine triples, 128 stolen bases, and a batting average of .256. She was chosen for the All-Star Team that year and was on the South American tour of the AAGPBL. Tiby last played with the Fort Wayne Daisies and completed her career in the league with 966 games and 674 stolen bases. She had a lifetime batting average of .224 and 11 career home runs.

Anita Foss, who was born on August 5, 1921, in Providence, Rhode Island, was informed that her husband, who was in the U.S. Navy, had been killed. She had to find a new route for her life. Her excellent speed earned her a spot on second base in a team in the AAGPBL. Anita played only 28 games, before deciding to look in other directions for the solace she needed. Her batting average was .118.

Blanche Schachter was born in Brooklyn on September 20, 1926. Her family was Orthodox and she played for the temple team. When she heard they were having tryouts in New Jersey for the AAGPBL, she asked her mother what she should do. Her mother said, "Blanche, go." The young woman made the team, the Kenosha Comets. It was the proudest day of her life. Blanche was a catcher. But her career was to last only nine games. In her final game, she tore a cartilage in her right knee and her playing career was over. Blanche had a batting average of .040. Following her playing days, she coached a girls' high school tennis team.

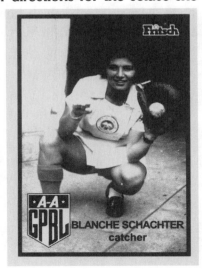

Margaret M. "Wiggie" Wigiser was born on December 17, 1924, in Brooklyn. Her parents were Herman and Pauline

(née Fabian) Wigiser, both of Hungarian origin. She graduated from Seward Park High School, where, in 1942, she received the Underhill Certificate for outstanding athlete. In 1944, she began her three-year career with the AAGPBL with the Minneapolis team. While playing for Minneapolis in Rockford Park, the home of the Peaches, she hit the longest home run ever hit at the park. This must have impressed the Peaches' management, for they traded for Wiggie, who spent the rest of her career at Rockford. Wiggie played centerfield for the Peaches and was the regular member of the team in that position when the team won the League Championship in 1945. Wiggie had a lifetime batting average of .227 and 4 career home runs.

Even before she started playing with the AAGPBL, Margaret began attending Hunter College; she holds both a B.A. and an M.A. After her retirement in 1946, she maintained her interest in women's athletics. She was a physical education teacher in New York from 1948 to 1969 and director of the city's high school sports programs from 1969 to 1982. She has been an important factor in persuading the New York School System to fund athletic programs for high school girls. Wiggie also takes a keen interest in golf. She is a member of the Halls of Fame of Hunter College, the Hunter College Alumni Association, and the New York City Public Schools Athletic Association.

A hero of our own day is fast-pitch sensation David Blackburn, of California, the fifth-ranked pitcher in the country today, and the only one of the top 25 pitchers who is Jewish. David is 37 years old and has been pitching for about twenty years. He estimates that he has probably pitched a thousand games and that he has won about 750 of them. In 1985, David pitched for the U.S. team at the Maccabiah Games in Israel, leading the team to victory. He did the same in 1989. David was chosen as the top American athlete of the 1989 games. In 1993, he again competed, but the U.S. team lost a squeaker to Canada.

Softball, throughout its history, unlike baseball, has remained principally—with the notable exception of the AAGPBL—an amateur sport. Therefore, the carefully kept records of major and minor league baseball do not have parallels in the annals of softball. Nevertheless, there have always been Jewish heroes and heroines, sung and unsung, who have enriched the softball diamonds of the land.

Chapter 8
Scandals, Scoundrels, and Little Boys

There is a passage in F. Scott Fitzgerald's novel The Great Gatsby (1925) that makes a good introduction for the first subject of this chapter. The narrator of the Fitzgerald story has just been introduced by his friend Jay Gatsby to a man named Meyer Wolfsheim. When the friends are alone, the narrator asks Gatsby who this man is, suggesting, perhaps, that he's a dentist:

" 'Meyer Wolfsheim? No, he's a gambler.' Gatsby hesitated, then added coolly: 'He's the man who fixed the World's Series back in 1919.'

" 'Fixed the World's Series?' I repeated.

"The idea staggered me. I remembered, of course, that the World's Series had been fixed in 1919, but if I had thought of it at all I would have thought of it as a thing that merely happened, the end of some inevitable chain. It never occurred to me that one man could start to play with the faith of fifty million people—with the single-mindedness of a burglar blowing a safe.

" 'How did he happen to do that?' I asked after a minute.

" 'He just saw the opportunity.'

" 'Why isn't he in jail?'

" 'They can't get him, old sport. He's a smart man.' "

The character Wolfsheim is based on the real-life Arnold Rothstein, the Jew who, perhaps, has had more impact on the history of our national sport than practically any other. Certainly, it was directly through the efforts of Rothstein that baseball lost some of its greatest players in the prime of their talent, men like Joe Jackson, Benny Kauff, and Ed Cicotte; that the baseball commissioner was created; and that the in-nocent American public, which had managed to survive the

Arnold Rothstein

First World War untouched by cynicism, finally experienced it. Rothstein's influence on Ameri-can society in general went far beyond this. He was not only a fixer of baseball games, he was also a visionary who conceived and developed most of the methodology and organization of the modern Mafia.

Arnold Rothstein was the product of an Orthodox Jewish upbringing in New York's Lower East Side. His father, Abraham, was a prosperous merchant in the garment industry, as famous for his piety as for his business acumen. To his employees and business associates he was known as "Abe the Just." In 1919, the very year of the Black Sox scandal, Abe Rothstein was given a testimonial dinner in honor of his handling of an industrial dispute. This dinner was attended by, among others, the governor of New York, Alfred E. Smith, and Louis D. Brandeis, a justice of the U.S. Supreme Court.

But Abraham Rothstein had very little influence on his son Arnold. Indeed, it was as if Arnold was seeking to be everything his father was not—except rich. Arnold was a bad stu-

OGDEN'S CIGARETTES.

ABE ATTELL.

dent in school (except for math). He was cruel and cunning. He would steal his father's money and use it to play craps in the street. But when he was very young, Arnold, with his acumen with numbers, figured out that if he could manipulate the odds just a little in his favor, gambling was not the even chance or fair bet it was supposed to be, but a surefire way of making money. Arnold Rothstein was often referred to as a gambler, but "The Big Bankroll" never bet on any game he hadn't already rigged.

When he was still a teenager, Arnold had amassed a few thousand dollars. Some of his money he loaned out at exorbitant interest. If you missed a payment, Arnold had a friend named Monk Eastman who would come around and pay you a "visit." You would not miss another payment. Monk, also Jewish, later went on to form his own large organization of Jewish thugs and killers. Arnold made friends with Tammany Hall politicians and the policemen who followed their directions. He soon had two private casinos, not only safe from police raids but actually guarded by city police.

Soon, too, Arnold used his money to open a luxurious restaurant and gambling resort in Saratoga, New York. This spot became the hit of the rich and powerful and Arnold was soon the toast of New York.

One excellent source of money for Rothstein was betting on baseball games. This was very popular at the time, probably the most popular form of betting in this country, up to the time of the scandal. The Yankees, then the Highlanders, had always been a good team and, in New York, the hometown favorites. Therefore, it proved a very good source of income for Rothstein to simply have a member of the team throw a game. Arnold, of course, would know what game and bet heavily on it. He would clean up.

One of the real heroes of the early Highlanders was Harold "Prince Hal" Chase, who had been the team's first baseman from 1905 to 1913. It is said that Hal Chase received more money from throwing games for Rothstein than he did for playing. Chase's popularity and the spectacular quality of his play, when he wasn't having an "off day," kept him from real trouble. Undoubtedly, it was the ease by which he'd made money through his association with Chase that inspired Arnold to attempt the biggest fix of all time: the rigging of the 1919 World Series. Chase would be banned from baseball for life in the aftermath of the Black Sox scandal.

It is not clear precisely where the idea for the throwing of the Series first originated, although it was indeed Rothstein's money and power of corruption that were behind it. Rothstein's right-hand man in developing and executing the plot was a Jewish boxer, a former featherweight champion of the world, Abe Attell. Attell was born in San Francisco in 1884, the son of Russian Jews. Abe's neighborhood was Irish and tough and Abe, who was small and slim, was the toughest of all. His fighting soon took him far beyond his neighborhood. He reigned as champion from 1901 to 1912. Many who saw him fight considered him, pound for pound, the toughest fighter who ever lived. Abe retired from fighting in 1917. Several attempts to open restaurants failed, so he depended for his livelihood on "the kindness of strangers." (The hundreds of thousands of dollars Abe had made over the years were mostly lost in gambling.) Arnie Rothstein particularly enjoyed the company of the spunky pugilist, and the two men became close friends.

It is believed that Abe acted as the bagman for the conspiracy, though the players were never paid the full amount they had been promised. For a while, in 1920, when the story first broke, Abe had to hide out in Canada. Eventually, he could come home and bask in his newfound infamy, to go along with his hard-won fame. His involvement in the scandal did not prevent him from being installed as a member of the Boxing Hall of Fame in 1955.

Arnold Rothstein was known in his day by various names. Sometimes he was "The Brain," the man who had organized all the rackets in New York; sometimes he was "Mr. Big," the man to whom all others were beholden; sometimes he was "The Man Uptown," referring to the political connections that kept his empire afloat; and, sometimes, he was just "A.R." One of Arnold Rothstein's greatest talents was in arranging the settlement of criminal cases. This won for Arnold his title "The Fixer."

Rothstein used this talent particularly well in the Black Sox affair. However, he was outflanked by the owners, who now created the position of commissioner of baseball and appointed Kenesaw Mountain Landis to the job. This brought integrity back to the sport, but it also kept it segregated until after Landis' death, in 1944.

We wonder whether Arnold Rothstein was aware that he had been immortalized in Scott Fitzgerald's classic novel. He was still alive when the book was published. Perhaps he was too busy with his bootlegging, rum-running, loan sharking, book-making, and other enterprises to find time to read a novel. Arnold was found shot dead in a New York hotel room in 1928. There are various theories concerning his death, but nothing has ever been proved. Abe Attell died in 1970, six days before what would have been his eighty-sixth birthday.

In 1923, there occurred a kind of mini–Black Sox scandal that is today practically forgotten. One of the central figures in this event was Sammy Bohne, Jewish second baseman of the Cincinnati Reds. In that year, a sports magazine called Collyer's Eye announced to its readers that two baseball players on Cincinnati had been offered bribes, by gamblers, of $15,000 each to throw an upcoming series with the New York Giants. Besides Bohne, the other player named by the magazine was Pat Duncan, an outfielder. The president of the National League, John Heydler, immediately called Bohne and Duncan into his office. Both players denied that anything in any way resembling the story had ever taken place. Heydler then ordered the men to bring suit against the magazine for libel. The players did file suit, winning the case for $100, plus court costs.

In 1933, in Toronto, Canada, on a warm summer evening, there was a game held to determine the city championship among teenage boys' clubs. The finalists were Harbord, a Jewish club, and St. Peter's, a Catholic club. As the game progressed, it became clear that there was very little goodwill between the teams or among the mob of spectators. There had been a great deal of trouble during the preceding months. Pro-Nazi groups had been flagrant in their propaganda and demonstrations in the city and in nearby resorts. Jews had registered complaints with the police, but many people were uncomfortable with the growing tension. Jews had been attacked in the streets and graffiti of an anti-Semitic nature had appeared on Jewish business windows. The game was being held at Christie Pits Ballpark, a favorite gathering spot for young people of all ethnic groups.

Harbord, the Jewish club, won the game. The victory was not well accepted by St. Peter's or its supporters. There were boos and catcalls, and there was no effort on the part of the spectators to disperse. Overlooking the field on one side was a hill. A boy on the hill suddenly shouted, "Heil Hitler!" and unfurled a Nazi flag. The members of Harbord, elated by their victory, charged the hill. Not far behind swept a hoard of their supporters. They reached the young Nazi and beat him to the ground. But this boy was not without his own supporters, who dove into the fray, often with baseball bats and pieces of lead pipe.

Soon the scene was one of universal struggle. Some of the onlookers fled the ballpark back into the streets of Toronto. But it was a hot night and many people were milling about. As word of the struggle at Christie Pits spread, more and more people came to break up, or join, the fight. Young Jewish boys ran to their homes, screaming, "They're beating the Jews!" Elder brothers and fathers ran out on the streets. In the households of the numerous supporters of anti-Semitism, the sons came home, also screaming, "They're beating the Jews!" and they, too, ran out in the street. Police were called and forces that were off-duty were called back to duty. Much of the night passed before order was restored. In the morning, the toll seemed to show that the Jews had inflicted more damage than they had suffered.

Many young Jewish men and boys swaggered about with black eyes and bandages, but they walked the streets without fear. Old Jewish men shook their heads and lamented the hooliganism of the young and their impatience. "Such things should be handled by the police," they mumbled. But assaults on elderly Jewish men—easily recognizable and vulnerable targets—which had grown, alarmingly, in the months before Christie Pits, now practically ceased. The mayor of Toronto declared that the public display of a swastika would, in the future, be considered a crime and be dealt with harshly.

In April 1973, a rather curious incident occurred. The Jewish Defense League (JDL) took umbrage at the two New York baseball teams, the Mets and the Yankees. Their argument was that Jews formed one quarter of the population of the city, and probably more than one quarter of the audience for the teams. They demanded that proportionate representation be given to Jews on the two teams. On April 30, the JDL staged sit-ins at both Shea Stadium and Yankee Stadium. Their demand was six Jewish players on each team, 25% of the 24-player roster.

Between ten and fifteen protesters showed up at the Mets' offices at Shea; they were met by Arthur Richman, the team's promotion manager. He explained to the protesters that when they scouted players they did not take into consideration the question of their religion. The protesters at Yankee Stadium were met by Michael Burke, the team's president. The group was asked to leave, but refused. Neither group used any violence and no arrests were made. The Yankees, by the way, did have a Jewish player on their staff: Ron Blomberg.

Before the first game of the American League Championship Series for 1996 began, on October 9, Baltimore was heavily favored to take it. The world's opinion did not change until the bottom of the eighth inning of that game. At that point an incident occurred that caught the attention of the nation and focused it on a 12-year-old Jewish boy, a Little League centerfielder from Old Tappan, New Jersey.

Jeffrey Maier was playing hooky from school that day, with his father's permission and in his father's company, for the once-in-a-lifetime chance to see a major league playoff game. Although Jeffrey had still a month to go until his thirteenth birthday, he had already fulfilled his bar mitzvah just a week before. Jeff's father had gone along with Jeff's excuse for staying away from school—a nonexistent orthodontist appointment—little dreaming that both of them would be shown up as fabricators on nationwide TV.

The Maiers were sitting in the first row of section 31, overlooking right field at Yankee Stadium. Baltimore was leading, 4 to 3, four outs away to a victory. The Yankees' rookie shortstop, Derek Jeter, hit a high fly ball toward the right-field wall. The ball was falling at a sharp angle and looked as if it was destined for the glove of Baltimore rightfielder Tony Tarasco. But as the ball came down, young Jeff Maier stretched out his hand, wearing his black Mizuno fielder's mitt, into fair territory and deflected the course of the ball so that it bounced into the stands. Right-field umpire Rich Garcia did not see Jeff's interference and declared Jeter's shot a home run. Oriole protests brought consultation with the other umpires on the field, but not one of them was at a position to have seen the play. The ruling of home run stood and the game went on. But the TV cameras had caught the event exactly: The ball looks certain to fall into Tarasco's mitt, when Jeff's hand darts out above him and deflects it into the stands, where it is grabbed by a middle-aged man from Connecticut. On seeing the videotapes after the game, Rich Garcia freely admitted he had blown the call.

The Yankees had tied the game and went on to win it in the eleventh inning. The game was protested by the Orioles, but the president of the American League upheld the call. The Yankees also went on to win the series against Baltimore and the World Series against Atlanta.

For the week or so after his attempted catch, Jeff was the toast of New York. He was honored by the mayor and the governor of the state. He was on television, both late-night shows and morning shows. The Yankees gave him a uniform and a place in the stands. Upper Deck promised to make a card of him in its 1997 series. (They did not keep this promise, but, later, changed their minds.) Jeff made a number of public appearances alongside Umpire Garcia.

The strangest thing about the whole incident is that it became the subject of editorials, both in newspapers and in the broadcast media. Many, particularly residents of Baltimore, found the incident symptomatic of the moral decay of Western Civilization and the decline of baseball. Others, mostly residents of New York, found the whole thing very joyous, even Huckleberry Finnish.

Chapter 9
The Jewish Contribution to the Integration of Baseball

Isadore Muchnick

The coming of Jackie Robinson to the major leagues, in 1947, is one of the seminal events in the history of the United States. It marked the end of the forward advance of prejudice and racial privilege in this country and the real beginning of the civil rights movement that eventually would bring real changes and real advancements in racial justice.

Many others before Robinson had requested, demanded, begged, or insisted on change in the condition of the black men and women of this country. Nevertheless, through the nature of his own talent, the nobility of his own character, and the convergence of certain historical events, Jackie Robinson opened a door for himself and his people that had never been opened before, and opened it in a way that it could never again be shut.

Most people believe that the story of Jackie Robinson begins with the name of Branch Rickey. Branch Rickey certainly was to become the major mover in Robinson's arrival. But he was not the initiator of the idea of introducing black players into the major leagues with the introduction of Jackie Robinson. This honor must go to Isadore H. Y. Muchnick (1908–1963), a Jew and a member of the Boston City Council from 1941 to 1947 and the Boston School Committee from 1948 to 1953.

Isadore Muchnick was a native of the Boston area. He was a graduate of the Boston Latin School, Harvard University, and Harvard Law School. From 1932, he was a practicing attorney. Muchnick was elected chairman of the School Committee in 1952, making him the first Jew to head the Boston school system. Among other reforms he proposed was the opening of public schools after school hours for the use of the school gym facilities by teenagers. This was proposed as a positive way of combating juvenile delinquency.

Muchnick, who first expressed his opposition to segregated baseball in 1944, threatened to push for a bill banning Sunday baseball unless the Boston Red Sox hired a black player. The Sox organization agreed to give tryouts to three.

In consultation with Wendell Smith, sports editor of the Pittsburgh Courier, an important black newspaper, arrangements were made for tryouts for Sam Jethroe of the Cleveland Buckeyes, Marvin Williams of the Philadelphia Stars, and Jackie Robinson of the Kansas City

Monarchs. Smith accompanied the players to Boston for the tryouts, which were scheduled for April 12, 1945. But that day President Franklin Roosevelt died and the tryouts were rescheduled for April 16.

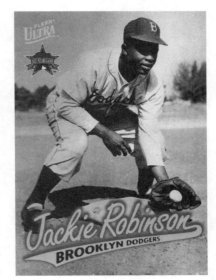

Eddie Collins, general manager of the Red Sox, set as a condition of the tryouts that no photographers were to be present and no prior publicity for them must appear in any newspaper. The only witnesses to the tryouts, outside of the three players themselves and the Red Sox organization, were Muchnick and Wendell Smith. The three players were allowed to show what they could do.

The three fielded and then batted. Williams and Jethroe did nothing spectacular, but Robinson was terrific. "You never saw anyone hit the wall the way Robinson did that day—bang, bang, bang, he rattled it," said Muchnick. When the workout was over, Muchnick went over to Joe Cronin, the Red Sox's manager, and Cronin said to him, of Robinson, "If I had that guy on this club we'd be a world beater." Cronin stated to Muchnick that he would be willing to sign Robinson.

Afterward, all three men were complimented and given application forms to complete. None of the men ever heard again from the Red Sox. Somewhere between Cronin's initial enthusiasm and hard reality something had happened. But at least the organization had done just enough, it felt, to get Muchnick off their backs.

Later in 1945, during a press conference with Branch Rickey, Wendell Smith asked the president of the Brooklyn Dodgers some questions concerning Rickey's newly announced Negro League team, the Brown Dodgers. After the conference, Rickey took Smith aside to discuss various matters. In the course of the conversation, Rickey asked Smith about the recent events in Boston and about how the three players—whom Muchnick's pressure had brought to Boston—had looked. Rickey particularly wanted to know if any of the three was really ready for the major leagues. Smith's reply was, "Jackie Robinson is."

Rickey sent his scout Clyde Sukeworth to Chicago to take a look at Robinson, who was playing there with the Monarchs. Sukeworth didn't get to see Robinson play, because he was injured, but on the strength of what he had heard about Robinson at the Boston tryouts and elsewhere, he arranged a meeting in New York between Robinson and Branch Rickey. At that meeting, Rickey explained to Robinson his ideas concerning the integration of baseball and the type of man who would be necessary to achieve the final goal. Robinson accepted the challenge that Rickey proposed to him and signed a contract.

Jackie Robinson spent the year 1946 with the Montreal Royals, Brooklyn's AAA minor league team. The world held its breath and waited to see what would happen. There was little doubt now that Rickey intended to introduce Robinson into the Brooklyn Dodgers. In April, 1947, the call came and Jackie Robinson became a full-fledged member of the Dodgers. This first step, itself, had not come without conflict. A cabal among the Brooklyn players had circulated a petition to keep Robinson off the team. Rickey, however, took a tough line and threatened to fire anyone who might attempt any action against his policies.

Then the problem spread throughout the National League. Votes were taken in many of the teams to see whether they should boycott play with Brooklyn. St. Louis outfielder Enos Slaughter had circulated a petition to this effect in his club. Baseball Commissioner "Happy"

Hank Greenberg

Chandler, with the support of Ford Frick, the National League president, declared that any player who boycotted play against Brooklyn or failed to play on opening day would be banned from baseball for life. With memories of what happened to "Shoeless" Joe Jackson and the other Black Sox still a living memory, this resistance completely collapsed.

Jackie Robinson was welcomed to the Dodgers with little warmth, but the Brooklyn resistance was mild to what Robinson would face from opposing teams. In every city to which the Brooklyn team traveled, Robinson was met with jeers, taunts, and racial epithets. These came not only from the stands but also from the opposing benches. The players launched into him the moment he came to bat, but so did the managers of those teams. But words were not all that Robinson had to face. Never in the history of baseball has a batter faced so many knockdown pitches or an infielder so many spikings. Jackie Robinson was fair game.

Ben Chapman, manager of the Philadelphia Phillies, is said to have threatened to fine any member of the team who didn't try to take out Robinson at second. Chapman, who had a reputation as a vicious and vocal anti-Semite, was certainly the worst of the managers. His obscene and racist harangues against Robinson drew down the ire of the league and forced him to a public apology. It was during a three-game series in Philadelphia, which started on May 9, that Robinson seriously considered giving up the struggle and quitting baseball.

That he did not may have a lot to do with a series that Brooklyn played in Pittsburgh starting May 16. On May 18, 1947, The New York Times published an article with a headline HANK GREENBERG A HERO TO DODGERS' NEGRO STAR. The story went on:

"Jackie Robinson, first Negro player in the major leagues, has picked a diamond hero—rival first baseman Hank Greenberg of the Pittsburgh Pirates.

"Here's why: Robinson and Greenberg collided in a play at first base during the current Dodger-Pirate series. The next time Jackie came down to the sack, Hank said, 'I forgot to ask you if you were hurt in that play.'

"Assured that Robinson was unharmed, Greenberg said: 'Stick in there. You're doing fine. Keep your chin up.'

"This encouragement from an established star heartened Robinson, who has been the subject of reported anti-racial treatment elsewhere and admits he has undergone 'jockeying—some of it pretty severe.'

" 'Class tells. It sticks out all over Mr. Greenberg,' Robinson declared."

Elsewhere, Greenberg also recollected this conversation, which included an invitation on Greenberg's part to dinner. Jackie turned down the invitation because he didn't want to put Greenberg on the spot. But from that time to the end of Robinson's life, the two men remained friends.

Others have portrayed this incident somewhat differently, but the result was the same. This was the first positive gesture that Robinson had received from an opposing player since he had entered the sport and the first truly unselfish and ungrudging welcome he had received in major league baseball.

In 1970, Jackie Robinson and Hank Greenberg joined together on the same team to fight against a basic injustice of the baseball system: the reserve clause. In that year, player Curt

Flood, with the support of the Major League Baseball Players Association, under the leadership of Marvin Miller, brought suit against the owners of the teams to break the reserve system. Flood and Miller both believed that the reserve system was a form of slavery intolerable in a modern society. Flood's attorney, paid for by the Players Association, was former Supreme Court Justice Arthur Goldberg. Greenberg and Robinson provided forthright and compelling testimony in behalf of Flood's cause. Unfortunately, Flood lost the case, but his example in bringing the case was instrumental in the eventual appearance of free agency.

Greenberg was not the only Jewish friend that Robinson found in major league baseball. In 1947, following the regular season, Sid Gordon joined Jackie on a barnstorming team organized by Charley Dressen. During the late 1950s, William Klein, a friend of the ever mysterious Moe Berg, was witness to a strange encounter between Berg and Jackie Robinson in a coffee shop in Newark, New Jersey. Berg went over to Robinson and whispered in his ear; then he came back to Klein and left the restaurant. Berg never offered an explanation of what he had said.

Lou Boudreau and Larry Doby

When Jackie joined the Dodgers in 1947, the team had no Jewish players. On April 20, 1949, some two years after his debut, he was joined on the Dodger team by Cal Abrams. And June 24, 1955, marked the Dodger debut of Sandy Koufax.

Jackie Robinson's arrival in Brooklyn was particularly well received by the team's Jewish fans, and the yells of encouragement Jackie heard from the stands were as likely to be in Yiddish as in English. While it's probably true that Jackie was generous and kind to all his young fans, he certainly went beyond mere courtesy, to real generosity, to a number of his young Jewish fans—who remembered, and left literary records. Here is just one of many such stories: In 1953, Jackie sent an autographed picture and an invitation to meet him after a game, in reply to a letter sent by 14-year-old Ronnie Rabinovitz. One feature that comes through in all these stories is Jackie's way of always treating children as if they were adults, as equals. It was the moment of a lifetime for all these children.

Through all his difficulties in 1947, Jackie Robinson held his head up and continued to play the best baseball he was capable of. His hidden anger was transferred to his bat, his glove, and his legs. His fellow Brooklynites began to develop a grudging respect for Robinson's dignity, fire, and determination. But the reactions of opposing teams only grew more vicious as the season progressed. It was in May 1947 that Enos Slaughter of the St. Louis Cardinals attempted to organize a protest strike against Robinson. This failed, but later in the season Slaughter spiked Robinson in the leg, inflicting the worst injury he was to receive during the season. Other players who spiked Robinson include Joe Garagiola, "Ducky" Medwick, and Richie Ashburn.

The dignity that Jackie showed in the face of such adversity won the admiration of the fans and the respect of his fellow players on the Dodgers. This helped immensely to ease Jackie's way. Then, as the success of Robinson became more and more apparent, new black players were recruited, easing his isolation.

One day after the Fourth of July, 1947, Larry Doby became the first black player in the

American League. Bill Veeck, the flamboyant owner of the Cleveland Indians, avoided the slow-entry method that Branch Rickey had imposed upon Jackie Robinson and put Doby into the lineup on that very first day. Most of Doby's teammates received him with coldness, though no open hostility was displayed. But the manager of the team, Lou Boudreau, who also served as the team's shortstop, received him with courtesy and even warmth.

Boudreau, unlike Hank Greenberg and Al Rosen, fellow members of the Indians staff, made no display of his Jewishness. Lou's mother had been Jewish and so, by Jewish law, to every other Jew in the world he is a Jew. His father was of French origin and Catholic, and Lou practices his father's religion. Nevertheless, some members of the Indians staff were aware of Lou's background. A number of players on the team were heard to refer to Boudreau, Rosen, and Greenberg as "those three Jews."

Boudreau, a warm and caring man in any case, was good friends with both Rosen and Greenberg, and he went out of his way to introduce Doby to every member of the team and take him under his wing. He always treated Doby as an equal, without condescension, and constantly displayed his awareness of Doby's difficulties as a pioneer. Boudreau did all he could to smooth the troubled path that Doby had to follow.

Doby saw little action in the 1947 season. At first he appeared at first base, then was tried at second. On two occasions, Boudreau even gave Doby the opportunity to try his own position, at shortstop. But Doby did not do well at any of these positions. Furthermore, his hitting was poor.

Still, Boudreau did not give up on the young player, who, he felt, had great potential but was overanxious to succeed and, so, not patient enough at the plate. Boudreau began to have Doby work out in the outfield, for there he saw that his future lay. Furthermore, he felt that the overanxious Doby would ripen into a fine batter if he were not overexposed, so he kept his plate appearances down while continuing his encouragement and nurturing. In the meantime, Doby kept in contact with Jackie Robinson. This helped to prevent him from giving up, while it undoubtedly also encouraged Robinson.

In 1948, Doby found his rightful place in the outfield and his natural rhythm as a batter. He also found a fellow black player beside him on the Cleveland Indians staff by the name of Leroy Paige, known to the world as "Satchel."

For years, Satchel Paige had been the leading pitching star of the Negro leagues. By the time he tried out for the Indians, he was already a seasoned veteran, and forty-two years old.

It was Abe Saperstein, the owner and creator of the Harlem Globetrotters, as well as the owner of a Negro league baseball team, the Chicago American Giants, who first suggested to Bill Veeck that Paige still had plenty of good years left in him and that he should be given a chance to try out for the major leagues. Saperstein made the arrangements and accompanied Paige to the tryout.

On July 7, 1948, Veeck secretly brought Paige to Cleveland's Municipal Stadium and asked Boudreau to do batting practice "against a young pitcher" who might help the team. When Boudreau came on the field, he asked Veeck where "the kid" was. When Veeck pointed out the lean, tall, and certainly not young or unknown black man, Satchel Paige, sitting next to the portly Jew, Saperstein, in the dugout, "Lou almost dropped," according to the irrepressible jokester Veeck.

Boudreau stood up to bat against Paige. At that time, Lou was batting near .400 and his only rival for the batting title in the American League was Ted Williams. Paige pitched 19 pitches and, despite a strike ratio of four strikes to one ball, as Boudreau admitted, he was unable to get a single hit. By mutual agreement of Veeck and Boudreau, Paige was immediately signed.

Paige and Doby became roommates, and it was felt that the presence of another black player would take pressure off Doby. In one way, this seems to have worked, for Doby blossomed into a truly fine player. By the end of the season he had a .301 batting average, with many important clutch hits to his credit. In the 1948 World Series, he would have a batting average of .368, the highest of any batter in the series. But in another sense it didn't, for Doby discovered that he personally didn't like Satchel Paige. The two men were of different generations and of completely different temperaments.

Nevertheless, under the management of "Mr. Lou," as Paige always affectionately called Boudreau, both the flamboyant Satchel and the colorless but intense Larry were able to make their contributions to the 1948 American League pennant-winning, World Series champions, the Cleveland Indians. And under Boudreau's aegis, both men were also able to make their contributions to American history—as the first black player in the American League (Doby) and the first black pitcher in that league and in a World Series (Paige).

Bud Selig, the acting commissioner of major league baseball, and the first Jew ever to hold such a position, said of Jackie Robinson: "It is still baseball's proudest moment and I believe it will always be baseball's proudest moment." On April 15, 1997, the fiftieth anniversary of Jackie Robinson's first major league game, Selig announced the unprecedented action of the retirement of Jackie Robinson's uniform number, 42, from all teams in the majors, both National and American Leagues. The only exception would be in the case of players already wearing the number, who would be allowed to wear it until their retirement. No future player will ever be issued number 42.

Chapter 10
Sam Spade on the Basepaths

Harvey Blissberg, a fictional Jewish baseball player on a fictional American League expansion team, is the creation of novelist Richard Rosen. Harvey is an outfielder, and the star of the team. He is known to his teammates as "The Professor," because of his wit and intelligence.

Harvey is a veteran player who has spent most of his career on the Boston Red Sox. Unexpectedly, the appearance of a new expansion team in Providence, Rhode Island, leads to his being traded away from his dear Boston. He is not happy in the squalid streets and alleys of Providence. But he also finds consolations in his new home. Here he meets local girl sportscaster Mickey Slavin; the two hit it off and Mickey becomes the love of Harvey's life.

When we first meet him, Harvey is beginning to become weary of the life of a baseball player. He is beginning to feel the aches and pains of encroaching age and is aware of various other reminders of his own mortality. Despite this, he is having a good year. His batting average is the best in the club, above .300 throughout his inaugural year with Providence. But his team, the Providence Jewels, is one of the worst in the league. The team is owned by Marshall Levy, who also owns a company that manufactures costume jewelry—hence, the team's commercial name. The home stadium, Rankle Park, is a dilapidated and inadequate hole, and the entire inaugural year, Harvey realizes, is a waiting game for future plans.

Harvey, who has a reputation of being uncooperative with reporters, is also aware of his position as that rare creature, a Jewish major-leaguer. In the first of four Blissberg novels by Rosen, Harvey gives an interview to a reporter from a New York—based Yiddish newspaper. The reporter gives Harvey a summary of some of the highlights of the history of the game in the 1920s and '40s. "Harvey was smiling at this unlikely fount of baseball lore. 'You were here during those years?' 'No. After the war. The second one. But I like baseball. A peaceful game.'"

Harvey Blissberg
PRIVATE INVESTIGATOR

Strike Three You're Dead (1984) is the first Harvey Blissberg mystery novel by Rosen. This novel—the only one in the series with a baseball background—won the 1985 Edgar Award for the best first mystery novel of the year. Harvey is forced to become a detective to solve the murder of his room-mate, relief pitcher Rudy Furth. Rudy has been murdered in the team clubhouse and is found soaking in the whirlpool. Harvey uncovers a complex plot with the help of his girl-friend, Mickey Slavin.

Fadeaway (1986) finds Harvey retired from baseball and attempting to make a living as a private investigator. He is hired by the Boston Celtics basketball team to find a player who has disappeared. Shortly afterward, the Washington Bullets hire Harvey for a similar reason: one of their players has vanished. Soon, both players are found dead and Harvey is retained by the teams to clear up the ensuing mess. Harvey soon finds himself back in Providence. Complications ensue, and Harvey is soon mixed up with a politically ambitious retired basketball coach and a female reporter with a maimed hand.

Saturday Night Dead (1988) finds Harvey retained to baby-sit an ex-teammate with a reputation as a boozer, who has been hired to guest-host a live Saturday-night comedy show. Harvey becomes acquainted with the show's quirky cast and even more quirky creative crew. During a cast party, Roy Ganz, the producer of the show, is pushed out of a high-rise window, and Harvey is hired to supplement the police in their investigation. He finds all kinds of strange, hidden links between the members of the cast and crew and discovers what a serious business it can be to make people laugh.

The most recent Blissberg novel is World of Hurt (1994). When Larry Peplow, a regular member of Norman Blissberg's pickup basketball game, is found shot to death in an empty field and the police are baffled, Norman turns to baby brother Harvey to investigate. Harvey travels from Cambridge, Massachusetts, to the Chicago suburbs to look into the affair. There he unravels deeper and darker secrets about Peplow, a psycho-therapist turned real estate agent. Rosen gives as much care to bringing life to the main locales of the story—suburban Chicago and Portland, Maine—as he does to the array of surly policemen, former ballplayers, sinister suspects, and wounded casualties of life's battles. Even though the background of this story are the worlds of real estate and psychotherapy, there is still here, as in all of the Blissberg series, much to remind us of Harvey's baseball background. Rosen writes: "At moments like this, Harvey liked to recall that he had once been able to hit ninety-five-mile-per-hour fastballs over four hundred feet" and "I was anxious to see what kind of dick an old beat-up ballplayer would make." and " 'I used to play baseball.' 'The majors?' 'Boston Red Sox and Providence Jewels.' " The authentic baseball flavor permeates every one of these novels.

But here we are going to have the temerity to make a suggestion, which we hope Mr. Rosen may consider. Many of the Jewish major-leaguers have returned, at some point, to coach, manage, or work in upper management, either in the majors or in the minors. Why not Harvey, just to get him back to a ballpark for his next case? Or, if not that, how about a card show or signing as a background? As excellent as all these books are, the first, with its wonderful baseball background, is still our favorite.

We wrote to Richard Rosen and asked him if he could provide us with some background on Harvey Blissberg. Mr. Rosen very generously provided us with the following:

> Harvey Blissberg is in part a product of the 1981 major league baseball strike. The sudden silence of summer—and the need to compensate for it—coincided with the urge to write a novel after many years of journalism and non-fiction. I was determined to write about what I knew. The result was a mystery novel about a Jewish baseball player whose allegiance to his room-mate and his natural curiosity compel him to solve a murder.

> From the moment I conceived and named him, Harvey Blissberg was an alter ego—the man I might have been had I been less of a writer and more of a hitter. In that regard, I think of a paradigmatic moment during my freshman year at Brown University in Providence, a city that would later provide me

with the sordidly romantic setting for my first two mysteries. I was returning from baseball practice in the spring of 1967, where I was the slick-fielding, poor-hitting starting first baseman on the freshman team. As I walked toward the campus with some teammates, I passed the window of a bookstore in which was displayed a college literary magazine in which I was prominently featured. Unable to summon the modesty required to ignore this fact, I pointed out the magazine—and my name on its cover—to my teammates. Their reaction, as I recall, was something between non-comprehension and indifference.

It was the first moment in my life when I truly realized that my intended careers as an athlete and a poet were not going to be easy to reconcile. As it happened, my weak hitting and a conflict with my coach over my flouting of some training rules soon decided the matter for me. Fourteen years later, I resumed my baseball career vicariously, through Harvey.

Ironically, it was during the writing of Strike Three You're Dead that my interest in major league baseball, already strained by the Red Sox loss to the Yankees in the 1978's one-game American League playoff, seemed to die. It was as if the invention of my own baseball world had made the real baseball one unnecessary. Today, I am amused by how little I follow baseball, a sport to which I devoted 47 percent of my waking hours between the ages of ten and eighteen.

Part III
Diamond Tales

Cal Abrams

During his first year with the Dodgers, 1949, when the team had reached Cincinnati, Jackie Robinson received a threat that he would be shot during that afternoon's doubleheader. In the 7th inning of the first game, Jackie hit a home run, and not taking the threat seriously, took his stroll around the bases. When he crossed the plate, Cal Abrams grabbed him anxiously and pulled him towards the safety of the dugout, blocking Jackie with his own body and saying, "Get into the dugout quick, before they take a shot at you." Jackie chided Cal for taking the threat seriously, but was touched by Cal's courage.

ⓧ ⓧ ⓧ

During the 1950 season, the Brooklyn Dodgers started a television series in which a member of the team would pick a child, from a group of three, who had the best potential to make it to the big leagues. The one picked as the best chose his favorite Dodger to talk to in the dugout. The show was called the Knot Hole Gang. On one program, Cal was asked to pick the young future ballplayer. Cal told one kid beforehand that if he should pick him, then the kid was to choose Cal. The reason Cal wanted to be picked was that the ballplayer who was picked was paid $50. The kid was given some candy and an autographed baseball. Cal picked the kid, gave him some candy and an autographed baseball, and when the kid was asked who he wanted to talk to in the dugout he said, "Carl Furillo." Cal was steamed, but he couldn't say anything.

ⓧ ⓧ ⓧ

When asked what his most embarrassing moment in baseball was, Cal Abrams told of a time in the minor leagues when he was playing for Mobile. He was getting just $5,000 a year and times were tough. He was having breakfast in a café and the bill came to $1.50. One of Cal's companions slipped a dime under his plate. Cal reached into his pocket and felt for change and then placed what he thought were three nickels on the table. But when he looked down, to his horror, he saw three quarters. Cal quickly removed two of the quarters back to his own pocket. Cal felt like a terrible heel—and still managed to overtip the waitress.

Franklin P. Adams

Newspaper columnist and radio personality Franklin P. Adams (1881–1960) didn't have a very Jewish-sounding name, which goes to prove that names can be deceptive. He was Jewish and very proud of it. While he was attending a baseball game in 1906, between the New York Giants and the Chicago Cubs, he became more and more frustrated as his favorites, the Giants, saw every prospective rally turned into a double play. The demise of the Giants' hopes that day led F.P.A. to compose the following mini-lament:

> Baseball's Sad Lexicon
> These are the saddest of possible words:
> 'Tinkers to Evers to Chance.'
> Trio of bear cubs and fleeter than birds,
> Tinkers and Evers and Chance.
> Ruthlessly pricking our gonfalon bubble,
> Making a Giant hit into a double—
> Words that are heavy with nothing but trouble:
> 'Tinkers to Evers to Chance.'

These verses caught the popular fancy like no baseball verses had since "Casey at the Bat." They led the "trio of bear cubs" directly into the Hall of Fame, and the refrain is almost as often quoted as "Take Me Out to the Ballgame."

In 1951, the refrain was just as widely parodied when the Cubs infield was a set of bumblers, rather than the infallible trio of 1906: "Miksis to Smalley to Addison Street." Addison Street is the thoroughfare that runs past Wrigley Park, parallel to the first base line. The first basemen who should have been receiving the throws was none other than Chuck Connors, later famous as TV's "The Rifleman."

Franklin Adams wrote one other baseball verse that deserves to be better known than it is. It's entitled "Baseball Note":

> In winter, when it's cold out,
> Appears the baseball holdout;
> In spring, when it is warm out,
> He gets his uniform out.

Mel Allen

Mel Allen

Following the death of Mel Allen, the Yankees' longtime sportscaster, during the early part of the 1996 season, the entire team wore black arm bands. The Yankee participants in that year's All-Star Game also wore the arm bands. Mel was also the host of "This Week in Baseball."

Morris Arnovich

Before America entered the Second World War, Morris Arnovich tried to volunteer for the Army, but was turned down because he was missing a pair of molars, which he had replaced with false teeth. After Pearl Harbor, he volunteered again and this time was accepted.

Jake Atz

Ring Lardner once wrote of Jake Atz, "He kept the whole bunch in good humor and earned his salary thus whether he played or not. But no one was pulling for victories on the ball field more than this game, old Mr. Atz's son."

Jake Atz

Jake Atz was a great fan of the horse tracks. Once he was contemplating laying a small wager on a particular horse that would be running in his hometown of New Orleans. Before placing the bet, however, he inquired about the condition of the track. When he was told it had been raining, he placed the bet. A friend of his asked him whether the horse liked the mud. Atz replied, "Sure, that baby is a real mudder if there ever was one. If you put a pail of oats and a pail of mud in front of him, he'd eat the mud every time."

Jake Atz told this story about his times on the road: "One day I was in a restaurant in Beaumont, Texas. I ordered chicken broth. When it came over, it had feathers in it. 'What's the idea?' I asked the waiter, 'Feathers in the soup?' "

" 'That just shows we do as we say—serve only genuine chicken broth—don't them feathers prove it?' the waiter replied."

When Jake Atz was traded from Raleigh, North Carolina, to the New Orleans team, around 1901, he refused to report to the latter. Abner Powell, manager of the New Orleans Pelicans, went to see Jake to convince him to join the team. Powell told him, "We will give you $125 a month."

Jake asked him to repeat that. Powell did.

"To play baseball?" Jake stammered, not believing his ears.

"Sure," said Powell. "Will you come and play in New Orleans?"

Atz replied, "For that much money, I'd play in Alaska!"

In 1916, Jake Atz was manager of the Fort Worth Panthers. The pitcher in one game was getting hit hard, but Jake decided the game couldn't be saved, so he'd let the pitcher go the route. Frank Weaver, the majority owner of the club, ordered Atz to yank the pitcher. Jake refused. Weaver went out, on his own, and relieved the pitcher. Jake immediately quit. His reputation was such that he quickly got a job managing Galveston. The following year, the minority owners of the Fort Worth team bought Weaver out and brought Jake back to captain the Panthers. Jake would manage the team for 12 years.

Once, Jake Atz, when he was skipper for the Fort Worth Panthers, won a game before it was over. It was the bottom of the ninth; the Panthers were leading San Antonio by one run. There were two outs, when San Antonio's Jim Galloway, one of the best hitters in the league, stepped up to bat.

At that point Jake started packing up his gear—something he never did until the game was over. Someone asked Jake why he was packing up at such a dangerous moment. Jake explained that the other team had made a mistake, Galloway was batting out of order. Jake knew the rules, and the rules stated that if a batter batted out of order he was considered out. Jake thought he might have an argument if Galloway got a hit, but he knew he had already won the game. As it happened, Galloway popped out.

Jose Bautista

While pitching on the Oklahoma City team in 1991, Jose Bautista roomed with Wayne Rosenthal. Wayne, at first, had trouble believing Jose was Jewish—even when he saw Jose's large, gold Star of David, a gift from his wife.

Bo Belinsky

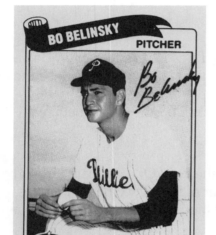

Bo Belinsky spent much of his misspent youth as a pool hustler. His golden rules of hustling were, one, never carry your own cue, it makes you look like a hustler; always use the house cue. And two, at least once a night, drop the chalk. Belinsky would continue to hustle pool games throughout his minor league and major league careers. He was also a dedicated poker player.

While he was playing in Venezuela, Bo Belinsky was shown a clearing in the jungle that was used as a softball field. A batter had sent a pop fly into the bush and the outfielder went back to retrieve it. They found his remains three days later. Jaguars had been waiting behind the outfield for just such an occasion, and when he went to find the ball they ate him.

While Belinsky was in Venezuela, an insurrection broke out in Caracas. Bullets were flying everywhere. Bo had been seated at a café sipping champagne with a beautiful señorita. Bo retired under the table with his guest, where they continued to sip their wine until the shooting stopped.

It was while in Venezuela that Belinsky was put into a game before he felt he was ready to pitch. He had not yet gotten over the rigors of the long trip south. Not feeling that he had his best stuff, he experimented with an off-speed pitch that he'd never tried before. He won the game and the new pitch became his famous screwball, one of the keys to his success.

Bo Belinsky had a Jewish mother and a Polish, Catholic father. During his early days in Los Angeles whenever Bo scored a victory, the papers reminded their readers that Bo was Jewish. When Bo lost, they reminded their readers that Bo was Polish. Bo's mother had little patience for reports that Bo was Catholic. She insisted that Bo had been circumcised and, to her, this alone settled any question in the matter.

When Bo Belinsky heard, in 1966, that Sandy Koufax had retired, he joked, "I knew I'd make him quit. Los Angeles just wasn't big enough for both of us."

Bo Belinsky, who made his reputation, when pitching for the Angels, with a no-hitter against the Orioles on May 5, 1962, pitched a second no-hit game. This one was during 1968, at the AAA level, for Hawaii against Tacoma. This game was considered by those who saw it to have been a true pitching masterpiece. Chuck Tanner, manager of the Hawaii team, said of that game, years later, that on that day Belinsky was overwhelming.

Moe Berg

Moe Berg kibitzing with Donald Davidson, the Bosox batboy.

Moe Berg, sometimes catcher and America's leading nuclear spy during the Second World War, paid a visit to Albert Einstein in 1945. Berg indicated that he had read a recent article by the physicist on "Atomic War or Peace." The usually unflappable spy was taken aback when Einstein, who rarely displayed interest in topics outside of physics and music, showed equal familiarity with an article that Berg had written on the art of catching.

Moe Berg was a great admirer of Dave Harris of the Washington Senators, when Moe was catching for that team. Harris' education, unlike Moe's, was significantly deficient, Harris having dropped out of school quite early on. But Dave could make contact with the ball. Dave used to kid Moe that he was too smart to be a hitter. Moe seemed to agree. "He may have been right because I liked to try to guess with the pitcher. Dave wasn't burdened with too much imagination; he'd just step up there and take a beautiful cut."

Irving Berlin

Irving Berlin might be more famous for "Always," "Blue Skies," and "God Bless America," but for us his most relevant work is "Jake, Jake, the Yiddisha Ball Player." The words to this ditty were written by Blanche Merrill, Irving composing the music. The song was composed in 1913, introduced by Lillian Shaw, and published by Waterson, Berlin & Snyder Co. This song doesn't seem to have been one of the better sellers of Berlin's own publishing company, despite a beautiful cover by E. F. Pfeiffer, for early catalogs published by the company don't list it.

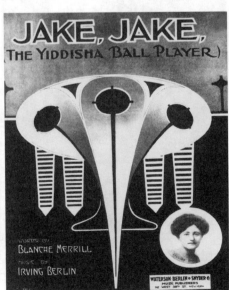

Cover of sheet music for Berlin's "Jake, Jake the Yiddisha Ball Player."

Cy Block

In 1944, when Cy Block, then in the Coast Guard, read of a contest to choose Miss Subway for New York, he sent a photograph of his beautiful wife Harriet. She won the contest and posters were printed and distributed to decorate the trains. But somehow the authorities discovered that Miss Harriet Block was really Mrs. Harriet Block, wife of the Chicago Cub. Harriet was quickly dethroned and her lovely visage ceased to decorate the clanking subway cars.

Ron Blomberg

Ron Blomberg, a native of Atlanta, Georgia, particularly loves New York. Why? For its bright lights and Broadway shows? No. Ron loves New York for its fine knishes. A cartoon of Ron eating away at a mountain of knishes is featured on the back of his 1973 Topps card.

Wade Boggs

Christian slugger Wade Boggs, when he steps to the plate, instead of crossing himself as some players do, makes the sign of the Hebrew letter "chai," which symbolizes "life."

Lou Boudreau

Lou Boudreau (center) managing from the bench.

During the 1942 season, Lou Boudreau was serving the dual role of manager and shortstop for the Cleveland Indians. One day, Lou was suffering from a cold. He felt too bad to place himself in the lineup, but despite his throbbing sinuses and open faucet of a nose, he felt that he could handle managing the team.

Among the signals of the team was one where Lou would put a towel to his face. This was the signal for a double steal.

The game progressed, but Lou's cold gave him no relief. His team had gotten two men on board. On second was "Fat" Pat Seery, one of the Indians' slowest runners. The man on first was also slow.

Lou's sinuses throbbed and he relieved the pressure by blowing his nose in the towel hanging around his neck. When he brought the towel down, he could not believe what was going on before his eyes. "Fat" Pat and his equally lummoxy teammate were both trying to steal. They were, of course, immediately picked off.

Lou was furious at the third base coach for instituting such a play. But, the coach calmly explained, it was Lou himself who had called for the play—when he gave the signal for the double steal by putting the towel up to his face. Then Lou remembered blowing his nose and the signal he had forgotten to remember.

Brothers in the Lineup

Six pairs of Jewish brothers have played major league baseball: Andy and Syd Cohen, Harry and Ike Danning, Erskine and Sam Mayer, Jacob and Lipman Pike, Harry and Lou Rosenberg, and Larry and Norm Sherry. The last two named were the most recent brother battery in baseball history.

Harry Chozen

While playing with Memphis, Harry Chozen, twenty-nine years old, was considered to be an old-timer. Players would frequently come to him for advice. One day, a pitcher on the opposing team, John Hetki, who was to pitch against Harry at the next day's game, asked him what he thought of his pitching. Harry told Hetki that he had a great fastball, but what he really needed was a good change-up. "After all," Harry said, "a pitcher can't survive on just one pitch."

The next day, Harry stood up to bat against Hetki. The first pitch was a fastball, so fast Harry couldn't even see it. "Strike one," the umpire said. The next pitch was another fastball, perhaps faster than the first. "Strike two," the umpire said. Harry knew his Hetki, knew he would have to prove what a wise fellow he was. Harry swung just in rhythm with the change-up that he knew Hetki would pitch. Harry belted the ball to left field, for all he was worth. When he looked back at Hetki from second, the pitcher was examining his shoes.

Andy Cohen

Once, when Andy Cohen was playing for Minneapolis, in the minor leagues, he played a game in Louisville, Kentucky. During the whole game, a large man in the stands kept yelling at Andy, "Christ killer," "Christ killer this," and "Christ killer that." Andy, finally, had had enough of this. He picked up a bat and walked over to the stands, as close as he could get to the heckler. He looked directly at him, bat in hand, and said, "Yeah, come down here and I'll kill you, too."

Cohen Stadium, home of the El Paso Diablos, named in honor of the Cohen brothers, Andy and Syd.

The minor league baseball stadium in El Paso, Texas, home of the Diablos (an AA team owned by the Milwaukee Brewers), is Cohen Stadium. Considered one of the most beautiful and modern facilities in the country, it was named in honor of major leaguers Syd and Andy Cohen. Both of the brothers had played on local El Paso teams and

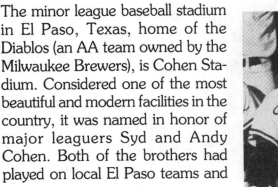

Syd had ended his 37-year pro career as a coach there.

Hy Cohen

When pitcher Hy Cohen played on Denver against Des Moines, the manager of the latter team was Andy Cohen. Hy was asked repeatedly by his teammates if he was Andy's son. Later, Hy played on the New Orleans Pelicans, under Andy's management. The same thing happened again. The two men, not related, did become lifelong friends.

While he was growing up in New York, one of the heroes of pitcher Hy Cohen's youth was Giants catcher Harry Danning. It appears that Hy was not aware that Harry was Jewish. In 1996, Hy was inducted into the Southern California Jewish Sports Hall of Fame. He was surprised to find his fellow inductee was Danning. Hy was thrilled to get to meet Harry "The Horse" and be able to share with him such a special honor.

Jim "Fireball" Cohen

Considering our subject, one name in the roster of players in the Negro League stands out, that of Jim "Fireball" Cohen.

Jim Cohen, who was born in 1918, began his baseball career in the Army, but his professional career was with the Indianapolis Clowns. He pitched for the Clowns from 1946 to 1950. A right-handed pitcher, he was noted for his blazing fastball, but he also had command of the curve, the change-up, and the knuckle-ball. Jim's ERA was 3.90 in 1948 and 3.64 in 1950. In the latter year, he was picked for the Negro League All-Star Game, but he did not get to pitch. However, when a second All-Star game was held that year, Jim pitched three innings. He remained with the Clowns organization until 1952 as a business manager and bus driver.

We contacted Mr. Cohen and discussed with him the provenance of his name. He indicated that he was not aware of any Jewish ancestry. His father had been Cohen before him, and Jim was aware that the name was usually a Jewish surname. It had been suggested to him that his name might reflect that of a Jewish master before the Civil War.

Harry Danning relaxing on a day off.

Converts

Six major league baseball players have converted to Judaism, although none of these had any Jewish ancestry. These six are: Lloyd Allen, Joel Horlen, Skip Jutze, Elliot Maddox, Jeff Newman, and Steve Yeager. Despite rumors, Rod Carew has never converted to Judaism.

Harry Danning

Perhaps no child was ever more prophetically named that the star reliever of the 1940s Giants, Ace Adams. Yes, that was his real given name. One of Adams' greatest achievements was the invention of the slider. Adams first used the pitch in

1942, pitching against Whitey Kurowski. The receiver of that first slider, which was the third strike for Kurowski, was Harry Danning. Danning ran across the field, embraced Adams, and declared, "That's the best damned pitch you ever threw in your life."

Barney Dreyfuss

Barney Dreyfuss, owner of the Pittsburgh Pirates, did not like tobacco, did not like it at all! When he learned that his new prospect for an outfield position, whom he had had scouted in Texas, was a cigarette smoker, he passed on the deal. The young outfielder's name was Tris Speaker, who would then be signed by the Boston Red Sox. Speaker played for 22 years and had a lifetime batting average of .345. He was elected to the Hall of Fame in 1937. Pretty good for a smoker.

On another occasion, Barney was recommended to look at a young pitcher. But the man who made the recommendation was a cigar salesman, so Barney decided not even to look. The pitcher was Walter Johnson, the "Big Train." Johnson would pitch for 21 years for the Washington Senators, with a winning average of .599, but with often mediocre support. His lifetime ERA was 2.17. Johnson got into the Hall of Fame with the initial group, in 1936. Sometimes cigar salesman can be trusted.

⚾   ⚾   ⚾

Honus Wagner may have been one of the sharpest shortstops of all time, be he was not quite so sharp as a mathematician. Barney Dreyfuss, the president of the Pittsburgh Pirates, once offered him a $2,000 contract.

"Not on your life," Honus replied, "I won't play for a penny less than fifteen hundred dollars." Barney immediately acceded to Honus' demand.

This story was a favorite of Barney's, who retold it often. But he would never tell it when Wagner was anywhere about, lest he hurt the old man's feelings.

Tiby Eisen

Thelma "Tiby" Eisen of the All-American Girls Professional Baseball League once played a charity game, in Chicago, for the benefit of a Jewish Hospital. Tiby's name and picture appeared in all the local Jewish newspapers. She heard from her uncle, "You shouldn't be playing baseball. You'll get a bad reputation, a bad name." Nevertheless, on the day of the game, Tiby's uncle was there in the stands, rooting for her for all he was worth.

Harry Eisenstat

In the next to last game of the Tigers' 1938 season, the year Hank Greenberg almost, but did not tie Babe Ruth's home-run record, pitcher Harry Eisenstat faced Cleveland star Bob Feller. Birdie Tebbetts, the Tigers' catcher for the game, found it funny that Bob Feller set the major league record for strikeouts in that game, pitching, he estimated a 105-mile-per-hour fastball and striking out 18 players. Eisenstat's fastball Birdie estimated at a mere 81 miles per hour and Harry struck out only 3, but it was Harry who won the game.

Harry Feldman

The lights used for night games in the North East Arkansas League were quite dangerous. Harry Feldman pitched for Blytheville in 1938. In one game, against Paragould, Johnny Martin was at-bat against Harry. Suddenly the lights went off, right after a pitch. Both Martin and the catcher, Angel Aragon, hurled themselves to the sides as the invisible ball came towards them. The sphere ended up striking the umpire on his chest protector and knocking him to the ground.

Eddie Gottlieb

What major league baseball player played basketball with an all-Jewish team? Sandy Koufax. Yeah, but so what? He's Jewish. But what about Art "The Great" Shires!

It was during the winter of 1929–30 that Art Shires, first baseman for the Chicago White Sox and then at the height of his popularity (a popularity he'd gained during the preceding season by twice ending disputes with his manager, Russell Blackburn, by knocking him to the ground), was invited by Eddie Gottlieb, their coach, to play for the Sphas (South Philadelphia Hebrew Association). Alas, Art, who claimed to have played basketball in college and who was promised $200 for the game, proved in practice that he couldn't hit the basket. At first, Eddie kept Shires out of the game, but the crowd went wild until he was put in. Then the Sphas kept the ball away from Shires until the opposing team started passing the ball to him themselves. Shires couldn't score.

The whole thing might have seemed a fiasco, but Eddie and the Sphas were delighted with the extra gate that Shires brought that night. Gottlieb sent Shires a check for $250, more than was agreed, and his thanks.

Shawn Green

Shawn Green's grandfather, wishing to make the family name sound less Jewish—perhaps so that he could ease the way for his eventual grandson to enter his eventual career, baseball—changed that name to Green. The original family name was Greenberg.

Besides Hank, other Greenbergs in baseball include Hank's brother, Joe, a minor leaguer, and Hank's son, Stephen, a minor leaguer and Deputy Commissioner of Major League Baseball under Fay Vincent.

Hank Greenberg

In 1935, the year when Hank Greenberg was first elected MVP for the American League, the Senators' Buddy Myer, who led the league that year in batting with an average of .349, was fourth in the balloting.

⊗   ⊗   ⊗

During the late 1940s, the New York Yankees hired a professional heckler to razz the visiting teams during weekends. This heckler was a real pain and made himself extremely unpleasant throughout the games. The guy particularly got on the nerves of General Manager Hank Greenberg when he accompanied the Cleveland Indians to Yankee Stadium. By accident,

Hank found out that this heckler worked for Gimbel's Department Store in Philadelphia and that he came to New York for the weekends. The next time the Indians were playing a weekend game in Yankee Stadium, Hank went up to this heckler and introduced himself. Then he told the heckler that his wife was a member of the Gimbel family and that if he heard one peep out of the guy during the game, he would be returning to Philadelphia without a job. The Indians never had any problems with that heckler again.

Hank Greenberg in military uniform.

⚾ ⚾ ⚾

Hank Greenberg stated that during 1938, when he was making his run on the home-run record, he didn't pay much attention to politics and what was going on in Germany. As the year progressed, of course he was forced to become more and more aware. By the end of the season, he felt that every home run he hit was one against Hitler.

⚾ ⚾ ⚾

When Hank Greenberg was playing, it bothered him when next to his name in the newspaper they would print "the Jewish ballplayer." Near the end of his life, with all his great achievements, however, it was this very thing of which he was the most proud.

⚾ ⚾ ⚾

Hank Greenberg's nickname during his youth, when he was playing baseball in Crotona Park in the Bronx, was "Bruggy." This name had come about from a misunderstanding of Hank's pronunciation of "groggy," for he would practice his swing day and night until he was groggy. The nickname came to be known to the public and later haunted Hank.

Once, while riding a subway in New York, he heard a man boasting to his friend that he had played with "Bruggy" in Crotona Park. Hank didn't know the man from Adam, and he stepped into the conversation and made it clear, in no uncertain terms, that he was Hank Greenberg and that this fellow had never played with him or known him.

The storyteller looked abashed, and Hank suddenly realized that he had stolen away a bit of reflected glory, the very kind that makes going on with life possible. He felt bad about this petty incident for the rest of his life.

After then, whenever anyone claimed to have played with Hank in his youth or to have known "Bruggy," he always pretended to recognize the man. Though only twenty or thirty people could really have made such a claim, Hank estimated that by his seventies, he had recognized some 10,000 childhood buddies from Crotona Park.

⚾ ⚾ ⚾

When Hank Greenberg was fresh to the minors, in Raleigh, SC, a strange incident occurred. He was standing out in the field when one of his teammates, a rustic, as most of his teammates were, started circling him and looking him over intently. Hank asked the farm boy what he was staring at. The player told Hank that somebody had told him that Hank was a Jew and he had never seen a Jew before. The yokel kept circling and looking until Hank asked him if he saw anything interesting. The player replied, "I don't understand it. You look just like anybody else."

"Thanks," was all Hank could think of to answer to that.

Cuban card of Hank Greenberg.

Benjamin Shibe invented the modern baseball with its two interlocking figure eight pieces of horsehide and its cork center. He was also a pioneer in the construction of ballparks and in the use of scoreboards. Shibe was also the co-owner, with Connie Mack, of the Philadelphia A's. After his death, in 1922, Shibe's interest in the team was passed on to his sons.

It was always Hank Greenberg's custom to come to the ballpark early to put in some extra practice before the regular practice period began. Once, in Shibe Park, in Philadelphia, the groundskeeper came over to Hank to tell him he was too early and that he'd have to leave the park. Hank and his helpers started to gather their equipment together, when an elderly man, sitting about twenty rows up in the empty stands, called to Hank to come up. He told Hank, "I very much admire what you are doing, young man." He then told Hank to tell the groundskeeper he had permission to stay and, if the man had any questions, he should go see Mr. Shibe. In Philadelphia, at least, Hank never again had any trouble with his early practices.

Hank Greenberg once volunteered to help a rookie Tiger improve his batting stance. The rookie declined Hank's offer of help; he told him that he was hitting .225, while Hank was hitting .315. The rookie also told Hank that he was being paid $5,000 for the year, while Hank was making $30,000. "My batting is all right, Hank. The way I figure it, you should be hitting six times better than me."

While playing for Detroit, Hank Greenberg became friends with the other most famous Jew in the city at that time, Abe Bernstein, head of Detroit's infamous Purple Gang, a band of bootleggers, rum-runners, and killers. Abe was Detroit's equivalent of Al Capone, but without Al's flair for publicity.

Abe once asked Hank for a favor and Hank agreed to it. While in the Army, Hank had refused all requests to play baseball, but Abe asked him to make an exception and play in an exhibition game between Michigan's Jackson Prison, where Abe's brother, Joe, was serving a life sentence for murder, and the Army team from Fort Custer, Michigan. Hank even volunteered to play for the prison team, rather than with the Army team.

Hank had a perfect day at bat, hitting two singles, a double, and a home run. The home run was the longest ever hit at the prison, sailing over the prison's outside wall—the first time this had ever been done. There wasn't a member of the prison audience who didn't volunteer to go get the ball. The prison team won, thanks to Hank, and the prisoners gave him a rousing cheer before he left.

This was the only baseball that Hank played between May 6, 1941, when he left the Tigers to join the Army, and July 1, 1945, when he returned to the Tiger lineup.

⊗   ⊗   ⊗

In 1949, Nate Dolin and a group of other businessmen purchased the Cleveland Indians from Bill Veeck and made Hank Greenberg the team's general manager. One winter, the American League winter meetings were being held in Phoenix, Arizona.

When Dolin and his associates were signing in at the large hotel where all the American League meetings were being held, they were told by the desk clerk that Mr. Greenberg could not register. Dolin asked what the problem was. The clerk told Dolin that Greenberg was Jewish and that the hotel did not accept Jews. Dolin replied that he and all his partners were also Jewish.

The party immediately left the hotel and checked into the hotel where the National League was staying—which was not restricted.

⊗   ⊗   ⊗

In 1955, Hank Greenberg was general manager of the Cleveland Indians and Spud Goldstein was the team's traveling secretary. One evening, when the team had arrived in Baltimore after an exhausting trip, Hank was surprised to discover that the team's five black players did not get off the bus to go into their hotel; he learned that black players had to room in private houses there in Baltimore, as well as in Washington and St. Louis. Hank ordered Spud that in the future he was to write to every hotel he booked that they either had to accept the entire team or they would get no business in the future from the Cleveland Indians.

Spud found that most hotels replied positively to the team's ultimatum, the first such in the major leagues. After that time, the team was always housed together.

⊗   ⊗   ⊗

One day, Hank Greenberg was playing with the Tigers in Yankee Stadium, just a short distance from his old home in the Bronx. After the game, as Hank was leaving, he was surprised to find his father outside the gate, surrounded by a bunch of kids. Someone, apparently, had recognized Hank's father and children were getting autographs from the elder Greenberg. But the children seemed confused by the autographs they received. Hank asked a boy to look at the autographed ball his father had just signed. Hank was nonplused to find his father had signed the ball in Hebrew.

⊗   ⊗   ⊗

The year 1997 marks the beginning of inter-league play in major league baseball. But Hank Greenberg had first proposed this idea in 1952, when he was general manager of the Cleveland Indians. Hank was even able to get a vote of support for his idea from the American League owners. However, the idea was tabled when the National League owners voted against it and the Commissioner of Baseball, Ford Frick, passed the buck back to the owners—many of whom changed their votes to kill the idea.

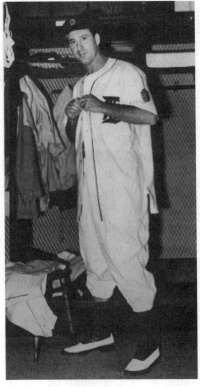

Hank Greenberg suiting up.

⊗   ⊗   ⊗

When, in 1956, Hank Greenberg was inducted into the Hall of Fame, all he received was a photograph of the plaque. He wondered why he wasn't given a replica of the plaque (as is given today). He was told by the president of Cooperstown that they couldn't do that because if they did give out such replicas, many of them would end up in pawn shops or in junk shops, sold because their recipients needed the money.

This made Hank realize how insecure the life of the average baseball player was, that financial security was not even guaranteed to its greatest masters. At that time, Hank began efforts towards a pension plan for retired players, pioneer efforts that would contribute to the existing pension plan and strong financial base that current players now enjoy.

⊗   ⊗   ⊗

Around 1940, the Detroit Tigers paid for a trip of the city's United Hebrew Schools to see a baseball game. During the game, Hank Greenberg waved to the kids and one of the students yelled down to Hank, in Yiddish, as a joke, that he was hungry. Hank called over one of the peanut vendors and had him bring peanuts over for the kids. The vendor told the kids that Hank had told him that the peanuts were on Greenberg.

⊗   ⊗   ⊗

"Lefty" Gomez once announced to a newspaperman that he had discovered a sure-fire way to strike out Hank Greenberg: If there was a man on second, get two quick strikes on Hank; then, call the catcher in and consult with him; then, send the catcher back and start to walk Hank by throwing three balls. But, before the fourth ball, the catcher would sneak back behind Hank and Lefty would throw in the last strike. The newspaperman eagerly asked Lefty if this worked. "I don't know," Lefty replied. "I never got two strikes on Hank Greenberg."

⊗   ⊗   ⊗

Everyone agrees that Hank Greenberg was a very nice man, nice to practically everyone. To fans, he was always ready with an autograph or a kind word. To those he worked with, there was often a pat on the back, an offer of a cigar, a drink, or even dinner.

Hank was known to go up to drunks in the street and hand them a five-dollar bill and, instead of a lecture or an offer of a meal, he would tell them to buy themselves a bottle. To everyone he liked, Hank was nice. And Hank liked umpires. He felt that they were honest, hard-working men, whose work went mostly unpraised. He was always ready with a word of encouragement and approval, an inquiry about their family, or a thank-you for a "good" call.

And, if Hank should run into an umpire in a hotel, which often happened, he was delighted to treat for dinner and a conversation, which, of course, was laced with his considerable charm. He always had an extra cigar, and drinks after dinner were, as always, a necessity.

Hank's usual nickname during his years of play was "Hammerin' Hank." But he had other nicknames as well. Sometimes a pitch that on another batter would look like a strike, to an umpire who just couldn't help remembering what a really nice guy Hank was, it would look like a ball. Hank became known as "Four Strike Greenberg" and, sometimes, even "Five Strike Greenberg."

⊗   ⊗   ⊗

Moe Berg was the great spy off the baseball field, but Hank Greenberg was probably the greatest Jewish spy within the game. The subject of Hank's espionage was the other team's signals. This intelligence work occupied Hank, both as a player and as a general manager, throughout his career.

Ⓧ   Ⓧ   Ⓧ

In 1947, while a member of the Pittsburgh Pirates, Hank Greenberg took a special interest in the progress of teammate Ralph Kiner. Hank had been Kiner's boyhood hero when he was growing up in Los Angeles. When Ralph met Hank, Hank invited him to join his daily ritual of extra batting practice. The two men soon became fast friends, and even roommates on the road. Ralph attributes much of his Hall of Fame career's success to Hank's influence and guidance.

Ralph, who became a sportscaster after his playing career was over, was broadcasting a ballgame in 1986, when he received the news of Hank's death. He announced, "This is the worst day of my life. My dearest friend, and the man who was like a father to me, Hank Greenberg, has died."

Ken Holtzman

When Ken Holtzman's contract with the Oakland A's expired at the end of the 1973 season, he was up for salary arbitration. Team owner Charlie O. Finley defended himself in the arbitration. Finley's defense was that Ken didn't deserve any higher pay because all of his 21 wins in 1973 were attributable to the work of the great closer Rollie Fingers. The next day, there was a salary arbitration hearing for Fingers. In that case Finley defended himself by saying that all of Fingers' saves were a result of the excellent starting pitchers on the team. Finley lost both of the arbitration cases and had to raise both men's salaries.

Jewish Baseball Players Who Became Authors

There have been many Jewish authors who have written about baseball. But there has also been a lot of writing done by Jewish baseball players themselves. Moe Berg wrote an article for Atlantic Monthly on "Pitchers and Catchers." Steve Stone is a published poet. Scott Radinsky's lyrics are published with his recordings. Here are some of the players who have published books:

MAJOR LEAGUERS

Al Shacht: Clowning Through Baseball, etc.
Hank Greenberg: The Story of My Life
Bo Belinsky: Bo (by Jewish sportswriter, Maury Allen, "with the
     uncensored cooperation of Bo Belinsky")
Max Patkin: The Clown Prince of Baseball
Sandy Koufax: Koufax
Bill Starr: Clearing the Bases
Cy Block: So You Want to Be a Major Leaguer
Lou Boudreau: Player-Manager, etc.
Steve Stone: Teach Yourself to Win
Al Rosen: Baseball and Your Boy

Sandy Koufax

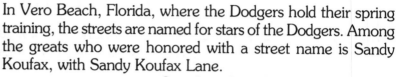

In Vero Beach, Florida, where the Dodgers hold their spring training, the streets are named for stars of the Dodgers. Among the greats who were honored with a street name is Sandy Koufax, with Sandy Koufax Lane.

Sandy Koufax's grandfather, Max Lichtenstein, was a plumber, but also a great maven of the theater, movies, and fine music. His proudest boast was that he had been present at Paul Muni's first appearance in the Yiddish theater under his real name, Muni Weisenfreund, and he had immediately predicted Muni's future greatness. We wonder if Max made any similar predictions about his grandson, Sandy?

When Sandy Koufax was 10 or 11, he was attending a function with his parents (mother and stepfather) at the local high school. Mr. Koufax sat Sandy down and explained to him the importance of good grades in school, how they might lead to a scholarship. Sandy was amazed. The idea of getting good grades had never entered Sandy's head. Sandy replied, "Gee, Dad, maybe an ath-a-let-ic scholarship." Sandy's family teased him about that line for years.

In 1951, Sandy Koufax played baseball in Brooklyn's Ice Cream League, a grouping of local teams of boys of high school age. Sandy was the catcher for the Tomahawks. No one had told him that lefties don't catch. The team's pitcher, Mike Fields, later became a surgeon. One team the Tomahawks faced was a team of Chinese boys, who had crossed the bridge to Brooklyn from Manhattan's Chinatown. They weren't too good, but they had a unique way of giving the signs: They merely called them out aloud—but in Chinese.

At the end of the season, awards were given out to players on the team. Sandy's award was "To the Best Basketball Player" on his baseball team.

Sandy Koufax was never much of a hitter. Once, at a crucial moment in one of his high school games, the coach pulled him and put in a pinch-hitter. This might not sound so bad, but the pinch-hitter they put in had been sitting on the bench with a broken kneecap. The coach, rather than let Sandy bat, sawed off the kid's cast, wrapped his knee in an Ace bandage, and sent him hobbling up to the plate.

⊗   ⊗   ⊗

In 1963, Yogi Berra batted against Sandy Koufax in the World Series. After the experience, Yogi was asked what he thought. He said that now it was no mystery to him that Sandy had won 25 games that year. What he couldn't figure out was how he had lost 5.

⊗   ⊗   ⊗

Late in 1994, at a signing being held in Atlantic City, Sandy Koufax was asked to autograph thirty yarmulkes that were going to be presented to kids who were attending a Hebrew school. Sandy was touched by the story, so he agreed to sign the yarmulkes for free. Some six months later, he was upset to learn, from a newspaper collectibles column, that the items were sold for $75 apiece. Sandy commented that it made him wonder if trying to be nice to people wasn't the same as asking for trouble.

⊗   ⊗   ⊗

Sandy Koufax might have been a Yankee, if the team management hadn't been over-subtle. When Sandy was just a kid phenom and teams all over the country were trying to sign him up, the Yankees sent a Jewish scout to try to hook him. Sandy and his parents thought this was just too obvious, were offended, and they looked elsewhere.

⊗   ⊗   ⊗

Sandy Koufax was the last pitcher to ever pitch for the Brooklyn Dodgers. After Sandy pitched in relief at the end of the team's final game of the 1957 season, they packed up their gear and moved to Los Angeles.

⊗   ⊗   ⊗

Sandy, at the end of the 1961 season, was the last Dodger pitcher to pitch at the team's first Los Angeles home, the Coliseum. Sandy was also the last person to ever pitch at Milwaukee's old County Stadium.

⊗   ⊗   ⊗

In 1962, Sandy Koufax got the first home run of his career off Warren Spahn. Koufax had a terrible reputation as a hitter, and Spahn had just tossed him his best screwball. Sandy swung at it with his usual half-hearted swing, but this time it went sailing into the left-field stands. As Sandy slowly trotted around the bases, Spahn followed his motion on the mound, cursing him over and over again as he went around. The third baseman, Eddie Matthews, asked Sandy, "What are you trying to do, make a joke out of the game?"

⊗   ⊗   ⊗

Sandy Koufax once remarked, "Any player who gets himself into a controversy by either downgrading the opposition or criticizing an umpire is off his head." Another quote from pitcher Sandy: "Never believe anything a batter says. They are a most untrustworthy lot."

⊗   ⊗   ⊗

Dick Sisler, manager of the Reds, discussing reports of Sandy Koufax's arm troubles in the 1965 season, said: "Yeah, some sore elbow! It's sore except between the first and ninth innings."

Ⓧ   Ⓧ   Ⓧ

Sandy Koufax, along with his pitching buddy Don Drysdale, was once scheduled to star in a feature-length movie. The movie was to have been entitled Warning Shot and to have been filmed in 1966. Don was to have appeared as a detective and Sandy was supposed to be an announcer (or, possibly the other way around). The movie was also to have starred David Janssen of TV's "The Fugitive" fame. The deal fell through when Koufax and Drysdale re-signed with the Dodgers, after holding out for some time in a salary dispute.

Kosher at the Concession Stands

Baltimore's Camden Yards is the only major league ball park in America to sell glatt kosher hot dogs at their concession stands. They also have a minyan on staff to pray, if necessary.

Barry Latman

Stan Williams, who played between 1958 and 1972, was a 6'5", 230-pound, right-handed pitcher with a very nasty temper. He used the bean ball like other pitchers used curves. And like the legendary mule of the pope, he never forgot a wrong. Once, during a spring-training game, Barry Latman accidentally hit Williams with a pitch. For years Williams seethed, but circumstances never allowed him to face Latman. Then both men retired and it looked as if Barry would escape scot-free. But, then, the two men found themselves coaching on the same minor league team. One day, Williams was pitching batting practice and Barry stepped up to take some swings. Williams hit him.

Jesse Levis

In 1993, the Pinnacle card company issued a card that was entitled "Rookie Team Pinnacle" and showed a picture of Jesse Levis on one side and Rookie of the Year Mike Piazza on the other. While talking to Jesse, he told us that this card was now worth $100. Jesse estimated that that was one dollar for his side, and $99 for Mike's.

Ⓧ   Ⓧ   Ⓧ

When Jesse Levis was planning his wedding with Joan Greenspan, there seemed no reason that the date October 29, 1995, would not be a good date. But then Jesse's team, the Cleveland Indians, went to the World Series. It was a tight thing and Jesse and his wife sweated it out in the press. "You try all your life to get to this point, to be on a team that plays in the World Series. And you never know if you'll get to be there again. But at the same time, you want to be able to go to your own wedding." Fate smiled on Jesse, as it frowned on the Indians. The Indians lost to the Braves in 6 games and Jesse made it to his wedding.

Ed Levy

Ed Levy, who played with the Phillies in 1940 and the Yankees in 1942 and 1944, is not Jewish. His parents were both Irish. But Ed's mother, when Ed was just a boy, got a divorce and married a Jewish man named Levy. Somewhere along the line, Ed changed his name from the original Whitner to Levy. Years later, Ed had a reconciliation with his real father and decided to change his name back to Whitner. When Ed reported to the Yankees business office in 1942, to sign his contract, he signed his name "Ed Whitner." When Edward Barrow, President of the Yankees, looked at the contract he became livid. He wanted to know what the meaning of this was. Ed carefully explained to him the whole touching story of his reunion with his father. Barrow replied, "There are two million Jews in New York who like to go to baseball games. You will play for the Yankees as Ed Levy or you won't play for us at all." Ed played as Ed Levy.

Eddie Waitkus

Eddie Waitkus, a Catholic of Lithuanian descent, first baseman for the Chicago Cubs in 1949, received a strange note that lured him to a room in a Chicago hotel. As he entered the room, he was met with the blast of a shotgun. Eddie's assailant was a crazed female fan who was obsessed with the idea that if she couldn't have Eddie, no one would. He survived the assault and went on to become the leadoff hitter with the 1950 Philadelphia Phillies, the famous "Whiz Kids."

Eddie's story was the major inspiration for the 1952 novel, The Natural, by Jewish novelist Bernard Malamud. Malamud's novel is considered by many critics to be the finest ever inspired by the sport. In 1984, a movie based on Malamud's novel appeared, starring Robert Redford as Roy Hobbs, the character based on the real-life Waitkus.

Brett Mandel

According to minor leaguer and author Brett Mandel, "The Bible actually begins with a baseball verse—'In the big inning.'"

Moxie Manuel

When Moxie Manuel was with the White Sox, in 1908, the team's manager was Fielder Jones. Once, in Jones's hearing, Moxie remarked that pitching in the major leagues was the same as pitching in the minors. Jones snapped back, "It is for you, all right." Moxie found this very funny and wasn't satisfied until he had made the round of the team and told everyone the story.

⚾   ⚾   ⚾

Jake Atz, who came to the Sox with Moxie, was disappointed that Moxie never was as successful in the majors as he had been in the Southern League. He always contended that "Mox never showed half his real possessions while with the Chicago bunch."

Duke Markell

Duke Markell found fulfillment in his police work, as well as in his pitching. In 1953, he was walking his beat and a boy stopped him and asked him what it was like to be a policeman. Markell said that it was fine and that the police department was a wonderful place to work. The boy elaborated, saying that he wanted a job with security, because he was a professional baseball player; he then told Duke that he probably couldn't understand what it was like to be a ballplayer. Duke then told the kid that he was the pitcher Duke Markell and that he knew all about the insecurities of a baseball career.

Duke investigated, and found that the boy was playing for an "outlaw" league. Duke intervened and got the boy out of his contract with the "outlaw" league, arranging to get him a tryout with Portsmouth, Virginia—a team run by Frank (Pop) Lawrence, an old friend of Duke's.

Erskine Mayer

On June 9, 1914, Erskine Mayer yielded Honus Wagner's 3,000th hit. Nevertheless, Erskine won the game for the Phillies over the Pirates, 3 to 1, and held Pittsburgh to only five hits. Joe Conzelman took the loss for the Pirates, at Philadelphia's Baker Bowl.

Marvin Miller

Marvin Miller relates in his book A Whole Different Ball Game that in 1971 he was invited to throw out the ceremonial first ball of the Puerto Rican Winter League All-Star Game. He expected to throw a ball down from a field box. To Marvin's surprise he was led out onto the field, past a glut of photographers, to throw the ball from the pitcher's mound. The catcher, Elrod Hendricks, crouched for a ball right over the plate. Marvin threw a ball that took a short hop before the catcher caught it. Hendricks lanced it right back, insisting on a strike. The next pitch Marvin threw was a strike.

After the game, Marvin returned to New York with a pile of photographs that were taken of his windup and pitch. Mets ace Tom Seaver stopped by his office, and he noticed the photographs on his desk and asked him what they were. Marvin told him about the game, then asked, "Care to comment on my delivery?"

Seaver played it straight. He studied the pictures carefully, looked up with a serious expression, and said, "Do you always pitch with your wristwatch on?"

Walter Miller

Walter Miller, the great Jewish jockey from 1904 to 1912, fancied himself as talented as a baseball player as a jockey. Early in his racing career, he fielded a team composed of racetrack workers and played against a semi-pro team. Walter was his team's captain and pitcher.

Walter once wangled a tryout with Giants manager and well-known Judeophile John McGraw. McGraw claimed he liked what he saw, but politely declined the offer, stating that Walter was too short.

After retiring from jockeying, Walter played baseball for a while with a semi-pro team in Emeryville, California. Walter, as a jockey, is a member of two athletic halls of fame. In 1957, he was inducted into the Jockey Hall of Fame. He was inducted into the Jewish Sports Hall of Fame in Netanya, Israel, in 1983.

Sam Nahem

Sam Nahem has said, "I've been mentioned, in the same breath as Sandy Koufax. The breath usually is, 'Sam Nahem is no Sandy Koufax.' "

Max Patkin

MAX PATKIN

THE CLOWN PRINCE

Here's a trivia question for you. When Tiger pitcher Bob Cain walked the midget Eddie Gaedel, on August 19, 1951, who was the Browns' first base coach, waiting to greet Bill Veeck's latest sensation? Answer: Max Patkin. Eddie was quickly replaced with a pinch-runner and his major league career was over. This incident has one other Jewish connection. The original story, "You Could Look It Up," by James Thurber, which presumably inspired Veeck and which first appeared in The Saturday Evening Post in 1935, has the following passage concerning the pitcher who pitched to the midget. In Thurber's story, by a strange twist, it is St. Louis who is pitching to the midget, rather than putting the midget in: "I wisht I could call the pitcher's name—it wasn't old Barney Pelty."

⚾ ⚾ ⚾

When the 1984 movie version of Bernard Malamud's classic The Natural was first shot, it included a sequence with Max Patkin. Alas, this entire sequence was left on the cutting-room floor. Max was later featured, to excellent effect, in the 1988 movie about life in the minor leagues, Bull Durham.

⚾ ⚾ ⚾

Once, during a minor league game between Toledo and Rochester, held in Toledo, Mike Epstein, who was playing first base for Rochester, sent a foul ball right into the dugout. The scorcher nailed Max Patkin, who had been entertaining at the game, on the shoulder. Max bore a bruise for two weeks. With probably only two Jews on the field that night, what were the odds?

⚾ ⚾ ⚾

Max Patkin, who was quite a good dancer—à la Ray Bolger, elastic and comic—won an opportunity for a Hollywood tryout in the early 1950s. He had even received the encouragement of Busby Berkely. The movie mogul, himself a Jew, was also holding the tryout. After watching Max's routine, he dashed the clown's hopes with the words "You're too Jewish-looking."

⚾ ⚾ ⚾

Max Patkin, in the late 1930s, had a tryout as a pitcher with the Boston Red Sox. After watching Max, the Sox management passed on the high-kicking young prospect. Someone later told Max that he hadn't had a chance with the Red Sox, because he was a Jew. Max didn't believe this, as the team already had Moe Berg.

Max Patkin and Al Schacht

Max Patkin wasn't the only "Clown Prince" with movie experience. Shortly after the turn of the century, Al Schacht, then just a lad, got a part in a motion picture being filmed in the Bronx. The title of the silent picture was East Side, West Side. Al played a newsboy and appeared in only one scene. Like Max in The Natural, Al's entire contribution was edited out of the final cut.

No one doubts that Max Patkin was the "Clown Prince of Baseball." But, throughout his life Al Schacht was also known as the "Clown Prince of Baseball." Schacht performed his pantomime routines in his trademark battered top hat, dilapidated frock coat, and giant mitt. Both "Princes" performed before millions of fans and both have been honored in Baseball's Hall of Fame.

Barney Pelty

The lowest lifetime ERA of any Jewish pitcher is not that held by Sandy Koufax, 2.76. The record is held by Barney Pelty, the original "Yiddish Curver": 2.63. If Pelty's winning average, .440, seems disappointing compared to Koufax, .655, this is due in large measure to the fact that Pelty played much of his career with the hopelessly inept St. Louis Browns.

The Philadelphia Phillies

The lackluster Philadelphia Phillies of the period 1916 to 1949 never won a pennant. During that period, much of the right-field wall of their home park, the Baker Bowl, was dominated by a large advertising sign for Lifebuoy deodorant soap. The sign announced that the Phillies bathed with the product: "Health soap stops B. O." The telegrapher for the stadium, "Shorty" Levin, used to like to point out this sign to visitors, with the comment, "And, brother, can they use it!"

It was also during this period that the team was almost bought by a Jew, Dr. Leon Levy, owner of radio station WCAU. Dr. Levy was a bit concerned, when the deal was offered to him, that there might exist some unwritten agreement against Jews owning major league teams. (Perhaps he was unaware that there had been a number of Jewish team owners before that time.) Levy sent an emissary to ask about the possible sale to Ford Frick, President of the National League. Levy's representative was received rudely by Frick, who refused to discuss the matter, and the deal fell through. The team was bought, instead, by William D. Cox, who was later thrown out of major league baseball for gambling. Instead of buying the Phillies, Dr. Levy used his money to build the Atlantic City Race Track.

Lipman Pike

Lipman Pike, the first Jewish major league player, was so fleet afoot that he raced a racehorse, a trotter. He did this on a $200 bet. This event took place on August 27, 1873. The race was a hundred-yard dash. The horse was allowed to start twenty-five yards before the starting line, to get into a good pace. When the horse crossed the starting line, Lip joined in. For most of the race, the pair ran neck-and-neck. When, near the finish line, Lip began to draw ahead, the horse broke into a run. Nevertheless, Lip beat the horse by 4 yards.

⚾ ⚾ ⚾

Lip Pike was the first player to hold the record for most home runs in a year, a record that he set—as part of a three-way tie in 1871—of 4. In 1872, he set a new and undisputed record: 6.

Jake Pitler

Dodgers first base coach and minor league manager Jake Pitler was not only known for his deliberate witticisms, but also for funny remarks that were quite unintentional. This happened, sometimes, when he talked with the well-spoken Branch Rickey. One day, while Jake was manager of Newport News, Rickey asked him what had happened to his star pitcher.

Jake responded, "I don't know what happened to him, Mr. Rickey. He can't even bend his arm. It's as hard as a rock. I can't even think of a word to describe it."

Rickey suggested the word "ossified."

"Oh, no, Mr. Rickey," said Jake. "That ain't it at all. This boy don't drink. He never touched a drop in his life."

Another such incident occurred when Rickey asked Jake what his opinion was of the oldest player of the team. Rickey asked Jake, "Can he hit? Can he run? Can he throw? Can he do any of those things we look for in a young ballplayer?"

"No, Mr. Rickey," Jake replied in a small voice. "But he's the only one old enough to drive the bus."

⚾ ⚾ ⚾

Jake was generally friendly with the other Dodger personnel, but he was quite vicious when it came to his responsibility of looking after the bag of practice balls. The practice balls would constantly disappear, especially for autographing purposes, and it was up to Jake to see that there was an "honest count."

Steve Ratzer

Pitching batting practice one day for the Expos, Steve Ratzer broke the bats of Warren Cromartie, Tommy Hutton, and Larry Parrish consecutively, while pitching coach Galen Cisco was watching. "Hey, Galen," Parrish shouted over to Cisco. "If you're ready, you better take over. We're running out of bats here."

Jimmie Reese

One year after his death, in 1994, Jimmie Reese's locker at Anaheim Stadium was encased in Plexiglas as a permanent memorial to the great fungo hitter. This was not the first honor the California Angels had paid Reese. The team had already retired his number, only the third number so retired by the Angels. (The other two were the numbers of Nolan Ryan and Rod Carew.)

But perhaps the greatest tribute paid to Jimmie was one paid during his

JIMMIE REESE

Reese Ryan (l.), named in honor of Jimmie Reese, walking with father Nolan Ryan.

lifetime, and a living one at that. Nolan Ryan, who served on the Angels with Reese from 1973 to 1979 and who became very close to him, named his younger son Reese Ryan, in honor of Jimmie. The young Ryan is currently a pitcher at Texas Christian University.

Replacement Players

During the 1995 strike, there were five Jews who were replacement players: Steve Wapnick, Lou List, Howard Prager, Barry Goldman, and Jason Friedman.

Jackie Robinson

In 1962, Jewish businessman Frank Schiffman planned to open a low-cost restaurant in Harlem. Black entrepreneurs in the same area instigated a protest against Schiffman's planned establishment, which they feared would cut into their businesses. These protests quickly took on a very anti-Semitic tone. Black leaders around the country were united in their response; they ignored the situation. But one black man did not ignore what was happening; he was appalled and said so publicly. This was Jackie Robinson. Jackie spoke out loud and clear that such behavior from anyone, black or white, towards any other group, Jew or gentile, was intolerable.

Jackie's statement struck fire, but not the kind he wished. The protesters were sent to picket Chock Full O'Nuts shops. Jackie was a vice-president of the company. Then, even more protesters were sent to picket a banquet being given in honor of Jackie's induction into the Hall of Fame. This proved too much and, one by one, other black leaders began to rally behind Jackie and his cause. First there was Roy Wilkins of the NAACP, then Dr. Martin Luther King. Eventually, practically all of America's black establishment rallied to Jackie's call for a firm stand against anti-Semitism.

In 1947, Jackie Robinson showed the way to his people and his nation. He never ceased to be a pathfinder and leader in social issues and in questions of clear moral sense.

Saul Rogovin

Saul Rogovin was best known, by most of his teammates, for something other than his pitching. He was known to be a sleepwalker. In 1950, Saul roomed with Joe Ginsberg. Joe didn't know about Saul's problem. One night, Joe woke to find Saul with his arms outstretched over him, as if to strangle him. Joe screamed and picked up a shoe to defend himself, but Saul had returned to bed. The next night, Joe opened the windows, which Saul always locked for safety reasons, and said, "If that so-and-so starts walking tonight, let him go right out the window."

On November 17, 1947, pitcher Saul Rogovin had the surprise of his life. The 24-year-old had just arrived the day before to pitch for Caracas, in the Venezuelan Winter League. Despite a tired arm and his protests, he was put into the game for relief by manager Oscar Yanes. He walked the first three batters he faced. When he then walked the fourth, he felt frustrated. But his frustration was nothing compared with Yanes'. Yanes called over four local policemen and had Rogovin arrested. Rogovin was held at the Caracas prison until after midnight, when Yanes had him released. After Yanes apologized, Rogovin continued pitching for Caracas, but with none of the success he would later have in the majors.

Al Rosen

Al Rosen seemed destined to take the Triple Crown in 1953. He led the league by a big margin in RBIs and homers, and he was virtually tied with Mickey Vernon of the Washington Senators for batting average.

Al Rosen working out.

In the last game of the season for the Senators, in the final inning, it was clear, as Al's season was already over, that if Vernon could get a hit in his last at-bat, he would win the batting-average race. On the other hand, if he flubbed, he would lose it. But the catch was: If Vernon didn't get to bat, he would also win. Vernon was scheduled to be the fourth batter up in that 9th inning.

With one out, Mickey Grosso hit a double. Then, "absent-mindedly," he stepped off the bag and was tagged out by the second baseman. The next batter, Kite Thomas, hit a single, but, "unexpectedly," tried to stretch it into a double and was easily tagged out. Vernon had been "robbed" of his last at-bat and Al was robbed of the batting average title by .0011 of a point.

Goody Rosen

When Babe Ruth was a coach with the Dodgers, he had the locker next to Goody Rosen's. The two men got along famously, but one time the Babe got mad at Goody. The Babe discovered that someone was stealing cigars from his locker. He accused Goody, but the Canadian was able to prove himself blameless by pointing out that he smoked a different brand. However, Goody helped Ruth set a trap for the thief. The two changed the top row of Ruth's cigars with exploding ones.

That evening, the team was traveling by train. Goody spotted the team's trainer about to light up an exploding cigar. The thief had been found! Instead of warning the trainer, Goody ran to get Babe. Just as they got to the car, the cigar exploded. The Babe had promised to murder the cigar thief, but all he could do was laugh, seeing the trainer's shocked face all covered in tobacco and soot.

⚾ ⚾ ⚾

Goody Rosen's first minor league team was Louisville, where he started in 1933. When Goody first reported for training camp, he was met by the trainer, Hump Pierce, a tobacco-chewing old-timer. Pierce took a look at the small, thin Rosen and told him, "Sorry, we don't need any more batboys." When Rosen explained that he was a player and was there for a tryout, Pierce told him he didn't have a uniform small enough to fit him. Nevertheless, Goody made the team.

Louis Rosenberg

Lou Rosenberg once played in a game with the infamous Ty Cobb. Lou saw Cobb get into an argument with the umpire. Cobb didn't like one of the umpire's calls and got into a fight with him. The umpire, who had graduated from Harvard, soundly thrashed Cobb and tossed him from the game.

Despite this occasion, years later, when he was asked to name the greatest baseball player of all time, Lou replied, "Ty Cobb."

After the death of Louis Rosenberg, a researcher contacted the wife of his brother, Harry, to find out what his middle name was. Mrs. Harry Rosenberg told the researcher that Louis did not have a middle name. The researcher pointed out that the records showed his middle initial as "C." Mrs. Rosenberg insisted that that was a mistake, that he didn't have a middle name. She then went on, "There were eleven Rosenberg children and none of them had a middle name. They were lucky to have a first name."

Rosenblatt Stadium

The minor league ballpark in Omaha, Nebraska, which first opened in 1948, was renamed in honor of Omaha's second Jewish mayor, John Rosenblatt, who served from 1954 to 1961. Besides serving as an AAA park, home of the Omaha Royals, for more than 40 years Rosenblatt Stadium has been home to the NCAA College World Series. It is affectionately known around the college circuit as "the Blatt."

Appropriately, Rosenblatt Stadium has witnessed some of the greatest triumphs of one of the greatest Jewish baseball coaches of all time, Skip Bertman. Skip's Louisiana State University teams won the College World Series in 1991, 1993, 1996, and 1997.

Sy Rosenthal

When Sy Rosenthal first signed with the Boston Red Sox organization, Hugh Duffy was the manager. Sy told the story like this: "Duffy wanted me to change my name to Rose because it would fit easier in box scores. But I told him that I wouldn't do it. I was born with the name Rosenthal. It won't make any difference if my name is Rose, Rosenthal or O'Brien. I'll rise and fall on my own name."

Marv Rotblatt

When "Marvelous" Marv Rotblatt first started high school, he stood only 4'11" (compared to his adult height of 5'6½"). Marv had been playing ball for years. He had once organized his own ball team at the Neighborhood Boys' Club at River Park. Marv pitched for the club and his brother, Lenny, was the catcher.

Marv immediately signed up for Von Steuben High School's baseball team, but as soon as Coach Chuck Goldstein took one look at him, he sent him home, telling him he was too short. Still, Marv was persistent, and every practice he would show up. Every time, Coach Goldstein would send him home; but finally he grew tired of this. One day, Marv showed up and the coach handed him a uniform in his size. He would be the team's batboy. As time went along, the coach got used to the diminutive player and gave him chances to pitch. In his junior year of high school, Marv's record was 11-3 and, in his senior year, 8-3. In later years, Coach Goldstein became one of Marv's closest friends.

Larry Rothschild

On June 7, 1997, Larry Rothschild, pitching coach of the Florida Marlins, wore a microphone during a game broadcast on the Fox television network. It seemed like cruel and unusual punishment to make him wear the microphone that day, because the game against the Colorado Rockies was played in Coors Field, known as the worst ballpark in the league for pitchers. Larry was forced into this miking by an agreement between major league baseball and Fox. If Larry had refused to wear the mike, his team would have been fined $100,000. Larry, with tongue in cheek, said that Coors Field "is a great place to be miked. But during the course of a game, you don't use the most eloquent language."

⊗ ⊗ ⊗

When Larry Rothschild went to spring training with the Detroit Tigers in 1981, he was considered the look-alike of fellow pitcher Mark Fidyrich.

Harry Ruby

Harry Ruby, the great songwriter and baseball fan, actually got to play in four official Pacific Coast League games, probably in the early 1950s. Harry played in games between the Los Angeles Angels and the Hollywood team, in the last innings of the last days of the seasons. The umpires turned their backs and pretended not to notice, for this was not legal.

In one of these games, Harry hit for Hollywood and made a good hit, a "Texas Leaguer" that seemed sure to drop, but Carl Ditmar, the Angels' second baseman, made a diving catch to come up with it. Harry wouldn't talk to Ditmar for two years after that, although later he forgave him and they became friends again.

⊗ ⊗ ⊗

In 1919, when Al Schacht was pitching for the Washington Senators, the team won a particularly crucial game against the Yankees to clinch first place. Al met his boyhood friend Harry Ruby after the game and invited him home to have dinner with his family. As they were driving to Schacht's home, Harry couldn't stop talking about the wonderful game that he had just witnessed. As they drove up to his place, Al warned Harry not to mention the game. His mother did not like baseball and Al and his brothers never talked about the game in front of her. "Not a word!" Al warned him.

The dinner dragged on, one hour, two hours. They talked about everything in the world, but no one said a word about baseball or about the results of the day's critical game. Harry was becoming visibly more and more uncomfortable, for he was like a pot trying to boil, but with the lid being pushed down harder and harder to prevent it. Finally, dinner was over and Al and Harry went out and down to Al's convertible, parked at the corner, so that Al could drive Harry home. As they were about to pull away, Al's mother stuck her head out the window. "So," she called out, "who vun today?"

J. D. Salinger

The 1989 movie Field of Dreams, which starred Kevin Costner as Ray Kinsella, was based on the novel Shoeless Joe (1982) by W. P. Kinsella. The movie features James Earl Jones as Terence Mann, portrayed in the film as the leading novelist of the revolutionary generation of the 1960s. This movie character is black and, obviously, is not supposed to be Jewish. The equivalent character in the novel, however, is the quite real J. D. Salinger, author of The Catcher in the Rye. Salinger's father was Jewish, his mother Christian. Many of the other characters in Shoeless Joe were historical figures, including the great Joe Jackson of the title and "Moonlight" Graham.

Abe Saperstein

Abe Saperstein, the creator and first owner of the Harlem Globetrotters, as well as owner of the Negro League Chicago American Giants, also owned an all-black barnstorming team, the Zulu Cannibal Giants. This was during the 1930s. The members of the team played baseball in grass skirts and war paint, so the team's outfits were similar to extras in early Tarzan movies, with trunks and sliding pads under the skirts.

    The team emphasized good ballplaying, as well as entertainment. The show featured shadow ball before the regular game would start. This was a make-believe batting practice, but without the ball—a very funny shtick. Among the fine players on the team were Goose Tatum, who later became a star of the Globetrotters, and Buck O'Neil, who in 1962 became the first African-American coach in the major leagues. The manager of the team was Charlie Henry, a former player in the Negro Leagues, and the team's publicity was handled by Syd Pollock, a Tarrytown, New York, vaudeville theater owner. The team had its home base in Louisville, Kentucky.

Al Schacht

In 1912, Al Schacht, then a young hurler with the Metropolitans, a New York semi-pro club, pitched against the recently retired Cy Young at Lenox Oval in New York. Cy was forty-five at the time and lost the game to the promising young Schacht. Cy hung it up after that game and never pitched again.

Al Schacht did not like to bet, but one thing he was confident in was his knowledge of the game of baseball. So once, when he was offered a wager on a question of the fine points of the game, he couldn't refuse. The stake was a dinner for five at Al's own restaurant. This wager was proposed by Harry "Champ" Segal, a former boxer and a boxing manager.

    The question was "Does a manager have the right to pull a pitcher at any time during a game?"

Al Schacht (squatting) clowning with Nick Altrock.

Al insisted that a manager did have that right. Champ claimed otherwise.

That evening, Champ showed up at Al's restaurant for dinner. Al, admitting defeat, graciously treated the party. Champ revealed that he was aware of the rule that a pitcher, after being introduced into a game, must complete pitching to at least one batter, because he had seen the question arise at an actual game.

The game was in 1954, between the Giants and the Pirates. The Giants' skipper, Leo Durocher, had put in a relief pitcher, who threw one pitch to a batter. Before he could throw a second pitch to the same batter, Leo decided to change pitchers. The umpire was Jocko Conlan, and Jocko insisted, according to the rule, that the pitcher had to complete pitching to at least one batter.

Al joined Champ's party and enjoyed the evening. He said that in 44 years of baseball he had never heard of such a situation. He also said that this was the biggest bet he ever lost in his life.

Richie Scheinblum

Richie Scheinblum wasn't too fond of Cleveland, though he was an outfielder on the Indians. He once commented that the only good thing about playing for Cleveland was that one didn't have to make any road trips there.

Bud Selig

Bud Selig, commissioner of baseball tells a story that he finds inspirational. Around 1971, Bud was on a flight home from a meeting of the team owners. Aboard the same flight was John Fetzer, owner of the Detroit Tigers. Selig asked Fetzer why he had voted for some measure at the meeting, as that measure was sure to be bad for the Tigers. Fetzer told Selig that he voted for it because it was good for baseball. What was good for baseball, in the long run, would have to be good for the Tigers. Bud feels that too many of the today's owners don't have that kind of vision.

Larry Sherry

When Larry Sherry was pitching relief with the Tigers in 1966, one of the pitchers he had to work with was Denny McLain. Denny didn't have the most saintly of reputations even then, though it would be years before his shenanigans would get him long terms in prison. Nevertheless, McLain's favorite expression was "If I'm lying, may God strike me dead!" McLain would say this over and over again, spicing it through his conversation like punctuation points. Larry likes to tell how, when sudden thunderstorms would break out, any member of the team who might be standing near McLain would immediately try to put as much distance as possible between himself and the last man who won thirty games in a season.

Norm Sherry

When Branch Rickey first saw Norm Sherry bat, at a time when Norm first started playing for Santa Barbara, in 1950, he didn't like what he saw. "How many times have you swung that bat?" Rickey asked Norm. Norm said about 5,000 times. "Do you realize you've taken 5,000 bad swings? Young man, try batting left-handed." But Norm kept batting right. In 1960, 3 of his 5 home runs were game winners. On September 20, 1961, Norm hit the last home run at Los Angeles Memorial Stadium, the Dodgers' home from 1958 to 1961. Sandy Koufax picked up the 3-2 win against the Cubs.

⚾ ⚾ ⚾

When Norm Sherry was managing the Angels, he got hit above the eye by a wild throw. His head felt as if it was exploding and he thought he was going to die. He kept moaning, "My temple, my temple." Billy Muffett, an Angels coach, leaned over Norm and told him in comforting tones, "Norm, today is Sunday. Temple is on Saturday."

Harry Shuman

When Harry Shuman had a successful heart operation, he thanked and complimented the surgeon. The surgeon was less than pleased. "I really never wanted to be a doctor, that was my father's dream. Harry, you were a major league ballplayer. You lived my dream."

⚾ ⚾ ⚾

Harry Shuman was enjoying dinner with his beautiful wife in Toronto's Victoria Hotel. At a nearby table a party was gaily celebrating a Jewish wedding. At the very next table to Harry, a well-dressed drunk was spouting out a string of anti-Semitic remarks to his older dinner partner, another businessman. When the drunk turned to Harry's table to share his ideas, obviously not recognizing that Harry was Jewish, Harry rebuked the drunk, who then left the dining room.

When Harry was leaving the hotel, he was again confronted by the drunk, who took a swing at the 6'2" relief pitcher. Shuman replied in kind and decked the drunk. As Shuman was departing, he was informed by one of the witnesses to the fracas that the man he'd flattened was one of the richest and most influential men in Toronto. The story quickly spread. The next day, when the little-known reliever was called to the mound, he was greeted by a standing ovation, led by a large contingent of Toronto's Jewish community.

Fred Sington

Fred Sington's contributions to Alabama's 1931 victory in the Rose Bowl, 24–0 over Washington State, made him a national hero. Knute Rockne himself presented Fred with his All-American title and called him the greatest lineman in the country for that season. But the cap to Fred's collegiate football career was having a song dedicated to him by the popular entertainer Rudy Vallee. The song was entitled "Football Freddie." In 1930, Fred was also named an All-American baseball player.

Bill Stern

Bill Stern (1907–1971), the famous sportscaster, was especially noted for his tall tales. One story he told concerned the origin of Thomas Edison's deafness. According to Stern, this began when Edison was hit on the head by a pitched ball, while he was batting in a baseball game in his youth. The pitcher who beaned Edison, according to Stern, was none other than Jesse James.

Another story Stern told concerned the origin of the game of baseball. According to Stern's apocryphal version of the already apocryphal tale of Abner Doubleday's invention of the game was that it was Abraham Lincoln himself who, with his dying words, inspired Doubleday's invention. Stern had this dramatic story accompanied by organ chords. When Stern was criticized by other sportswriters for his lack of research, he replied that his show was entertainment. Then: "If there's a story that I know is not factual, I'll say so—but that's seldom the case."

Steve Stone

While Steve Stone was attending Kent State University, his favorite pool partner was his catcher on the school team, Thurman Munson. Munson fancied himself a pool shark. Stone says, "I was careful never to disillusion him—especially when I was in the process of beating him 25 matches in a row."

Elie Wiesel

In 1986, Elie Wiesel, the great Holocaust survivor and scholar, received the Nobel Peace Prize for his message "of peace, atonement and human dignity." Baseball Commissioner Peter Ueberroth must have thought these were just the things that that year's World Series could use, for he invited the Nobel laureate to throw out the ceremonial first pitch at the first game of the Series. But Wiesel, though he has lived in this country since the 1950s and has been an American citizen since 1963, had to answer the offer of this great honor with, "What's that?" Ueberroth thought he was kidding, but Wiesel wasn't. Nevertheless, the author accepted and opened the 1986 World Series. The reports on Wiesel's performance were that though he might belong in the company of Dag Hammarskjöld and Martin Luther King, Jr., he was not quite ready to join the ranks of Sandy Koufax or Ken Holtzman.

Larry Yellin

Player Larry Yellin went to the same high school as Sandy Koufax. This was Lafayette High School in Brooklyn.

Guy Zinn

Guy Zinn's six 1912 homers placed him fourth in the American League, after "Homerun" Baker, Tris Speaker, and Ty Cobb. An experimental radio broadcast of that year contained a memorable line, if it could be heard through the static of primitive receivers, "And Zinn zimmed the ball into the bleachers for a home run."

Major League Update

Frank Charles

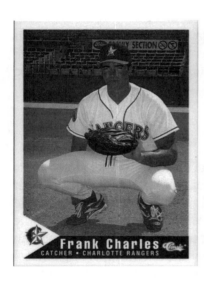

Franklin Scott Charles was born in Fontana, California on February 23, 1969. His mother is Jewish, his father is a gentile. Frank attended Pepperdine University, where he was named All-CIF and All Big West, and the University of California at Fullerton where he majored in public relations. In 1990, as part of Cal-Fullerton's baseball team, he participated in the College World Series.

Frank, a catcher who throw and bats right-handed, was selected by the San Francisco Giants in the 17th round of the June, 1991 draft. That year Frank played with Everett, hitting .318. Frank was named to play in the Northwest League all-star team for 1991. He spent 1992 with Clinton (Midwest League) and San Jose (California League). His total average for that year was .285. Frank was released by the Giants on March 29, 1993, but signed with the independent St. Paul Saints (Northern League). Frank hit .273 for St. Paul in 1993. His contract was purchased by the Charlotte Rangers on March 1, 1994. In 1994, Frank batted .264.

The following year Frank played with the Tulsa Drillers (Texas League) and batted .253, but with 24 doubles, 13 homeruns, and 72 RBIs, the best figures of his career. Most of that year he played at first base, rather than as a catcher. He led the league in games (123), total chances (1200), and double plays (117).

Frank split 1996 between Oklahoma City and Tulsa. He spent 1997 in Tulsa, where he hit 9 home runs. But 1998, which he spent with Shreveport and Fresno was another outstanding year. Again he hit 13 home runs. He tied for second in the Texas League with 39 doubles. For Shreveport he had 118 hits in 108 games. On December 18, 1998, he was signed as a free agent by the Las Vegas Stars. During the 1999 season he batted .246, with 19 doubles and 28 RBIs.

Frank began the 2000 season with the New Orleans Zephyrs (Pacific Coast League), where he had an average of .261, with 5 home runs and 37 RBIs. On September 4, 2000 he was called up by the Houston Astros and he made his major league debut on September 5. Frank appeared in 4 games for the Astros, hitting .429, with a slugging percentage of .571. His fielding percentage was 1.000 in the only game he started in the position of catcher. At the end of the season, Frank was reassigned to New Orleans.

Years	Games	AB	H	R	RBI	HR	BA	OBP	FP
1	4	7	3	1	2	0	.429	.429	1.000

2000 Hou-N

Keith Glauber

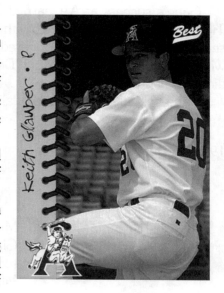

Keith Glauber played baseball at Montclair State University. He was drafted by the St. Louis Cardinals in the 42nd round of the 1994 draft. He began his professional career with the New Jersey Cardinals, in 1994, with an ERA of 4.19. This figure improved to 3.73, in 1995, with the Savannah Chiefs, with an ERA of only 1.42 for home games.

During the 1996, Keith became primarily a closer and he recorded 14 saves. He won the club's Bogard relief award.

In 1997, Keith went to the Cincinnati organization through the Rule 5 draft. Keith was injured during the pre-season and spent most of the year in rehab and in making the rounds of the Cincinnati farm system. Keith was called up to play for the Cincinnati Reds for the last two weeks of the regular season. Keith made his debut on September 9, 1998, the same day Mark McGwire set a new home run record. Keith's game was against Houston and he allowed only 1 run in $3\frac{2}{3}$ innings. The 6'2", right hander appeared in three games, before the close of the season, and was used strictly as a reliever. The numbers he produced in his brief stay were impressive, with an ERA of 2.35. In $7\frac{2}{3}$ innings, he had 4 strikeouts and only 1 walk.

Keith makes his home in Marlboro, New Jersey.

Years	Games	IP	W	L	GS	SV	PCT	ERA
2	7	15	0	0	0	0	NA	3.00

1998, 2000 Cin-N

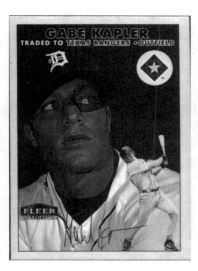

Gabe Kapler

Gabe Kapler attended Moorepark Junior College in California. The Detroit Tigers chose Gabe in the 57th round of the June, 1995 draft. It was Dennis Lieberthal, Mike's father, who signed Gabe. In 1995, his first season, he batted .288 and he has consistently improved on that number.

Gabe is a weightlifter and considered one of the strongest men in the minor leagues. He is not fast on the bases, but his power has usually more than made up for this. Gabe has a good eye and he often draws a walk, when he doesn't hit. In the field, Gabe's speed limits his effectiveness, but he does have a good arm.

During the 1998 season, Gabe played with the Jacksonville Suns (AA). Gabe batted .322, with 28 homers. He set a new record for RBIs for the Southern League, with 146. This number was also the highest in all of the minor leagues. Gabe led his league in homers, hits (176), extra-base hits (81), and runs (113). His 47 doubles tied for the league lead. Gabe was named by both Baseball Weekly and USA Today as the Minor League Player of the year for 1998.

Gabe's success at AA earned him a brief appearance with the parent club, the Detroit Tigers. Gabe made his debut with the Tigers on September 20, the last home game of the season. The 6'2" slugger appeared in 7 games with the Tigers. His batting average was .200, with 5 hits, including one triple. Despite his reputation for slowness on the base paths, Gabe did steal two bases.

Gabe, who lives in Reseda, California, played in the Arizona Winter League during 1998.

Years	Games	AB	H	R	RBI	HR	BA	OBP	FP
3	253	885	241	122	115	32	.272	.335	.975

1998-99 Det-A, 2000 Tex-A

Mike Lieberthal

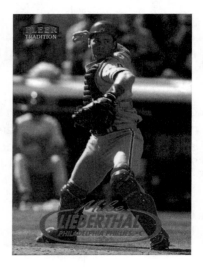

Michael Scott Lieberthal was born on January 18, 1972 in Glendale, CA. Mike's father, Dennis Lieberthal, a baseball scout, is Jewish, his mother is not. Mike's parents are divorced. Mike, guided by his father, began playing baseball at 8. He played in youth leagues, Little League, Pony League, and Babe Ruth League. Though now 6' tall, Mike was slow in growing, and he was always the smallest player on his various teams. Through his first three years at Westlake High School in Ventura County, CA, Mike was considered too small to catch and he played various infield positions. By his senior year, he was the star of the baseball team as its catcher, the position he continues to play. In that year, Mike was chosen as the MVP for all of Ventura County and the Cal Hi Sports Magazine's California State Player of the Year. In 1990, the Philadelphia Phillies picked Mike as their first round draft pick. Mike was the third player chosen overall in that draft.

Mike, who bats and throws right-handed, had an outstanding career in the Phillies farm system. In 1992, he was awarded the Paul Owens award as the best player in all of the Phillies minor league system. In the same year, he appeared in the Eastern League (AA) All-Star game. The following year, Mike threw out 47% of all runners attempting to steal a base.

On June 30, 1994, Mike made his major league debut. He served the Phillies as their backup catcher behind Darren Daulton and Benito Santiago, until 1997, when he became the team's first string catcher. Mike turned in excellent numbers that year both offensively and defensively. Mike hit 20 homeruns, including his first grand slam, on August 18, 1997. He had 77 RBIs. During the month of July, he had a .400 batting average, the best in the National League. Mike was considered the fastest bat on the Phillies. Mike allowed only .64 steals per 9 innings, the third best record in the league. The league leader was Brad Ausmus.

Mike had an excellent start for the 1998 season, as did the Phillies. But, on July 23, Mike suffered a pelvic injury, which ended his season. The Phillies, without Mike's defensive and offensive abilities, faded and dropped out of contention. At the end of the season, Mike's status for 1999 was still unclear, with the possibility of surgery still under consideration.

Mike is unmarried and he makes his home in Westlake Village, CA.

Years	Games	AB	H	R	RBI	HR	BA	OBP	FP
7	563	1959	528	265	321	82	.270	.331	.991

1994-2000 Phi-N

Jason Marquis

Jason Marquis was born August 21, 1978, in Manhasset, New York. Jason participated in Little League and pitched in the Little League World Series. He attended Tottenville High School in Staten Island, New York, where he was a member of the National Honor Society and the baseball team. As a right-handed pitcher, Jason led his school to two straight New York City titles.

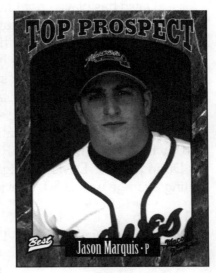

Jason was drafted right out of high school as a special selection between the first and second rounds of the June, 1996 free agent draft, by the Atlanta Braves organization. He was signed on July 18, 1996. Jason's first minor league team was the Danville rookie league team, where, in 1996, he pitched in 7 games, with a 1-1 average and an ERA of 4.63. Since that first year, Jason has only been used in the minors as a starter. In 1997, he pitched for Macon (A), where he pitched 28 games, with a 14-10 record and 4.38 ERA. 1998 saw him with the Danville 97s (A—Carolina League,) the youngest pitcher in the league. His record, at first seems, unimpressive, with 2 wins and 12 losses and a 4.87 ERA, but he had a remarkable 135 strikeouts for $114\frac{2}{3}$ innings, with only 41 walks. In 1999, he pitched for the Myrtle Beach Pelicans (A—Carolina League) and the Greenville Braves (AA—Southern League), with a combined 6 and 4 record. He had 76 strikeouts in 87 innings and a 3.00 ERA. During the season, Jason was hampered by a pulled oblique stomach muscle, which cost him five weeks and some overall effectiveness in all but his final two starts.

Jason is recognized, with his fast ball in the mid-to-high 90s and an excellent curve and changeup, as one of the most promising young pitchers in the Braves organization, an organization remarkable for its outstanding pitching. He began the 2000 season with Greenville. On June 5, 2000, when the quirky John Rocker was sent down to the minors for threatening a reporter, Jason was called up to the parent Atlanta Braves team. Jason made his debut on June 6, when he was called on to relieve the starting pitcher, Tom Glavine, at the beginning of the 7th inning. He walked one batter and struck out one, in a single scoreless inning. The Braves won the interleague game over the Toronto Blue Jays, 7-6.

Years	Games	IP	W	L	GS	SV	PCT	ERA
1	15	$23\frac{1}{3}$	1	0	0	0	1.000	5.01

2000 Atlanta-N

David Newhan

David Matthew Newhan, the son of The Los Angeles Times baseball writer Ross Newhan, was born on September 7, 1973 in Fullerton, California. David graduated from Los Angeles's Esperanza High School in 1991 and attended Pepperdine University. He was chosen in the 17th round of the June, 1995 draft and was signed by Ron Vaughn for the Oakland organization. In 1997, David's contract was acquired by the San Diego Padres.

Dave Newhan

David has played right field and second base. He bats left, but throws with the right hand. During the 1999 season, he spent most of the year with the Las Vegas Stars (PCL), where he batted .286, with 14 home runs and 49 RBI's. For three brief periods during the season he appeared with the parent club, the Padres, in a total of 32 games. David made his major league debut on June 4, 1999. During this season, David had a total of 43 at bats, with a batting average of .140, with two homers and 6 RBI's.

During 2000, David has again appeared with the Padres. After his first 14 games, his batting average was .150. David makes his home in Yorba Linda, California.

Years	Games	AB	H	R	RBI	HR	BA	OBP	FP
2	56	80	12	15	8	3	.150	.236	.981

1999-2000 San Diego-N, 2000 Phi-N

Mike Saipe

Michael Saipe attended San Diego State University. He was chosen by the Colorado Rockies in the 12th round of the June, 1994 free agent draft. After he entered professional baseball, Mike continued his studies and he received his degree from San Diego State in December, 1996.

During the 1997 season, Mike, who stands 6'1", was 12-8 in 29 starts for the New Haven Ravens (AA) and the Sky Sox (AAA). As a reward for outstanding work, Mike attended spring training for the 1998 season with the parent Rockies club. Before his call up to the parent club, Mike was having a fine season at the AAA level. Following his major league stint, Mike rejoined the Colorado Springs Sky Sox (Pacific Coast League). Mike was noticeably weaker after his return. Perhaps he had lost some confidence as a result of his trip to the majors. His final record for the Sky Sox in 1998 was 5-11, with a 5.16 ERA. Mike did lead his team in strikeouts, with 124.

Mike pitched in the Arizona Winter League in 1998. Mike makes his home in San Diego.

Years	Games	IP	W	L	GS	SV	PCT	ERA
1	2	10	0	1	2	0	0.00	10.80

1998 Col-N

Scott Schoeneweis

Scott David Schoeneweis was born on October 2, 1973, in Long Branch, New Jersey. Scott's mother is Jewish, his father is Christian. While attending Duke University, Scott, a left-handed pitcher, was chosen in 1993, his freshman year, as an All-American. But during the next two years he battled against two serious health problems, one life threatening, the other career threatening. He overcame a bout of testicular cancer and he received Tommy John-type reconstructive elbow surgery. On his graduation, Scott was chosen as their third-round draft selection by the Anaheim Angels.

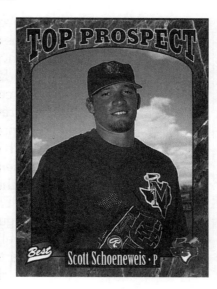

Scott began his professional career in 1996 at Lake Elsinore, where his record was 8 and 3. His second year, at Midland, yielded him a record of 7 and 5, with 3 complete games. In the 1997 Arizona Fall League, he had and ERA of 1.98. And in 1998, with Vancouver, he was 11 and 8.

Scott made his major league debut on April 7, 1999 with the Angels. During the first half of 1999, Scott served strictly as a middle reliever with the Angels. He appeared in 31 games and pitched $39\frac{1}{3}$ innings. He was transferred for the second half of the season to Edmonton. There he suffered a second bout of elbow problems and his year ended with an operation for a torn medial collateral ligament in his left elbow.

In 2000, Scott made a second great comeback and became a starter for the Angels. The early part of the year found him pitching with considerable success. From his first 12 starts, he won 5 and lost 3, with an ERA of 4.93. Scott makes his home, in the off-season, in Mt. Laurel, New Jersey.

Years	Games	IP	W	L	GS	SV	PCT	ERA
2	58	$209\frac{1}{3}$	8	11	27	0	.421	5.46

1999-2000 Anaheim-A

Jeff Stember

Jeffrey Alan Stember was born on March 2, 1958 in Elizabeth, New Jersey. Jeff was a right-handed pitcher and pitched in 1978 and 1979 with Cedar Rapids of the San Francisco Giants organization. In 1980, Jeff appeared with Shreveport, Texas, where his ERA was 2.65, and Phoenix, where his ERA was 3.44.

Jeff made his major league debut on August 5, 1980, in a game he started for the parent club Giants. Jeff pitched only 3 innings, giving up only one run, a home run. Jeff spent 1981 with Phoenix. Jeff currently lives in Roseland, New Jersey.

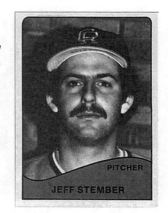

Years	Games	IP	W	L	GS	SV	PCT	ERA
1	1	3	0	0	1	0	—	3.00

1980 SF-N

Bob Tufts

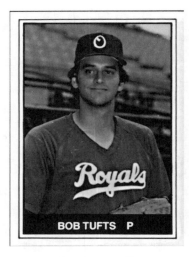

BOB TUFTS P

Robert Malcolm Tufts as born on November 2, 1955 in Medford, Massachusetts. Bob was born to non-Jewish parents, but he would convert to Judaism in 1982.

Bob graduated from Princeton University, before starting his career as a professional baseball player. Bob's first team was Shreveport, Texas (Texas League,) which he served as a left-handed pitcher in 1979. Bob led the league in wins that year, with 14. The following season found Bob in Phoenix (PCL,) where he pitched along side Jeff Stember. Bob also spent much of the 1981 season with Phoenix, where he won 9 games, with an ERA of 1.70. But on August 10, 1981, Jeff made his major league debut with the San Francisco Giants, when he came in as a relief pitcher. Jeff would relieve in 10 more games for the Giants before the end of the season.

Bob was traded in 1982 to the Kansas City organization. He appeared with the Omaha team and with the parent club. Bob relieved 10 games for Kansas City that year, with an ERA of 4.50. Bob appeared in 6 more games with Kansas City in 1983, before arm troubles forced his retirement. Following that, Bob took a graduate degree at Columbia University. He currently lives in Forest Hills, New York.

Years	Games	IP	W	L	GS	SV	PCT	ERA
3	27	42	2	0	0	2	1.000	4.71

1981 SF-N,1982-83 KC-A

1998, the first year of Bud Selig's official tenure as Commissioner of Baseball, was one of the most remarkable in the history of the sport. The year saw Mark McGwire set a new one-year home run record of 70, breaking the old record of Roger Maris, as well as Hank Greenberg's right-handed record. The Yankees were practically invincible and carried their winning ways through the World Series.

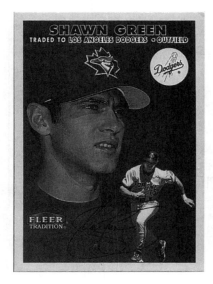

Exactly one dozen Jewish players participated in major league baseball during that season, including three new names. The outstanding Jewish player of the year was certainly Shawn Green, who for the first time in his career began to live up to his wonderful potential. Shawn hit 35 home runs that year, giving him the third best home run one-year record of any Jewish player in the majors. But this he bettered in 1999, with 42. His record for 1999 is only surpassed by that of Hank Greenberg's 58 in 1938 and Al Rosen's 43 in 1953. In 1998, Shawn also stole 35 bases, setting a new record for a Jewish player and making him the first Jewish player to achieve a 30-30 year, in his case 35-35. Shawn had 630 at bats during the same year, the most ever for a Jewish player. One of Shawn's most endearing qualities is his pride in his Judaism. Before the beginning of the 2000 season, Shawn was traded to the Los Angeles Dodgers. Shawn is now one of the highest paid players in the majors.

Other outstanding performers during 1998 include Ruben Amaro, who retired from playing, but was named the Assistant General Manager of the Phillies. The Phillies, with two, had more Jews on its staff than any other 1998 team.

Brad Ausmus did a great job, in 1998, catching for Houston. Despite a slow start in his hitting, he ended the year with a .269 batting average. On January 14, 1999, Brad was traded to the Detroit Tigers. Brad appeared, along with Shawn Green and Mike Lieberthal, in the 1999 All-Star Game.

Mike Lieberthal won the Golden Glove Award (for catcher) for 1999, a year he would bat .300. Mike would also be selected to appear in the 2000 All-Star Game.

Micah Franklin did not make it back to the majors in 1998, but he played an excellent season for the Iowa Cubs (AAA). His slugging average of .655 was the best in all of the minor leagues. His batting average was .329 and he hit 29 homeruns. In 1999 and 2000, he played in Japan, with the Nippon Ham Fighters.

Scott Radinsky ended the 1998 season with a 2.63 ERA. This was his third straight season with an ERA below 3.00. Scott was traded for the 1999 season to St. Louis, where his ERA was 4.88. He began the 2000 season on the disabled list.

Gabe Kapler hit 18 home runs in 1999. He was traded at the end of the season to the Texas Rangers. During the 2000 season, Gabe had a 28-game hitting streak.

Al Levine, after some shaky pitching in the past, has turned in some solid middle inning relief work with the Anaheim Angels at the beginning of the 2000 season. Al spent 1997 with the Chicago White Sox and 1998 with the Texas Rangers. He joined Anaheim in 1999.

Andrew Lorraine began the 2000 season as the 5th starter for the Chicago Cubs. In 1997, Andrew was with Oakland and in 1998 with Seattle. He was traded to the Cubs in 1999.

New Jewish minor league players include Scott Albin, a right-handed pitcher; Greg Belson, a right-handed pitcher; Jeff Blitstein, a right-handed pitcher; Tony Cogan, a left-handed pitcher; Jason Robert Crews, a pitcher; Jake Epstein, 1st base; Darren Fenster, 2nd base; David Glick, a left-handed pitcher; Josh Goldfield, an outfielder; John Grabow (Jewish Mother,) a left-handed pitcher; Damon Katz, a shortstop; Glenn Katz, an outfielder; Mike Koplove, a right-handed pitcher; Justin Martin, a 2nd baseman; Ryan Moskau (Jewish Mother,) a left-handed pitcher; Adam Neubart, an outfielder and brother of Garrett Neubart; John Novak (Jewish Mother,) an outfielder; Jeff Pickler, a 2nd baseman; John Powers (Jewish Mother,) an infielder; Tony Schrager (Jewish Father,) an infielder; Cameron "Cam" Smith (Jewish Mother,) a pitcher; H. Hamilton Wayne, a left-handed pitcher; Justin Wayne, a right-handed pitcher; and David Wolensky, a right-handed pitcher.

In 1999, we saw a major movie documentary on Hank Greenberg. Sports Illustrated declared Sandy Koufax to be the athlete of the century. A major motion picture was in the planning on the life of Moe Berg. Never before has there been more interest in the history of Jewish baseball. Meanwhile, the future for Jewish players and executives in the sport has never seemed more promising.

Index

Photo Credits

Taussig, Don (Courtesy The Topps Company, Inc.)
Turchin, Eddie (NATIONAL BASEBALL HALL OF FAME
    LIBRARY, COOPERSTOWN, NY)
Wapnick, Steve (Courtesy Fleer SkyBox)
Wineapple, Ed (Courtesy Yury Arkadin)
Yeager, Steve (Courtesy Mother's Cookies)
Yellen, Larry (Courtesy The Topps Company. Inc.)
Zinn, Guy (NATIONAL BASEBALL HALL OF FAME
    LIBRARY, COOPERSTOWN, NY)
Zosky, Eddie (Courtesy Fleer SkyBox)

PART II-TOUCHING OTHER BASES

Amaro, David (Courtesy Judy Amaro)
Ashkinazy, Alan (Courtesy Fleer SkyBox)
Asinof, Eliot Photo by Nick Lacy (Courtesy Eliot Asinof)
Blumberg, Rob Jr. (Courtesy Scoreboard)
Borowsky, Erez (Courtesy Fleer SkyBox)
Boudreau, Jim (Courtesy Fleer SkyBox)
Cohen, John (Courtesy Scoreboard)
Cohen, Tonny (Courtesy Fleer SkyBox)
Friedman, Jason (Courtesy Best Cards)
Gershberg, Howie (Courtesy Scoreboard)
Goldstein, Ike (Courtesy Fleer SkyBox)
Greenberg, Steve (Courtesy Fleer SkyBox)
Horowitz, Ed (Courtesy Fleer SkyBox)
Kantor, Brad (Courtesy Fleer SkyBox)
Kolinsky, Steve (Courtesy Scoreboard)
Komer, Stuart with Pete Gray (Courtesy Stuart Komer)
Lipson, Marc (Courtesy Best Cards)
Mandel, Brett (Courtesy Sport-Pro)
Oliphant, Dave (Courtesy Dave Oliphant)
Pill, Leonard (Courtesy Leonard Pill)
Rosenthal, Todd (Courtesy Star Images Inc.)
Silverman, Aaron (UPPER DECK and the Upper Deck
    Logos are trademarks of The Upper Deck Company,
    LLC. © 1997 The Upper Deck Company, LLC. All
    rights reserved. Used with permission.)
Silverstien, Allan (Courtesy Fleer SkyBox)
Steinberg, David (Courtesy Larry Fritsch)
Weinberg, Barry (Courtesy Mother's Cookies)
Arffa, Steve (Courtesy Fleer SkyBox)
Bair, Dennis (Courtesy Best Cards)
Buxbaum, Danny (Courtesy Fleer SkyBox)
Epstein, Ian (Courtesy West Michigan White Caps)
Feuerstein, David (Courtesy Best Cards)
Garber, Joel (Courtesy Best Cards)
Gerstein, Ron (Courtesy Scoreboard)
Glauber, Keith (Courtesy Scoreboard)
Hunter, Scott (Courtesy Sport-Pro)
Kapler, Gabe (Courtesy Best Cards)
Kleiner, Stacy (Courtesy Best Cards)
Levey, Joshua (Courtesy Joshua Levey)
List, Lou (Courtesy Scoreboard)
Myrow, John (Courtesy Best Cards)
Neubart, Garrett (Courtesy Best Cards)
Prager, Howard (Courtesy Fleer SkyBox)

Saffer, Jeffrey (Courtesy Best Cards)
Saffer, Jon (Courtesy Fleer SkyBox)
Saipe, Mike (Courtesy Best Cards)
Siegel, Justin (Courtesy Best Cards)
Solomon, David (Courtesy Fleer SkyBox)
Solomon, Steve (Courtesy Scoreboard)
Stein, Ethan (Courtesy Lansing Lugnuts)
Waco, David (Courtesy Scoreboard)
Weinberg, Todd (Courtesy West Michigan Whitecaps)
Weiss, Marc (Courtesy Sport-Pro)
Wolfe, Joel (Courtesy Best Cards)
Zimmerman, Mike (Courtesy Fleer SkyBox)
Kaye, Danny (Current Biography 1952)
Miller, Marvin (Courtesy Marvin Miller)
Herman Goldberg Jersey in The Baseball Hall of Fame
Bertman, Skip 1 (Courtesy McDag Productions)
Bertman, Skip 2 (Courtesy McDag Productions)
Weinstein, Jerry (Courtesy Scoreboard)
Rosen, Coon 2 (Courtesy Coon Rosen)
Eisen, Thelma (Courtesy Larry Fritsch)
Foss, Anita (Courtesy Larry Fritsch)
Schachter, Blanche (Courtesy Larry Fritsch)
Wigiser, Margaret (Courtesy Larry Fritsch)
Robinson, Jackie (Courtesy Fleer SkyBox)
Blissberg, Harvey (Courtesy Richard Rosen)

PART III-DIAMOND TALES

Belinsky, Bo (Courtesy Fleer SkyBox)
Cohen Stadium (Courtesy El Paso Diablos)
Greenberg, Hank 1 (UPPER DECK and the Upper Deck
    Logos are trademarks of The Upper Deck
    Company, LLC. © 1997 The Upper Deck
    Company, LLC. All rights reserved. Used with
    permission.)
Koufax, Sandy (Courtesy Fleer SkyBox)
Levis, Jesse (Courtesy Pacific)
Patkin, Max (Courtesy Fleer SkyBox)
Reese, Jimmie-Reese Ryan and Nolan Ryan (Courtesy
    Pacific)
Reese, Jimmy (Courtesy Mother's Cookies)

MAJOR LEAGUE UPDATE

Charles, Frank (Courtesy Scoreboard)
Glauber, Keith (Courtesy Best Cards)
Kapler, Gabe (Courtesy Fleer SkyBox)
Lieberthal, Mike (Courtesy Fleer-Skybox)
Marquis, Jason (Courtesy Best Cards)
Newhan, David (Courtesy Best Cards)
Saipe, Mike (Courtesy Scoreboard)
Schoenweis, Scott (Courtesy Best Cards)
Stember, Jeff (Courtesy Fleer-Skybox)
Tufts, Bob (Courtesy Fleer-Skybox)
Green, Shawn (Courtesy Fleer-Skybox)